For

Doug Cjak

Blessings (

+ fun chck

10/7/10

A Journey of Grace

A Journey of Grace

The Formation of a Leader and a Church

Herbert W. Chilstrom

AN AUTOBIOGRAPHY

Foreword by Martin E. Marty

Huff Publishing Associates / Lutheran University Press
Minneapolis

Published under the auspices of the full service publishing consultants
Huff Publishing Associates, LLC
www.huffpublishing.com

by
Lutheran University Press
PO Box 390759
Minneapolis, MN 55439

Cover photo of "Rondel" image by Robert Kusel
Design by Dorie McClelland, www.springbookdesign.com
Printed in the United States of America

Scripture quotations are from New Revised Standard Version Bible, copyright ©1989, Division of Christian Education of the National Council of the Churches of Christ in the United States of America.

ISBN: 978-1-932688-61-0
Library of Congress Control Number: 2011929543

To my brother Dave and to all who live with developmental challenges. He entered hospice care two weeks before this book went to print. His days are numbered; his faith is strong. May the Lord teach us all "to count our days that we may gain a wise heart" (Psalm 90:12).

Contents

Foreword

Martin E. Marty

A legendary rabbi, reflecting on the experience of being among "the chosen people" and mindful of the wilderness experience of Israel and centuries of travail, prayed in thanks to the Holy One for having chosen Jews. Then, reflecting on their suffering, he switched and prayed that, if it be God's will, "next time, choose someone else."

The first draft of *A Journey of Grace* was called *I Have Chosen You: The Formation of a Leader and a Church,* but author Herb Chilstrom, perhaps fearing misinterpretation of the title, did well to change it to what the book really is about. It *does* tell of a journey, long and tortuous, but also one whose highways deserve celebration. And it goes without saying that "grace" works better in a title than being "chosen."

"Grace" fits because it has been so needed in the lives of Herb and Corinne Chilstrom, as the following story makes clear. Does a couple look "chosen" if, as this one did, the story had to include the loss by suicide of a troubled son? Does a pastor and then presiding bishop, though often elected by pastoral peers and others ordained by baptism to lead, get to feel and appear to be chosen in the face of always complex and sometimes vicious assaults by members of his own church body? Dare he look chosen to lead in a time of great uncertainty, when no one knows in advance where the path will lead—and only naysayers who attack are sure that *they* know what they would have done? The answer is "yes."

Grace, unmerited, usually unforeseen and often unseen, works its surprises on page after page of this account. My favorite paragraph, quoted from a Chilstrom address on a Seminary Day in 1985, provides the foundation for defining and interpreting this grace, when the author describes himself as "an evangelical conservative, with a radical social conscience":

> An evangelical is simply one who believes the good news about Jesus Christ and becomes a bearer of that message of hope. The moment you get beyond that core . . . you begin to drift from the center. . . . it's important for me to be a conservative. I'm a trinitarian Christian—that's conservative. I believe God reveals himself to us in Jesus Christ—that's conservative. . . . I believe we are justified by grace through faith—that's conservative. I believe that the church is the creation of the Holy Spirit—that's conservative. . . . The prophetic word can only be spoken by those who have a radical social conscience. . . . the most radical word we can speak is a word of hope.

That paragraph is packed with other evidences of grace-full faith, as any reader of any chapter, including those marked by tumult and tension, will soon find out.

Eugen Rosenstock-Huessy provided me with a vision of good writing: "One book is about one thing, at least the good ones are." Once again, this *is* all about a "journey of grace." One feature of the story and the personality revealed in it that helped guide the plot of the book is its juxtaposition of rough stretches on the road of the journey followed by clear paths, which is a good description of how life appears to most of us. The other feature that kept impressing me was the portrayal of Chilstrom's vulnerability. By this I certainly do not mean that he comes across as someone afraid to take chances or who expects to be and is a victim. Rather, he simply did take chances in that "evangelical" and "prophetic" course of life, without taking pains to foresee all the hazards along the way.

This is the story of a student, then a pastor, a bishop, and finally presiding bishop at the founding of the Evangelical Lutheran

Church in America. Leaders in almost every denomination one can
think of this side of Mormons, Jehovah's Witnesses, and some—but
only some—of the still-thriving evangelical churches, will read this
account in efforts to find their parallel experiences to what occurs
in the ELCA, since they are equally vulnerable. I am not sure that
being aware of them would have spared Chilstrom and will spare
them, given our times. All denominations are threatened, some are
broke, most are torn, not a few lack guidance and perspective. No
matter what course leadership takes in these divided and at-risk
church bodies, their journeys will not be protected in any ordinary
sense of the word. Too many conflicting forces in the surrounding
world and, more painfully at hand, movements and personalities
in their own church bodies come with or quickly develop mutually
antagonistic stances. A wise leader may be tempted to give up.

A *Journey of Grace* shows that Chilstrom is in the company of
those who, not appreciating the tumult and personal attacks, find
ways to be guided by grace and, yes, to enjoy life and ministry. A
concept that courses through the book is that of a calling, which
is the best defense against moroseness, defeatism, and defeat. That
calling may take the form of an evening walk with Corinne, without whom grace in human form might have appeared remote from
Herb's life. It may be shaped by the not-few notes of cheer and
recognition, which could give wall-upon-wall decoration to the
Chilstrom country and town homes alike.

The horse St. Paul rode on the way to Damascus, a stock figure
in many portraits of the apostle's conversion, has long been retired.
Martin Luther, writhing in penance on a monastery floor, appears
almost histrionic compared to most modern acceptances of an
apostolic call. Each person's comes in a distinctive way, and author
Chilstrom here carefully and sometimes entertainingly revisits his
steps along the journey.

One assignment, or at least one element in the agenda of those
who write forewords, is to get out of the way of the plot. Our task

is to provide a frame for the author's pictures, to do some pointing toward significant elements and features, and leave the detail and suspense—yes, there is some of that here, too!—to the author. A feature that I consider to be significant and worthy of being pointed out to others is the nature of the steps Chilstrom has been taking through life. He does not appear to be pretending when he avers that he had not readied himself for the leadership roles into which he has been cast.

For example, he confesses that very late in his career—but never too late for his vocation!—he had to acquaint himself with ecumenical leadership and practices. He comes across not as a naïf but still as a provincial. His journey has taken him through the main roads of Lutheran and upper-midwestern life more than on shuttles to Canterbury, Rome, Jerusalem, or Cape Town. But he shows himself to be a quick learner. Long schooled in *Robert's Rules of Order* he has often had to preside in the church as if *Rules of Disorder* were singly in evidence.

Could anyone on Pastor Chilstrom's course have prepared for the "Big Three," which, he says, latterly preoccupies church existence: a) money, b) sex, and c) the (ecclesiastical) in-laws? A lack of support for the church's mission threatens almost all religious bodies, but hits hardest the newly-formed bodies that have not had a chance to address suspicions, celebrate victories, or make new plans so early in their life together. As for sex—Chilstrom, like every church leader from pope to peon learns—it remains an obsession. One hopes with the author that "grace" can be perceived on that front, too. It will be a long journey.

Since he heeds a call, Chilstrom *has* been chosen.

Introduction

I fully intended to begin working on my autobiography shortly after I retired in 1995. I thought it would be well to write while events were fresh in my mind. That never happened. Now I'm grateful I waited. Time allows for a degree of objectivity that only the passage of years can bring.

When I began writing I asked two friends, Martin Marty and Harold Lohr, if they had any advice. Both were to the point. Be as objective as possible, they suggested. Above all, they said, avoid vindictiveness, the bane of too many autobiographies.

I have tried to do that. One soon realizes, however, that absolute impartiality is beyond any autobiographical writer's reach. One writes as a participant, not as an outside observer. The life of a bishop—including mine for almost twenty years—brings one into controversy almost daily, sometimes a minor skirmish and often a major conflict. So while I have written about many high and inspirational moments, I also have, of necessity, revisited some major battlefields. The record would not be complete without this. In these instances I have tried to support what I have written with solid factual evidence. Nevertheless, even at best, nuances as well as personal opinions and perspectives inevitably seep into the narrative and shape how the story unfolds.

So I ask for patience from those who find errors in fact, forgiveness from those who are offended by anything I have written, and indulgence from those who think I have been too uncritical of myself.

Why write?

Maybe Richard Paul Evans answers best:

> I find myself astonished at [humankind's] persistent yet
> vain attempts to escape the certainty of oblivion, expressed
> in nothing less than the ancient pyramids and by nothing
> more than a stick in a child's hand, etching a name into a
> freshly poured sidewalk. As we chronicle our lives and the
> circumstances that surround them . . . it is our own reflec-
> tion. It is the glance in the mirror that is of value . . . if we
> write but one book in life, let it be our autobiography.

So why did I write?

First, because persons for whom I have a high regard urged me to
do so. Months before I retired in 1995, Philip Natwick, a respected
member of the Church Council of the Evangelical Lutheran Church
in America (ELCA) and an excellent penman in his own right,
expressed his hope that I would

> . . . do some writing about this moment in the history of
> the Lutheran church. Looking back at it truly is going to be
> a task for future communicators to unsnarl. You are a key
> person to do some of that.

Another prod came from Theodore Bachmann, one of the leading churchmen of the generation before mine. Parish pastor, theological professor, Lutheran World Relief resettlement officer, head
of the Board for Theological Education for the Lutheran Church in
America (LCA) and author of a history of that church, Bachmann
had a lifelong passion for preserving the past. I had been retired
less than a month when he asked:

> Would it not be a valuable gift to the church at large as
> well as to our church body, if there could be a Chilstrom
> account of the ELCA in the making? Such an account
> could be a splendid exercise of what I'd call the steward-
> ship of experience. You do indeed have something timely

and winsome to share—precious contents of a ministry for
Christ and [his] church.

And, of course, both of these men were right. I had the unusual
privilege of serving as the first presiding bishop of the ELCA from
1987 to 1995. That placed me in a unique position. I had a ringside
seat in the formative years of that church and one in the center of
the ring in its first years. It compels me to want to share an account
with those who may be interested in my story and in how my life
has been intertwined with the church. My wife Corinne shared
fully in that unusual venture.

What should the title be?
Many authors will tell you that the title for a book often does not
emerge until the book is finished. That was true in this effort. As I
looked back over my life and the life of the church as I had experienced it, I could only conclude that it had been, first and foremost,
"a journey of grace."

Does that mean that I believe in predestination, that it is determined before birth that we are to play certain roles in life? That
seems too rigid. It infringes on our personal freedom to make
choices about the direction our lives will take.

And yet—and yet, I have this strong conviction that God is, in
fact, intimately involved in our unfolding lives. I'm convinced that we
are not simply drifting along like a dry leaf on the surface of a swift
stream, without God knowing or caring about what happens to us.

Isn't it somewhat of a paradox: certain that we have freedom to
choose, yet equally certain that we are chosen?

". . . all human work is imperfect," wrote Toynbee, "because
human nature is." Should this keep us from doing things like
writing an autobiography? No. Because, as he also said, ". . . this
intrinsic imperfection of human affairs cannot be overcome by
procrastination.

So, I exercised my free will. I stopped putting it off. I wrote.

The story yet to come

As for the ELCA, the definitive history of its formation and early years will not be written for at least another quarter century or more. That's the way it is. The best accounts of an era seldom come from those directly involved. They stand too close to the action. Instead, the complete histories are only written when sufficient time has elapsed, giving an author the necessary perspective to write that more complete, objective, and dispassionate account. I can only hope that this effort will be helpful in that larger account.

My resources

Some readers will be impressed by the amount of detail I have included. That comes of a penchant to be a collector, inherited from my mother, Ruth. Ever since college I have maintained an annual file for each year. Whenever I thought something might be important to preserve, I inserted it into that file. My mother also saved every letter we sent to her over many years, giving me another important resource for recovering times and events. These resources, along with my fairly intentional habit of keeping a journal, have been my major sources for writing this autobiography.

Thank you

I owe a word of thanks to those who have encouraged me to write, and not least to Corinne. She lived through most of these experiences with me. Without her companionship I could never have sailed these seas. She, too, has had a sense of history and of the importance of this effort for future generations.

Longtime friends Joseph Wagner, Martin Marty, and Paul Edison-Swift were of invaluable assistance. Wagner and Marty patiently read through hundreds of pages and made insightful suggestions. Edison-Swift advised me on baffling computer issues. Mary Hetland graciously gave permission to use the "Rondel" image on the cover. Her late husband David created it for the entrance to the ELCA Church Center in Chicago. It is a warm, inviting symbol that greets staff and visitors each day. Sonia Solomonson and Susan Niemi, accomplished editors in Lutheran publication circles, helped to reduce the text to a readable size and, without infringing on content or style, aided in shaping the final text. Finally, publisher Bill Huff always had a word of wisdom and encouragement when the effort bogged down.

As I approach my eightieth year the words of an old Celtic prayer seem just right:

> As thou wast before
> At my life's beginning,
> Be thou so again,
> At my journey's end.
>
> As thou wast beside
> At my soul's shaping,
> Father, be thou too
> At my journey's close.

Chapter 1

My parents:
good, ordinary, pious, Swedish

An early history

I was blessed; my family was a good family. I was blessed; they were ordinary. I was blessed; they were pious. I was blessed; they were Swedish.

For the first years of my life I was, as much as anything else, self-consciously Swedish.

My father's and mother's ancestors in Sweden were mostly farmers, with a sprinkling of innkeepers, sheriffs, musicians, shoemakers, soldiers, and other ordinary folk. On my father's side I've traced our lineage back to one Mikael Kjöllerström, born in 1612 and a farmer and colonel in the army of the illustrious King Gustavus Adolphus. The first to come to America were my father's grandparents, Johan and Kristina Nilsson and Magnus and Katrina Kjöllerström. The Nilssons came in 1852 and the Kjöllerströms in 1853. The sea voyage for the Kjöllerströms and six of their seven children lasted sixteen weeks. Nilsson soon became Nelson, and, because of the impossibility of pronouncing and spelling Kjöllerström, that family eventually changed the name to Chilstrom. These two families settled first near Milwaukee, Wisconsin, and then moved on to the Minnesota frontier north of Willmar. After nearly being killed in the Great Sioux Uprising in the early 1860s, the Nelsons and Chilstroms resettled near Cannon Falls, Minnesota.

Eventually John, the son of Magnus and Katrina Chilstrom, married Hedda (usually called "Hattie"), the daughter of Johan and Kristina Nelson. John and Hattie moved to the Beckville community near Litchfield, Minnesota, where my father Walfred, the youngest of seven, was born in 1888. A detailed history of the Chilstrom and Nelson families is included in a volume I wrote and published in 2005 titled, *The Story of Two Families and Their Times—the Chilstroms (Kjöllerströms); the Nelsons (Nilsons).*

My mother, Ruth, was born in Mälmo, a seaport city on the southern coast of Sweden, just before Christmas 1900. She was carried to America in the spring of 1901 as a babe in the arms of her parents, Arvid and Hedda Lindell. Hedda had trained as a midwife. Arvid was in the military. Ruth was so desperately ill on the long and tumultuous sea voyage that the ship captain suggested that Arvid and Hedda begin to think about burial at sea. Fortunately, little Ruth not only survived but grew to become a strong, energetic woman.

The Lindells came to the Litchfield area where two of Hedda's sisters had settled earlier. Arvid worked for other farmers for one dollar a day until he could eventually rent and then own a spread. His Elgin pocket watch, purchased in 1905 for $5.00 and still in perfect working order, sits on top of my desk. Hedda took up her midwifery practice in the Beckville area and helped bring many babies into the world. Though she lived in this country for more than fifty years, Hedda never learned to speak English. Her world was confined almost entirely to the Swedish-speaking Beckville community. She died when I was eighteen. Over all those years on my frequent visits to her home, she spoke to me in Swedish and I understood her; I spoke to her in English and she understood me.

As for John and Hattie Chilstrom, unbelievable tragedy stuck on a warm July afternoon in 1892. John and his oldest son Edward were making improvements to the well. Edward was overcome by methane gas. In an attempt to rescue him, John also perished. Just when the promise of their dreams was breaking out, the family was cast into despair. With the help of her other sons, Hattie survived and even prospered on that farm.

Beckville Lutheran Church, a strong Swedish congregation in the open country seven miles south of Litchfield, Minnesota, was the center of life for both the Lindells and Chilstroms. Still a viable congregation today, it is named in honor of the pioneer pastor, Peter Beckman, who organized Beckville and dozens of other Swedish churches along the Minnesota frontier in the last half of the nineteenth century. Worship, religious education, social life—most everything happened at the church. Since marrying outside the Swedish church community was strongly discouraged, many romances germinated at these gatherings, including that of my parents.

As I reflect on my memories of my grandparents and as I probe the history of my great-grandparents and their antecedents, I find families who represent the best of Swedish Lutheranism. They are Christians who loved their church and its worship life. They are also believers who enriched their personal and family life with regular reading of the Bible and prayer in their homes. This is what they carried with them to America. And it is the best of the Augustana heritage: love of good liturgy and personal piety. This is my inheritance from them. What could be better? I did nothing to earn it. It is gift.

Wally and Ruth: a mismatch that worked

Had Wally and Ruth visited a marriage counselor during their courtship they probably would have been told, "You two have much in common. But I'm afraid your differences are so great this marriage will never work. You're the youngest of seven, Wally, and rather shy and laid back. And you, Ruth, are the oldest of five and very aggressive and outgoing. You better think again about getting married."

Well, maybe it's a good thing there were no marriage counselors in that rural community. The marriage did work. They went on to survive the worst economic times in the history of the country and raise eight children.

Yes, there were many differences. For starters, Ruth was only twenty and Wally already in his early thirties. With an age gap of more than a dozen years and a late start for Wally, one would not necessarily expect this couple to have a very large family. They had other ideas. Nine months and two weeks after their marriage, Adeline, the oldest child, arrived. Fifteen months later Lorraine appeared. And soon Winnifred and then Virginia. Hard times or not, the babies kept coming. I was born in 1931, David in 1933, Martha in 1935, and Janet in 1940.

In the first nineteen years of their marriage Ruth was pregnant almost half of the time (she miscarried three times). Yet she worked hand in glove with Wally in the barn, the fields, and the garden. She tended flocks of chickens and turkeys for extra cash. And all the while she cooked, baked, and managed the household.

Wally and Ruth never owned a farm, always renting and share-cropping. By 1935 the Great Depression drove them and their family off the land.

In her diary Ruth has a simple three-word entry to describe the trauma that unfolded on March 16, 1935: "Came to folks." On the previous day all of their machinery, cattle, and poultry were sold at public auction. The morning after the sale Ruth took four of us and moved in with her parents, Arvid and Hedda Lindell, and their adult son Clarence, on their farm on the west shore of Swan Lake. Wally gathered up the other two and went to live with his single brother Sig and widowed mother Hattie on another farm three miles down the road on the north shore of the same lake. Less than three months later Martha, the seventh child, joined the already over-crowded Lindell household.

Wally and Ruth and their family lived this way for the next

eighteen months. Day after day Ruth would record in her diary, "W. no work. W. no work. W. no work." On February 16 she noted: "W. home. I got $6.00 from W. got groceries—$1.50."

At long last, Wally and Ruth found a small two-bedroom, bedbug-infested rental house near the outer edge of Litchfield. On November 30, 1936, they gathered up their scattered family and moved to the city. With roots in the rural countryside that reached back for many centuries in Sweden and America, they would never again be farmers. And I, as the oldest son, would be the first such in several hundred years who did not at least try to make a living as a farmer.

On May 20, 1983, I entered some notes in my journal about Wally and Ruth's differences:

> Was it a good marriage? Yes and no. Dad was not the kind of man who was prepared to be the head of the family. Brought up under the protective eye of a strong & domineering mother & older brothers, he never reached his full potential. I think of him as a sheltered, hothouse plant who never was exposed to the kinds of experiences that bring one to maturity & a full sense of responsibility.

Wally: kind, steady, decent, easygoing

In spite of many hardships during my growing-up years, I carry good memories of my father. All eight of us recall times in early childhood when he would cross one leg over another and invite us to ride on his shoe while he pumped his knee up and down and recited the Swedish rhyme, *"Rida, rida ranka, Hesten heter Blanka,"* which roughly translates as *"Ride, ride on my knee, The horse is named Whitey."*

Wally's first steady job after the move to Litchfield was with the Works Project Administration (WPA), a Roosevelt era New Deal program of building parks, sidewalks, golf courses, and many other civic projects. Now when I play a round of golf and think at times about him and his co-WPA workers, I can almost see him standing there next to the fairway, leaning on his shovel, and looking in amazement and humor at his boy chasing a little white ball with those uppity fellows from high society.

Wally was one of more than three million who were employed by the WPA program. Most men were deeply grateful to Roosevelt for creating jobs and income. Some of his detractors suggested that Roosevelt did it to win votes. His landslide reelection to a second term in 1936 may well have been linked to his New Deal programs. Wally, however, was not one of his admirers. He remained steadfastly Republican his entire life.

Eventually he got a job at a powdered milk products company where he worked for many years as a common laborer. Unfortunately, one day he absentmindedly walked into a restricted area with his ever-present pipe in his mouth. Most of the time he carried it unlighted between his teeth. That day, however, it had a spark in it. With fine milk powder dust in the air it ignited a minor explosion. There was no damage to the building. Yet the manager fired him. It was an emotional upheaval for Wally, a tenderhearted man who "wouldn't hurt a flea." Though he was already in his late sixties and might have retired by that time, he needed the income. After all those years of faithful and steady devotion to the company, to have it end in this way was distressing for all of us in the family. The manager said he had to do it. I didn't believe him. I remember feeling intensely angry at him for not giving Wally another chance.

For added income to feed and clothe their growing family, Wally and Ruth were the custodians at our church. Though Wally carried the title, my memory is that Ruth worked at least as hard at the task as he did. And, of course, all of us children got into the act as well, sweeping, mopping, dusting, cutting grass, shoveling snow, and, in my case, filling the furnace stokers with coal on wintery days. While I enjoyed working at the church, especially with my dad, my favorite activity was ringing the bell. In my journal years later (5/20/83) I wrote about that duty:

The bell was rung every Saturday evening at six o'clock sharp. We would wait for the six o'clock whistle from the power plant & then ring the bell. It was a large, heavy bell that took some effort for a boy to get going—but what a feeling of exhilaration once it began to toll. Then on the very last pull I would hang on to the rope & it would carry me up about 4–5 feet in the air & I would step off on to a large box that covered the motor for the pipe organ.

There was never any expectation that there would be pay for the work at the church. It was just sort of understood that one did this together as a family to help pay for the groceries.

The annual salary in 1944 was $360.00. By 1950 it was $602.50. Because Wally often worked on Sundays, it fell to my mother and one of us children to sit near the thermostat at the back of the church to make certain the sanctuary was comfortable during worship. Because it was all but impossible to control a coal-fired furnace, we often scurried to open the stained glass windows with a long stick and hook.

Wally never held a leadership position in any organization to which he belonged, which to my recollection numbered only two: the church and the labor union. There was nothing in him by way of word or example that would have inspired or motivated me to pursue education beyond high school or to be open to leadership opportunities.

Wally was short and rugged, probably only about five feet and seven inches at most. He was kind, decent, gentle, and loving; and we shared a deep emotional bond. When we worked together he gave me free reign to do things in whatever way I thought best. He never criticized or suggested I might have done it better.

I heard him swear only once. He was fixing some barbed-wire fencing on his brother Sig's farm. The wire snapped and scratched him. "You bastard," he exploded. I was stunned, never having heard anything even close to profanity from him.

Saying "I love you," of course, would have been considered quite odd and entirely inappropriate in a typical Swedish family. Yet I never doubted for a moment my dad's love and affection for me and for all of his children.

Wally was quiet and reserved in any group. He preferred to listen. Yet when you were alone with him you were always surprised at how lively the conversation could be.

Family finances were of little interest to Wally. Any major decisions invariably originated with Ruth and were carried through by her. He brought home his paycheck, placed it on the dining room table in front of Ruth, and got enough cash from her to purchase a few pouches of his favorite Velvet pipe tobacco. Once he got his tobacco money he was content. If he got a tall can of Velvet for Christmas he had all he wanted. I have one of those old Velvet tins sitting on a small shelf above my desk. The faded inscription reads: "Aged in wood, an old time process which takes out all rawness and harshness. Velvet is mild and mellow and smokes smooth."

"Mild and mellow"—good words to describe who he was. I can almost smell the pleasant aroma that wafted up from behind the newspaper every evening.

Wally died as he had lived—quietly and peacefully—while taking a nap in his seventy-sixth year. I was living in New Jersey at the time. I wept quietly for much of the flight back to Minnesota for his funeral. Yes, the bond was deep, tender and loving. He was a good father.

Ruth: loving, strict, hardworking

Like Wally, Ruth had only an eighth-grade education. She told of missing school many days because of the need for her as the oldest child to help with farm and fieldwork. Not until I was an adult did she share with me that her father had been an alcoholic and harsh during some of those years. Eventually he changed and lived as a faithful church member, decent husband, and good father.

In spite of her minimal education, Ruth read and spoke both English and Swedish fluently. As I reread letters she sent to me over the years and as I review the entries in diaries she kept, I'm impressed with her good spelling and grammar. No, not perfect, but better than many college-educated folks I've known. For all of her adult life she corresponded with cousins in Sweden, relatives she had never met. With the help of an English/Swedish dictionary she would sit at the dining room table and labor for hours over a single letter, making certain it was grammatically correct.

Ruth was, first and foremost, an exceptional homemaker and a good mother to all of her children. She gave special care and attention to my developmentally-challenged brother, Dave, and to her aging parents.

Ruth was aggressive, hardworking, a marvelous cook, a friend to many, and the leader in our family. Tall and physically strong—she towered over Wally by at least two or three inches—she could outwork most men I've known. When something heavy needed to be lifted or moved she seldom asked for help. She had some part-time jobs over the years—child care, cooking at a restaurant, cleaning homes, seasonal work at a canning factory, and other low-paying employment. Her culinary skills, along with a good sense of humor, won the hearts of younger children, including her grandchildren.

Ruth was the primary disciplinarian. She never threatened me or my siblings with words like, "You just wait until your father gets home." When I needed a "licking"—which was fairly often—she administered it on the spot. On occasion, when Dave and I teased each other and giggled at night and kept him awake, Wally rose from his bed and removed the leather belt from his trousers. In our small house we could hear it. We knew what was coming. We flipped on our tummies, froze stiff, and prepared for the worst. We knew the slaps on the butt would smart. Unfortunately, he usually threw the blanket over Dave, thus giving him double coverage and leaving me exposed to the full benefit of the belt. He knew, of course, that I was the most deserving of the smacks. No, they were never hard enough to give more than a temporary sting.

Other than that, I recall only one spanking from Wally. It was Ruth who kept a yardstick above the door between the kitchen and the dining room. During one of my "lickings" the stick splintered over my butt. I suppose by today's standards she might be accused of child abuse. I've always said, however, that I fully deserved every spanking I got and never harbored any bitter feelings toward her for them.

Ruth and Wally kept a huge garden on their corner lot, a necessary mainstay for the family and a plot where everyone was expected to pull weeds, hill potatoes, and harvest vegetables and fruits. It was not unusual for Ruth to rise early and spend an hour or two with her flowers and vegetables before preparing breakfast for her family. At the end of a day of hard work, Wally found enjoyment in the garden as the sun was setting. Again and again, however, he went to the garden with a stern warning from Ruth not to let his hoe get too close to her flowers. He couldn't tell a flower from a weed. When his hoe leveled one of her cherished flower seedlings there was a price to be paid.

Ruth was a strong advocate of organic gardening. Long before they became broadly popular, she was a faithful devotee of the Rodales from Allentown, Pennsylvania. She pored over *Organic Gardening* magazine as soon as it arrived, searching for new ideas in gardening, including insect control without pesticides. A billowing compost bin was a staple in one corner of her garden. She entered lovely flowers and vegetables at the Meeker County Fair each August and had dozens and dozens of blue, red, and white ribbons to show for her efforts, all tacked to an old cupboard door in the basement.

Much of the harvest from the garden was destined for canning and the fruit cellar, a partitioned corner of the basement where everything was kept cool. For almost every meal during the winter one of us was dispatched to fetch a jar of beans, pickles, applesauce, carrots, corn, jelly, or something else of the dozens of other items she had lovingly preserved the previous summer.

From her small eight-by-eight-foot kitchen she produced a sumptuous meal not only for her family of ten but also for my sisters' boyfriends and other guests who were often with us for Sunday dinner. During the late 1930s when hobos still roved the countryside, they were never turned away from her kitchen door. In spite of her large family and Wally's meager income, she always had something for the homeless men to eat. I took all this hard work and efficiency for granted, of course. I assumed most mothers did these things. Only later did I realize what others saw in her, how much she was able to do in such a seemingly effortless way.

My children remember her as an affectionate, fun-loving, and engaging grandmother. She took absolute delight in all of her eighteen grandchildren.

Ruth labored over the family budget. I grew up knowing that there were always substantial bills to be paid, especially at the doctor's office and the grocery store. I recall one day when Wally came home with some bags of groceries, set them on the kitchen counter, turned to Ruth, and said quietly, "Hoel says we have to pay down on our bill." Little wonder all of us children grew up knowing it was important for us to work in order to make ends meet.

They were, indeed, a rather mismatched couple, Ruth and Wally. She was the engine, full of fire and steam, always eager to move ahead. He was the caboose, content to follow and always grateful for her energy and enthusiasm.

There was seldom an obvious show of affection. Yet, I have pleasant memories of evenings when they would dismiss us from kitchen duties. Ruth would wash the dishes while Wally rinsed them from the teakettle of hot water on the stove and dried them. They would talk and banter. He would giggle and give her an affection pinch.

In contrast to working with my father, I found it quite difficult to work with my mother. We clashed at times over how to do something in the garden, in the yard, at the church, and in the house. I was as determined as she, insisting that mine was the better way. We were simply too much alike. I found it a great relief when I was old enough to get a part-time job away from home.

When I left home after high school I was intensely homesick for some days. As I reread some of her letters I saved from those years I realize how much she loved me and cared for me. Though it often went unspoken—that was the Swedish way—I could feel that she was intensely proud of me when I graduated from college and seminary and when I was elected to leadership positions through the years.

A cruel end to a difficult life

After Wally died, Ruth lived on with Dave in the family home, devoting herself to him in every way. She often said to me, "No one knows what it's like to raise a handicapped child." From the moment he was born and through the rest of her life, he was constantly on her mind. Dave could not have had a better, more caring mother. She always made the best of things. She saw avenues to move out of impossible corners, to find a way when all doors seemed closed.

By the time she reached her late sixties she was beginning to show small signs of senility. I had been instrumental in arranging for her to win a free trip to Sweden, her lifelong dream. She celebrated her seventieth birthday with cousins she had corresponded with but never met. When she returned, however, she seemed confused about many details of the venture.

As she moved into her seventies we found it necessary for her safety and for Dave's sake to bring her to the local nursing home. Within a year or two she was confined to her bed. For years we visited her and looked into her vacant, searching eyes, conversing with her but getting almost no response. The only time she roused ever so slightly from her deep, distant isolation was when Dave walked into the room on one of his frequent visits. All those years of care for him, all the love, all the devotion—that and only that brought a response. He would go to her bed, take her by the hand and say, "Hello, Mother. How are you?" She would grunt and move, seeming to want to speak to him, to reach out and hold him one more time.

We prayed earnestly for her death. It finally came just three days before her ninety-second birthday. At her funeral service it seemed only appropriate that we sing:

> When peace like a river, attendeth my way;
> When sorrows like sea billows roll;
> Whatever my lot, thou hast taught me to say,
> It is well, it is well with my soul.

A combination of Wally and Ruth

It can be said, on the one hand, that it is nearly impossible to see ourselves as others see us. Yet who knows us as well as we know ourselves? When I try to envision myself, I see someone who is a combination of many of the characteristics of Wally and Ruth. If I am more like one than the other, I would have to say that I am somewhat more like my mother.

I often said of my dad that if you told him it would be a nice, sunny day tomorrow he could shed a tear just thinking about it. He really was a tenderhearted person, never ashamed to let a tear flow. I feel that same way. Tears come easily. Feelings run deep.

At the same time, Wally could be insensitive, not because he meant to be, but simply because that's how he was. He could overlook things that needed to be said, obvious to others but not to him. He found it difficult to talk about differences of opinion. It was the Swedish way to think that if you ignored them they would go away. It took me a long time to break out of that same mold.

Like Ruth, I'm intensely aggressive about many things. Like her, I've always paid attention to details in my work. I've initiated many creative and innovative programs. Once asked to lead or do a task, I have an enormous capacity for hard work. Others tell me that, like her, I seem to be able to do many things effortlessly. Like her, I can get enormous satisfaction from raising a tender flower from a tiny seed and bringing it to full delicate bloom. Like her, I make friends quite easily and count them by the hundreds.

Yet I can also be cool and even stern at times. People who have worked with me know something about the rigid, icy demeanor that comes over me, how my eyes turn a steely grey, how my jaw becomes fixed when I'm displeased with something they have not done as well as I thought it could be done.

If you asked me where I might place myself on an extrovert/introvert scale, I would tell you that I sit at the middle, probably just slightly tilted toward the introvert side. I'm comfortable in my own skin. I need and love time alone. Yet I don't want too much of it. I also love to be with my family and friends.

I guess I'm a bit of both Wally and Ruth. I was born bone of their bone, flesh of their flesh. And I still am.

Thank you, Lord

I give thanks for my heritage. No, they weren't perfect parents by a long way. And neither am I. I can only pray that I will pass along to others what has come down to me.

> We give Thee thanks, our Father,
> for all those who, passing this way before us,
> have beautified the highway of our earthly
> pilgrimage with the splendor of their lives;
>
> For all who have turned the commonplace into
> the Holy of Holies; who have lifted the burden
> of the weary and spilled the fragrance of their
> lives to sweeten the scene of our human anguish;
> We give Thee thanks.

As we partake of the inspiration and strength which
their lives have bestowed upon us . . . let the
remembrance of them rest as a living benediction
on all our days, so that in our days we too may be
the ministers of light and strength, peace and comfort.

So let it be, O Lord. Amen

—Donald Houston Stewart

Chapter 2

Birth and early years:
big family, big garden, big bills

O happy day!

I was born two minutes after midnight on October 18, 1931. Later that same day inventor Thomas Edison died, prompting cities across the land to turn off the lights for five minutes in his honor.

The local newspaper account of my birth is simple:

> Mr. and Mrs. Walfred Chillstrom, residents southwest of town, are parents of a son, born Sunday at the hospital.

There is something sobering and mysterious about my birth. My mother had a miscarriage in July of 1930, probably precipitated by jumping from a hay wagon. She recorded it in her Bible. I assume she was in the early stages of pregnancy or she would not have been in the hay field. The bed of those wagons stood about four feet off the ground. If there was hay on the wagon, the distance may have been higher. Why did she jump, knowing there could be consequences? Was she unaware that she was pregnant? There are no answers. Had my mother carried that pregnancy to full term and delivered a baby in late 1930, I surely would not have been conceived in January of 1931.

Who can probe the mystery of life? Did God intend for me to be? And if so, what about the one who might have been except for that accidental miscarriage? Of course, anyone can wonder why that one particular sperm, out of tens of thousands, penetrated that egg at that moment and gave them life. There is no answer to this mystery of why we came to be. We simply have to say that we *are* and then live life to the fullest.

In 1969 when I celebrated my thirty-ninth birthday my mother wrote a letter to us describing the days around when I was born:

> Dear Herb, Corinne, Mary Lee, Chris & Andrew: Happy Birthday. Much the same weather we had the year 1931. Was a beautiful day the day I came in to the hospital. But after four days it was raining and by the 26–27th we had some 4–5 inches of snow. The wind came along and blew that snow into drifts and it was cold and freezing. It was good to come home to a good warm house and four sisters who couldn't wait to see that "Brother." Everyone busy helping to get the blankets opened up. Chile was 3 years 5 months and quick as lightning, she was the first one up on the davenport and almost sat right on your head. Believe me there were maids and nurses, all willing workers. Adeline was 8 years and she set table for supper. Dad had a roast in the oven and potatoes peeled. Grandma C had sent an apple pie over. So that was such a happy welcome home dinner party. And what joy having such a big fine son. Dad stayed close to basket as watchman over the "peepers" the rest of the evening.

With four delightful, happy daughters already under their roof and in heart of the Great Depression, Ruth and Wally surely didn't need another hungry mouth to feed. I've often said that had they had access to birth control I may never have seen the light of this world.

All of my older sisters had been born at home. Because she must have expected an unusually large baby, Wally and Ruth decided that this time they better go to the hospital in Litchfield. They were right. I weighed in at ten pounds, twelve ounces. My oldest sisters still remember the broad, happy smile on Wally's face when he returned from town to announce that they had a little brother. For a farmer, of course, having a son meant more than just having another child. At that time Wally and Ruth probably still harbored dreams of one day having a quarter section of their own land. The arrival of a son was a sign of hope for the future, the promise that there would be one to till the soil on what would lovingly be known as "the home place."

Becoming a child of God

On November 29, 1931, I was baptized at home by Pastor J. Gottfried Larson, a small man with a heavy limp caused by the ravages of polio. I became a child of the kingdom that day. My baptismal sponsors, in addition to my parents, were Ruth's brother and his wife, Reuben and Cornette Lindell. For all of their lives I felt a special bond with my godparents. As a boy I enjoyed many visits in their home. They often celebrated Christmas Eve with our family. I would lie on my parents' upstairs bed and watch for their car to make the turn a block away on Highway 12. The moment I spied them I raced down the stairs and heralded to the household, "They're here! They're here!"

Why was I baptized at home? I suspect it may have been because Reuben and Cornette were not able to arrive until after lunch. Men worked six days a week in those times. It would have taken them most of Sunday morning to drive out to the country.

My older sisters recall vividly standing wide-eyed about the dining room table as Pastor Larson splashed the water on my head. I still have the etched crystal bowl that was used as a font that afternoon. With each advancing year I treasure my baptism all the more. Little wonder that my favorite Scripture verse is Romans 6:4:

> . . . we have been buried with [Christ] by baptism into
> death, so that, just as Christ was raised from the dead by
> the glory of the Father, so we too might walk in newness
> of life.

Earliest memories

Other than growing up poor and needing to be disciplined quite often, I have mostly good recollections from my first years and through grade school. Given that most of the families we knew were as poor as ours, I have no recollection of feeling sorry for myself.

As I mentioned earlier, we lived with my grandparents, Arvid and Hedda, for more than a year when I was a stripling. One day a shout rang through the house, "There's an airplane in the sky!" We stumbled over each other rushing out to see this wonder of wonders! I couldn't imagine that a human being could actually soar above the earth in what looked like a small, fragile feather floating in the skies. Little did I know that I would eventually fly completely around the world twice and pile up millions of miles in the air, enough to circle the earth more times than I could have imagined on that summer day.

Another early memory brings a smile. My dad and I were having a "peeing contest" in the woods. Little boys have enormous bladder power and I was no exception. Wally was having a ball trying to out-distance his young sire. He was never vulgar or profane. But he loved good humor and a hearty laugh.

I have no doubt that my early spiritual formation stems from those days in my grandparents' home. Each evening after "supper" grandmother Hedda, afflicted with crippling rheumatism, rose slowly and painfully from the table to reach for her well-worn Swedish Bible and *Psalm Bok,* the latter a collection of hymns and prayers. A gentle silence descended over the room as she read from Scripture and then prayed in whispered tones. Rambunctious as I was, I knew this was a reverent moment.

Hedda was a product of the great awakening that swept through Sweden in the nineteenth century as a result of the work of the lay evangelist Carl O. Rosenius.

After they retired and moved to Litchfield, I stopped at Hedda and Arvid's home every week, usually while going to or coming from some custodial duties at the church around the corner. If it was mealtime, the Bible and prayer book invariably came to the table. Though I understood common Swedish words, biblical and devotional usage was out of my ken. Yet an impression was made each time I visited in her home and it was good.

I was a busy, industrious little lad. With little or no money for toys, we had to be inventive. As soon as the table was cleared after breakfast and noon lunch I would go to the silver drawer and remove forks, knives, and spoons. The forks were horses, the knives cows, and the spoons calves. For hours the tabletop was my "farm." I would plow, reap, and harvest with my teams of horses. The cows would go from the "barn" to the pasture and back again for milking. The calves would gambol in the barnyard. I was lost in my imaginary world until it was time for another meal. Now when I watch a commercial on television for the latest offerings for children, I wonder what we're doing to the world of imagination and fantasy.

Duties for everyone

All of us children had our chores after we moved into the house in Litchfield. My sisters aided with cooking and cleaning. My major tasks were to see that the wood box and the coal/corncob bucket beside the kitchen stove were always filled. We kept our "ice box" in the basement. Fashioned from fine hardwood with a metal interior, it looked a bit like a fine safe, which, I guess, it was: a safe place for food in the hot summer months. Because there was no floor drain, my often-neglected duty was to carry out the pan of water that collected from the melting ice. Because it was usually ready to run over by the time I remembered to tend to it, the trip up the narrow basement stairs and over to the kitchen sink was an acrobatic feat. More often than not, water sloshed over the edges on the stairs and kitchen floor, bringing on another scolding for neglected duty.

My most detested chore was to care for the flock of laying hens we kept in the backyard. Because we had no car, half of the garage was partitioned off for a chicken coop. Chickens have to be the most stupid and uncooperative of all of God's creatures. Cleaning their smelly coop was easy to neglect and brought constant reprimands from my mother.

My most frightening duty was to fetch a gallon pail of milk each evening from Mr. Kramer, a dour man who had a small barn and a cow about four blocks from our home. I didn't mind this trek in the summer. In the winter, however, I was terrified as I pulled my sled through deep snow along the dark woods at the edge of town. The fiercer the winds blew, the louder I would sing, "Jesus loves me, this I know, for the Bible tells me so . . ."

Because I always needed to be busy doing something, I would hound my mother with the question, "Mama, what can I do? What can I do?" I drove her to near exasperation. Of course, I had no interest in more chores. I simply wanted her to think up enjoyable things to keep my busy fingers occupied. If she suggested something, such as building a birdhouse, it always turned into a disaster. My dad simply had no decent tools or the ingenuity to create a place for a workshop.

Time for fun

After our duties were done we were free to play. On long summer evenings our large corner lot was the gathering place for all of the kids in the neighborhood. Pump-pump pull-away; hide and seek; captain may I?; ante-I-over; football, softball. My folks gave up any hope of ever having a green, verdant lawn in those years. In the winter we did our homework, listened to the radio, and played games. I often played Monopoly by myself. Later I learned that Corinne did the same on the farm in South Dakota. Too bad we didn't know each other, I thought. Then again, with my propensity to tease, she may have lost all interest in me by the time the romantic juices began to bubble.

As I got a bit older, the boys from the neighborhood organized football, basketball, and baseball games. I would wolf down my food as fast as possible, usually to the consternation of my mother and older sisters, and dash off to engage in the current sport. Wally, at whose left hand I always sat at meals, never slowed me down unless prompted by Ruth.

At the top of the list of my favorite things were the summer days I spent at Uncle Sig's farm. Sig was Wally's older brother, the bachelor who lived with their old mother on the "home place" five miles in the country. It was always comfortable to be with him. He was a good, respected farmer in the community, a long-time deacon at Beckville Church and, like Wally, almost always jovial. What seemed like drudgery at home was a delight at Sig's side. I was eager to do whatever he asked of me and even pestered him for added duties. Shelling corn and tossing it to his flock of chickens, leaning on the fence and watching the pigs wallow in the mud, searching for clutches of eggs that wayward clucking hens tried to hide until the eggs hatched, stroking the noses of Sig's huge horses, pitching hay to the cows, standing in the barn alley watching Sig and Wally lean their heads against the warm bellies of the Holstein cows while they pulled milk from their udders, lingering around the kitchen while Grandma Chilstrom finished a batch of my favorite date-filled cookies. It was always an adventure at Sig's farm.

Time for prayers

Our home was small. Until some of my older sisters graduated from high school, they would at times sleep three in a bed, while Dave and I had our bed in another corner of the room. We were years ahead of colleges that thought coed housing was a novel idea. It was usual for all of us to say our evening prayers together, led by Adeline, our "bedroom chaplain." We began with the Lord's Prayer, followed by:

Now I lay me down to sleep,
I pray the Lord my soul to keep;
If I should die before I wake,
I pray the Lord my soul to take.

The last prayer would be:

God bless Momma, Daddy, my sisters and my brother(s),
and all the children of the world. Amen.

Haroldie, my best friend and compatriot in mischief

Haroldie (Harold Gunter) and I (Herbie) were the best of friends.
Haroldie was the toughest kid in our class, making him especially
nice to have as my buddy. Though he struggled in school, he was
the closest thing to a nature boy I've ever known. On summer
days after chores Haroldie and I wandered far and wide, hiking to
Chicken Lake and Rush Lake, following the Great Northern rail-
road tracks, shooting pigeons near the towering grain elevators,
and, most of all, meandering along "The Crick," a small stream
that snaked its way through fields and ponds for fifteen miles from
Chicken Lake to the Big Crow River.

We fashioned Y-shaped slingshots out of strong tree limbs, cut
rubber strips from worn auto inner tubes, and fashioned stone
grips from the soft leather tongues of discarded shoes. Haroldie
was an ace. Over the summer he would shoot as many as sixty-five
birds; I would do well downing twenty. We shot only "bad" birds—
sparrows, black birds, and robins, which devoured strawberries.

Three or four times each summer Haroldie and I rose before
dawn, took our twelve-foot bamboo cane poles and a can of worms,
and walked Huck Finn-like seven miles to Lake Richardson. We
heisted up our pant legs and waded into the water as far as possible.
If we caught a dozen or two sunfish and a sizeable largemouth bass,
it was a good day. We lingered as long as we dared, believing, like
all good fishermen, that the biggest fish always went for the worm
just as you were ready to call it a day. The long trek home in time

for supper before the sunset was always rewarded with oohs and ahs from our proud parents.

I suppose I was about ten years old when Haroldie introduced me to the fine art and pleasure of smoking. We couldn't afford to buy a pack of cigarettes, of course, even though they cost only ten cents a pack. So on summer days we walked on the curbs on Litchfield's main street, pretending we were doing a balancing act. When we came upon a cigarette butt we deliberately faltered a bit, clutched the butt under our toes, and limped off to the shelter of a bush where we extracted it and deposited it into an empty Prince Albert tobacco tin. Then we were off to the safety of the country-side or someone's backyard shed where we indulged in our sin. We were always careful, however, to smoke from the burnt end of the butt so as to avoid germs!

One night when I came in after a smoking foray my mother asked if I had been smoking. "No," I replied. "Come over and breathe in my face," she demanded. It was the end of my smoking career.

Six wonderful sisters

Though we had our occasional spats, my relationship with my sisters was very good. Each, in her own way, was a very cute child who turned into a good-looking young woman. Some were home-coming queen attendants in high school. Given the need for my mother to attend to the needs of Dave and to help with outside work, all four of my older sisters had a hand in caring for me when I was a baby and young lad.

Adeline, the eldest, was almost like a second mother—and a good one at that. Like Ruth, she was the aggressive, hard-working sister who set the pace for all of us who followed in her footsteps. When her friends started calling her "Addie" it also took hold in the family. She went to a secretarial school and eventually rose to become the executive secretary to the head of an insurance firm in Minneapolis. She and her teacher husband Earle Christenson had one son.

Lorraine, next oldest, was the quiet, sweet one. Like Wally, she said little when we were all together, but talked freely one-on-one. Her delicate good looks won her the title "Miss Litchfield" at one of the community's annual events. She worked as a telephone operator after high school and then assisted her husband in his pharmacy business. Lorraine and Dick Juul had three children.

Winnifred (Winnie) was always cheerful and fun loving. Even to this day our children often say they can't imagine that Auntie Winnie could ever be angry at anyone. She was primarily a homemaker, rearing four children with her husband, Clyde Christenson, an electrician in the Minneapolis area. Later she became a teacher's aide.

Though most of my sisters were called "Chile" outside the family, *Virginia*, the next sister, was the only one who got and kept that moniker within the family. She was also the only one who came with natural curls, the envy of her sisters. Three years older than I, she had to endure most of my teasing, much to her dismay. She became a registered nurse, went off to California where she met Bill Francis, a sailor from South Carolina. After they married, Bill pursued medical school and practiced family medicine in Pickens, South Carolina. They had two children. Chile devoted much of her life to volunteer activities in her community.

After *Dave*, two years younger than I, came *Martha*, the busy, industrious, and creative sister who often rearranged the furniture in the living room and loved to play games with her older brothers and their friends. She trained as a beautician and had her own business for many years. She and Chuck Anderson, a teacher and coach, had four children.

Janet, the surprise package, came along almost five years later. Jan became an elementary teacher and an education specialist, married a pastor, Fred Sickert, and had two children. As with all of her sisters, she has been deeply involved as a volunteer in every congregation where they have been members.

Each of them passes along a legacy of deep faith and good works to future generations.

My brother Dave

I could write much more about each of my sisters.

I need to single out my brother Dave for special and lengthier attention. He was born at the home of Ruth's sister Gerda in Litchfield on November 11, 1933, just a bit more than two years after me. Wally and Ruth were still living in the country at the time. Apparently they could not afford to go to the hospital for this birth. Given the uncertainly of winter weather, they probably opted for Gerda's home as the second-best choice. When the doctor arrived it was clear that this would be a difficult delivery. Most of the details of that day have been lost. Rumors persisted over the years that the physician was inebriated when he arrived. Whatever the case, Dave suffered significant brain damage that left him developmentally disabled for life.

Dave had periodic convulsions in early childhood. My older sisters recall that Ruth placed him between them in bed so that they could alert her when a convulsion was coming on. Ruth wrapped him in warm blankets to reduce the effects of a convulsion. Winnie recalls holding a clothespin between his teeth to keep him from biting his tongue. The convulsions continued on occasion into adulthood. Even now in his 70s he uses medication to control them.

I recall Dave's difficulties in learning to do the things we all take for granted—tying shoes, telling time, making change, understanding the rules of children's games. Everything he did took far more time than it did for other children.

When Dave got excited he pumped his arms and jumped in place. Children can be cruel. There were those who teased him. I got intensely angry at them and had more than one fist fight in defense of Dave. He eventually outgrew this problem.

With no provision for special education in the schools, Dave was simply passed from grade to grade without significant improvement. By the time he reached fifth or sixth grade it was clear that he would have to go off to the State School for the Retarded at Owatonna.

It was decided that Ruth and I would ride with the social worker to bring Dave to Owatonna, four or more hours from Litchfield. Our family had no automobile. I have no idea why Wally did not go instead of me. I can't believe he was unable to get the day off from work. Was it because he was just too softhearted to make that difficult journey?

Except when my son Andrew died, the day we took Dave to Owatonna looms large as the most wrenching moment of my life.

All of the buildings on the grounds of the State School for the Retarded were grey and cold-looking. Nothing like our little shingle-covered house at Litchfield. That house was too small; this place was too large. Inside the front door of the administration building one looked up at high, institutional ceilings, rooms that seemed to echo even when you were just breathing. And I was breathing hard.

We were introduced to the superintendent. He was a kindly, white-haired older gentleman. After a brief tour of the school the superintendent put his arm around Dave and said it was time for his family to leave. Dave began to shake and broke into a desperate sob. Though he had been prepared for this moment and knew what was going on, he was inconsolable. My mother wept and hugged him tightly. I thought I had to be strong. I stood ramrod straight and rigid. The lump in my throat hurt so much that I can feel it even as I write these words.

On the long ride back to Litchfield there was very little conversation, especially the first miles. It was like a car in a funeral procession following a hearse. I was in the back sitting close to my mother. I could feel her body trembling with quiet sobs. My throat was too tight to speak. I was sad to the core of my being.

In the weeks and months that followed, little was said about what my mother and I experienced that day. Nor was I encouraged to speak about it, especially if it meant sharing my feelings. It was the Swedish way. One walked the difficult passages of life in stone silence.

At night, however, my pillow was wet with tears as I cried myself to sleep. No loud sobs, of course, in a room where others were sleeping, too. Just tears. Now the bed we two brothers had shared seemed a mile wide and cold as a frozen prairie. No more poking each other, no more teasing, no more wrestling, no more giggling. Just silence.

I wondered, "How can this be? Where is God in all of it? Why couldn't this have happened to me instead of him? Surely that would have been easier." Dave and I had done so many things together, playing ball, shooting baskets into a wastebasket in the corner of the bedroom with a ball of socks, tickling each other until we were weak from laughter, working in the garden, and much more. At the table, Dave was the one who eagerly and gratefully ate whatever the rest of us didn't like. We joked about him being the family garbage can, and he didn't mind at all. He had a wonderful sense of humor. When he said something funny he laughed at himself harder than anyone else laughed at him. It took a long time until we laughed again around the table. Indeed, it was like death, with all of the stages of grief that follow.

How did I, a twelve-year-old, handle all of this? Though it surely took years for it to become clear, I believe this experience was the beginning of what I later came to understand as the theology of the cross. I could not believe that God, as I had come to understand God in family and Sunday school, would cause things like this to happen. Instead I came to see that God comes to us at our most distressing moments in life, helping us to see that Christ, the Suffering Servant of God, understands our deepest sorrow because he has taken it to the cross. No, all of that wasn't clear to me at the time. But bit by bit the curtain parted and I found comfort.

After more than two years at the State School it became apparent that it, too, was not the right place for Dave. He was brighter and better adjusted than most others. Much to our relief, the community came to realize that it needed to support children like Dave. He returned home and came under the care of Mrs. Niels, a marvelous tutor. He made good progress and was able to function at an early elementary school level. It also made it possible for him to do common labor.

Like the rest of us, Dave was expected to work. For a time he pulled his sled or wagon around town collecting newspapers, magazines, and cardboard boxes. He sorted and packaged them in the garage. Periodically, he sold his collection to a recycling company.

Eventually he got a job at the local turkey processing plant where he worked for more than twenty-five years, spending most of the time on an assembly line, tucking wire prongs into the legs of turkeys. He also had a Saturday evening job cleaning the bakery on Main Street.

When the plant closed I helped Dave secure a position as a custodian at a local church-related retirement center and nursing home. It was the ideal place for him. He has a special way of relating to the elderly. He brought sunshine into their lives as he swept and mopped floors and emptied wastebaskets. At times, when I was a bishop, I stopped to visit him. As we walked the halls together we stopped and chatted with those sitting along the way. They wondered who I was. When I explained it to them they lit up and said, "Oh, you're Dave's brother! He's wonderful. He does such a good job." It made no difference whatever that I may have had some prominence in other places. The only thing that mattered was that I was Dave's brother. I was roving the world, meeting the high and mighty across the country and around the globe. His world was mostly six square blocks in my hometown. Yet, in that world he had become as important, and more so, than I was in mine.

Litchfield has an annual Watercade celebration. One year, as one of the town's supposed famous sons, I was invited to be the commodore. That meant riding down Main Street in an open convertible. Corinne was unable to be with me so I invited Dave to share the ride. Folks all along the way called out, "Hi Dave! Great to see you." Having been away from Litchfield for more than forty years, I was known by very few. They might well have asked, "Who's that fellow with you, Dave?"

Jim Klobuchar, a popular columnist for the *Minneapolis Star Tribune*, wrote an article about the day. It soon spread across the country and the church and became one of the most memorable Jim ever wrote in his long newspaper career.

Dave has always had a deep faith. I often referred to him in sermons as an example of simple, uncomplicated trust. Typical of those references was what I said at Luther Northwestern Seminary in January 1977:

> Last Saturday night my only brother, Dave, did his usual thing. He went down to the local bakery on Main Street in my hometown and cleaned it. That's right, cleaned it. He swept the bakery from one end to the other and scrubbed it until it glistened. He does this every Saturday night because it's one of the few things he can do.
>
> You see, Dave had brain damage when he was born that left him somewhat developmentally disabled. He can do little beyond routine things. He couldn't finish high school like his brother. He couldn't go to college and seminary and graduate school like his brother. He's never been on TV, radio, or had his picture in the newspaper. No one will ever call him bishop.
>
> But he has a calling. And if you could hear him describing how important he feels about cleaning the bakery on Saturday night, how important it is to make certain every corner is spic and span, how important it is to have it ready for an

unexpected visit by the health officer, if you could hear him
tell it, you would understand what it means for one of God's
precious children to use his gift; and you would forever
forget about belonging to an elite group of professionals in
the church.

When I was elected the first bishop of the ELCA in May 1987, I
called him immediately from Columbus, Ohio, site of the constituting convention. I wanted him to get the news straight from me.
He was quiet for a moment and then said, "I know." "What do you
mean?" I asked. "Has someone called you already?" "No," he said,
"but I know." "Well," I said, "who told you?" "You know," he said,
"you know." Then he was quiet again. Finally it dawned on me. He
was telling me that he had had some conversations with God about
all of this and he simply knew it was going to turn out that way.

When he was diagnosed with prostate cancer after his retirement, Martha, Chuck, and I took him to the surgeon to find out
what procedure he would recommend. Dave and I had time that
day to drive out into the Beckville community where our folks once
lived. We walked the cemetery where so many relatives are buried.
As we moved among the graves, chatting about various ones we
knew, Dave said, "It's going to be a big gathering up there, ain't it?"

As I write, Dave continues to live in an apartment at the retirement
facility where he was employed. This is his family. For years he volunteered in the kitchen, cutting up empty cardboard boxes and preparing them for recycling, just as he did more than fifty years earlier.

Again and again through life Dave has reminded me by his
example of what Jesus said about faith like that of a little child.

Dave has had a profound impact on my life and the life of our
family, including our children. If I have some sense of working for
justice for others, some sensitivity for those who are developmentally challenged, some courage to speak out on issues of fairness, I
owe much of that to Dave.

Grade school: an average student

We lived nine blocks from the elementary school. The way Haroldie and I walked those blocks—via alleyways, across the courthouse lawn, through Central Park, past the entrance to the Presbyterian Church—reduced the distance to about six blocks. Our direct line took us near the Roman Catholic Church and the nuns' residence. If we saw the priest coming down the sidewalk, we stepped into the gutter; if some habit-clad nuns happened along our way, we crossed the street.

Had you suggested to that young lad that he would one day have a priest as a good friend, that he would know Catholic bishops in Minnesota and across the country as respected colleagues, and, wonders of wonders, that he would have a private audience with the pope some fifty years later, he would have laughed so hard he would have fallen to the ground. Yes, it all happened.

My record in elementary school can only be described as lack-luster. In fourth grade I received an "unsatisfactory" in speaking well before a group. It was probably related to stuttering. At that stage of life it was quite pronounced. I was petrified at the thought of standing before the class to read or recite. By the time I reached junior high school the problem was mostly gone. In those days, of course, there was no speech therapy for cases like mine. I simply seem to have outgrown stuttering. Even now, however, there are certain combinations of words and syllables that are difficult for me to pronounce. When I start to speak them I subconsciously stop and substitute other words or phrases.

I don't recall what was behind it, but in fifth grade some of my classmates were teasing me incessantly about something. I came to a slow boil. One day when the teacher stepped out of the room for a moment I walked over to the worst heckler and punched him in the chest so hard that he flew across the aisle and against a chalkboard. That ended the teasing. I suppose it was part of the formation of a future bishop, one who would need to administer discipline on occasion.

Years later, when I was bishop of the Minnesota Synod, *Lutheran Partners* magazine invited me to write an article about my three all-time favorite teachers. I chose Margaret Schmid, my sixth grade teacher, as one of them. Like all school children I thought she seemed ancient when I had her as a teacher and assumed at the time I wrote the article that she had long since died. To my surprise, someone who knew Margaret informed me that she was indeed still very much alive and retired in New Ulm, Minnesota, her hometown. I got in touch with her and arranged for a visit on one of my trips through that area. We had a delightful time. Among other things, she recalled what an excellent student I had been. I didn't have the heart to demolish her illusion. My report card, saved by my mother, told a different story.

Junior high school

In junior high school, which included grades 7–9, I was preoccupied with sports, especially basketball. I was on the first ten traveling team when I was in eighth grade. My prayers were centered on asking God to help me make that team each week. Either God answered or else I was quite good. When a new coach took over in ninth grade he asked me which other fellows I thought should be on the first five with me. I was of average height until then and enjoyed good coordination and fine athletic skill.

My academic record in junior high school was much like that in grade school—very average. Though I was far from the top student, I seemed to be quite popular among my classmates who elected me "Snow King" in seventh grade. I remember asking myself, "Why me?" It was a question I would be asking for the rest of my life.

Everyone works

As we reached junior high school age, all of us children in the family were expected to find a part-time job. After school, on Saturdays, and during the summer months we were busy earning money for our own clothes and school needs. My first regular part-time job was filling beer and soda pop dispensers at the Travelers' Inn before and after school and sorting bottles on Saturdays. The best thing about that job was the Saturday noon meal that came as part of my three dollars and fifty cents per week remuneration. How I loved *two* pork chops, mashed potatoes smothered with white gravy, creamed corn, and a generous slice of pie à la mode. I was in heaven. Unfortunately, the owner was an alcoholic. I watched as he came to the basement and spiked glasses of Coke with whiskey. I witnessed his degeneration. It was my introduction to the curse of alcoholism. Ironically, his brother was a highly respected Lutheran pastor in Iowa.

When the Traveler's Inn changed ownership I got a job at Harding Dry Cleaners, sorting dirty clothes and putting them through the cleaning machine. The owner said I could keep any small change I found in pockets. For a time I also worked at a local poultry processing plant, walking a moving track and pulling malodorous feathers from steaming chickens and turkeys before tossing them into huge cold bath tubs.

Confirmation class: a boring time

Confirmation class was a total bore for me. I put little effort into it. On Friday evenings, when I should have been preparing for the Saturday morning class and in spite of repeated pleas from my mother, I occupied myself with playing Solitaire, a card game I had learned from my godfather.

In the class, old Pastor Franzen would begin in the front row and go from one student to the next asking us to recite from memory the answers to questions in Luther's *Small Catechism*. A few of us boys soon learned that if we sat in the back row we could figure out which question would be ours. We memorized the answer on the spot and rendered perfect responses, forgetting it as quickly as we had learned it. I looked forward to the end of confirmation classes and a time when I might decide for myself if I wanted to go to worship on Sunday mornings.

World War II

I was just ten years old when World War II broke out with the attack on Pearl Harbor. In those pre-television years the most vivid images of the war came in the newsreels that preceded movies. It was awesome to hear President Roosevelt declare war on the Japanese and then the Germans, to see actual footage of battle scenes, to imagine what it must have been like to fly those planes that battled the enemy.

At the beginning, no one in my immediate family was involved in the war as a soldier. Annie, my dad's cousin, gave us detailed accounts of the letters that came from her son Ray, an infantryman in the South Pacific. She pored over the daily newspaper to see if she might catch a glimpse of him in one of the photographs from the front lines.

My friend Haroldie's older brother Jim joined the Navy Seabees. His father, a veteran of World War I, suggested that he bring back Tojo's ear, no doubt a way of using humor to cover his fear for his son.

Everyone, of course, got caught up in the war in one way or another:

> I recall buying two war bonds. They cost $18.25 each and would mature in ten years to a payout worth $25.00. I recall cashing them in when I was at Augsburg College.

> We collected anything that might be used for the war effort—cooking grease, foil wrappers from sticks of gum and cigarette packages, tin cans, newspaper, and other items.

> Gas was rationed. Depending on your personal situation, you got an "A," "B," or "C" stamp that was affixed to the windshield on the passenger side. We had no automobile. But I recall peering at the stamp on my Uncle Sig's car. On

every stamp was the question: "Is This Trip Necessary?" It occurs to me that we could use those same stickers to save the earth today!

In the front of our church hung a banner with blue stars, each representing a son of the congregation who served in the military. I recall the sobering chill that settled over the congregation on the Sunday when a gold star appeared. A son of the congregation had been killed.

Families with sons in the military also hung a flag with a star on it in the street-side window. When a gold star appeared in the window of the one home it gave me an eerie feeling. Art had made fun of brother Dave. Now he was dead. I felt very sad for the family. I was certain he must have felt sorry for having teased Dave.

Every Saturday Elmer, a bachelor neighbor, would crank up his old Model A coupe and take me along to the creamery to get a gallon of buttermilk. I suppose my mother used it for baking bread. On the way home he would stop a grocery store to get his Copenhagen snuss supply for the week and treat me to a candy bar.

Hate for the Germans and Japanese was encouraged in subtle ways. Ash trays had an image of Hitler on the bottom where one could snub out a cigarette butt in his face. The dislike for Hitler spilled over into our treatment of people of German descent in the community. Just a block from our home lived an old man, a widower, named Kalkbrenner. I recall with shame the night my friends and I, for no reason other than that he was German, tossed dirt bombs at his home from his garden.

Poor families were given tokens that we could exchange at the Relief Office for food and clothing. The thin jacket I wore until my senior year in high school came from that office. I recall bringing home foods of various kinds in my coaster wagon.

When the war ended I walked with pride down Litchfield's main street, proud at the sight of a flag inserted in a pipe hole in front of every business place.

Because of the shortage of young men in the community, laborers like my dad and I would go out to farms after work and school to shock grain and help with harvest. After our work in the field we would be served a sumptuous meal. I enjoyed the "grown up" conversation and thinking that I was helping the war effort in some small way. It was at one of those dinners that I first heard the awesome report about a new kind of bomb that had been dropped on Japan killing tens of thousands of civilians. I could not have known that one day I would walk over that ground at Nagasaki and remember those who perished.

I recall hearing my mother express concern that the war might last long enough for me to be involved. I don't remember feeling any sense of dread over that thought.

A very average lad

If one of the aims of an autobiography is to look back and try to find sparks that would later flame up into something significant, I'd have to say in all honesty that nothing from this period of my life took on anything beyond suggesting that I was a very average lad.

Chapter 3

Youth: finding faith and a career

Beginning a spiritual quest

I had many spiritual guides during my childhood and youth. My parents made certain we attended Sunday church school and worship. There was always a prayer before meals and, at times, family devotions. First Lutheran Church at Litchfield was an important part of my spiritual odyssey.

I grew up not only as a Lutheran, but as a self-conscious Swedish Lutheran. There was a German Lutheran Church one block to the east and a Norwegian Lutheran Church one block to the north, but they may as well have been on different planets. Though each had a proper name—"First," "Zion," "Redeemer"—each was more commonly identified by its ethnic identity—Swedish, Norwegian, and German.

If you had asked me as a young lad to describe the difference between these three churches I may have suggested that beer was the clue. While cutting the grass at our Swedish church I noted that the local beverage company often delivered cases of beer to the German Lutheran parsonage. In contrast, I knew that most of the Norwegians were strict teetotalers. As for the Swedes, I knew that some of them quaffed a glass now and then, but only after pulling the shades.

As I said earlier, my grandmother Hedda was a major influence on my spiritual journey. One Sunday school teacher also stands out. Though her body had been ravaged by polio, necessitating heavy leg braces, Luella Nelson's cheerful faith made a lasting impression on our fourth-grade class. Our "classroom" was the front pew in the church. We could hear her coming down the aisle, braces and feet clomping with each step. We were aware of her disability. But the moment she turned to the class and broke into a broad smile, we forgot that she was disabled in any way. She radiated Christian hope and joy.

Earlier I said that confirmation class meant little to me. On our confirmation day, June 9, 1945, we were presented with Bibles. In mine one of the Scripture references Pastor Franzen penned into the front was Romans 5:1:

> Therefore, since we are justified by faith, we have peace
> with God through our Lord Jesus Christ.

Like most thirteen-year-olds I paid little attention to it that day. How could I have known that this verse would come to life in a very personal way in the week that followed?

An unexpected week of grace

When I learned that my friends were going to spend a week at Green Lake Bible Camp near Spicer, Minnesota, following our confirmation day, I decided to join them. I had no special interest in the Bible I had received the previous Sunday. Strong sexual feelings were beginning to stir. My motivation had more to do with girls than with the Bible.

To my surprise, that week turned out to be the most significant week of my young life, and possibly of my *entire* life. I began to hear the Word of God in a new and fresh way. Paul Lindell, a lay leader with theological training, and Pastor Wallace Setterlund were especially influential. Both men exuded joy and excitement about the Christian faith.

In the evenings cabin counselors from Gustavus Adolphus

College, Robert Johnson and Donald Johnson, made an indelible impression on me during our devotional time. I said a free prayer during one of those sessions, a first for me. I recall looking up from my top bunk bed one night and out into the starry nighttime sky. I was overwhelmed with the thought that a loving God came to us in Christ to forgive sin—my sin.

The camp experience changed me. It was my Damascus Road moment. I came home with a determination to live the faith. In retrospect, it is difficult for me to imagine the direction my life might have taken had I not gone to that camp. I began reading my Bible daily. Because our home was so small and because it usually cooled down in the house in the winter when it was bedtime, the only comfortable place I could find for my devotional reading was the bathroom. So I usually waited until the others had gone to bed before doing my Bible reading and prayer. I would close the stool cover and use it for my chair. I often knelt by the bathtub to pray.

By the time I finished high school I had read my Bible from cover to cover, including every "begat" in Numbers and every "selah" in the Psalms. As I read I underlined passages that were especially meaningful to me. It is difficult to find a page in that well-worn Bible that does not have a passage that is underlined. In 1947 my mother inscribed a short note on the flyleaf in the front of the Bible:

> Be careful how you live. You may be the only Bible some
> people ever read. Mother 1947

On blank pages in the back of my Bible I jotted down pithy sayings that I reaped from a variety of places. A few samples:

> I see that a man cannot be a faithful servant until he
> preaches Christ for Christ's sake, until he gives up striving
> to attract people to himself and seeks only to attract them
> to Christ.
>
> —Robert McCheyne

What are churches put into the world for except to do the impossible in the strength of God?

—George Armstrong

He who kills time mortgages eternity.

God's mercy holds back what we do deserve; God's grace gives us what we don't deserve.

Prayer is the opening of the channel between our emptiness and God's fullness.

If we do not trust God *with* all we do not trust him *at* all.

It was also during those cabin devotions at Bible camp that one of the counselors suggested that we begin praying that God would guide us one day to the person we should marry. That made good sense to me. I did so until I met that special one several years later.

Tithing, a lifelong practice

When I was a junior or senior in high school, I learned about tithing. Though I was beginning to think about attending college and needed to save every dime toward that possibility, I decided to take a leap of faith. Each week I set aside ten percent or more of my part-time income and gave it to my church or a church-related cause. That start proved to be the beginning of a lifelong practice of tithing. It has been a source of enormous blessing. In a journal entry in early 1973, nearly twenty years after we were married I wrote:

> Last year we gave . . . well over a tithe. It really is a thrill to
> see how God blesses. We don't know what the future has
> in store—but the blessings that have come since I began
> tithing in 1949 have been beyond my wildest imagination. I
> hope we will be able to stretch even more in '73.

Tithing, and many times well beyond the ten percent plateau, has been a way of life for Corinne and me for all of our years of married life.

Is God calling me to be a pastor?

Beginning at the Bible camp and through my high school years I kept thinking about the possibility of becoming a pastor. At first the idea seemed so preposterous that I never mentioned it to a soul. When asked what I might seek as a career I usually said, "civil engineer," though I had not the foggiest notion what such a person actually did.

My pastor, A.H. Franzen, surely saw no qualities of leadership in me and gave me no encouragement to think about the ministry. My friend and confirmation mate Don Anderson and I were acolytes nearly every Sunday. Again and again Franzen would turn to Don in the sacristy and urge him to think about studying to be a pastor. And for good reason. Don was at the top of our class in school and an all-around stellar young man. Eventually Don became an engineer, a senior official in the Iowa Highway Department and an ordained deacon in the Episcopal Church. Not once, however, did Franzen ever make a comment like that to me. And also for good reason.

In high school I continued to be a very average student. My report cards show no indication of academic promise. Our small home was not an environment conducive to study. With only an eighth-grade education at best, and with Swedish as their primary language during their own childhood and youth, Wally and Ruth had little sense of how to encourage disciplined study habits. Among my many relatives, only cousin Ed had attended college. We were a working-class family. There were no expectations that any of us would go to college or rise to places of leadership.

Physical changes, more work

After ninth grade I moved into a sudden growth spurt, shooting up almost a foot in a matter of two years. Having been so well-coordinated and agile, I became awkward and gangly, stretching up to more than 6 feet 3 inches and weighing only 140 pounds. Now others passed me up in athletic ability, and I dropped out of competitive sports in school.

I continued to play basketball in the community league with a few friends one night a week. In my senior year some of the play-off games in the community league fell on Wednesdays, which conflicted with Lenten mid-week services. Much to the dismay of my teammates, I opted for church. Was that a wise thing to do? Might I have made a stronger witness if I had upheld my commitment to the team? I wonder now. Then, it seemed the right thing to do.

It was in high school that I had my longest and most favorite part-time job. The Litchfield Greenhouse was just a block from home. How I loved to come into the warm, colorful tropics of the greenhouse on a frigid Minnesota winter afternoon, shed my coat, and care for the plants. My lifelong love for flowers was fostered by my mother, of course, but also by Al Marohn, the burly florist. He took great delight in creating a lovely bouquet or a delicate corsage with his ham-hock fists. Often when I passed through the preparation room he would hold up a masterpiece and ask, "Herb, isn't this beautiful?" Al taught me that loving flowers is as masculine as it is feminine.

Halfway through my senior year Al informed me that his business had grown and he needed full-time help. Out of courtesy and somewhat half-heartedly he offered me the job, knowing that it would mean quitting school. Though it was a kind gesture, we both knew it was out of the question.

Fortunately, a new restaurant opened just a few blocks away, the Nel-Dix Post House. I got a job as a waiter. Part of my remuneration was a free meal after closing and clean-up time. In a matter of three months I added twenty pounds to my skinny frame. One evening Mrs. Dixon, who was more like an army sergeant than her retired military husband, suggested that I eat a little less. I must have been cutting into their profit margin.

These folks also owned an A&W root beer stand near the restaurant. In the summer of my senior year I managed the enterprise, informing them of supplies that were needed and riding herd over carhops, the teenagers who carried root beer, Pronto Pups, and ice cream to the waiting cars. Good preparation, I guess, for a bishop-to-be.

Early clues to a future of leadership

It was in my tenth-grade English class that I got my first hint that I might have some potential for leadership. We were assigned to give a short, humorous speech. Being a bit more of an introvert than an extrovert, I was amazed at how comfortable I felt in front of others. They seemed to pay careful attention to what I said. They enjoyed my humor. The teacher, a grumpy curmudgeon by the name of Floyd Warta, seemed stunned and a bit bemused that this shy boy from the edge of town had done so well.

The next year it was another teacher, Jesse McClure, who played what was probably the most significant role in my unfolding life toward leadership. I was on my way to the balcony of the school auditorium to be a spectator at a basketball game when she caught me on the stairs and urged me to come to her room where there was rehearsal for extemporaneous speaking. I had no idea what the term meant, but decided on the spur of the moment to give it a try. Again, I discovered I had gifts for communication. That led to involvement in both extemporaneous speaking and original oratory at area speech contests. I earned "Superior" ratings at contests.

My original oration was entitled "Alcoholism." When I reread it I can understand why my mentors suggested that I concentrate on extemporaneous speaking. For a high school student it wasn't all that bad. But it had an unnecessarily negative and judgmental tone. Speech judges would not have reacted kindly to it.

In my senior year I was elected class vice president. Marion Scudder, social studies teacher, penned a note in my senior yearbook:

> I expect to come into a church some day and see Herbert in the pulpit.

I was stunned. How could she have been so certain of my future when I myself still felt so unsettled about it?

At First Lutheran Church my friends must have seen some potential in me when they elected me president of the Luther League in my junior year. Now my principal spiritual guides were Mildred Oslund and Myrtle Oslund, single twin sisters who worked as bank tellers. They were counselors to our youth group. It was they who encouraged me to attend Mount Carmel Bible Camp one summer. I returned to Mount Carmel every summer for the next five years. There I became acquainted with the work of the Lutheran Bible Institute in Minneapolis, sponsors of the camp. Each year I looked forward to another week or two at the camp. It was always a place for spiritual renewal.

When First Lutheran Church celebrated its seventy-fifth anniversary it was decided to have a youth night. Pastor Franzen suggested we invite the Rev. Melvin Hammarberg, pastor of a large congregation in St. Paul, to be our guest speaker. I made all the arrangements and introduced him to the congregation prior to his address. I was surprised and a bit embarrassed when he said in his introductory remarks that he hoped Herbert would consider becoming a pastor. How could he have known that I was thinking about it? Little did I realize that one day Hammarberg would play a major role at critical times in my life.

Academic life—no shining star

In school I continued to be a mostly average student, struggling especially with courses in math and science. In tenth and eleventh grades the record shows mostly Bs with a few Cs in courses like algebra and chemistry. I simply assumed that I could do no better. Yes, I worked after school a great deal. Yes, our home was a difficult place to study. Yes, I devoted much time to the youth program at church. My major problem, however, was that I simply did not know how to study. I graduated thirty-third in a class of one hundred and six.

In spite of that less than brilliant academic record, I seem to have had a rather strong sense of confidence in myself. In an essay written for an English class in twelfth grade I was assigned to describe my life. Among other things I wrote:

> I greeted this new and fascinating world with a bright and smiling face and have tried to keep it as such all of my life. All in all I think that my life has been quite exciting and interesting so far, and I'm looking forward to it being even more so in the future.

In my senior year I made one of the most important decisions in my academic journey. Along with a couple of other classmates I decided to take the typing class as an elective. Once we learned the basic skill all three of us dropped the course. I have been forever grateful for that decision. It meant that all through college, seminary, and my years of ministry I have been able to type my own papers, to type letters when necessary, and to use a computer with ease.

Girls and special friends

I had many good friends, male and female, both at church and in school. I dated sporadically and exchanged letters with several I met at youth conferences and Bible camps. All were fine Christians, and, in my opinion, good-looking young women. There were girls in our church youth group that gave signs that they would be pleased if I dated them. They were more like sisters to me. I surely had a strong interest in girls. But I kept thinking and praying about that special one. I knew I hadn't met her as yet and was content to wait.

Among male friends whose relationship lasted for a lifetime were Fred Erson and Don Lehti. Both were several years older than I. Both eventually became pastors. Their letters were like what Paul's letters to Timothy must have been. I found encouragement and inspiration in each of our exchanges. Erson's wife and children became close friends. Lehti never married. Only after his death did I learn that he was gay. Never during our long years of friendship did we ever discuss his sexual orientation. We were simply brothers in Christ.

I also found delight in singing in the church choir. Surrounded by the deep bass voices of Lowell Wilson and Walfred Lund, and with my own voice changing rapidly, I reveled in the blended tones of the choir. Lowell's wife, Margaret, was not only the director and a superb musician, but also a beautiful woman with an engaging personality. I dreamed that I might one day have a wife just like Margaret.

You're going to a *Bible* institute?

Because of doubts about my academic ability and because I wasn't certain I had the gifts needed to become a pastor, I decided it would a good idea to spend a year at the Lutheran Bible Institute (LBI) in Minneapolis, Minnesota.

My decision distressed my parents. Though they gave their children absolute freedom to make our own decisions, including the choice of a career, this was a bit much. One night Wally and Ruth and one of my older sisters sat down with me and tried to persuade me not to attend LBI. They spoke about obnoxious people from the school who went about buttonholing people and asking if they were saved.

Pastor Franzen also weighed in. On the Sunday before I left for LBI he cornered me in the sacristy and told me that I was wasting a year of my life. I remained resolute. I had met others from LBI who were not as abrasive as those my pastor and parents had met. Though I was reluctant to displease them, I felt certain it was the right next step for me.

It needs to be said here that Wally and Ruth eventually changed their minds. By the end of my year of study at LBI they were fully supportive of me and of the school. They even attended Mount Carmel Camp themselves more than once.

A year at the Lutheran Bible Institute

Attending the Lutheran Bible Institute proved to be a good decision. I've never regretted it. Yes, some of the faculty and quite a few students were fundamentalist in their biblical views. But there were also those who were quite progressive and well-balanced in their thinking. Little or nothing was said in the classes about social concerns or justice issues. The major value for me was that I became better acquainted with the content of the Bible. I memorized hundreds of Bible verses, writing the verse on one side of a three-by-five card with the reference on the other. These disciplines were a gift that has served me well for my entire ministry. Dr. Alvin Rogness, president of Luther Seminary in St. Paul, Minnesota, once commented that he wished all seminary students would spend a year or two at LBI simply to give them a better knowledge of the content of the Bible. I agree.

I worked in the bookstore mail room during my year of study, wrapping and mailing books and Bible study materials. In a note written more than fifteen years later, manager Anne Peterson said that she remembered me for "your efficiency, in spite of your youth . . . I count you as one of the two outstanding and dependable helpers (I have had) in that department."

The most important benefit from my year at LBI was that I finally learned how to study. My grades for the year were mostly As and Bs with only a few Cs. At the end of the first year I was offered the school's only scholarship for a second year of study. It was an enormous boost to my confidence. But I was ready to go on to college.

Letters to and from home

My mother was faithful to write during the year I was at LBI. In the first letter, written in early October 1949, she begins with a reference to Psalm 27:14:

> Wait for the Lord; be strong, and let your heart take cour-
> age; wait for the Lord!

This was usual practice for pious Swedes. The letters I have that
grandmother Hedda Lindell sent to her parents in Sweden and the
letters they sent to her commonly began with a Bible reference.

Ruth's letter to me is mostly about my work at LBI. I had
arranged for the mail room job before I enrolled. After I arrived the
frenetic business manager, tried to persuade me to give the job to
another student he deemed more needy than I. Ruth, as might be
expected, urged me to persist in holding the business manager to
his promise, reminding me that I had worked hard to accumulate
enough money to attend LBI and that it would be unfair to give the
job to someone who may not have been as diligent as I had been.

In another letter in early November she devotes much of it to
concern for her mother Hedda:

> Grandma's days are very limited, and as far as that goes
> grandma is happy and ready to meet her savior. She has
> had a thorny path to walk all through this life nothing but
> suffering. Yet so patient.
>
> Love from all here. Mother

In a letter home a month later I mentioned that I was working as
much as five hours a day in the mail room. I also noted that I had
brought my laundry to sister Adeline. All through my years at LBI
and Augsburg College one of my older sisters, all of whom were
living in Minneapolis at the time, did my laundry for me—a magnificent gesture on their part. And, of course, almost every time I
delivered or picked up laundry there was a delicious meal waiting
for me. I owe so much to them and their husbands. I ended the letter home with a reference to 1 Corinthians 1:4–6:

> I give thanks to my God always for you because of the
> grace of God that has been given you in Christ Jesus, for

in every way you have been enriched in him, in speech
and knowledge . . .

There were sprinkles of humor in the letters. In one I suggested
that my mother worried too much about me, especially the trips
to and from Minneapolis. After riding back to the Cities with my
Uncle Clarence I wrote:

> I thought I should drop you a line to let you know that we
> had a terrible trip. We had ten accidents in all. At Dar-
> win a car sideswiped us and we nearly ran into the ditch.
> When we got to Dassel we had a head-on collision with a
> new Cadillac. At Howard Lake we ran into the ditch and
> at Rosemont we nearly knocked an old man down. And to
> top it off the bridge just outside of Mpls caved in just as we
> were crossing it! Even if all those things had happened, it
> would have done absolutely no good for you to have wor-
> ried. So the moral of the story is: Don't worry!

Yes, I will study to become a pastor

My sense of call to ordained ministry came to a head one Sunday
morning. Pastor Franzen had retired from my home congregation at Litchfield. The Rev. J. Henry Bergren, a faculty member at
LBI, was preaching on weekends at First Lutheran Church, part
of a two-point parish. One day he asked me if I would go with
him to conduct the liturgy while he did the preaching. I agreed.
All that previous week I went to the cold, musty attic of the old
dormitory and rehearsed the liturgy, turning first to an imaginary
altar and then to an imaginary congregation. I was nervous but
well-prepared.

Sunday dawned—March 26, 1950. As we drove out into the
country for the first service at Ostmark Lutheran Church near Wat-
kins, Minnesota, Bergren pulled up to a stop sign a mile from the
church. He turned to me and asked, "Herb, may I tell the congregations this morning that you plan to study to become a pastor?"

Without hesitation and with strong confidence I was able to say, "Yes, you may do so."

I had "put my hand to the plow." Now there was no turning back. With one brief exception that I will write about later, there has never been a moment of doubt since that day that God had called me to the ordained ministry.

Pastor Bergren invited me to accompany him again less than a month later. This time I was to preach for the first time. It was April 16, 1950. The text was John 21:3–7. Again, we went first to Ostmark Church in the open country. I preached from an outline. Like all good Lutheran sermons, it had three points: A Dark Night, A Dawning Day, and A New Day. I prepared what I thought was an adequate sermon of appropriate length.

The sermon wasn't all that bad. The problem was that in a day when the minimum length for a sermon was at least twenty-five minutes, mine lasted only ten to twelve minutes. I'm certain the brevity was due in part to my nervous state of mind and rapid pace. All the way to Litchfield I combed my mind to think of illustrations I might add to extend the sermon for another five minutes. I managed to stretch it to almost twenty minutes.

I think Wally and Ruth were quite proud of me that day, though Swedes would have a hard time expressing such sentiments. I remember that my dad told me that he was impressed that I was able to preach from notes and look at the congregation as I spoke. As for my mother, she expressed her pride in a letter that I received the last week of April 1950. She had just returned from a Minnesota Conference (Synod) meeting and wrote:

> I got a kick out of Mrs. Hulterstrum. She kept saying after hearing each preacher, oh, Herbert's first sermon was wonderful comparing with these four ministers. Some were older and yet I guess were not cut out to be preachers.

A time of doubt

At some point in the year at LBI I wrestled with a time of doubt—what some call a "dark night of the soul." Several years later, in February 1954, I reflected on that experience:

> I was very discouraged about everything. But from my classes and past experience I knew that God could meet my need in his Word. I knew that I would have to spend time *alone* with the Lord in his Word. I determined that I would spend this time during the noon hour. "Instead of waiting in the long line for lunch why not go to my room and be alone with the Lord?" I thought to myself. This I did for several days until I finally found the release and assurance that I wanted to regain.

Corinne—the best gift of all

There was, however, another wonderful gift that I received during that year at LBI. I met the one I would marry—that special one I had been praying for—Corinne Hansen from Vermillion, South Dakota.

Corinne had graduated from Augustana Academy, a church-related high school at Canton, South Dakota, the previous spring. She was among the top students in her class. She was beautiful. Her classmates had elected her homecoming queen. She was on the girls' basketball team, the debate squad, and in the a cappella choir. She sang solos. I garnered all this data from Charles Ekanger, my roommate at LBI and one of Corinne's classmates at the academy. He knew she would come the second term.

Had she done as I had done—defied her parents' wishes—she would not have come to LBI. Her dream had been to go to St. Olaf College at Northfield, Minnesota, to major in English and possibly go into teaching. Having attended the academy where Bible and religion courses were required, she saw no need to attend LBI.

Her parents, however, were adamant. "You will no doubt get

married and have a family," her domineering father said. "There's
no need for college." This seemed strange, given the fact that his
wife, Edith, had had a year of college and his daughter Dorothy had
spent two years at Augustana College in Sioux Falls, South Dakota.
Nevertheless, his word was final. Then, because Corinne's mother
had been ill during the summer months, her father also insisted
that she stay home on the farm in the fall. Only then would she be
free to go to LBI after the New Year. She agreed half-heartedly and
came to LBI with the intention to simply endure it.

Corinne and I have often said over the years that her father
was half-right. She did become a wife and mother. But eventually
she also graduated from college—Minnesota State University at
Mankato, summa cum laude—and, ironically, served for several
years on the Board of Trustees at St. Olaf College. So, in spite of
him, she not only earned a college degree but also got to St. Olaf.

Charles Ekanger, my roommate, had a composite photo of the
academy senior class mounted on the dresser near his desk. When
he wasn't in the room I would often wander over and take a closer
look at that special girl in the small oval insert. I wondered, "Could
she be the one I've been praying for?" The more he told me about
her, the more determined I was to be first in line to date her when
she arrived in January.

I moved rapidly. The very first week I called and invited her to
go to an evangelism rally the following weekend at a church in
south Minneapolis. The fact that it was Friday the thirteenth made
no difference to me. I was not superstitious. A light, fluffy snow
was falling as we walked to the streetcar line at Chicago Avenue,
a few blocks east of LBI. The trolley was full so we stood, hang-
ing on to straps as we chatted for most of the half-hour ride. The
church, Trinity Lutheran of Minnehaha Falls, was hosting a visiting evangelist. I have no recollection of what he said. All I recall is
that he pounded heavily on his Bible to make his points, a gesture I
thought quite odd.

I knew from the moment I met her that she was indeed a very special person. And she says that her feelings were the same. She found herself wondering, even on that first date, if this tall Swedish boy might be the one she had been praying for. She recalls how those gentle snowflakes settled in my big ears on the walk back from Chicago Avenue. She noticed that they didn't melt. "A cool guy," she thought. Twenty-eight years later, on the anniversary of that first date, Corinne wrote on a card, "I remember the warm happy feeling I had that evening. I knew you were different from anyone I'd dated . . . special."

We dated on occasion for the remainder of the year. Both of us knew, however, that we had many years of education ahead of us. We didn't even hold hands during that time. When we parted in the spring of the year I had no idea whether our relationship would continue in the fall. I simply hoped and prayed that there was more to come.

The negative side—legalism

As important as my spiritual journey had been during my years in high school and at LBI, there was also a negative side to it. LBI was an enclave of piety, shielding us from many of the problems in the culture that surrounded us in the Twin Cities and the broader world. We learned nothing about issues such as racism, abuse, prostitution, poverty, and other pressing questions. The extent of our contact with the world outside the Bible school was an occasional visit to a gospel mission in the Washington Avenue "red light" district, then the center for bars and houses of prostitution. Our aim was to convert, not to understand the underlying problems that festered in that world. In a letter home in March 1950, I describe one of those outings:

> Last Friday night I was the leader down at one of the gospel
> missions on Washington Avenue. It's really an experience
> to go down into the filth of that section of town. Some of

those men are certainly in a terrible condition. You often
wonder how men can go down so far into sin. Some of
them have been real Christians at one time in their lives.
It just goes to show what happens when we stop seeking
the Lord. It's amazing how changed the lives of those men
become when they accept the Lord. Some of them come
back there afterwards and you can really see the difference.

I became quite legalistic and somewhat judgmental of others
during that time. Wally and Ruth had never forbid us to go to movies or dances. We played cards in our home, especially when my
sisters brought their boyfriends to the house. Unfortunately, my
contacts with more legalistic Christians at Mount Carmel Camp
and at LBI attracted me to their more rigid, narrow way of life. I'm
sure I made others, including members of my family, feel uncomfortable at times. In a letter to my family in December of 1951 I
gave some advice to younger sister Martha, encouraging her to
avoid dances and movies. It took me several years to move away
from that attitude and practice.

Many former LBI students spoke regretfully of the time they
spent at the school. As they moved on to other educational settings,
they saw that the environment at LBI was not conducive to academic growth and that the heavy accent on the *don'ts* rather than
the *dos* of the Christian life had actually been detrimental to their
growth in the faith. Some, in fact, abandoned the faith in reaction
to these influences.

I never felt that way. Yes, I had to unlearn some of the things I
had accepted uncritically at LBI. And I had to drop some of my
legalistic practices. But I have always given thanks for the good
things that I garnered from that year: knowledge of the content of
the Bible, accent on the global mission of the church, devotional
practice, and, though LBI was independent from the organized
churches, faithfulness to the church and its mission.

The attitude of the organized churches toward LBI, including the Augustana Synod, was always mixed. Like Pastor Franzen, many in Augustana thought negatively of LBI. Others were positive and supportive. The Augustana Seminary Chorus, of which I was a member, gave a concert at LBI in the spring of 1955. Dr. Hjalmer Johnson, a member of the seminary faculty, gave the message that evening.

In summary, this part of my life's journey was crucial for all that followed. But it was only the beginning. It was time for me to move on, to broaden my perspective on life, to move into the larger world.

Chapter 4

College and a life partner:
two good choices

Gustavus Adolphus or Augsburg?

Having deep roots in the Augustana Swedish tradition, it might have been assumed that I would enroll at Gustavus Adolphus College in St. Peter, Minnesota, after my year at LBI. The national youth organization of the Augustana Lutheran Church offered scholarships for study at any of the colleges supported by that church. I applied. To no one's surprise, including mine, I was not one of the recipients. I took it as a sign that I needed to look elsewhere.

Augsburg College struck me as a good possibility and a logical option. I liked what they had to offer for seminary preparation. I knew financial help from my parents would be minimal at best. I needed to work my way through college. The Minneapolis area offered good part-time work opportunities. With my four older sisters living in Minneapolis at the time, I knew their generosity to me during my year at LBI would continue—more free laundry service and delicious meals nearly every week.

Looming even larger, however, was the hope that my budding relationship with Corinne Hansen might blossom. She was ready to begin study at Fairview Hospital to become a registered nurse. It crossed my mind, of course, that Augsburg College was only two blocks from Fairview!

On a sunny spring day while still at LBI, I strolled through the Augsburg campus. I spoke to no one. At the end of the walk I sat down on the soft green grass in Murphy Square, a small postage-stamp-size park in the middle of the campus. I prayed, "Lord, this seems right. If it isn't I will trust you to close the door and lead me in another direction."

A place to work and a place to live

I returned to the Augsburg neighborhood a few days later and set out looking for work and a place to live. First, I applied and found a part-time job at Fairview Hospital. That was a good sign. They hired me to clean and run elevators, sweep halls, and handle central supply duties on Saturdays, beginning in September. That meant I would see Corinne.

Down the street on seedy Riverside Avenue I stumbled on to the Walter Anderson Funeral Home, a block east of Cedar Avenue and directly across the street from the Triangle Bar, given that name because it was wedged into an intersection where two diagonal streets converged. Cedar Avenue was still known as "Snuss Boulevard"—a reference to an earlier era when Scandinavian men nestled a wad of chewing tobacco in their cheeks and expectorated streams of juice in the gutters. Yes, the funeral home would be pleased to offer me a room if I would handle night phone calls. Another door cracked opened. I was certain that God's hand was in all of this.

A summer of valuable experience

During the early summer between LBI and college I taught vacation church school for six weeks in southern Minnesota, hitch-hiking my way from one assignment to the next. At American Lutheran in Windom they were laying the foundation for their new sanctuary. Pastor Floyd Lein, a wiry and energetic little man, thought I should spend my days as he did: mornings teaching vacation church school, afternoons balancing wheelbarrow loads of wet concrete, and evenings preparing for the next morning. Those weeks proved to be the beginning of a lifelong friendship with Floyd, his wife, Orena, and their son, David. Floyd was one of my models for what a parish pastor should be.

The next two weeks I moved out into the countryside between Windom and Jackson to teach more vacation church school at Bethany and Hauge Lutheran Churches. Large edifices that loomed over the flat prairie only a mile or so from each other, they represented the deep divisions in Norwegian Lutheranism that plagued some immigrant communities. Though it would have been difficult for them to articulate their differences by the mid-twentieth century, the members of these two churches continued to insist that they could never worship at the same altar. In spite of their assumed differences, I taught the same materials at each church.

I hitchhiked across southern Minnesota to do a third two-week stint at Garness Lutheran Church, a rural congregation nestled in the hilly and wooded southeastern corner of the state near Canton. The only thing I recall from that assignment is that a couple from the church tried desperately to get me to be interested in their daughter. I had my mind set on someone else.

I spent the balance of the summer working at First Lutheran Church, my home congregation at Litchfield. Pastor Bergren, who had been my teacher at LBI, took the call to the congregation and became my mentor, and a good one. I lived at home during those weeks. My time with my parents was good. My relationship with my mother seemed much more comfortable. I'm sure the year away had reminded me of many of her good qualities. Not least, I feasted again at the table of a wonderful cook.

Having said that, I also learned the truth of the old adage, "You can't go back home." I could not wait for the weeks to fly by so that I could get on with my studies at Augsburg College.

Walter Anderson Funeral Home

My accommodation at the mortuary might well be described, à la Gary Cooper, as "A Room *without* a View." There was a small window too high on the wall from which to look out. The room was barely wide enough to fit the bed. The ceiling rose to about fifteen feet. Between the foot of the bed and the other wall was just enough space to wedge in a small wooden desk and chair. I often speculated that if I could just turn the room on end it would be exactly right.

It was also *a room with an odor*. The pungent smell of formaldehyde from the preparation room next to mine wafted through the ventilation system. Eventually I adjusted to it. Besides taking phone calls, I had to unlock the back door when bodies arrived in the night. When the undertakers finished their work, I locked the door and returned through the room where the dead were laid out. Those first nights I heard every sound.

When business was good I had company. Bodies would spill from the preparation room to be laid out in the anteroom next to mine. I had to leave my door open in order to hear the phone. Yes, it was a bit unnerving at first. In time, however, I got accustomed to having "guests" and gave thanks to God for free rent. Nevertheless, I always appreciated it when Corinne or one of my sisters called. They all noted that I seemed unusually eager to extend the conversation as long as possible.

Because the Triangle Bar was directly across the street, it was not unusual for a drunken man to wander over for a "visit." One night an inebriate walked in and challenged me to a fistfight. I suggested that it would be better to fight outside. As soon as he cleared the door I slammed it shut and turned the lock. Good preparation for the kinds of diplomacy I would need to practice in my future career.

In a letter to my folks I expressed my gratitude:

> When I stop to think of how . . . things have worked out
> for me this year I certainly need to thank the Lord. It really
> was marvelous to get a place like this to stay and also to get

work so near. It really pays to trust in him even though it seems very hard at times.

Through all of these years I kept a careful account of my income and expenses. In the front of my financial record book I wrote the reference from Hebrews 13:5:

> Keep your lives free from the love of money, and be content with what you have; for he has said, "I will never leave you or forsake you."

Augsburg, the right place

I hit the college campus and community running. I decided that I would major in sociology. That was a good choice. Joel Torstensen, head of the department, was a fine Christian man who believed that one's faith needed to be lived in commitment to one's community, both local and in the wider world. Torstensen and his colleagues in the department made certain we became aware of prejudice against blacks, Jews and other minorities, family life matters, economic problems, environmental questions, rural issues, and much more. This was exactly what I needed after growing up in Litchfield and my year at LBI. I needed to become more aware of the changing world around me and of the explosive tensions that tear communities and nations apart. I was being ushered into the real world. From that point and on there was no turning back.

Other shapers of my new world

Anne Pedersen, professor of English, played an important role in my intellectual formation. She was known to be the best in her department. We were tested as freshman and placed in English sections according to our scores. Much to my surprise, I made it into her class. A petite woman with a sparrow-like appearance, Pedersen was a no-nonsense, exacting grammarian. Every paper was scrutinized with scalpel-like precision. Even out of class, she would gently but firmly correct us. I recall the exact spot on the stairs of

Old Main where she stopped me one day after I had given a chapel talk. "Herbert," she said quietly, "I'd like to have a word with you." She proceeded to patiently explain why something I said was grammatically incorrect and how it should have been stated. Then she turned and was on her way. Where else but at a small liberal arts college could one expect to have such an encounter?

She was, of course, more than a grammarian. Prose and poetry came alive in her class. She taught me how to find themes and patterns in novels, how to appreciate poetry, what marked the difference between great and run-of-the-mill literature.

Unfortunately, I didn't have Carl Chrislock until he arrived on campus in my senior year. Had I had him as a freshman I'm certain I would have tried for a double major in both sociology and history. Carl was the archetype of the rumpled, absent-minded professor who was so caught up in the subject for the day that he forgot to wash or comb his hair for days on end. He loved and lived what he taught. Characters and eras in history came alive in his class. Until then I was a Henry Ford student of history, thinking it was all but worthless to reflect on the past. Chrislock helped me to understand that one cannot know what is happening today or forecast where trends may lead unless one has a firm grasp of what has transpired in the past.

Being a pre-seminary student, I was eager for the courses in New Testament Greek. When Bernhard Christensen, president of the college, met Mario Colacci he decided that this refugee from Roman Catholicism deserved a chance to teach at Augsburg. Colacci had been a rising star in Rome. Gifted with a keen mind and enormous physical energy, he was the quintessential Italian: bold, engaging, forthright, decisive, demanding, and explosive. One day when I made a particularly gross mistake in translating a word from Greek to English he leaned back in his chair, roared with laughter and exclaimed, "Brother Chilstrom, have mercy on us a *thousand* times."

I had no idea at that time that Colacci and I would become close friends after I was ordained. He came to the parish I served in Pelican Rapids and to the college where I taught in New Jersey to teach courses in Roman Catholic–Lutheran relationships. Corinne and I enjoyed getting to know his Italian wife and three bright children. Unfortunately, that was in pre-Vatican II days. Colacci was entirely negative in his attitude toward the church he had left. Later in his career he shifted ground as Catholicism changed and as he underwent movement in his own theological journey.

Ray Anderson, professor of speech, played an important role in my evolution as a public communicator. My gift for speaking extemporaneously made it possible for me to prepare and orate on short notice. One day our class was assigned to give a five-minute humorous speech. I was very busy at the time and prepared my comments as I walked across campus. My classmates were impressed. Anderson, however, saw through my smoke screen. As soon as I was seated he walked to the front of the class, turned a piercing eye on me, and asked how much time I had spent preparing my little contribution. I could not lie. I learned that day that, indeed, one cannot fool all of the people all of the time. From then on I determined to prepare my public remarks as carefully as time permitted.

Though I worked with Bernhard Christensen, president of the college, to a limited degree when I was student body president, I never felt especially close to him. He was an introvert in an extrovert's job. What I treasure most is the memory of how he would handle a chapel service when a speaker failed to appear. He spoke out of the depth of a meditative man of God, often citing from memory lengthy passages from his trove of favorite poetry.

My academic record at Augsburg was respectable, considering the amount of time I invested in working my way through college and the extent of my involvement in extracurricular activities. My grade point average for four years fell just a fraction short of what I needed to be an honor graduate.

Preparation for seminary

Though the course in New Testament Greek prepared me well for future biblical study at the seminary, the Augsburg religion faculty, with the exception of Paul Sonnack, had not yet come to grips with changes that were happening in the world of biblical theology. The Bible was treated, more or less, like a text in which all books, chapters, and verses were of equal value.

Comparative religion was taught with the idea that the Christian way was the only true way and that other religions had little or nothing to offer. Biblical criticism, the authority of the Bible, how to use the Bible when dealing with complicated social issues, the contribution of other religions to our understanding of the nature of God and the universe—these issues would have to wait until I moved on to seminary and graduate school.

Extracurricular activities

Student Council

The first week at Augsburg I was one of five freshmen elected to the Student Council. Though I had no idea I would succeed him in two years, Stan Tousaint, a senior pre-seminary student, became a role model as president of the student body.

Debate

My excellent experience with extemporaneous speaking in high school encouraged me to think that I might find a good extracurricular outlet in debate. I was right. Vernon Jensen, coach for the debate program, thought Bill Halvorson and I might be molded into an effective team. He was right. Bill was a senior, an outstanding student, a clear thinker, an accomplished speaker, and a fine mentor.

We entered debate contests all over the Upper Midwest at colleges and universities, including a major one at the University of Minnesota. I took the first speaker position, laying out our case. In all of these contests we consistently finished among the top five or six teams out of many dozens that competed. After a tournament in Moorhead, Minnesota, a note in the campus newspaper read:

> Augsburg's number one debate team consisting of Bill Halvorson and Herb Chilstrom took fifth place in the Red River Valley Speech Tournament held at Concordia and Moorhead State. . . . This team won five out of six debates, losing to Duluth branch of the University (of Minnesota).

The Luther League

I also joined the Luther League, Augsburg's equivalent of Lutheran Campus Ministry, as soon as I arrived on campus. It was the largest student organization. I traveled to churches with teams of students to give programs. I was usually the speaker or preacher. It was a fine way to hone my speaking skills.

At the end of my freshman year it was assumed that Gordon Thorpe, a junior who came out of Lutheran Free Church background, would be the next president. I was shocked when it was announced that I had been elected to that post. Merton Strommen, the campus pastor, was advisor to the League. He was to be gone the next year on sabbatical leave. I invited Paul Sonnack to fill that slot. We had a wonderful year under his guidance.

After Augsburg Thorpe and I went our separate ways until the early 1980s when both of us were elected to serve on the Commission for a New Lutheran Church (CNLC). Over those next six years our relationship was renewed. We remain good friends.

Student body president

At the end of my sophomore year friends urged me to run for student body president. In early April 1952 I wrote in my diary: "Nominated for Pres. of Student Body. Hard time deciding but felt it was God's will so agreed to [run]." I was reluctant, knowing that it was customary for seniors to be in that place. Quentin Goodrich, who eventually became my chief opponent, wrote in the student newspaper that "an outstanding possibility from the sophomore class is Herb Chilstrom, an extraordinary statesman." I thought that was a bit of a stretch for a college sophomore.

Several of us formed a party called the Crusaders and adopted the campaign theme: "Herb's Superb—Vote for the Crusaders." My friend and roommate Jerry Trelstad was the vice presidential candidate. Our entire slate won handily.

Besides being the focus for various student committees, the council took on an energetic fundraising program for the new college library. In my diary I note that on some days I had as many as five separate meetings related to my role as student body president. It was quite amazing—given this level of involvement on campus, my part-time work at Luther Memorial Church, long hours sorting and delivering mail at the U.S. Post Office during Christmas break, and my time dating Corinne—that I was able to maintain a fairly decent academic record.

In those years Augsburg had no Phi Beta Kappa chapter. The same was true at Gustavus Adolphus College in St. Peter, Minnesota. Daniel Borg, student body president at Gustavus, proposed that we establish an honor society at our two campuses. It became known as The Guild of St. Ansgaar, singling out a dozen or so students each year who were noted for achievement in scholarship, leadership, and extracurricular activities. I was pleased to be one of eight seniors elected to The Guild. More than fifty years later The Guild still exists on both campuses.

The issue that consumed us that year more than any other was the question: "Shall we allow for folk dancing on campus?" No, not ballroom dancing, but *folk* dancing. President Christensen opposed it and so did I. Within a year, in spite of that heavy opposition, we were folk dancing on campus. Fifty some years later it is difficult to believe that an issue like that could have roused so much furor.

I was encouraged to run for a second term. I weighed it carefully.

By now Corinne was my confidant. We prayed about things and discussed them thoroughly. In my diary I wrote:

> Talked over S.B.P. (student body president) with C. & decided not to run again. On the day that I turned responsibility over to my successor I wrote: Thanks for helping me Lord. You've been good to me and I've learned a lot of valuable, lifetime lessons.

Basketball

My love for basketball continued. I played on intramural teams all four years, fitting the games into my work schedule. An article in the *Echo* noted that our team won a game 51 to 20 and that "Chilstrom scored 24 points on a variety of shots." Their center must have been a midget.

Devotional life

I continued to maintain a strong personal devotional life. When I was living at the funeral home I tried for a time to take a full hour for Bible reading and prayer. That proved to be more challenging when I moved into the dormitory at Augsburg in my sophomore year. Yet even then I tried to keep this part of my life vital and active. In a diary entry I wrote, "Neglected prayer this A.M. & it was to my chagrin until this afternoon when I had devotions." Later I noted that I was reading *A Faithful Guide to Peace with God* by C.O. Rosenius and that "the grace of God became new and fresh to me again."

Opportunities for work in congregations

When I came to Augsburg I prayed that God would give me opportunities to share my faith. Whenever I mention this to Corinne she laughs and agrees that God answered this prayer "above and beyond anything that you could ask or think!"

In the summer between my freshman and sophomore years I was invited to work with Pastor Bergren again in my home congregation at Litchfield, a city of some 4,500. Among other things, I did a survey of the entire city to ascertain the church membership of every home. This was daunting. Knocking on doors cold turkey was not an easy assignment for someone who was somewhat of an introvert. I soon learned, however, that my reluctance to meet new people would be minor compared to my encounters with mad dogs!

My home congregation was very good to me all the way through college and seminary. At least once a year Pastor Bergren invited me to preach. On that day the loose offering was designated for my education. On those occasions, State Senator John and Hilma Simonson always lingered after the service to give a special word of encouragement and handed me an envelope with a newly-minted, twenty dollar bill. With no children of their own, they took a special interest in my progress.

Early in my sophomore year I got a call from Pastor Carl O. Nelson at Luther Memorial Lutheran Church in the northwest corner of Minneapolis. He invited me to join his staff as youth director. Confirmation classes were always a challenge for me. In my diary I wrote, "Class wasn't too good today. Maybe it was just me." The next week I wrote, "Class very good today (except for Bradley). Praise God!" It was a pattern that would persist through all my years of teaching confirmation students! On Sundays I would assist Pastor Nelson with the services, preach when he was gone, and do more youth ministry. On one occasion I noted that I had "worked on my sermon in the evening. It didn't 'come thru' until after I went to bed; praise the Lord!"

After my summer of construction work in Litchfield in 1953, I got a call in November to serve in a similar capacity at Hope Lutheran Church, still farther out into the northwestern corner of Minneapolis. My mentor was Pastor Carl Zimmerman, a former military chaplain and a man deeply interested in the scientific aspects of the Christian faith. Again I was blessed with a good example of what a pastor should be. Though highly disorganized, Zimmerman was a man with passion for his flock.

At Augsburg College doors continued to open for leadership roles. I was master of ceremonies at college events. On one occasion our guest speaker was Pastor Melvin Hammarberg, the man I had introduced at an event at my home congregation several years earlier. After the event many of my friends commented on the similarity between Hammarberg and me: tall, blond, Swedish, similar speaking styles. I took it as a fine compliment.

Though I felt confident that God was calling me to ordained ministry, I cannot forget the challenge Dr. Oscar Benson, president of the Augustana Lutheran Church, laid out for a room full of pre-seminary students one evening. The occasion was a gathering at a Minneapolis church for all young men of Augustana background who had indicated an interest in the ministry. We were, of course, all eagerly expecting that we would hear only words of encouragement. Benson was not the main speaker but was asked if he had any comments for the group. A short, rotund man with a somewhat Napoleonic mien, Benson stood at his place, glowered at our young faces and said, "If you can stay out, stay out," and sat down.

The advice seemed strange and inappropriate at the time. Yet over the years I came to appreciate what he said. He wanted pastors in the church who were so certain they had a call from God, who felt such strong conviction about ordained ministry, that they would not be easily discouraged when inevitable times of testing would come.

A budding romance, engagement, and marriage

I once ordered a seed for the bird of paradise plant. The seed looked like a small, hard pebble. It took weeks to germinate and then seven years to bloom. Some romances grow and blossom like the first flowers of spring. Others mature very slowly. For Corinne and me it was the latter.

It was more than four years from the time we first dated until we married. Our love for each other grew almost imperceptibly at first.

But the end result was a lovely flower that has lasted for more than fifty-seven years.

When I enrolled at Augsburg I had no idea whether my relationship with Corinne would continue. Our early letters were stiff and formal. There was not even a vague hint of passion. Our dates consisted mostly of going to church meetings, long conversational walks, and times with mutual friends. I had no doubt that I wanted our relationship to flourish, but I was fearful that I would lose her if I moved too quickly. Because I was so strapped for money and had no car, we never went out for dinner or drove to an event.

When the moment seemed right I asked if she would consider going steady. She said she needed to think about it. At that same time I told her about my brother, Dave, that he was developmentally challenged. Though I thought I had explained carefully that it was caused by a brain injury at birth and was not a genetic fault, she became concerned, wondering if she really wanted to continue our relationship.

A few days later she called and asked if I would come over and chat with her. I tried to feel optimistic, but an ominous feeling came over me. She told me our relationship was over. She had met a young man from Luther Seminary and was enjoying his friendship. The fact that he had a car and could afford to take her to dinner and concerts was in his favor.

In a long journal entry, written in late November 1951 I poured out my disappointment and grief. At the top of the notepaper was the verse from Romans 8:28: "We know that all things work together for those who love God." I wrote:

> The reality of the verse at the top of this page seems very hard tonight. Breaking up with Corinne seemed so easy at the time. When I got back to the dorm I tried to laugh it off. But when I went to bed I got a very strange feeling. I thought back over our last two years—the joys, the prayers

together, the places we went together, the plans that I made
in my own mind. . . .

Last night I didn't sleep very well. That funny "lost" and
"lonely" feeling came over me. I finally went to sleep. But
when I awoke this morning I found that I was thinking
about the same person—Corinne.

Today has seemed like a week. I couldn't concentrate very
well. It's funny how a person becomes attached to another
and how hard it is to break with them. The thought came
to me tonight, "Maybe Corinne will be mine after all. Do I
dare pray for such a thing?"

In the weeks that followed I tried dating other girls. I found that
I had no feeling of attraction for any of them.

What I didn't know at the time was that others were telling
Corinne that she had made a terrible mistake, including her sister
Devona, five years older and a staff nurse at Fairview, and Corinne's
roommate Audrey Bergh, her soul sister and most trusted friend.

Shortly after New Year's 1952, Corinne left for affiliation at the
Fergus Falls (Minnesota) State Hospital. Though I don't recall it,
apparently I said to her when we broke up that she should call
sometime. That gave her the confidence to write a letter to me in
late January. She went into great detail about what it was like to be
at a mental hospital.

When I received her letter I was, of course, both puzzled and
encouraged. During that month she also attended a conference in
Minneapolis where I was one of the speakers.

By the way . . . your message, I tho't was *wonderful*. . . . God
is using you in a powerful way, already as you seek to serve
him. If you have a spare minute, drop me a line—and in the
meantime I'll appreciate your prayers.

I did, of course, "drop her a line." In an early March letter she
describes in detail what it was like to work with the mentally ill.

Then she added:

> Well, there's lots more that could be said about this place and
> things I wonder about. Maybe we can have a chat sometime.
> Guess I'll always like to talk things over with you.

I was reading between the lines that she wanted to reopen our
relationship—and I couldn't have been happier over that prospect.

As soon as she returned to Minneapolis, she and some friends
came to a youth rally at Augsburg. We started chatting and soon
wandered off by ourselves. On April 17, 1952, I wrote in my diary:
"Called Corinne Hansen to line up date for Sat. nite." After the date I
wrote, "All things work together for good. . . ." A week later we went
to see the Lakers beat New York for the world basketball champion-
ship. On the walk home we sat on a bench in Murphy Square on the
Augsburg campus and agreed to go steady. Now we were back on
track. Now I was certain that this relationship would endure.

What I also learned only later was that though her friend from
the seminary was a very fine young man, Corinne had come to
realize that he was not right for her. Apparently she unconsciously
talked about *me* when she was on dates with him. He finally told
her that he thought she should "go back to Herb Chilstrom."

In a letter to my folks in early May 1952, I wrote:

> A couple of weeks ago Corinne Hansen and I started going
> together again. One of these times it will stick! Seriously,
> she really is a wonderful girl and I wouldn't mind having
> her for a wife someday.

My brother Dave continued to be on Corinne's mind. She asked
questions in class and did extra reading to try to understand his
condition. She came to the conclusion that his problem was truly
an accident of birth and not a genetic disorder. This gave her freedom to pursue our relationship without that fear.

In early June she left on a trip to the national nurses' convention
at Atlantic City, New Jersey, as the chosen delegate from her class.

One night just before she left, we sat on a park bench in the north-east corner of Murphy Square on the Augsburg campus. I described the evening in my diary:

> Bought Corinne a leaf rhinestone pin for $5 at Morgans.
> Gave her the pin and *first* kiss in Murphy Square! I also
> gave her my high school ring to wear.

Now there would be no hesitation on the part of either of us. Now it was full steam ahead. We were deeply in love.

Shortly after she returned from the trip, we both went to the Wood Lake Bible Camp in Wisconsin as counselors. I was there with youth from Luther Memorial Church. In my diary I wrote that early one morning we rose at five a.m. and went fishing. ". . . didn't catch any! Went for hike across lake. Sat by old log for awhile. Second kiss!!"

At Thanksgiving time in the fall of 1952 Corinne thought it was the right moment for her to take me for a visit to her home on the farm in South Dakota. One night a few days before we left she said she needed to tell me more about her family. Until then I had only a positive impression of her parents. She had talked about their piety, daily family devotions at the breakfast table, faithful attendance at worship and prayer meetings, their practice of tithing, and their support for missionaries.

Now it was time for her to share the negative side of their lives. She talked at length about their critical attitude toward the organized church and, in particular, their dislike for some pastors. She described her older brother, Harold, who lived on an adjoining farm, as even more intense in his criticism of the church and of pastors. Bringing home a young man who was planning on becoming a pastor roused deep fears in her. She wondered how I might be received by them. I assured her that I had no fear about meeting her family.

When the day dawned for us to leave, Minnesota was in the grips of a major winter blizzard. Corinne's mother called and questioned whether we should travel. Corinne reassured her, falsely, that the weather conditions in Minneapolis did not seem so serious and that we intended to set out. In truth, it was a very reckless and senseless thing to do. But Corinne knew that there was no time in the foreseeable future when we could make this trip. She was determined that we must go.

After a day with them I noted again in my diary that "Mr. Hansen 'approved' of me at one a.m. after I had gone to bed!!"

Needless to say, it was a strange and stressful first visit. Nevertheless, I seemed to have passed muster with Corinne's parents.

I could never be accused of spending money for exotic and expensive gifts for my girlfriend. On one occasion it was a lamp that she needed for her room. For Christmas 1953 I noted that the gift was "some nylon boots with fur up the front." I think her friends, who were getting fine jewelry must have wondered about this much-too-practical suitor. She, however, was equally practical. Her gift to me was an electric shaver.

Near the end of my junior year I sensed that it was time to ask Corinne to marry me. On May 11 I borrowed a car from a friend. We stopped near Riverside Park just east of Fairview. I asked her if she would marry me, noting that I also felt that with all her talent and potential for more academic work, I would understand it if she might choose otherwise. She was not hesitant in the least bit. She said that her number one goal in life was to be a wife and mother and that she would be mine.

Now came the question: If we are to be engaged soon, where will I find the money for a ring? It was the end of the school year and I was just barely keeping my head above water financially. I decided to ask my dear sister Chile if she might loan me $40. She was happy to do so.

It was customary in those days for a young suitor to ask the girl's father for her hand. I knew Corinne's parents were coming to Minneapolis for her graduation in late May. So I wrote a note to them, giving my intentions and asking if it would be all right with them. I must have struggled more than a little with that letter, given the fact that I note in my diary that "I finished it at one a.m."

There was no time for them to reply before coming for her graduation. When they arrived in Minneapolis I had a few moments alone with them and asked if they had received my letter. Yes, they had and, yes, it would meet with their approval. It was the last hurdle.

On the eve of Corinne's graduation from nursing I borrowed a car from another Augsburg friend. We drove to Riverside Park. I pulled over to the curb, reached into the glove compartment, and took out the ring. She was completely shocked, knowing that I had no money for it. When we returned to the Fairview dormitory the place exploded as the news rolled through the halls from room-to-room and floor-to-floor. I sat in the lobby savoring every moment of the celebration I had ignited.

In a note to my folks the next day I described what it had been like:

> Well, I took a pretty big step last weekend, didn't I? It's a good thing a guy doesn't have to do that more than once because it's really nerve wracking—getting a father's consent. Seriously, though, I know that Corinne is going to make a wonderful wife for me. Our engagement has been an answer to many years of prayer on the part of both of us. Now it is only the grace of God that can keep us faithful to him so that our lives can be used to help spread the kingdom of God. I don't have any idea when we'll be married. Tomorrow would be fine with me!

Shortly after we were engaged, Corinne wrote a note to my folks:

> Our engagement has been such a wonderful experience, especially because it seems that God has so definitely guided us together. Words seem feeble at this point, but I just want to express my gratitude for your Christian

home that God has used largely, as the tool, to make Herb what he is today. It is with much joy that I look forward to becoming part of your family. "God is able to do exceeding abundantly above all that we ask or think."

As I moved into my last year at Augsburg the big question was whether I should study at Luther Seminary in St. Paul for a year or go directly to Augustana Seminary in Rock Island, Illinois. Staying in the Twin Cities would have given us a chance to accumulate a nest egg before our marriage. But it also would have meant waiting for two years to get married. Corinne's dad suggested that two years was too long to be engaged. I don't think he was worried about his daughter having a child out of wedlock. But it was probably obvious to him that our relationship had heated to the point where waiting another year was inadvisable. On January 9 I wrote in my dairy: "We set June *12 as the Day!!* Had good devotions on Rom. 8."

Our romance was not without its bumps now and then. One diary entry says "C. & I had a misunderstanding so had a long talk. Everything came out fine though & we parted loving each other more than ever." It would be a pattern that has characterized our relationship all through the years—a commitment to talk out differences.

I continued to consider spending a year at Luther Seminary in St. Paul. In mid-March I went over to the headquarters for the Minnesota Conference of the Augustana Synod and had a chat with Dr. Emil Swenson, president of the Conference. It was not a very pleasant visit. I found him cold and quite uncaring. He did, however, suggest that it would be better to go directly to Rock Island for seminary. I took his counsel and enrolled immediately at Augustana Seminary.

As for Corinne and me, our relationship deepened with each passing week. When she went off for a weekend to visit her friend Audrey in South Dakota two months before our marriage I wrote in my dairy that it "surely was a long weekend without having her around."

One of the more interesting venues for our romance in the months prior to our wedding was the elevator at Fairview Hospital. In the fall of my senior year I resumed my work there as an evening elevator operator. In those days it was the crank version, requiring an operator to open and close the door on each floor. If Corinne were on duty when I was working, she would eagerly volunteer to run any errand that was needed for her station. If we were alone on the ride I would stop the elevator between floors and we would have some moments for an intense embrace and refreshing kisses until the buzzer called me to another floor.

In the course of my work at Hope Church, Pastor Zimmerman indicated that he would be leaving for a call in Texas and asked if I would continue at Hope through the summer of 1954. He said that Corinne and I could use the apartment in the parish house. It was another sign to us that this was the time to get married. On June 7 we bought our first automobile from Fenton's at Litchfield for $57—a used 1948 Pontiac. Corinne had saved enough for the $190 down payment.

A South Dakota wedding

St. Peter Lutheran Church, an open country congregation on the flat prairies of southeastern South Dakota, was Corinne's spiritual home. It would be the site of our marriage. My brother, Dave, would be my best man and her sister Devona the maid of honor. The ceremony was simple and beautiful. Bridal wreath was in full bloom and cascaded from tall vases about the altar. Corinne looked lovely in her wedding dress, loaned from sister Dorothy. We sealed all those years of preparation with our promises: "I plight thee my troth till death do us part."

Honeymoon at Crosslake

We spent our honeymoon at a cabin on Crosslake near Brainerd, Minnesota, given to us for the week by the Glenn Miller family from Luther Memorial Church. I had stayed with them for part of the summer of 1952. A kinder gesture or more wonderful wedding present we could not have imagined. From there I sent a postcard to Martha, David, and Janet:

> We went fishing yesterday and really got sunburned! Oh, yes, we also caught some fish.

For the rest of the summer Corinne worked at Fairview Hospital and I cared for Hope Church. Part way through the summer we took a trip to Rock Island to find housing for the fall.

The Augsburg years were nothing less than wonderful. God had opened many doors for me to study, witness, and serve. But best of all, I now had Corinne for my wife—the choicest gift of all.

Chapter 5

Theological formation: Augustana Seminary

You're sleeping in the bathroom?

With our limited financial resources Corinne and I knew we couldn't be selective about an apartment when we moved to Rock Island, Illinois. We found an upstairs set of two small rooms and a large bath. Since it was located about a mile from the seminary, I could easily walk to classes, making it possible for Corinne to have the car for work.

The owners assumed that we would sleep on the fold-down davenport, just as other renters had done. We learned the first night that those renters must have been midgets. It was absolutely impossible for me to get comfortable. We scarcely slept a wink all night. When we explained our dilemma the next morning, the landlord agreed to secure a fold-down bed that we could store in the bathroom during the day and wheel into the living room each night. That, too, proved quite inconvenient. After experimenting a bit, we discovered that the three-fourths size hide-a-way bed just fit in the large bathroom if we shut the door before we unfolded it for the night. What could be more convenient? That was our unique sleeping arrangement for all three years that we lived in Rock Island. If nothing else, it was a good tidbit for conversation with friends and family.

Theological maturation

I had been forewarned before entering Augustana Seminary that
it was different from Luther and some other Lutheran seminaries.
They were right. But they were also wrong. Whereas they had tried
to convince me that Augustana was a dangerous seminary because
it was too liberal, I found that in biblical theology Augustana was at
the cutting edge of change in many mainline seminaries.

Much of that change was due to the towering influence of Dr. Eric
Wahlstrom, professor of New Testament. One might describe Wahlstrom as deceptively progressive. He leaned humped over the lectern
like a great blue heron, often looking at a pencil that he twirled in his
fingers as he lectured. With his gentle manner, slight Swedish accent
and disarming honesty, he was not out to destroy our faith by shock-
ing us with new ideas about how to interpret the Bible. Instead, he
patiently took us by the hand and invited us to explore new and fresh
ways to look at a biblical text. He helped us to see that the heart of
the Bible, the good news about Jesus Christ, need not and could not
be destroyed by any question we might raise about a particular passage. If we came to his classes with any vestiges of a fundamentalist
approach to the Bible—such as regarding every chapter and verse to
be of equal value—he helped us to understand that the Bible is, first
and foremost, about the great moments in history when God broke
onto the human scene to bring hope to the world. And, of course, it
was in Jesus—his life, death, and resurrection—that this good news
of the kingdom of God was seen most vividly.

Dr. Carl Anderson was known among students as *Hoshek*—the
Hebrew word for "darkness." And for good reason. He droned on
and on in a most boring tone of voice. Like an eagle, he gazed back
and forth across the classroom. But one had the feeling that, unlike
Wahlstrom, Anderson did not necessarily like to be interrupted
with questions about the subject matter.

At that time the study of Hebrew was an elective. I decided to
take the plunge with about a dozen of my erstwhile classmates. It

proved to be a wise choice. In this small class the stolid Anderson came to life. When we probed into the Hebrew words in books like Amos and Micah, he got so animated that we feared the man, already with a history of heart trouble, might die on the spot. Scripture came alive. Anderson instilled a passion for the message of the Old Testament.

Dr. A. D. Mattson, professor of social ethics, was another pace-setter. He entered the room and took his place behind the desk like a great horned owl. He peered out at us, seldom rising from his chair. Though he was a most tedious lecturer, often reading long passages in a droning voice from his textbook on the subject, he made his mark. This good news we would be commissioned to preach was for the *whole* world, not just for those who occupied the pews on Sunday mornings. He put his philosophy to work by serving as chaplain to the labor unions at the local farm machinery factories.

Dr. Arthur Arnold, professor of homiletics, was like a song sparrow. Though small in stature, when he entered the pulpit he sang the good news of the gospel with force and clarity, setting a good example for us future preachers. I was selected as his assistant in my senior year. Though the work involved was minimal, making me feel almost guilty for the remuneration, I formed a strong bond with Arnold that continued for a lifetime. In class Arnold was a strict taskmaster. He expected clarity in our preaching and was sternly critical of students he thought were slack in preparation.

Dr. Paul Lindberg's specialty was pastoral theology. He was the most handsome man on the faculty. His white egret-like mane made him stand out in a crowd. He was a man of deep piety and pastoral care. He spearheaded the program that later flowered in the church into clinical pastoral care and became a requirement for all students. Little wonder that when I came to serve First Lutheran Church in St. Peter, Minnesota, in 1970 and learned that he was ready to retire, I invited him to join the staff. It proved to be a good partnership with my former professor.

Dr. Hjalmer Johnson was probably the object of more jesting than any other faculty member. Always clad in black and with the shape of a penguin, students wondered if even his underwear was that hue. His style of teaching was such that one either sat in awe of what he was saying or was bored and confounded by it. Harold Lohr was in the first category and took copious notes in every class. He still cites things that Johnson said more than a half century ago.

The weak link in the academic program at Augustana Seminary was systematic theology. The professor for that subject had died suddenly the year before our class arrived. The seminary imported a Latvian refugee to take over the class. Between his discomfort with the use of English and his heavy reliance on the notes of the deceased professor, the classes were a near total waste of time. In our senior year Dr. Arnold Carlson came on the scene and rescued the department. It was, however, too little and too late. For most of my ministry I had to play catch-up in systematic theology.

Dr. Karl Mattson, president of the seminary, looked like a bulldog. In fact, he had one that resembled him. When one of the seminary students stayed at the Mattson home, he slipped a clerical collar around the dog's neck and took a photo that got wide circulation. Unlike that characterization and a somewhat grumpy mien, Mattson was actually a very tenderhearted fellow. Though he only taught on rare occasion, he was instrumental in helping us to keep abreast with the foremost theologians of the time: Karl Barth, Rudolf Bultmann, Reinhold Niebuhr, Paul Tillich, and others. He was a man very much at the vanguard of Lutheran theologians.

The overall impact of my study at Augustana Seminary was a move away from a narrow view of faith and of the Bible. There was no lessening of my concern to bring people to a living relationship with Christ. But as I was exposed to a variety of religious views, I became more tolerant of others. My changing view of the Bible is seen in a couple of papers I wrote in my senior year:

> In the Hebrew-Christian tradition history is a straight
> line with a purpose. . . . As you move toward both ends of
> this line you move more and more into the realm of myth.
> Creation and eschatology are both expressed in terms of
> symbol.

In a report on Joseph Sittler's book *The Word of God* I wrote approvingly of his conclusion that

> It is the message of the Bible and not the Bible as a book
> that impresses itself upon Luther. The Word of God is in
> essence God's 'self-disclosure and self-communication.' We
> cannot equate the Bible with the Word of God. To do so
> would be to limit the doctrine. Christ is the very content of
> the Word. Whenever and wherever we meet Christ we are
> in contact with the Word of God.

Over the course of my future ministry this view remained constant. Even after I retired and was asked to deliver one of the Hein Fry lectures I continued to make reference to Sittler's work.

More calls to leadership

At the first meeting of the freshman class I was elected president. It was a fine honor. I discovered, however, that what Dr. Oscar Benson, president of the Augustana Synod, said about Augustana pastors, was already true when they entered the seminary. Every pastor, said Benson, is a "walking declaration of independence." After my good experiences of leadership at Augsburg College, I found that conducting meetings of the class and organizing events of any kind were most unpleasant. A large part of the problem was that most of the members of the class were married. Other than attending class, their focus was elsewhere, on family and work.

Part of my responsibility as class president was to preach at a welcome event for our class, attended by the entire faculty. Corinne describes my uneasiness in a letter to my folks:

Herb had been asked to represent his class and to give the
evening message. He was kinda scared—speaking in front
of all classmates, seminary professors, etc. I was scared right
with him—in fact, I was sort of out of breath too during the
last song before the sermon. Well, as usual—he *hid* his stage
fright. He did very well and we were blessed by the Word.
I'm sure you feel as I do, that God has given Herb a real gift
for sharing the Word in such a simple and practical way. We
must pray that God will really guard the gift he has given!

Singing in the Seminary Male Chorus was one of the more
satisfying extra-curricular activities I had in the Rock Island years.
Elmer Copley, our director, was a giant, both physically and as a
musician. Copley stood at least six feet and six inches and weighed
well over two hundred and fifty pounds. In my senior year my chorus mates elected me to be manager. That meant organizing individual concerts, a weekend tour, and a major spring tour. Working
out all the details of those events was a magnificent administrative
learning process for me. When the year was over and I handed in
the final financial report, President Mattson commended me, indicating that it was the first time in his memory that a chorus manager had completed that report before leaving campus.

Making ends meet

Both Corinne and I needed to work. She found a position in the
obstetrics department at St. Luke's Hospital across the Mississippi
River in Davenport, Iowa. She traversed the river via a unique
bridge that turned on a center pivot, allowing barges and other
river traffic to maneuver through the lock system. At times this
meant waiting for up to twenty minutes for the creaking bridge to
swing back into position for vehicular traffic.

We joined Calvary Lutheran Church in Moline, the city next east
from Rock Island and also part of what was known as the Quad
Cities. That included Davenport and Bettendorf, Iowa; and Rock

Island, Moline and East Moline, Illinois. In those days farm machinery manufacturing dominated the valley: John Deere, International Harvester, Case, and others. The pungent effluence from the factories earned the area the epithet "The Armpit of the Nation."

During the last half of my middler (second) year I tried my hand at selling Cutco cutlery door-to-door. Though I had times of discouragement after several evenings with no sales, I discovered that if I just persisted the sales came. In addition to the money I earned, I learned the kinds of lessons for evangelism that would benefit me in my future ministry:

> Never be afraid to go to any door. Most people will receive you kindly.
>
> Be persistent. Sometimes it takes more than one call to make a sale.
>
> Attend sales meetings for inspiration and encouragement from others. You can't do it on your own.
>
> Be positive. Encourage your customer to keep saying "yes" until they say "yes" to your product.

In 1995, almost forty years later, I returned to the Quad Cities and spoke at a rally attended by ten thousand people from area ELCA congregations at the Moline Arena. My message, well-suited to the text for the day, was based on those four points. Dr. Conrad Bergendoff, former president of Augustana College and highly-respected theologian of the church, was in the audience. He came to me after the rally and pronounced it one of the best sermons he had heard. A treasured compliment.

During the summer months I took assignments in congregations. The first summer Pastor Bergren asked Corinne and me to come to Litchfield to care for First Lutheran Church while he and his family took an extended trip to Europe. This meant living in the huge four-bedroom parsonage and caring for Mrs. Bergren's extensive flower gardens. It proved to be a good summer, further helping me to hone my skills for future ministry.

Near the end of my second year of seminary I saw a note posted on the seminary bulletin board asking if anyone were interested in spending the summer at Nathaniel Lutheran Church in Alcester, South Dakota. I had never heard of the place. But when I mentioned it to Corinne she erupted in surprise and delight. Alcester was only a few miles from her parents' farm near Vermillion, she said. Her grandfather was dying and her mother needed help to care for him. Furthermore, her parents planned to move to their retirement home that summer. Living in Alcester meant we would be able to assist them. It was the perfect arrangement.

We had three delightful months with the folks at Nathaniel Church. In the parish newsletter I tried to set the members at ease with this comment:

> Many women make excuses for what they think is an untidy house. But there are three reasons (at least) why you shouldn't feel bad: 1. It usually does not look as bad as you think. 2. It's hard to keep the house spic-and-span with so much work to do outdoors. 3. We "ain't no different." And you men—I don't mind a greasy handshake one bit!

It was extremely dry that summer in South Dakota. Crops were failing. Farmers were cutting corn for silage rather than for harvest. I wrote to the congregation:

> "... he makes his sun to rise on the evil and on the good, and sends rain on the righteous and on the unrighteous" (Matt.5:45b). God is absolutely impartial in his love—there is no respect of persons. He loves all equally. So many have commented this last week that maybe there is a purpose in the lack of moisture. Maybe we have been taking things too much for granted. And this may well be true. We forget to "count our blessings, name them one by one." Yet, it is also good for the Christian to know that we have something

solid to lean on—"Therefore do not worry, saying, 'What will we eat?' or 'What will we drink?" or 'What will we wear?' For it is the Gentiles who strive for all these things; and indeed your heavenly Father knows that you need all these things" (Matt. 6:31–32).

Another unexpected blessing from that summer was that my supervisor was Pastor Dallas Young from Sioux Falls. It was the beginning our friendship with the Young family, one that remains strong and important to this day.

When we returned from internship for the senior year at seminary, I was offered a position as youth director at Calvary Church. In a letter to my family Corinne wrote about one of my experiences that might well have been a forecast of similar times in my future ministry. She describes my turmoil in preparing and delivering a sermon:

> Saturday Herb spent all day working on it. When I came home from work at 3:00, he sure seemed discouraged! He tried three different texts and nothing came! Saturday evening he had something ready, but it didn't seem to satisfy him. On the way to church he looks like he's deep in thought and I dare not disturb him! It seemed to me to be one of those times like the apostle Paul talked about, "When I am weak, then I am strong." After the service Pastor Edquist came over and shook my hand and said, "My, but you have wonderful days ahead of you!" And when we got home I couldn't help but cry some tears of joy.

Internship—any place but New York City or Chicago

Almost from the beginning of the second year at Rock Island there was talk among classmates about our year of internship. We had no input into that decision. It was simply announced and we went wherever we were told to go. I expressed the opinion to friends that I would be happy with any assignment *except* New York City or

Chicago. My hope had been that I might be assigned to a growing suburban congregation.

I should have known better. The faculty knew what I needed most. When the assignments were announced I learned that I would be going to Trinity Lutheran Church, an old Swedish congregation on Chicago's near north side. Organized in 1883, the congregation had flourished when that area was considered to be a fine middle-class neighborhood. By the end of the century an imposing brick structure was erected at the corner of Barry and Seminary Avenues. Until 1926 Swedish was the primary language at all services, with English reserved for the Bible class and evening vespers. When English became the primary language, Swedish was still used at occasional services. A highlight of the year was the annual Christmas morning Swedish *Julotta* service broadcast over WMAQ radio and heard on that clear channel through much of the nation.

I was the first intern to be assigned to Trinity Church. In a letter of welcome my supervisor, Pastor Vernon Ryding, wrote:

> We have been hoping for a long time to have an intern at Trinity and now our prayers are answered. I wouldn't be honest if I said that work in the city is easy. It isn't. It is difficult, but it is also rewarding. You will like it, I'm sure.

Before the end of the school year Corinne and I made a visit to the site. In a letter to our families Corinne gave this description:

> The church is very old. So are all the big frame houses in the neighborhood and all of the buildings sit out on the street almost. You don't see a spear of grass and that is going to really be an adjustment for a couple of kids who like wide-open spaces! But behind those walls we know there are a lot of wonderful people . . . an old established church is almost becoming like a new mission. So we see a great challenge—the more we learn about the place, the more we see what a great deal there will be for us to learn.

Vernon Ryding was a good supervisor. He allowed me plenty of room to be creative and to organize my own areas of responsibility. That suited me well. In my final report at the end of the year I apparently stated that Ryding had offered little criticism of my work. He responded in a personal letter by suggesting that

> I could see from the start that you were no novice at it but that you took right ahold of things like a veteran. I was grateful for the fact that I could leave many things in your hands and know that they would all be taken care of and that I could just forget them afterwards.

Though Vernon Ryding was my supervisor, Corinne and I soon realized that Mrs. Ryding—Grace—would be a force to be reckoned with. Yes, she was "really nice" as Corinne had written. Like my mother Ruth, Grace was kind and generous to a fault. But, also like Ruth, she was forceful, demanding, and controlling. She had her own desk in the parsonage, just beyond Vernon's office. We soon learned that most everything that passed over his desk would also pass over hers. Grace was deeply involved in activities beyond the local congregation, including the national Women's Missionary Society, the board of American Missions of the Augustana Church, and the board of the National Council of Churches. We often said that she would have been at ease running a major Chicago corporation. Both Corinne and I had to stand our ground with her. In time, as she realized we had strengths of our own and were not easily overpowered, we developed a comfortable relationship.

Ryding worked hard to try to move the congregation to embrace its changing community. Emigrants from Cuba were beginning to move into the neighborhood as younger Caucasian families moved to the suburbs. At a council meeting one evening the pastor laid out a plan for reaching out to the community. One member responded briskly by saying, "The door is open. Let them come." Unfortunately, that was probably typical of the outlook of most members. By 1970, some twenty-five years later, the congregation was unable to sustain itself. It merged with nearby Messiah church to form Resurrection congregation.

While I worked at Trinity Church, Corinne was employed as a nurse at nearby Children's Hospital. In a letter to my family she describes it as a place where one sees the most unusual cases— "things you wouldn't see more than once in a lifetime." She goes into detail about a tragic Christmas Eve accident when a drunk driver slammed into a family in another car, injuring a three-year-old boy. Later he died on her shift.

> I couldn't help but think of all the liquor ads we'd seen in the paper right before Christmas. "Beer belongs" and "The kind that grandma used to make" and "Make this the merriest Christmas ever." As I wrapped up his cold and stiff little body I thought, if *this* picture could only accompany those ads instead of the false pictures. . . . And then I thought of the poor young parents in another hospital who should have to lie there with this Christmas sorrow on their hearts.

In another letter from Chicago Corinne tells of a time when I was rather ill with a cold and asked her at the last moment to take my place in giving a report on a book about missions to the local Women's Missionary Society.

> Oh, me! I was afraid that would happen, so I had given him extra special care the day before, but it didn't help. I probably told those ladies things that weren't even true, but anyway they had a book report! I pleaded that he'd never try this trick on a Sunday morning! Can't you just see me in a robe in a pulpit?

Little could we have known that some twenty-five years later that's exactly where she would be—in a robe in a pulpit!

Babies for others—but not for us

Many of my classmates were older and came to the seminary with children. Others soon began to announce that babies were on the way. After each meeting of the Seminettes, the wives of seminary students, Corinne would come home with news about the stork's impending visit to more seminary couples.

By the end of the second year at Rock Island Corinne and I began to think that maybe we could somehow handle beginning our family. We had dreamed of four as the ideal number. By that time many of our siblings had children. We never imagined that *not* having children would be a daunting issue for us.

Our longing to have children grew even stronger as we looked toward the end of internship. Now we were involved in fertility studies. I wrote to my family in April of 1957:

> We've been going to our "family" doctor lately to see why we don't have one. We had hoped to have at least one or two by now. But it seems that we will have to be patient— and that is a hard thing sometimes. We will appreciate your prayers in this matter.

At graduation time in 1958 only twelve of seventy were not married. We referred to them as "The Apostles." By the time we were ready to be ordained the number of children reached no less than sixty-six.

Graduation

I was grateful to complete my seminary work with a strong academic record, good enough to qualify me for honors. I give Corinne as much credit for it as I take to myself. Her hard work made it possible for me to devote more time to study. It was a shared honor.

Dr. Arthur Arnold, professor of homiletics, wrote of his vision for our class of seventy men. He likened us to the young and inexperienced prophet Jeremiah:

Those of us who have known these young men . . . have
sensed something of this hesitancy. It is not a mark of lack
of faith, but humility and an awareness of human insuf-
ficiency. . . . they pause before the task that is too big for
any human. To the youthful Jeremiah, the Lord said: 'I
consecrated you . . . I appointed you . . . be not afraid . . . for
I am with you. . . .'' This is the promise of God to youthful
prophets today.

St. John's Lutheran Church, Rock Island, was the site of our
graduation ceremony. My folks came by train. I was happy to have
them there with us, but also a bit troubled by it. Coming to my
graduation meant that they would miss my sister Janet's graduation
from high school. Since they planned to attend my ordination, I
felt it more important that they attend her event. I suspect Pastor
Bergren leaned heavily on them to come to Rock Island.

The graduation address was delivered by Dr. Henry Bagger,
president of Philadelphia Lutheran Seminary. He outlined three
demands God makes of a pastor:

The demand of personal fellowship with God.

The demand of personal integrity.

The demand of complete commitment to the causes of God.

He went on to suggest that:

You will never attain this ideal, but in holding this ideal
before you, you will go further in your ministry. Go forth,
not with a complacent spirit of academic achievement, not
with an assumption of prestige; but go as men of God to
show the world what it is to be a Christian.

A solid foundation

Over my years as pastor, teacher, and bishop I've probably had
as much contact with the seminaries as any other leader in the

church. All through the years of our history as a Lutheran church in the United States, we have had first-rate schools of theological learning. Augustana Seminary had a weak link here and there—as does every seminary. I must say, however, that Augustana ranked with the best of them.

Augustana Seminary: a gift to me and many others.

Chapter 6

Ordination and our first parish

Where will it be?

After all those years—years of searching for an understanding of God's will for my life, years of study and hard work to complete Augsburg College, marriage to Corinne and our years at seminary, including internship in Chicago—after all of that it came down to the questions: Where will we go to begin our ministry? Where will we be living in the next stage of our lives?

For most professions it becomes a matter of searching for a position and agreeing to a contract. For a graduate of Augustana Seminary in the 1950s it was quite different. The custom of the church was to let us suggest three conferences (the equivalent of today's synods) where we might prefer to serve. I entered Columbia as first choice; Minnesota as second; and left the third preference open, a clue that I would be open to assignment anywhere in the country.

My strong hope, of course, was that I would get my first choice. The Columbia Conference included several states in the Northwest: Washington, Oregon, Idaho, and Montana. Having grown up on the prairies of Minnesota and having interned in Chicago, I thought it would be adventuresome to "go west, young man" and do ministry in a completely new setting.

Once we had made our preferences known, my classmates and I searched out information about calls in those conferences where we thought we might be assigned. I learned that the Augustana Church was contemplating the start of a new mission congregation in the mountainous community of Arco, Idaho. There were rumors that the Atomic Energy Commission might establish a major facility in that area. I envisioned a fast-growing city and the potential for a solid population base for a new congregation. It looked exciting to us.

As for the Minnesota Conference, my preference centered in the hope that if nothing materialized in the Northwest I might be chosen to start a new congregation in one of the rapidly growing suburbs in the Minneapolis-St. Paul metropolis.

As for Idaho, I lived to thank God that I was *not* chosen for that call. Years later while on a retreat at Sun Valley, Idaho, Corinne and I happened to drive through Arco. It was a sleepy, backwater village. Plans for development never materialized. One of my classmates started a new church but it closed after a few years of futile effort. In that predominantly Mormon area, prospects for a Lutheran congregation were dim.

I learned that the powers-that-be had in mind for me something totally surprising and unexpected.

Pelican Rapids and Elizabeth

All through our senior year, my close friend Ralph Strand told me about his experience at Faith Lutheran Church in Pelican Rapids, Minnesota. He had served there for a summer stint. He described how a few members from Central Lutheran Church, a rural Augustana congregation just three miles from town, had decided to purchase an old church building in Pelican Rapids and start a new congregation. Most of the members of the country church thought it a ridiculous idea. They looked on those who left as traitors. Feelings were intense. Ralph wondered if he might be assigned to go back to that setting. I kept trying to reassure him that it probably would not happen.

On the evening assignments were announced, our class gathered in the seminary chapel. Each conference was called out alphabetically. Columbia—but I was not included. I thought that it would then surely be Minnesota. At that time the Minnesota Conference did not include the northwestern area of the state. That part was in the Red River Valley Conference and included not only that corner of Minnesota, but also all of North and South Dakota. When the Minnesota group was called and I was not summoned, I was baffled. I went through the rest of the alphabet in my mind. When Red River Valley was called, I heard my name. I was totally shocked. I had given no thought whatever to that possibility.

What I soon learned was that it would be Pelican Rapids and Elizabeth. I was completely unprepared for this possibility. And I must admit, having heard so much about Pelican Rapids from Strand, I was more than a bit chagrined at the news. Walter Carlson, president of the Red River Valley Conference, whom I now met for the first time, was a short, muscular man who might easily have been mistaken for a factory worker. He explained that because Faith Church in Pelican Rapids was so small, the Augustana Synod had classified it as a "mission aid congregation," meaning that it would receive financial support until the congregation could function on its own. As for Augustana Church in Elizabeth, he said that it had been linked to Faith Church because the congregation in Fergus Falls, Minnesota, that had been its partner, wanted to sever that relationship. Thus I was looking at a first call that included one orphan church and one infant church, both so small that they could not exist even in a linked parish

The prospects for this call got more dismal a week or two later when Dr. Theodore Matson, director of American Missions for the Augustana Synod, came to Rock Island to meet with all of those going to congregations receiving mission aid. Matson, known and even feared for his blunt and forthright manner, moved around the circle, asking our names and the places we were assigned. He gave a thumbnail sketch of each situation. Most were new mission congregations in suburban settings. The excitement of those going to these promising sites was palpable. They exuded confidence that the church had chosen them for good reason; that they had the skills needed to start vibrant new missions.

When Matson got to me and heard my name and place he paused for a moment and then said, "Mr. Chilstrom, there are seventy calls for this class. I would place Pelican Rapids sixty-ninth on the list." That's all I remembered.

When I shared the news with Corinne we both went into an even deeper state of dismay. We simply had not imagined anything like this. After a few days, however, our confidence that God was somehow involved in the process sustained us. We prepared ourselves for an unexpected venture. Corinne tried to console me by suggesting that after a couple of years at Pelican Rapids and Elizabeth, we could move on to greener pastures.

We accepted the calls from the congregations in mid-April and began to make detailed plans for our move. In a letter to John Granstrom, one of the pillars at the fledging Faith Church, I noted that I had spoken to several classmates who had connections with Pelican Rapids and had come to be optimistic about the future of the congregation. Granstrom assured me in a comment that came with the letter of call that not all members were of Swedish background. I replied:

> That suits me fine. I married a mixture of Denmark and Norway and I really think she's pretty nice! If I can't get along with the Norwegians I'll just turn them over to her!

A couple of weeks later, Matson sent a letter with an apology. Having learned more about the parish, he said:

> It appears now that the possibilities at Pelican Rapids are very good. The stewardship is excellent and I believe the members themselves stand ready to carry on a very effective evangelism program.

It also helped to receive a letter from Lorenze Mellgren, pastor at Central Church.

> We wish to welcome you to Pelican Rapids. We can assure you that it is a very nice place, filled with friendly people and we have wonderful fellowship among the five Lutheran pastors (six when you come) here in Pelican.

After alluding to the tensions between the two congregations at Pelican Rapids, Mellgren added:

> I feel that it is truly of God that you are coming here and I know we can work together and possibly find a solution to the situation. That is our task and it takes much love and patience.

In my reply to Mellgren I suggested:

> There may be many things to irritate and frustrate, but maybe that is when we will be forced to depend the most on the grace of God. One thing I know for sure—there is only one way to come to Pelican: on my knees. . . . as you say, if there is to be unity it must begin with us as cowork-ers. On the surface it seems that it is poor stewardship of manpower to have the witness of six Lutheran pastors in a community the size of Pelican, but at the same time I am of the firm conviction that my assignment is an answer to prayer. Maybe twenty years from now we will be able to see more plainly what God has in mind. Right now it is only seen "through a glass darkly."

We left for our trip to the ordination at Jamestown genuinely excited about the prospects for our future at Pelican Rapids and Elizabeth.

Ordination at Jamestown, New York

The Augustana Synod met in convention every year. It was the tradition to have the ordination for each new class at the convention. This meant that no matter where you were going to serve your first call, you were expected to attend the convention. If your first call was near the convention site, well and good. But if it was in a far corner of the country, too bad, the cost of travel was yours to absorb.

We invited my parents to join us for a circular trek that would take us down to North Carolina to visit sister Chile and her husband, Bill; to go to Washington, D.C. and New York City for sightseeing ventures; on to Jamestown, New York, for the ordination and then back to Minnesota. Ruth, an inveterate diary keeper, noted bits and pieces of the trip:

> In Kentucky: "Herb took picture of red soil. Got motel—$10.00."
>
> In North Carolina: "To Old Salem, museum and Moravian graveyard."
>
> In Washington, D.C.: "To Augustana Lutheran Church, Mount Vernon, Lincoln Memorial."
>
> In New York: "Sightseeing tour of New York City."
>
> At Jamestown, New York: "First Lutheran—sem boys sign book. Ordination—very impressive service. Beautiful day— cool 65 degrees."

The site for the ordination was the Chautauqua Institution just north of Jamestown. Called "the most American thing in America" by Theodore Roosevelt, it has been a cultural center for music, education, recreation, and religion since 1874.

The ordination at the Chautauqua amphitheater on Sunday, June 22, 1958, attended by six thousand, was indeed a very impressive service. Our class of seventy would be the second largest in the history of the church. It began at four in the afternoon with the majestic hymn "Holy, Holy, Holy, Lord God Almighty!" The lesson was from Romans 10: 8–15, including the words, "How beautiful are the feet of those who bring good news!" The gospel was from

John 21:15–17: "[Peter] said to him, 'Yes, Lord; you know that I love you.' Jesus said to him, 'Feed my lambs.'" Dr. Oscar Benson, president of the church, preached on Jeremiah 1:5:

> Before I formed you in the womb I knew you, and before you were born I consecrated you; I appointed you a prophet to the nations.

Benson said to us that

> The God that called Jeremiah is now calling you to serve him. You are not only called *by* God; you are also called *for* God. Be on guard lest you minimize your gifts, and they be wasted instead of used. Be on your knees often, asking God to make your gifts instruments for him. God wants you to be filled with the Holy Spirit. May we serve God with our short little days.

With a text and message like that, having my wife, my parents, and my pastor and his wife in the congregation made the event more meaningful than ever. The same was true for most of my classmates. However unlikely it may have seemed to others that we should be ordained and, in many cases, emerge as future leaders in the church, on that day we had the blessing of the church to do the work of ministry. On that day, as many times since, I felt a profound conviction that this could not have happened to me unless God was involved in it from the beginning. I had a deep and unshakable certainty that I had a call from God to be a pastor. And, no less, a feeling of gratitude for Corinne, my family, and my church.

After singing our class hymn "Thee We Adore, Eternal Lord!" there were prayers for the ordinands, charges from Scripture, and the confession of the Nicene Creed by the class. Then we were asked:

> Are you ready to take upon you this holy ministry, and faithfully to serve therein?

> Will you preach and teach the Word of God in accordance
> with the Confessions of the church, and will you administer
> the Holy Sacraments after this ordinance of Christ?

> Will you adorn the doctrine of God by a holy life and
> conversation?

After our affirmative responses the class knelt while President
Benson declared:

> The Lord bestow upon you the Holy Ghost for the office
> and work of a minister in the church of God, now commit-
> ted to you by the authority of the Church through the lay-
> ing on of hands; in the Name of the Father, and of the Son,
> and of the Holy Ghost.

At that moment each of our sponsors, in my case J. Henry Bergren, stepped forward, laid hands on our heads, prayed the Lord's
Prayer, and placed over our shoulders the green stole.

I might note that our class was the first in the history of the
Augustana Church to wear a white alb over our black robes at our
ordination.

Before we rose the congregation joined in singing:

> Lord of the Church, we humbly pray
> For those who guide us in Thy way,
> And speak Thy holy word;
> With love divine their hearts inspire,
> And touch their lips with hallowed fire,
> And needful grace afford.

In an article in the July 16 *Lutheran Companion*, Dr. Victor Beck
summed up the service by suggesting:

> One seemed to sense the prayers not only of this great
> assembly, including wives, parents, and loved ones, but
> also the prayers of the entire Church focused upon these
> young men.

It's important to note that the ordination service was only one part of the synod convention. The "spirit of Augustana" can be measured in some of the actions taken by the delegates.

That spirit was evident in actions that urged pastors to be engaged in politics, asked congregations to open their doors to people of all cultures, condemned corruption in labor unions and business enterprises, and suggested giving aid to rural and urban congregations in changing communities.

More significant for me than I could have imagined at the time was that the convention put itself firmly on record as favoring Lutheran unity. I could never have believed that I would play such a significant role in that unfolding venture. My only thought at the time was to be ordained and to serve in parish ministry.

A stop at Litchfield

Eager as we were to get to Pelican Rapids after my ordination, I had agreed to preach at my home church, First Lutheran, at Litchfield, Minnesota, on June 29. This was the eighty-fifth anniversary year for the congregation, and my preaching and an afternoon reception for Corinne and me were part of the year's celebration. The announcements for the day noted that I was the first son in the history of First Lutheran, confirmed at that congregation, to enter the ministry.

On to Pelican Rapids and Elizabeth

Our drive from Litchfield to Pelican Rapids was on a stormy July 1 morning. Threatening clouds accompanied us all the way. We noted that the fields between Fergus Falls and Elizabeth were black, as though no crops had been planted. We soon learned that a devastating hailstorm had swept through the countryside just ahead of us, leaving the young crops decimated.

We noted the simple, white clapboard Augustana Lutheran Church in Elizabeth as we passed through the village on U.S.

Highway 59. Its high steeple seemed almost too large for the tiny building. As we drove on we looked eagerly for our first glimpse of Pelican Rapids, our home for the next years. About four miles south of town we rounded a curve and caught sight of the town's water tower. Then we noticed a steeple with a clock in the tower. We had seen photos of the structure on covers of bulletins John Granstrom had sent to us. We knew this was Faith Lutheran Church.

As we turned the corner by the church we saw a cattle truck parked along the street. A driver seemed to sense who we were and got out. Slender as a rail and looking a bit like Ichabod Crane, Edwin Sundstrom was our first encounter with a member of the congregation. Over the next four years bachelor Edwin, a cattle trucker and kindly gossip, was a frequent visitor in our home. Under his arm was a loaf of bread from the local bakery. It was the first of many gestures of generosity from him, his single brother, John, and from many members of Faith Church. Edwin led us to the small apartment that was our temporary home in Pelican Rapids.

I hit the ground running. While Corinne busied herself with getting settled in the apartment the congregation had furnished for us, I set out to call on board members in both congregations. I wanted to see them before my first Sunday in the pulpit. Most of them were shocked when I showed up. I'm sure several thought I was a salesman of some sort and, like most reserved Scandinavians, their initial reaction was somewhat cool. When they learned who I was, they shifted gears quickly and welcomed me warmly.

Augustana Lutheran Church in Elizabeth

The village of Elizabeth had less than one hundred residents. The three churches, two Lutheran and one Roman Catholic, were outnumbered by six saloons. A small general store, a sleepy service station, and a creamery completed the downtown.

We wasted no time starting a variety of programs in both congregations. Augustana, as I mentioned earlier, had been the little

sister of a larger congregation—Augustana Lutheran Church in
Fergus Falls. They were accustomed to having minimal pastoral
attention. That would change dramatically.

Janet Petterson, a new young bride in the community, had some
musical gifts. We convinced her to start a senior choir. Their first
rehearsal was at the parsonage in Pelican Rapids. The walls must
still ache from the discordant vibrations of that evening. But she
persisted. In time they matured into a respectable choir.

Mildred Nelson, one of God's dearest saints, labored at an old
pump organ. She made no pretense of being a musician. But she
was all they had. Corinne convinced some of the promising young
girls in the congregation to take organ lessons. In time a new electronic instrument was purchased and Mildred yielded gladly to our
talented young musicians.

Corinne started a children's choir. As with the adults, the first
rehearsals can only be described as dreadful. But she persisted and
in time they were singing at worship services and special programs,
much to the delight of their pleased parents.

In the summers we held vacation Bible school. Children from
the community came out of the cracks and we had a marvelous
time with them.

As new members joined the congregation, I suggested very cautiously and on a one-by-one contact with board members that we
needed to add a parish hall to the building. First, however, the steeple, rotted out by years of neglect, had to be toppled. Now, instead
of being dominated by a steeple too large for the rest of the building, the structure looked more like a school than a church. Nevertheless, my suggestion for expansion germinated for some months
and surfaced at a congregational meeting. There were expressions
of doubt about the project. But folks like Carl and Mildred Nelson
and Stanley Norgren, known for their generosity, gave it their quiet
and generous support. We passed out slips of paper and asked each
giving unit to write down what they thought they could contribute

toward the project. We were all pleasantly surprised, and some shocked, when the total assured us that we could proceed. Over the next months, again with much volunteer help, the building rose and became a commodious gathering place for congregational fellowship. With hammer in hand, I spent many happy hours working side-by-side with members of the congregation.

Augustana is the site of my shortest sermon ever. One Sunday, just as I began preaching, I felt a wood tick snaking its way up my leg. I kept hoping it would make a U-turn. But it kept coming. I cut the sermon, concluded the service, and headed for the sacristy where I doffed my robe, dropped my pants, and extracted the pesky intruder. Had they known, I'm sure some members would have encouraged more visitors of that ilk.

Because Corinne and I were tithers and because Augustana members had become accustomed to giving very little to keep their church going, it soon became apparent that the young pastor and his wife were some of the largest donors to the ministry of the congregation. And this was only one of the congregations in the parish. We worked hard at stewardship education. By the time the building project was completed, Augustana had one of the highest per capita giving figures in the entire Red River Valley Conference.

No one told me that there had been some informal conversation prior to our arrival that the congregation might close once it severed its ties with Augustana Church in Fergus Falls. Good thing. Such a thought never entered my mind.

Faith Lutheran Church in Pelican Rapids

Pelican Rapids was a thriving agri-business/tourist community of fifteen hundred. There were two of most everything: hardware stores, pharmacies, implement dealers, furniture stores—both with mortuary service, grocery stores, lumber yards, restaurants, and much more. Otter Tail County has a thousand of Minnesota's ten thousand lakes. That made it a favorite destination for summertime visitors, mostly from the Fargo-Moorhead area.

In the fifty years since then, the community has changed dramatically. Now only one of each kind of store exists. The hospital, abuzz with activity in the 1950s, is closed. A turkey processing plant, started in the early 1950s to accommodate the local work force, has burgeoned into the largest employer in Otter Tail County today.

The makeup of the community has also been transformed in these years. When we arrived one could hear Norwegian spoken on Main Street. And most of those who didn't know Norwegian spoke English with an accent that suggested that it had not been long since they disembarked an immigrant ship. Because of the success of the turkey plant, hundreds of Hispanic families from south Texas found their way to Pelican Rapids. Each international conflict also brought a new wave of immigrants looking for entry-level employment at the plant: Southeast Asians, Bosnians, East Africans. Today, though the façade of its downtown looks much as it did fifty years ago, Pelican Rapids is a completely different community from what it was when we arrived in 1958. It is among Minnesota's most international cities.

The greatest challenge at Faith Church was to grow a congregation in a community that was already over-churched. Trinity Lutheran, with a staff of two pastors, had fifteen hundred members in a village with that many citizens. There was also a Lutheran Free Church in town with its own pastor. In every direction there were Lutheran country congregations, some with substantial memberships. And there I was, serving a new mission congregation that was expected to stand on its own after five years of mission aid from the national church.

There was only one thing to do: call, and call, and call some more. Every open evening I was out visiting members and new prospects. I often set out with no particular destination in mind except to see what was going on in the village. More often than not I ended up calling on a member family or discovering someone new who had moved to town.

That kind of aggressive calling would be a hallmark of my ministry at Pelican Rapids and Elizabeth. With only seventy-five members at Elizabeth and fewer at Pelican Rapids, it was easy to make frequent calls in their homes. I also earned the reputation of being the pastor who was "standing on the front porch when the suitcases arrived" to welcome a new family to the community.

Because we were in lake country, I printed posters that I distributed to cabins and lake homes, as well as to all of the resorts and country stores in a fifteen-mile radius of the city. Some of the lake residents had considerable resources and gave generously to the fledgling congregation.

The first major business for Faith Church was to find a permanent home for its new pastor and wife. Walter Carlson, president of the Red River Valley Conference, had visited the community, looked at existing home possibilities, and strongly recommended that the congregation build a new parsonage. The members accepted his advice and set out immediately to build. Though a carpenter was hired, it was agreed that volunteer help would do much of the work. Ground was broken in the fall and the house came up over the winter. Corinne and I were frequent visitors and volunteers at the site.

If having no choir at Elizabeth was one of its deficits, the choir at Faith Church was its strongest asset. With key voices in every section, it was by far the finest choir for a church that size that I have ever heard. It was a delight for Corinne and me to sing under the direction of Idell Granstrom, another of God's special gifts to us. John and Idell, in fact, became wonderful friends. We often visited them on a Sunday evening after the day's work was done and John had finished milking his six cows. It was a place of refuge and security for us.

The most dominant member of Faith was Everett Johnson, a partner with his brother in a furniture store and funeral home. Through thick and thin, through his divorce and remarriage, family stresses and economic ups and downs, Ev became one of my best friends. The chemistry was right. Whenever I returned to the area in later years, it was important to spend time with him. His major fault was that though he could give generously, it was difficult for him to receive.

The most pressing issue in the community was the use of alcohol. Unlike Elizabeth and thanks mainly to the work of the Women's Christian Temperance Union (WCTU), Pelican Rapids was dry. Its leader was Hannah Haugrud, a large and formidable woman in the model of Golda Meir and Margaret Thatcher. Whenever the issue arose it was expected that the clergy would support a dry vote. And we did. That caused some rifts with members of Faith who saw no problem in moderate drinking. It proved to be a time when I did some of my best pastoral work, helping those members to understand that though I preferred a dry community, I did not condemn those who drank alcohol responsibly. In retrospect, I'm not certain the issue was worth the effort we clergy invested in it.

More calls to leadership

Stewardship

At the first meeting of the Alexandria District, a network of about twenty churches in western Minnesota, I was elected district pastoral stewardship counselor. I thought it was an honor. I soon learned, however, that it was the task most pastors shunned and was often dumped on one of the newest and unsuspecting arrivals. I took it as a challenge. I was coupled with a marvelous and deeply dedicated lay counselor by the name of Walter Sundberg, a beekeeper from Fergus Falls. We traveled to any congregation that would have us and promoted the work of the church beyond the local congregation. Walter's unwavering theme was that he would rather have the joy of giving while he was living than to leave large sums after he died.

At Faith and Augustana churches I promoted giving to the church beyond the local scene. Though we needed every dollar for our own budget, I insisted that we set high goals for giving to the mission of the Augustana Synod.

Youth ministry

At my first meeting of the Red River Valley Conference Luther League, I was elected president. This meant doing my best to promote youth ministry in all of the congregations in northwestern Minnesota, and North and South Dakota that were part of the conference. I launched a newsletter to pastors and aggressively promoted leadership schools and the annual camp for the League.

This election led to my first airplane ride. I was head of the Red River Valley youth delegation to the national youth gathering in San Antonio, Texas, over the 1960 New Year. The flight from Fargo to San Antonio included at least five or six stops along the way. The weather was stormy. I was petrified. Little could I have envisioned the day when I would fall asleep before the plane left the runway.

At San Antonio I roomed with Don Sjoberg, president of the Canada Conference Luther League. It would be the beginning of a lifelong friendship. I could never have dreamed that he would be the first presiding bishop of the Evangelical Lutheran Church in Canada (ELCIC) and I the first presiding bishop of the Evangelical Lutheran Church in America (ELCA) and that he would be the preacher when I was installed as presiding bishop in 1987.

Writing

I was also getting invitations to do some writing. For its January 1958 issue of *Teen Talk*, published by the Augustana Book Concern and aimed at youth of the church, I was asked to write about my call to be a pastor. *Youth Programs*, a resource for program planning for youth meetings, also invited me to write articles.

LCA Constituting Convention

In 1961 at the Red River Valley Conference convention I was elected a delegate to the Constituting Convention of the Lutheran

Church in America. I believe I was the youngest clergy delegate at that event in Detroit, June 28–July 1, 1962. Little could I have imagined as I sat in the far gallery seats of the cavernous Ford Auditorium and observed the eminent Franklin Clark Fry preside over much of that gathering, that I would be elected to fill that role in the ELCA some twenty-five years later.

What's a pastor's wife to do?

Once the parsonage was up and we got settled comfortably, Corinne and I faced a question that I was not prepared to deal with. Here was a woman with enormous energy, talent, and intellect who was going crazy in the confined role of a pastor's wife in a small parish. She was actively engaged in the many aspects of the two congregations. And she entertained as many people as one could imagine. She took a special interest in single persons and those who had lost a mate. That has been a pattern for her all through the years. But here was a woman with a nursing degree, excellent experience in the field, and a local hospital that needed her skills.

When Corinne first brought up the idea that she might like to go to work I was stunned. I turned sullen. This was not my idea of what a pastor's wife should be and do. It didn't fit the role model I had come to think was appropriate. I was also dealing with some guilt. Corinne had worked so hard to help me get through seminary that I thought she should not have to be employed at all.

Corinne resolved the problem by simply announcing one day that she had been over to the hospital and learned that they needed help very badly. She would be going to work a couple of days a week. I yielded ever so grudgingly. I soon realized, however, that she found enormous satisfaction in caring for the sick. And I couldn't help but note that the added dollars to our bank account made a young pastor's life much more secure. In retrospect, it was an era of transition for the spouses of pastors. By the time I became a synod bishop in the mid-1970s it was common, and even expected, that a pastor's wife would have her own career outside the home.

Should we adopt children?

It had become clear to us by the time we settled in Pelican Rapids that we would not be able to have children born to us. That was a bitter pill for us to swallow. Each new announcement from family and friends that someone was pregnant was another bittersweet moment for us.

We decided to venture into the adoption scene. We contacted the Board of Social Ministry in St. Paul, Minnesota, our church's agency. Evelyn Bonander, the caseworker, visited us several times and walked with us through the tedious process. Month after month passed. It seemed like a long, painful pregnancy. In a letter to my folks in mid-July 1960 I wrote:

> It's been a long process. They don't leave any stones
> unturned. And even now we don't know for sure until we
> get a letter of approval—but there doesn't seem to be much
> doubt now. So you may be Grandma and Grandpa again
> before long. It really has us excited. We feel it is an answer
> to our prayers and the closer we come to it the more certain
> we are that this is God's way for us.

Finally after eighteen months, the phone rang in my office one day. Corinne was away. It was Evelyn. She said they had a little girl for us. We were ecstatic! I jotted some notes on a piece of scrap paper: a full head of black hair, bright dark blue eyes, birth parents with college background, a mixture of English, Irish, French, Norwegian, and German.

We could hardly wait to get to the agency in St. Paul on August 30, 1960. Our first sight of that little baby girl was the fulfillment of all those long months of waiting and dreaming. She was more beautiful than we could have imagined. It was customary to have a brief service of blessing at the Bethesda Hospital Chapel across the street from the agency. Pastor Norman Anderson from a St. Paul congregation conducted the service. Soon we were on our way to Pelican Rapids. It was a hot day. There were small beads of sweat on her face as we drove through the villages along Highway 12 on our way home.

The newspapers were filled with political speculation about the contest between John F. Kennedy and Richard M. Nixon. We sent an announcement to our family and friends:

ELECTION YEAR NOTICE

We've *adopted* a new platform and on it we're introducing our little candidate: Mary Lee joined the Chilstrom party on August 31, 1960, at the age of six weeks. Campaign speeches broadcast nightly. Campaign managers: Herb & Corinne Chilstrom

Just before Christmas that year I wrote a letter to Mary. Here are some excerpts:

Dear Mary Lee: What can a Daddy give a little girl who doesn't know what Christmas is all about? I guess the best I can do is write you a letter that you can read when you are a big girl. And even if you feel that Mommy and Daddy love you now, you'll be able to read about it and understand it better when you grow up.

On the back of a pair of pants you got from Eleanor Johnson it says, "My First Christmas." I was holding you up at Church Women this afternoon and showing it off. Pretty clever they all thought! But it's more than clever—because your "First Christmas" is the best one your Daddy has ever had. One of the ladies told your Mama today that I was just about bursting I was so proud of our little Mary. I didn't realize it showed so much—but that's how I feel.

I can only pray that this Daddy will bring as much happiness to you as you've brought to him.

You've got a wonderful Mama, Mary. No little girl has
ever been better taken care of—I can tell you that. And no
Daddy has ever been so lucky either.

Now I'm going to put this letter away. Maybe someday
you'll read it and you'll know how happy your Dad is and
how thankful he is this Christmas that God has given him
a wonderful little girl named Mary. God bless you and
keep you for his own always. May his very best purpose be
fulfilled in you!

Your Daddy
Christmas—1960

Where do we go from here?

Given our first impression of Pelican Rapids and Elizabeth, we
came to the parish with the thought that our time there would be
rather brief. Surely not more than two years before moving on to
greater challenges. We soon discovered, however, that we were in
love with the people and the community. With good response from
both congregations, we felt no need to rush off to what seemed like
more promising places.

The first hint of what the future held in store for us came less
than a year after we arrived at Pelican Rapids. Vernon Serenius
was serving at Evansville, an hour away. He was a large figure in
the Augustana Synod, having served as senior pastor at Augustana
Lutheran Church in Minneapolis and then as director of Immanuel
Hospital and Deaconess Institute in Omaha, Nebraska. He left that
corporate position to serve his last years in ministry in a small
town setting. He was a dour, opinionated man with very conservative tendencies. Yet I had learned that he also had a softer, more
pastoral side when one got to know him.

Serenius was on the national board of the Lutheran Bible
Institute association. At that time there were four schools in the

network: Minneapolis, Los Angeles, Seattle, and Teaneck, New
Jersey. In a letter dated May 27, 1959, he indicated that as chair of
the nominating committee of the board it was his responsibility to
look for pastors who might be prospects for faculty positions at the
schools. He wrote:

> I have been wondering recently whether you have ever had
> any particular interest in that type of teaching ministry.
> I have been impressed with your native intelligence, and
> evident good judgment. You impress me as one who could
> fit into a corporate situation like that very well.

In my response a fortnight later I wrote that I was "flabber-
gasted" at the thought that I might be regarded as worthy of consideration for such a ministry. I admitted, however, that I enjoyed
teaching "almost as much as preaching," and that I felt that more
could be accomplished in a teaching setting than in a preaching
arena. I wrote that I would be willing to keep the option alive,
knowing that God would open and close doors when and if the
opportunity ever became a reality.

In early 1961 inquiries began to tumble in from various places,
asking if I would consider a move. First, there was Grace Church,
Mankato, Minnesota, looking for an assistant pastor. Then First at
Parkers Prairie, Minnesota. Then First at Rush City, Minnesota,
where Carl Zimmerman, my supervisor when I was doing youth
ministry while at Augsburg College, was leaving the parish and
wanted me to succeed him. In mid-July one came that caused much
excitement at first. Augustana Church in Denver, Colorado, wanted
me to come as an assistant to Paul Noren, one of the great pastors
and preachers of the Augustana Synod. Was my seminary dream
of serving in one of the Western states coming true? Here was my
chance. But, like the others, I found I could not move beyond a
kind word of thanks and an affirmation of ministry where I was.

At some point in this time frame Harley Swiggum, married to

Corinne's sister Devona, talked to me informally about joining his staff with *The Bethel Series,* an adult Bible study program that would grow in the ensuing years to become one of the largest programs of its kind in the world. Nothing came of it and I doubt if I would have moved in that direction even if the offer had become concrete. Much as I admired him and the great work he was doing, I felt certain that I was destined for another kind of ministry.

Then in late August or early September of 1961 I received a phone call that eventually changed the course of my life and of our life as a family. It was from Philip Worthington, president of the Lutheran Bible Institute at Teaneck, New Jersey. He invited me to consider joining their faculty. I recall thinking after our conversation that of all the Bible Institutes, Teaneck was the one I would *least* want to consider. Los Angeles, Seattle, or Minneapolis, yes, but New Jersey? No, that had no appeal whatever. Nevertheless, for reasons I could not explain, I was unable to close the door.

Two weeks later Worthington wrote to tell me that my name would go to the board as a candidate for a teaching position.

In early October I wrote back, admitting that the number one question in my mind was whether I was really qualified to teach. "The task of teaching . . . is an awesome one. However, I know that God is able to supply the necessary wisdom and insight."

I suggested that among several factors that would discourage a move at that time, the most significant was the rumors I had heard about the conflict among LBI faculty members between those who were fundamentalist and those who were conservative. I made it clear to Worthington that I could not serve in a setting where a fundamentalist view was predominant.

I find it interesting now, almost five decades later, to see that the course of my theological journey has been so consistent. At some point I began describing myself as "an evangelical conservative with a radical social conscience." I'll have more to say about this later. This paragraph in my letter to Worthington was an early indication, however, of how hard I have fought over the decades to be faithful to Lutheran theological formulations while, at the same time, avoiding the pitfalls of fundamentalism that have infected so much of our church's history.

Worthington made no comment about my concern. In an early December letter he indicated that the Teaneck school was broadening its curriculum and applying for accreditation by the State of New Jersey. Like its parent in Minneapolis, Teaneck was moving toward becoming more than a Bible institute.

At this same time I was contacted by Leman Olsenius, pastor at the prestigious Gustavus Adolphus congregation in St. Paul, Minnesota, asking if I might consider joining his staff. In more normal circumstances, I would have jumped at this opportunity. Again, for reasons I cannot explain, I didn't even feel inclined to meet with Olsenius. I was being pulled in another direction.

All of these months of speculation and turmoil came to a head in mid-January 1962, inviting me to teach at Teaneck. I had thirty days to make a decision.

By early February I thought I had a clear answer. I would decline. For one thing, I learned that I had been unknowingly caught in the middle of the conflict at the Minneapolis school over the leadership of its president, Bernt Opsal. Though I was completely innocent of the charges that had been leveled against me—that I had supported Opsal in his conflict with certain faculty members—I had no desire to become more enmeshed in that turmoil by becoming a member of one of the faculties. I had also been thinking about using the *The Bethel Series* at Pelican Rapids, but hesitated to ask that small congregation to come up with the necessary finances. When two board members suggested that the congregation would fund the program I took it as a sign that I should stay in the parish. On February 10 I declined the call. I thought the answer was final.

What happened next is beyond easy explanation. First there was a call from Worthington, expressing his surprise and disappointment over my decision. Was there any possibility for reconsideration? I gave him no encouragement. Yet I couldn't concentrate. I couldn't sleep. I could scarcely pray. I felt deeply conflicted. Corinne was completely joined with me in my struggle. She, too, wondered if it may have been wrong to turn down this call to teach. We decided that the only thing to do was to fast and pray. For a whole day we did this, each in our own solitude. By sunset we knew we had no choice. Though we were filled with trepidation, we simply had to change our minds. We had to go east. In my letter to Worthington I said:

> I thought I was through wrestling with this call, when in reality it was only beginning. I guess I was looking for an excuse to stay in this pleasant place.

To the chair of the LBI national board I wrote:

> Like Jonah, I looked for excuses to run away from this call. But I found out that the psalmist is right—"Where can I go from your spirit?" It is with real joy and anticipation and excitement that I now look forward to beginning my work at Teaneck. . . .

To Walter Carlson, president of the Conference, I wrote:

> It is a humiliating thing to change a decision once made. For a couple of days after I declined the call I felt so glad that we were staying here. The people have been wonderful to work with in both churches and they have been more than good to us. But I found no release from the dilemma until I finally gave in and reconsidered.

Among those who wrote letters of encouragement following my decision to move to Teaneck was one from Dr. Oscar Hanson, former president of LBI of America and father of Mark Hanson, future presiding bishop of the ELCA and one of my successors in that office. Hanson said:

This comes as a real answer to prayer. God has equipped you by talents and experience and training for this great ministry. You will have open doors everywhere. God will use you to touch many congregations.

Another child?

When Corinne and I began to realize that a move was in the offing, we decided it was time to think about adopting another child. If it were to be a move outside of Minnesota, we didn't want to start from scratch in another state.

This time the process proceeded very rapidly. Having done so much preliminary work when we adopted Mary, we were able to move quickly into the final stages. By early March we were approved. A few weeks later came the call telling us that a little boy was waiting for us in St. Paul, Minnesota. The same surge of excitement came over us again. To Philip Worthington at Teaneck I wrote on April 5:

> We drove to St. Paul on Monday and returned on Tuesday with our little Christopher Paul. He is one month old and resembles our Mary a great deal. Naturally, we are all as happy as three can be! His name means, "Bearer of Christ," and our prayer is that he may grow up to be such a person.

As with Mary, there was a brief service of blessing at the Bethesda Hospital Chapel. This time my mother, Ruth, was with us to experience the process. Pastor Raymond Hedberg presided. Little could I have known that day that Ray would one day be a close colleague in the Minnesota Synod, a friend in Green Valley, Arizona, after we retired, and a lifelong confidant.

Final awkward months

The Teaneck school wanted a reply from me in February in order to make plans for the fall term. But they did not want me to come until mid-August. That made for an awkward final six months at

Pelican Rapids and Elizabeth. I learned then that no matter how much you love a parish and no matter how much you think they love you, it's never good to linger too long once you've resigned. We could not wait for the moving truck to arrive and to be on our way to the next chapter in our lives.

Our last visitor as we were about to leave town was George Sanstead. George and Dorothy like Idell and John, were those salt-of-the-earth lay members that every pastor cherishes. I fished and hunted with George. We were bonded at the heart. The tears flowed as he hopped into his pickup and returned to his brake shop.

As we drove away from Pelican Rapids in our new '62 Chevy Impala, we had no idea that we would be back in three years to buy property on Lake Lida just east of Pelican Rapids. For the next more than thirty years we continued to be linked closely to the community.

Chapter 7

Stretching years:
college teaching and graduate study

How extreme can change be?

That shiny new Chevrolet carried us in grand style to a radical change:

From the resort country of northern Minnesota to a densely populated, metropolitan center.

From a predominantly Scandinavian community to a veritable melting pot of cultures.

From an effective parish ministry where I did the kind of work I had been prepared to do in seminary, to the classroom and uncertainty about my skills in this new venue.

From a place where dear family and good friends were nearby, to a place where we knew scarcely a soul.

From the security of a call to a congregation of the Augustana Synod and close identity with that church, to a school that had no official connection with any of the Lutheran church bodies in the country.

Indeed, Corinne and I were like Abraham and Sarah venturing out into a new world. It was a step of faith into the unknown, certain only that this was a call from God.

The Lutheran Bible Institute

The Lutheran Bible Institute movement began in the Midwest after World War I. There was growing concern among some Lutheran pastors and lay leaders that Bible study was being neglected in a church that claimed its identity was rooted in the Holy Scriptures. The formal organization of the first school occurred in 1919. Its first permanent home was in Minneapolis. The prime movers came out of the more conservative and pious elements of Swedish and Norwegian Lutheranism.

As the movement spread, sister institutions were organized in Los Angeles, Seattle, and New York City. The eastern school met at first at Gustavus Adolphus Lutheran Church in lower Manhattan. When a large mansion came up for sale in 1951 across the Hudson River in Teaneck, New Jersey, the school moved to that site.

By the time we arrived in 1962, the school had constructed a women's dormitory and added an extension to the mansion for a chapel and dining room. Shortly after we arrived in the fall of 1962, a home next to campus was dedicated as a library. Two years later still another home was purchased and renovated for a men's dormitory. At its zenith in the late 1960s the campus covered about six acres.

The enrollment in the fall of 1962 was fifty-five. By the fall of 1964 enrollment had climbed to over one hundred. There were five full time faculty members when I was installed and a number of part-time teachers. From time to time well-known seminary professors such as Dr. Harold Floreen from the Canadian Lutheran Seminary and Dr. Gerhard Frost from Luther Seminary in St. Paul, Minnesota, taught at Teaneck while pursuing graduate studies in New York City.

Because the Bible schools were not directly related to any of the Lutheran church bodies, financial support had to come from student fees and contributions from a small cadre of enthusiastic supporters. The school was in constant financial difficulty. There were occasions when we had to wait for up to a week to receive our monthly salary. Harold Midtbo, an executive with Standard Oil of New Jersey and a widely known and respected lay leader, used his financial acumen again and again to keep the school afloat. This meant that it was essential for faculty members to not only teach, but also recruit students and carry out "deputations" in congregations—usually in the form of Bible teaching events.

What made the Teaneck school somewhat unique from the other three Bible schools was the support many congregations and members of the Lutheran Church—Missouri Synod gave to that school. Having come out of Minnesota, where LCMS congregations were completely disassociated from most other Lutherans, I could scarcely believe the warm welcome I received as I went to some of their congregations to preach and teach. Many of those churches in the East were part of the English District of the LCMS, a non-geographical alliance of congregations in all parts of the country that believed in fellowship and cooperation with other Lutherans.

What's in a name?

As I mentioned earlier, prior to my coming to Teaneck there was already a move at the school to add a broader spectrum of classes in the area of the liberal arts and to seek accreditation as a college from the State of New Jersey. That prompted a name change in early 1963, near the end of my first year of teaching. It was now the "Lutheran Collegiate Bible Institute." That change, however, never seemed to catch on with the constituency. Several years later I recommended and the board accepted the name, "Luther College of the Bible and Liberal Arts." Eventually it simply became known as Luther College.

The aim of the college was to remain true to its original purpose, namely, to be a place where students could come to concentrate primarily on biblical studies and closely related subjects.

While the school offered a course for women who wanted to go directly into parish work and youth ministry, the majority of the graduates went on to complete their degree work, usually at Lutheran colleges in the Midwest.

Because the school needed students to survive, entrance requirement were low. That meant that in every class the spectrum of academic ability was unusually broad. The brightest and best mingled with some who could never do serious college level work. Spanning that gap was a daily challenge. One of our greatest satisfactions was to see a marginal student begin to blossom and go on to complete a college degree.

Already in 1963 I had a clear vision of the purpose of the school. At the baccalaureate service address on May 26, 1963, after suggesting that the goal of much of secular education was to equip students for a job, I expounded on what I thought we were about at the Lutheran Collegiate Bible Institute. A few excerpts:

> Education is in danger of becoming merely a tool in the hand rather than an idea in the mind; an idea in the head rather than a burning passion in the heart; a way of doing something rather than a way of believing and living something.

> I would like to suggest some of the obligations that become yours because you have had the privilege of study here these two years.

> First, there is your obligation to God. Life is a stewardship. . . . your whole life is to be lived under the grace and judgment of God.

> Second, there is your obligation to others. . . . selfless love gives and gives and gives again. The wonderful thing about Christian love is that the more you give the more you receive. Our nation is being torn asunder by racial tension. Law by itself cannot resolve our basic problem—but Christian love can.

> The third obligation is the one you have to yourself. God has a plan for each of you that is good and meaningful. The time to set your course is now.

A fourth concern is your obligation to the church. Some think of our school as an institution outside the church. On the contrary, if we are true to our purpose and the Word we study, we will always find ourselves in the mainstream of the life of the church. . . . people will look to you for positive leadership, not negative criticism.

I left the college in 1970. Several years later, due to financial stresses and declining enrollment, the college closed its doors. Eventually, the Bible school movement and its four campuses either closed or transitioned into other kinds of operations.

The first two years—incredible pressure

Given that I had no aspiration other than to be a parish pastor, I felt totally unprepared to teach. I was assigned some subjects with which I had only minimal acquaintance. Evening after evening I was up long into the night preparing for the next day. I felt I was only a half step ahead of the students in most subjects. By the end of the first year I was thoroughly depleted. I tried hard to be a good father. But most of the parenting responsibility fell to Corinne. She was incredibly patient and efficient.

Graduate study: Princeton Seminary and New York University

The thought of graduate study had also been of no concern to me when I was ordained. I had all the education I needed for parish ministry, other than some short-term continuing education. Now, however, I was in an academic setting. All of my colleagues on the faculty were in some kind of advanced degree work. Both for the sake of improving my own teaching skills as well as for the stature of the college, I decided that I must pursue further study.

Princeton Seminary offered a fine program that made it possible for me to earn a master's degree in New Testament by going to the campus every Monday for a year and one-half and then writing a dissertation for my final semester of study. I began classes in the fall of 1964. One summer I also took classes at Union Seminary in New York City that transferred for credit at Princeton.

Now the need for a second automobile became urgent. It happened that a missionary on his way back to Africa left his 1957 Volkswagen Beetle at the campus with the request that we try to sell it. It was badly discolored. The lock on the window was broken, making it impossible to secure the vehicle. I offered him $125 and he took it. (When we left the East in 1970 I drove it to Minnesota. In 1972 we traded if off for a new Beetle and got $100 in the trade. One of our better investments!)

My academic experience at Augustana Seminary had been excellent. Princeton was even better. Professors were consistently superb. What a privilege to sit at the feet of such preeminent scholars as Bruce Metzger, an expert linguist and Bible translator; Johannes Monk, a Pauline specialist from Denmark; Matthew Black, a Scottish New Testament scholar; and Seward Hiltner, known for his insights into pastoral psychology, and others. Those classes were a respite in my hectic life at Luther College. Speer Library was a haven for quiet study and reflection. I was especially eager to take a course in Hebrews, a book of the Bible that I was teaching at Luther College. David Hay was a fine guide in that course. Over time that book became a favorite and led to the authorship of one of my books, *Hebrews: A New and Better Way*.

For my dissertation in the final semester I chose to research and write a major paper on "Current Dialogue Regarding the Meaning and Practice of Infant Baptism in the Early Church." I concluded that even though it may be impossible to construct "an irrefutable case" to prove that infant baptism was practiced from the beginning, the theology of the New Testament supported the idea that even infants were to be included in the family of faith and that baptism was the gateway to that family.

My view of the Bible, inherited from study at Augustana Seminary, was reinforced at Princeton. This comment from notes taken in Bruce Metzger's class illustrates that point:

> We feel assured that the early church has been very care-
> ful in transmitting the words of Jesus. True, there has been
> modification to suit the situation. But the basic material we
> can receive with confidence.

New York University (NYU) was the next stop on my academic
venture toward an earned doctorate. At least once a week I drove
my little VW Beetle into Manhattan to attend classes at the Washington Square campus at the lower end of Manhattan. Because
of its short wheelbase, I never failed to find a place to park. And
because of its ratty condition I never worried that anyone would
break into it, even though it could not be locked. The mid- to-late
1960s were the height of the Hippie era, and Washington Square
was the epicenter of that culture. My street mates represented every
expression of that tuned-out, turned-off generation.

Class work at NYU was less than gratifying. The contrast with
Princeton was significant. But I persisted, class by class, and by
the time we left the East I had completed all but one class for that
requirement. *All* I had left to do was to write a doctoral dissertation. More on that later.

My maturation in theological understanding and my view of the
Bible shows in a letter to my high school classmate Bruce Koerner.
Bruce had wandered about between various church bodies, always
keeping in touch with me to find out what I was thinking. In February of 1970 I wrote to him:

> I would have to be classified as a traditionalist. I accept the
> Bible as the standard for faith and action. This is not to say
> that my opinion of the contents of the Bible has remained
> static over the years. It has changed quite substantially in
> some areas—yet there remains the conviction that this
> document stands unique among all writings.

I go on in the letter to discuss the relationship between the Bible
and personal experience of the faith. I agreed that the Bible is not

. . . the exclusive source of our knowledge of God. Certainly the natural world and so-called natural theology are sources of revelation. And direct experiences of God . . . are to be included. But these . . . can only be accepted as trustworthy when seen and interpreted in the light of Christian revelation as we have it primarily in Scripture. I find in my own experience that this is not restricting. It seems to me that our religious experiences need the testing and correction of something that lies outside of us in a more objective sense.

Academic dean

When Ralph Holmin, dean of the college, left in 1965 to join the faculty at the Lutheran School of Theology at Chicago, the question of his successor came to the fore. I'm not certain why I was chosen over two women who had seniority and deserved first consideration. Yet given the times, it probably was the case.

I accepted the offer with some trepidation. On the one hand, I welcomed the challenge to grow in my administrative skills. One of the first things I did was to change the schedule for the weekly faculty meeting. Until then we had gathered in the president's office each Friday afternoon, beginning immediately after lunch and often continuing right up until or even into the dinner hour.

When I became dean I scheduled faculty meetings for two hours on Friday morning. Amazingly, we got our work done in the allotted time.

In a letter to my folks I described how I made my office more pleasant, underscoring my love for flowers and plants:

> I had our maintenance man build a wide shelf along one window and have that full of plants . . . gloxinia, fuchsia, geranium, bird of paradise, four varieties of begonia, and an orchid plant.

I put much effort into getting the school accredited with the State of New Jersey. I also spent considerable time getting the college approved for student loans. These efforts came to fruition in 1968 and gave our graduates greater access to other colleges with full or near-full credit for classes completed at Luther and access to government loans that not only enhanced their pursuit of a degree but also gave the college resources from tuition payments. In 1968 we also broke ground for a much-needed chapel and classroom building.

Our residence in Teaneck was a large college-owned house in a quiet neighborhood. Just a bit more than a mile from campus, I was able to walk to classes most days. My home study was a sun porch. Early in the evening, after some playtime with the children, one or more of them hopped on my lap for some of their own "study time" with daddy. Then it was off for a bath with Mom's help and prayers with both Mom and Dad.

Corinne's roles at college, hospital, and church

From the moment we arrived Corinne involved herself in the life of the college. She entertained faculty families and students on special occasions. Given her background in nursing, she soon became the college nurse. That brought her to the campus at all hours of the day and night.

At St. Paul's Lutheran Church in Teaneck, Corinne was an active volunteer. A note in the November 1968 parish newsletter gives a small glimpse of her efforts.

> Meet the new president of Lutheran Church Women. At Luther College the students know her as one of the school nurses. At Englewood Hospital she is known as Corinne Chilstrom, R.N., who works part-time, usually two or three evening shifts a week, and at times as the head nurse on the floor. The past four years Corinne has served LCW as program chairman, and we all have appreciated her interesting and unique programs for our general meetings. She also teaches a Sunday school class. And—most important of all—she is the mother of three young children.

In June 1968 I received an interesting and revealing note from Corinne's father, Jens, marked "Personal & Private."

> Dear Herb . . . you can share this with Corinne if you think she can stand it. Elna (married to Corinne's cousin Earl) told us that C. Matson (highly respected and long-time teacher of music and director of the Augustana Academy Choir) told her that Corinne was the finest all-around person he had ever known at Augustana Academy. Guess the genes came together just right that time, eh? Wonder what you think by this time. I know that she had privileges and opportunities that many kids don't have today. Well, be good to one another. Love, Dad

In retrospect, the letter is quite revealing. This would be typical of Hauge Lutheran piety. Any tendency toward pride was frowned upon. Even commending someone for a fine achievement would need to be quite muted. Jens needed to remind her that she didn't do it on her own—there were many "privileges and opportunities" others didn't have. One would think that Jens would simply have sent this note to Corinne, his daughter. Yet, also in true Hauge fashion, he takes some backward credit for her high achievements by suggesting that she had good genes, from her parents, of course.

What he said affirmed what I had observed over the years. Every time we attended a reunion of her classes or had contacts with those who had known her in her early life, there was uniform, positive affirmation of her as an outstanding person in every way. I could not have survived the difficult years in the East—or anywhere on our journey—without this caliber of person at my side.

Sunday, a time to go our separate ways

On most Sundays I was off preaching and promoting the college at a congregation. Those travels took me from Maine to Washington, D.C., and as far out as western Pennsylvania. Most visits, however, were in the northern New Jersey/New York City metropolitan area.

In a 1964 letter to our Midwest families, Corinne described what became a typical pattern.

> Herb had a full day last Sunday. He left at 7 a.m. for Conn. where he preached two morning services . . . spoke at an afternoon youth meeting, had a fireside Bible study, and then drove on up to Bridgeport for an evening Bible study. It was after 11 when he got home—kind of a tiring day for a "day off"!!

While we were members of St. Paul's Lutheran Church several miles away, it happened that Grace, a congregation of the Lutheran Church—Missouri Synod, was just around the corner from our home. Corinne ventured over there on occasion and fell in love with them. Her growing appreciation for the formal liturgy of the church blossomed in that setting. Like many other LCMS congregations in the East, Grace was a warm, loving, and progressive congregation. One of its pastors, John Damm, eventually became a key figure in the departure of many congregations from the LCMS and the formation of the Association of Evangelical Lutheran Churches (AELC), one of the partners in the eventual formation of the ELCA.

The death of my father—sudden and unexpected

Having helped Ruth and Wally remodel their home into a comfortable and accessible place for them to spend their retirement years, we all longed for them to have many more years together. I was home alone on the afternoon of March 9, 1965. The phone rang. It was the funeral director at Litchfield. In an even, sympathetic tone he said that my father had died suddenly that afternoon. He had been out shoveling the sidewalks. After lunch, as usual, he went to the basement to have a nap on a cot near the warm furnace. He never awakened. Though this was a peaceful way for a peaceful man to die, it caught us by surprise. Because Wally had so much longevity in his family, I assumed he would live well beyond his seventy-six years.

I felt great sorrow that Mary and Chris would never have the privilege of knowing their Grandpa Wally as Corinne and I had known him. So I sat down one day a few weeks later and wrote a letter to them. Some excerpts:

> Dear Children: Your grandpa spent his entire childhood and young adulthood on the same farm where he was born. His main responsibility was to keep the garden in shape. He carried a love for the garden through his entire life. I'm sure some of it rubbed off on me.
>
> Grandpa was a wonderful man. I miss him very much. It will be sad to go back to Minnesota this summer and not have him there.
>
> Grandpa's funeral was a wonderful experience. Even though we felt sad, there was a great peace and joy beneath the surface. Because of Christ we can look death in the face and believe there is victory.
>
> Love, Daddy

Lake Lida, a place to call our own

In the summer of 1965 we visited Pelican Rapids, the place that was still dear to our hearts. We had dreamed of having a lake cabin of our own, a place to retreat for a month in the summer. We found an old cabin that had been remodeled into a simple house with water but no indoor bathroom. With little or nothing to fund such a venture, it seemed like a foolhardy move. Corinne and I walked out on the long dock one afternoon, looked back at the cabin and shoreline, took a deep breath and said, "Let's do it." This would give us a roof over our heads immediately without any need to build from scratch.

About twenty-by-twenty when we made our purchase, the cabin consisted of a kitchen, bedroom, living room, porch, and two tiny upstairs bedrooms. Every room was small. For the first time in our lives we owned a piece of property.

Little could we have known that our decision was the beginning of a thirty-five year odyssey that would bring us back to that lovely spot again and again, and that it would become the place where we would first retire. I remodeled parts of it to make it more convenient. I landscaped the lot, planting perennials and trees almost every year. Finally in 1989 when we determined that we wanted to live at Lida after we retired in 1995, we razed all of the older structure and built our nest. Lovely Lake Lida became a place of precious memory for our family.

Why not adopt another child?

When Chris was two we started to think about adopting a third child. But we assumed that having two adopted children was the limit.

All that changed one day in the fall of 1965. As I pulled into the driveway, Corinne came rushing out to meet me. In her hand she held a copy of a newsletter from Lutheran Social Services of New Jersey. In breathless excitement she pointed to an article that announced that they would consider placing a third child in some homes.

We contacted the agency the very next day. In whirlwind timing we were approved. By the first days of February we learned that we would have another boy in our family. Only a bit more than a week old, little Andrew's arrival in our home was beyond our fondest dream. Mary and Chris immediately dubbed him "Andrew Bright Eyes" because of the alert look on his little face.

Two days after he arrived at our home I sat down to write a note to Andrew:

> Dear Andrew: It's late at night and I'm here in my study preparing a sermon for tomorrow morning. I was just upstairs a few minutes ago to help Mom settle you for the night. You are a precious gift from God! People sometimes tell us how wonderful they think we are to adopt you. That's not the point at all. We adopted Mary Lee and Chris and

you *just because we love you.* We asked God to send children to our home and *you are his answer!*

Work and family time

It seemed that my life got busier and busier as the Teaneck years unfolded: classroom teaching, administration, teaching missions in congregations, preaching, summer camp, fundraising, and graduate study.

When I became academic dean at the school I felt it important to be involved with the New Jersey Junior and Community College Association. Within a year or two I was elected president of the association. Though the duties were not substantial in themselves, it was one more responsibility.

I also tried to do a bit of writing. An article on the dangers of obesity and nicotine appeared in the April 8, 1964, issue of *The Lutheran* magazine. In June of 1966 I wrote an article under an assumed name—"Bert Strom"—in which I described an experience in conducting a healing service for Earl Frazier, a member of my first parish in Pelican Rapids. The *Lutheran Forum* invited me to write reviews for two books in its May 1967 edition. In that year I also submitted an article to *The Lutheran* magazine that was not accepted but shows my prescience in calling the church to admit younger children to the Lord's Supper. In it I describe how Corinne brought seven-year-old Mary to church one Sunday, left her in the pew while going forward to receive the Sacrament, and then, on returning to the pew, heard Mary ask, "Mommy, why can't I go up there just like you? I love Jesus, too." I argued in the article that it made little sense to withhold the Sacrament from younger children.

I also tried to stay somewhat engaged in community and political affairs. I wrote to Minnesota Senator Eugene McCarthy, whom I had supported as a candidate for president and who had lost the nomination, to give his endorsement to Maine Senator Edmund Muskie. I wrote to Senator Harrison Williams of New Jersey and

urged him to raise taxes in order to improve government services
for the poor. After the murder of Martin Luther King, I signed a
petition calling for gun control. And because African Americans
were moving into our area in greater numbers and were experiencing discrimination, I signed a petition calling for fairness for all
people in purchasing property in Teaneck.

A black family moved to a home a few doors down the street in
the late 1960s. One Saturday as I was raking leaves a man drove up
and rolled down his window. "Do you know that a black family has
moved on to your street?" he asked. "Yes," I said I knew that. "Well,"
he blurted out, "those people were born in a barn." "That's interesting," I replied. "One of my best friends was also born in a barn." He
blanched and drove off. It was one of those rare times in life when I
seemed to have the right word for the moment.

I tried hard to carve out time to be with my family. One of the
pleasant summertime activities for our family was to attend Camp
Winni at spectacular Lake Winnipesauke in the rolling White
Mountains of New Hampshire. I was named director of the camp as
soon as I arrived at Teaneck. That meant many weeks of promoting
the camp, planning all of the details for those weeks, correspond-
ing with guest speakers, and directing the program while it was in
session. Families from all over the East coast attended, most for one
week and some for both weeks.

These few excerpts from a letter Corinne wrote to our relatives
back in the Midwest in February 1964 give a glimpse into that corner of our life. Mary was three and one-half at the time and Chris
nearly two.

> Herb usually plays with the children after supper while I
> clean up the dishes. Their favorite game is, "Daddy, you be
> the big giant" . . . so he stalks around making a funny sound
> and they giggle and run away from him like they're scared
> and just have much fun.

We usually returned to Minnesota in the summer to visit family and friends. With no air conditioning, we often drove through the night.

Back to a parish?

Beginning in 1964 I made regular trips to Good Shepherd Lutheran Church at Pearl River, New York, about an hour's drive from Teaneck and just across the northern border of New Jersey. In December 1966, one of the leaders of the congregation called to inquire if I would be interested in a call to succeed the retiring pastor. I was tempted. It was one of the most affluent churches in the area. The congregation had great potential. The salary would be double what I was getting at the college.

I knew, however, that the timing was wrong. I had only been academic dean for a year, and I had just started work on my doctorate at NYU; if I were to return to a parish call, I felt certain that it should be back in the Midwest near our families. Simply being invited to consider the call evoked a deep longing that I knew would flower one day in a return to parish ministry.

As the 60s drew to a close, another equally strong sense was beginning to stir in me. Yes, the college was doing quite well in most respects. We had a new classroom/chapel building, my study for a doctorate was progressing well, and I was becoming increasingly known and respected in area congregations. Yet I knew in my heart of hearts that change was on the near horizon. There were many elements:

> We longed to be closer to our families in the Midwest.

> I was growing weary of working with a rather narrow segment of young adults of college age. I longed to be back in a parish setting where I could be a pastor to families from the cradle to the grave. I was invited to preach and teach in different churches almost every week. But it was all quite

superficial when compared to what I had experienced in parish ministry.

I was alienated from the organized church. I went to synod conventions and felt as though I were sitting "at the end of the bench guarding the water bucket."

My working relationship with the president of the college was difficult at best. We were simply too different in temperament, working style, and theological perspective to make for a comfortable partnership. I felt boxed in.

I had come to the point where I simply had to move on.

A stab in the dark

What was I going to do? Given my conviction, inherited from my Augustana background, that one must never seek a call, I could not bring myself to write to Dr. Melvin Hammarberg, president (bishop) of the Minnesota Synod, to inquire about a call to a parish in that area.

It got to the point where I wondered if I might serve in some way other than in ordained ministry. Preposterous as it seemed, I decided to test the idea. I knew that a new community college was being built at Fergus Falls, Minnesota. Given my background in sociology and course work in marriage and family, I wondered if there might be a faculty position at the college. I loved our place at Lake Lida. I dreamed of how we could remodel our old cabin into a year-round home and live at the lake while I commuted the half-hour drive to Fergus Falls.

On our trip to the Midwest that summer I decided to visit the college. I had no appointment, but the president happened to be in that day and welcomed me. I laid out my proposal. To my surprise, he liked the idea and encouraged me to apply for a position.

As I walked back to the parking lot where the rest of the family was waiting for me, I was overwhelmed with the sense that I had just done one of the dumbest things in my life. Leave the ordained ministry? It was preposterous! I had floated the ship and it sank in the harbor.

A class reunion: a twist of fate? Or the hand of the Spirit?

During that same summer trip to the Midwest I was looking forward to attending the twentieth anniversary reunion of my high school class at Litchfield. Though I hadn't kept in close touch with many of them, I thought it might be a good thing to renew some old acquaintances. The event itself was a huge disappointment. At that stage of life many graduates have a need to boast about their accomplishments. Others, unfortunately, saw the evening as a good time to get drunk. The small talk was boring. Corinne and I were square pegs in round holes most of the evening.

One conversation that evening, however, changed our lives forever. Classmate Arnie Hed had been a good friend in high school. We were active in the youth program at our church. Now he had his own business as an advertising agent for a network of banks. He and Carol were living in Chaska, a suburb in the Lake Minnetonka area just west of Minneapolis.

Arnie asked, almost offhandedly, if I ever thought about moving back to the Midwest. He said the congregation they belonged to, Holy Cross in Excelsior, was looking for a new pastor. My heart skipped a beat. Could this be the break I was looking for? For years I had peered out of the window of the Greyhound bus as it passed through those manicured western suburbs on its way from Litchfield to Minneapolis. I salivated over the lovely homes and pleasant lakeside communities, thinking of how wonderful it would be to live there one day.

Over the next several weeks everything moved very rapidly. Corinne and I were invited to fly out to Minnesota to meet with the call committee. The meeting went extremely well. We felt at home with them.

By mid-September the congregation met and extended a call. Everything looked good—a fine salary and benefit package, with a generous housing allowance for buying or building our own home. Yet there was a persistent unsettled feeling in my soul. What followed was a time of intense scrutiny, reflection, and prayer. Corinne described it well in a letter to our families:

> Herb is going through something and I don't know if I can or should try to describe it. It's almost a mystical thing and I couldn't give you any reason for we haven't a specific one. I know one thing for sure—that if we are to stay here Herb will have to find a new sense of call. And in the midst of finding it, you get to the place where money or opportunities become so second place that you give up trying to figure it out and finally just ask the Lord to make it clear what he wants!!

Out of nowhere—First Lutheran in St. Peter

I was sitting in my study one evening working on a letter to Holy Cross Church, informing them that I did not feel at peace about accepting the call. The phone rang. It was Dr. Hammarberg. He said he was calling to inquire how I was feeling about the call to Excelsior. I wanted to tell him that I felt good about it and was ready to accept it. If I turned it down, would I ever have a chance to move back to Minnesota?

I had to be honest. I told him that I was just at that moment in the process of writing a letter of declination. I expected him to say, "That's too bad. I had been hoping you would accept it." Instead, came the surprise. His next words were, "Would you be interested in exploring a call to First Lutheran in St. Peter?" Before he spoke another word I knew that my struggle was over. This was what I had been waiting for. I had no idea that this congregation was looking for a pastor, knew nothing about its ministry or building or anything else. Yet I knew this was it. Hammarberg went on to share some information about the congregation—its new building, its unique ministry in a town/gown setting, the salary range and housing situation. The details mattered little to me. I knew this was right.

The next day I wrote to Hammarberg:

> The opportunity at St. Peter strikes a responsive chord with me. My dilemma these past weeks has centered in the desire to return to the parish ministry while at the same time feeling drawn to the academic ministry. In a sense, the First Lutheran parish could satisfy both interests.

Again things moved rapidly. We flew to Minnesota to meet with the committee. It was a good experience for them and for us. Some years later Dr. Clair McRostie, chair of the call committee, recalled in a parish newsletter (*First Pages,* 12/82) what he thought was the key element of that meeting:

> We had asked (Chilstrom) to prepare a brief meditation. In that ten-minute meditation he did more to make the Bible a living document for each of us than any of us had experienced before. I think it was there that he really pulled it out and turned the matter into the whole committee's favoring him.

In the midst of all this maelstrom of activity, we received a letter from my mother with thus sage advice: "Better not make haste. Just one day at a time submissive to the Lord's command. Psalm 46:10—'Be still, and know that I am God!' Luther's favorite psalm." It was more evidence of her deep faith. Given how much we knew she wanted us to return to Minnesota, I thought this note was another example of her concern that we put the will of the Lord before all other considerations.

I responded positively. In my letter to the congregation I suggested that we pattern ourselves after the early Christians by devoting ourselves to "the apostles' teaching and fellowship, to the breaking of bread and the prayers" (Acts 2:42).

I had a letter from the chair of the board at the Seattle Lutheran Bible Institute inquiring whether I would be interested in being a candidate for president of that school. He hadn't heard that I had accepted the call to St. Peter. Given my longing to serve in the Northwest when I was ordained, one would think I might have had some regret that I was not available. I had none whatever. I wanted to be back in parish ministry. I wanted to be closer to the organized church. I knew where I wanted to go and where I was certain God was calling me.

A retrospective on the Teaneck years

I'm writing these lines from the perspective of my seventy-ninth year. Now I'm fifteen years beyond the Herculean task of bringing the ELCA together as its first presiding bishop. Others might think that those years were surely the most challenging of my career. I must say, however, that the Teaneck years were at least as formidable. From the moment I accepted the call to move to the East until the day I left, I was under intense pressure.

On the one hand, I thoroughly enjoyed all of the activities the position required. But it was becoming apparent that I was painting myself into a corner from which it was increasingly difficult to extricate myself. Indeed those years were incredibly difficult. But I must end my reflections on the Teaneck years by stating very forthrightly that had it not been for what I did in those eight years, I could never have even begun to measure up to the demands that would follow: senior pastor of a large town/gown congregation, bishop of the largest synod in the Lutheran Church in America, and the first presiding bishop of the Evangelical Lutheran Church in America.

Corinne and I were stretched to the limit during our Teaneck years. I thank God that we survived. And I give Corinne the greater credit for it.

Chapter 8

Return to the parish

Back to Minnesota

Leaving New Jersey proved to be more difficult than we had anticipated. Having arrived eight years earlier as virtual strangers, we
discovered that we had made many friends at the college, at our
church, and in the community. Four-year-old Andrew may have
expressed well our feelings. As the movers began to carry items
from our home, he broke into tears and railed against the men who
"broke my bed."

The shiny new Chevrolet that carried us to the East Coast in
1962 was now spotted with rust. With annual trips to the Midwest,
excursions to New England and Canada, and trips to places all over
the East Coast, the odometer had run up considerable mileage.
But after we purchased both the Lida cottage and our New Jersey
home, it would have to carry us back to Minnesota. I assumed we
would get rid of the Volkswagen Beetle, probably to a junkyard.
But Corinne was in love with it and wondered if we couldn't bring
it with us to St. Peter. The only way, of course, was for *me* to drive
it those long miles over mountains and across plains. It dawned
on me that this might be a good way to save my precious house-
plants—Corinne and the kids in the Chevy and me and my plants
in the Beetle, a mobile greenhouse. If it broke down on the way we
would simply junk it and toss my plants.

With little remaining horsepower, the Beetle struggled mightily like "the little engine that could" to get to the top of one side of a Pennsylvania mountain and then coasted merrily down the other. It got to be a gleeful adventure for the children. They would pass me on the up side and I'd pass them on the down slope. We were a modern version of the Okies and the Arkies heading west.

My portable greenhouse lasted only one night. When I hopped in the Beetle the next morning high in the Alleghenies I found every plant frozen stiff. I had not realized how cold it was in the mountains in mid-March. There was nothing to do but discard them all. Now with my plant companions laid to rest, I felt rather lonely for the remainder of the trip.

Where will we live?

Our options for housing in St. Peter were limited. After several months we seemed to be running into dead ends. When nothing seemed to be working out I reminded Corinne one day that we had never given a tithe on the profit we made on our Teaneck home. We needed every dollar of that money to invest in another home. Yet we also knew from experience that this was a step of faith we needed to take.

Some might say it was coincidence. Be that as it may be, doors started opening. I found a home plan that would fit nicely on a lot near the church. When we brought it to a builder the cost estimate was far above what we could handle.

Then someone suggested that we consider being our own contractors, thus securing materials at a much lower rate. Over the next months Corinne and I were busy chasing down every detail of the process, conferring with contractors, and doing as much of the work as we could ourselves. I would stop by the site while out calling and find out what was needed for the next stage.

We wanted the look of old Chicago brick on the front of the house. We learned that there was a large open pit at the state

hospital on the south edge of St. Peter where brick from a demol-
ished building had been dumped. It was exactly the kind we were
looking for. I descended to the bottom of the pit, unearthed bricks,
heaved them to Corinne half way up the bank and she in turn
tossed them to Mary, Chris, and Andrew at the top.

The end product was a handsome home on a quiet street. We
spoke of settling in and enjoying this place for at least the next two
decades.

A congregation in need of a pastor

First Lutheran Church had been without a senior pastor for nearly
four years. The congregation had come through some rocky times.
In 1960 the stately old church, located near downtown, was struck
by lightning and burned to the ground. The members decided by
a razor-thin margin to abandon that site and build on the edge of
town where a few scattered homes had been built.

The building itself was of a radical design. The architect's vision
was to create a church that would fit the landscape of the countryside, including its grain elevators that towered like tall square boxes
over the prairie. While some heralded the building as the cutting
edge of architectural innovation, others dubbed it "the God Box."

Donald Gustafson, a member of the congregation, wrote the
150th anniversary book for the congregation in 2007. He writes:
"First Lutheran Church was clearly a demoralized congregation."
The debt on the new facility was overwhelming. The congregation
seemed to be going nowhere.

My coming heralded a new day. I could feel the surge of enthusiasm. I felt warmly welcomed.

Setting the tone

In my initial greeting to the congregation I appealed to the wisdom
of keeping a balance between tradition and change:

> The mark of alert Christians is that, though they stand unflinching on the basic truths inherited from the past, they are always ready to adapt those verities to a changing world. . . . it is at the golden mean between thanksgiving for tradition and commitment to change that First Lutheran Church will find its purpose.

In one of my first newsletter offerings I tried to help the congregation take a peek into my personality:

> Believe it or not, I am not a natural extrovert. There is a shy side to my nature that makes it difficult for me to take the initiative in getting acquainted with other people. But I refuse to let that tendency govern my relationships with others. So I fight it by prodding myself in getting to know others.

The burden of debt

I soon learned about the monster I had inherited—an enormous building debt. It was so great that half of the annual budget had to be set aside for debt reduction. That left little for program and staff. We managed to find enough funds to call Judy Johnson, an energetic young woman who served as office manager, Christian education director, and youth minister. For a time retired Pastor Joseph Bergquist called on the sick and shut-ins. Then I learned that Dr. Paul Lindberg—one of my professors at Augustana Seminary in Rock Island, Illinois—was ready to retire from his work for the LCA in Philadelphia. He agreed to be our visitation pastor and occasional preacher. Christine Johnson was our highly talented but grossly underpaid organist and director of the senior and children's choirs.

We had a succession of congenial and competent part-time secretaries in the office: Carol Solberg, Dorothy Paulson, Donna Green, and Liz Sietsema. No one ever came into the office or called the church without feeling a genuine and warm welcome.

Setting priorities was crucial. Gustafson describes what I did (p. 57):

> Chilstrom (insisted) that at the end of the month the
> synodical dues were to be paid first, then the mortgage
> payment, then utility bills and the salaries of the rest of the
> staff, and only if there was any money left should the pastor
> be paid. To the amazement of many of the council mem-
> bers, the system worked. Only once did the pastor almost
> miss his monthly paycheck.

I convinced the congregation to give over and above its support
for the Minnesota Synod and the LCA by sponsoring missionary
families in Tanzania—the Stanley Bensons and Dean Petersons.
That program continues unbroken to this day.

Are we really that large?

I also soon learned that the membership numbers, stated as well
over 1,000, were highly inflated. Many members in the community
and across the country who were on the rolls had not been active in
the life of the congregation or contributed to its support for years.

I wrote letters to those living elsewhere, urging them to find a
church in their community and suggesting that we would drop them
from membership at First Lutheran Church if we heard nothing.

At the same time, I engaged in vigorous calling on prospec-
tive members. Membership began to grow. At times we received
as many as fifty or more new members at a time. Because of our
losses from those who transferred to other churches or were
dropped, however, the overall growth of the congregation was not
spectacular.

Administratively, I tried to use my experience to strengthen the
organization of the congregation. Though there was talent galore in
the membership, it had not been mobilized. For the most part, we
had good chairpersons for the church council. Among them, Helen
Carter was the first woman in the church's history to serve in that role.

Worship, preaching, teaching, calling, weddings, funerals

As I reflect on my years at First Lutheran Church, these elements stand out: worship, preaching, teaching, calling, weddings, and funerals.

Worship

Thanks to former pastors and persons like Christine Johnson, First Lutheran Church had a vital liturgical life. The sanctuary lent itself to good formal worship. Our biggest hurdle, both for leading worship and preaching, was the acoustics of the sanctuary. For music, it has been rated as one of the finest spaces in the country for sound reproduction. For that reason no one wanted to tinker with the material of the building or add carpeting.

Spoken words, however, echoed mercilessly off the hard brick walls and terrazzo floors. It was a constant strain for me. Until then no one had ever complained about not being able to hear me. But from day one in St. Peter, I heard over and over again that some folks could not hear me. One sound expert tested the sanctuary and told me that the tone of my voice was the most difficult sound to hear in that place. Though I kept trying, in the end, I harmed my voice and have had problems with projection for the rest of my ministry.

In spite of that handicap, I never tired of leading worship in that beautiful space. It lacked one thing—a prominent figure of the cross. For that reason, one day stands out in my early years at First Lutheran Church.

I sat in the sanctuary with sculptor Paul Granlund to envision the kind of processional cross he might fashion for us. Granlund liked to talk out his ideas with others. We engaged in animated conversation about the nature of the space. Suddenly it came to him like a moment of creative energy. He knew exactly what the sanctuary needed. It is, in my judgment, the most important worship element in the sanctuary.

At times I wrestled with the dilemma of baptizing children of parents who were inactive in the life of the congregation. On one Sunday I wrote in my journal that I had baptized Michael.

> A disappointing experience. The parents seem disinterested in the church and the faith. What does one do? Baptize, I guess, in the hope that this initial contact will blossom into further contacts in which the church will become meaningful.

Preaching

I've always been a bit suspicious of those who say, "I love to preach." Yes, I surely understand the joy of it. My satisfaction spilled over in my journal one Sunday evening:

> A great morning—Transfiguration Day. Why do some sermons meet with such a spontaneous response? A mystery—but today so many were grateful for the message. A needed encouragement.

But there's also great fear in it. At times I felt what Frederick Buechner describes as "The terror that someday in the middle of a sentence I would simply run out of things to say." I tried to work on my sermon through the week but often found myself in my study on Saturday evening doing the final touches.

First Lutheran Church was an especially challenging place to preach. Though I was reasonably confident of my homiletical skills, looking out on a Sunday morning congregation was always a bit frightening. Religion faculty, farmers, state hospital employees, business men and women, faculty with doctoral degrees in a variety of disciplines, a dozen retired pastors and spouses, homemakers—one could not address a more eclectic group of persons in any setting, secular or religious. I soon learned, however, that with rare exception they all came to be fed with the good news of the gospel. If I prepared well I had no need to be intimidated.

Adding to the privilege of preaching to the congregation was the weekly live broadcast of the service over our local radio station. This brought a special dimension to the Sunday morning experience, putting me in touch with listeners from across south central Minnesota.

Teaching

When I accepted the call to First Lutheran Church, I indicated that I had a strong desire to introduce the congregation to the Bethel Series, the Bible study course that had been written by my brother-in-law Harley Swiggum. Corinne agreed to be one of the eight to ten whom I chose to be the teachers.

By the fall of 1973 we were ready to launch the congregational phase of the program. It was one of the most satisfying and fulfilling aspects of my ministry at First Lutheran Church. We enrolled about one hundred and fifty in the classes. To walk the halls and see the teachers engaged in sharing their insights with so many members of the congregations was surely one of the high points of my ministry.

In his history of that period, Gustafson notes that

> First Lutheran Church certainly benefited from Chilstrom's skills in administration as well as his amazing knack for mediation, but for him personally it was the . . . *Bethel Series* that was among the highlights of his First Lutheran Church experience.

In contrast, teaching confirmation classes was a mixed blessing. There were twenty or more in each year's group. I often said that my forte was *not* teaching junior high kids. Some classes could not have been better. Others, however, left me almost totally exasperated. I was often surprised and pleased to meet some of those students years later and hear them speak appreciatively of their confirmation instruction.

I was determined to move the age of confirmation up one year, reasoning that an added year of maturity would make it a more worthwhile experience both for the students and for me. Most parents agreed. But there were a few who staunchly opposed the idea, even, in one case, threatening to cut their pledge in half. I stuck to my guns, but entered an uncharacteristically crude note in my journal:

> That's an irony—you work your ass off for the kids, only to
> get it kicked by the parents!

In spite of some frustration over the confirmation class, I was also pleased that several of our youth from those years went on to become pastors and leaders in the church: Mary Lou Baumgartner, Maria Erling, Scott Duffus, Carol Baumgartner, and Christian Johnson. And, of course, I'm grateful for others who are leaders in churches across the country.

Calling

As was true in my first parish, I continued to put strong emphasis on pastoral calling. With our need to grow, searching out new members was on my mind almost every day.

I discovered again that reawakening interest in lapsed members was a questionable use of my time. In my 1973 pastor's report to the synod under the category of "most pressing problem" I wrote:

> Having to move a number of people to the inactive membership list. The frustration of not being able to excite people about the gospel and the church.

Yet in spite of the frustration I kept at the routine of calling. I even did ministry of that kind in playing golf with men from the community and mingling with folks on Main Street. I often dropped in at Cook's Café at coffee time to visit with members who might be there. Rather than dropping them in the mail, I also walked Main Street to pay the monthly bills, looking for people from the congregation and chatting with them.

Weddings

One of the things I enjoyed least was preparing for and officiating at weddings. I often felt that either or both parties agreed only reluctantly to have premarital counseling. In my journal I note again and again that I had grave doubts about a good outcome for a couple.

It was also a time when living together prior to marriage was almost unheard of, especially in small towns and rural areas. I held to the ideal that couples should not live together and/or have sex prior to marriage. After meeting with a couple who spoke openly about living together I wrote:

> How does one handle this? They seem to have a very deep and beautiful relationship and seem very desirous of a Christian wedding. Yet—I had to frankly tell them I did not—from my point of view—think it was right for them to live this way. A real puzzle.

Within a decade it became the norm rather than the exception.

Funerals

In contrast to weddings and, probably strange to some, I enjoyed most funerals as much as I disliked most weddings. We had many fine old saints in the congregation. When I had the funeral for Elma Johnson, for example, I wrote that I was

> Not sad at all. She was 85 and longed to "go home." Eyesight and hearing had failed. A fine Christian. A joy to lay her body in the ground and know that her spirit was free.

Opportunities for leadership beyond First Lutheran Church

In my pastor's report to the Minnesota Synod for 1970, I stated that "I have devoted almost exclusive attention to parish activities." It didn't take long, however, before calls for leadership beyond the congregation started coming. At my very first meeting with the pastors of the St. Peter District I was elected dean. The district was a network of about twenty LCA churches in south central Minnesota.

In 1972 I was involved in the inauguration of the Hot Meals and FISH programs in St. Peter. I agreed to serve on the regional committee of the Minnesota Council of Churches, working to foster interdenominational activity in south central Minnesota. In that same year Dr. George Harkins, Secretary of the LCA, informed me that I had been appointed to serve on the Examining Committee of the Minnesota Synod, a group that interrogated and approved candidates for ordained ministry. Though I do not know for certain, I suspect the appointment came on the suggestion of President Hammarberg. Was he beginning to see me as a potential candidate to be his successor? Later that year I made four presentations at Spiritual Emphasis Week at Golden Valley Lutheran College in the Twin Cities. In 1973 I preached at the "Key '73" evangelism event at West Union Lutheran Church in Carver, Minnesota.

At the 1971 synod convention I was elected a delegate to the 1972 LCA churchwide convention in Dallas. It was a mixed experience. When I arrived at the convention hall there was no chair at a table for me. I had to sit in the aisle, balancing my materials on my lap. Though I tried my best to prepare myself for the event, I felt confused and somewhat disoriented as I struggled to follow the agenda of the convention. I watched from afar with admiration as President Robert Marshall chaired the convention, never dreaming for a moment that I would ever be elected to such a position or that he would one day be one of my confidants.

One striking memory lingers from that Dallas convention. I was standing in the lobby of our hotel. I looked up and saw Elizabeth Platz, the first woman ordained into the LCA ministry, descending the wide staircase. She was wearing a clergy collar. It caught me off guard. I thought I had moved a bit down the road in accepting women as pastors. In that moment I realized I had far to go until I was convinced this was right for the church.

By the beginning of 1973 I had come full circle. In my journal on January 5 I wrote:

To GA for pastors' conference . . . talking about the role of
women in the church. Without a doubt we have discrimi-
nated against women. . . . It seems strange three years ago
I had very serious doubts about the ordination of women.
Now I feel quite the opposite.

Again, even in my wildest imagination, I could not have
dreamed that Corinne would one day don a collar and be one of
the pastors of the church.

For a time I served on a synod Parish Education Task Force that
was examining materials for Sunday church schools. For the most
part, these kinds of extra-parish responsibilities were enormously
gratifying to me. After a Minnesota Synod deans' meeting I wrote
in my journal: "It's a privilege to be dean of the St. Peter District—
gives greater insight into the broader program of the church—and
also into the problems of the church and synod." Now I felt that I
was back in the organized church and part of the network of pastors and laity, the kind of relationship I had missed so much while
teaching in New Jersey.

At the 1973 Minnesota Synod convention Melvin Hammarberg
was overwhelmingly reelected to a second term as president of
the synod. At that convention I had a conversation with J. Henry
Bergren, the pastor who had been my ordination sponsor. I noted
in my journal that "He suggested that I might be a future synod
pres." Had I not written that note I would long since have forgotten
Bergren's comment. It seemed to be an early hint of a larger leadership role to come.

In the fall of 1973 I was invited to attend a theological sym-
posium at Waukegan, Illinois. Again I assume Hammarberg had
something to do with it. There were about fifteen to twenty prominent theologians from Lutheran colleges and seminaries. I was one
of a half-dozen parish pastors and was appointed to head one of the
subgroups. In my journal I suggested:

Apparently someone thinks I have some theological grasp
& expertise. I'm not sure that is true—& yet I felt I could
hold my own in the conversations.

I went on to make some interesting observations about some of
the theologians in attendance:

I was greatly impressed by Carl Piepkorn from Concordia
Sem. Obviously a genius. The same could be said for Robert
Jenson from Gettysburg Sem. Warren Quanbeck is also a
very brilliant theologian—but one of the worst gossips in
informal conversation. I was quite appalled at the way he
took others apart.

Corinne's educational and service ventures

Though she always put family first, and though she always did more
than one could expect as a pastor's wife, Corinne's deep desire to
earn a college degree never waned. With the children in school all
day she felt free to explore options to earn a degree. Mankato State
University (later Minnesota State University, Mankato) offered a
program for a bachelor of science degree in nursing. In December
of 1973 I noted:

Corinne has now finished her fall term at Mankato—and
it's been a very good experience. She got an "A" for sure
in biology, & I wouldn't be surprised if she did the same
in English. It has given her confidence in herself such as I
haven't seen before. And this is good for the whole family.

She went on to graduate *summa cum laude*. She was determined
to prove to her father that his judgment years earlier—that she
didn't need college—was faulty.

In 1975 she was elected to the Board of Directors at Bethesda
Lutheran Medical Center in St. Paul. With her nursing background,
her studies at Mankato State, and her good common sense, I felt
it was a natural place for her to serve the larger church and to

establish her own identity. She was easily elected and served for nine years. Prominent Twin Cities' lawyers and businessmen dominated the board. Some were male chauvinists. But she more than held her own and soon became one of the respected members of that board.

One of Corinne's most helpful contributions to First Lutheran Church was her willingness to take on teaching a class of confirmation students who had proved to be the undoing of many Sunday school teachers. She had a marvelous gift for relating to junior high students. At the first session she informed them that if any misbehaved in class she would contact their parents immediately and require that they be at the next class. If some failed to complete their assignments she invited them to our home and accompanied their make-up work with hot chocolate. In time she became their best friend and they turned into a model class. One of the most obstreperous of them even became a pastor!

As we moved into the mid-1970s and her work on her degree at Mankato State was winding up, Corinne was sought after to teach in the nursing program at Gustavus Adolphus College. This would be a marvelous opportunity for her to use her gifts. Not least, finding such a fine position right in the community where we were living could not have been more convenient.

As we will see, this dream would never be realized.

Just three days before my election as synod president the *Mankato Free Press* (6/2/76) ran a major feature story about us as a couple, highlighting our joint quest for more education.

> Going back to school for the Chilstroms was a decision based on the philosophy that "if it cheats us of quality of life, it wouldn't be worth it," according to Mrs. Chilstrom. She found, however, that there was much parallel learning. "It's enhanced other areas of my life." A frequent response, according to Mrs. Chilstrom, is one of admiration for their ambition.

Gustavus Adolphus College: a long and fulfilling relationship

In 1971, my second year at First Lutheran Church, I was elected at the synod convention to the Board of Trustees at Gustavus Adolphus College. It was the beginning of a relationship that stretches right down to the moment I sit here writing this auto-biography. I served on that board for several years as an elected member, then for eleven as an ex-officio member when I was synod president/bishop, and then again for one four-year term after I retired. In 1975 I was elected secretary of the board. Now that we live in St. Peter in retirement, I'm on the board of directors of the Gustavus Linnaeus Arboretum and serving a two-year term as interim director.

It was during my early membership on the Gustavus board that I became embroiled in controversy over the tenure decision for Dr. William Dean, a member of the college's religion department. The event shows something of where I was in my theological stance at the time and of my understanding—or lack thereof—of what it means for a college to be a *liberal arts* center for learning.

I was on the committee that, among other things, examined the credentials of faculty recommended for tenure. At the commit-tee meeting I voted against granting tenure to Dean, thinking he leaned too far to the left theologically and feeling the need for a better balance between liberal and conservative persons on the reli-gion faculty. By the time of the board meeting I decided not to vote against him, convinced that it would have been unjust to Dean and his family to deny tenure only on that basis. In my journal follow-ing the meeting I wrote:

> Had thought prior to meeting that I would speak against tenure for Dr. Wm. Dean. But did not have the guts to do so after both Hammarberg and Barth spoke favorably. Maybe it is just as well—now we can argue the case for balancing Dean & others in the religion dept. with some conservative men.

After the board meeting I wrote a long letter to Lloyd Englesma, chairman of the college board, stating my reasons for questioning the decision regarding Dean. I said I was not opposed to having a variety of views in that department; I simply wanted to balance it in a different direction. I suggested that my opinion was undoubtedly rooted in

> ... my centrist position theologically. As such, I can iden-tify closely with some members of the religion faculty. But it is my judgment that the religion faculty ... is weighted to the left side of the theological spectrum. There seems to be very little that would represent a more conservative posi-tion. If our concern, as was expressed at the board meeting, is to expose our students to the full range of theological viewpoints, then I have some doubt about how adequately this is being done.

I sent copies of my letter to Frank Barth, president of the college, and Robert Esbjornson, chair of the religion department.

My letter evoked a long response from Esbjornson. "Esbj" was a member of First Lutheran Church and I was his pastor. He and I and our spouses developed a strong and cordial relationship. He took umbrage, however, at my assertion that the department was becoming "too liberal." He chided me for using too loosely terms like "liberal" and "conservative." He wrote:

> I think the responsibility of a scholar in religion is to see to it that students have a chance to learn about as many varia-tions of theology as we can manage and that we are obliged to see that the several positions are presented fairly. It is quite easy to become dogmatic in any field, not least in the study of religion. I would hold strongly that there is a place for critical scholarship within the church.

Looking back some thirty-five years later I see several aspects of the discussion that continue to be relevant to the mission of

Gustavus and other colleges of the ELCA. I'm embarrassed, of course, by my journal note that singles out men as potential members of that faculty. I suppose that prejudice reflects the fact that there were so few women at that time who were prepared to teach religion on a college faculty.

More seriously, it's clear that I had a much too narrow view of what it meant to be a *liberal arts* college. I was surely convinced that we needed to open doors of understanding for students in every area of intellectual endeavor. Over the years, and especially when I was synod bishop and usually preached at the installation service for tenured faculty, I vigorously asserted that faculty members should be free to pursue truth wherever it took them.

But at the time I don't think I carried that view into the work of the religion department. I saw these professors as ones who needed to be, first and foremost, apologists for the faith and theology of the Lutheran church. In retrospect, I'm embarrassed. Certainly students need to be introduced to all aspects of religious thought, including that of other religions of the world.

In 1974 the Board of Trustees was working on a revision of the constitution. In a letter to Arnold Ryden, chairman of the board, I show some movement in my thinking. I expressed my conviction that we must state forthrightly that

> We are an "institution of higher education in the Christian tradition." This gives candid recognition to our tradition without implying that it is our purpose to promote an exclusive view of life in the classroom.

Having said that, I still wrestle with the question of how a college of the church, which has a constitutional mandate to uphold the faith and traditions of the Lutheran church, should carry out that charge. Is it sufficient to have ELCA chaplains and a daily or occasional chapel service? Is it being narrow and bigoted to insist that every student who enrolls at our church colleges should at some time be exposed to our theological roots? And what about balance? We have a huge religious grouping in the U.S. often identified as evangelical conservative. During my time on the board of the National Council of Churches (NCC) I headed a committee that explored relationships with those kinds of churches—Evangelical Covenant, Evangelical Free, General Baptist, etc. In the process I learned again, as I had discovered earlier, that there are many first-rate theologians in these kinds of churches. Do we have an obligation to our students to make certain that such views are represented on the religion faculty?

Many questions. Few answers. In 1974 Barth resigned as president of the college and I was elected chair of the committee to search for a new president. I charged into the task with enthusiasm. After beginning with more than one hundred candidates we quickly narrowed the field to a half dozen. In the end, our recommendation for Dr. Edward Lindell was unanimous. He proved to be exactly the right person to bring the college out of its near-fatal financial predicament and back to solid ground.

Writing endeavors

I continued to write during my years at First Lutheran. There were book reviews for the *Lutheran Forum* magazine. My article "Good News on the Sea of Galilee" appeared in the *Bible Society Record,* published by the American Bible Society. Rooted in the trip I had taken to the Holy Land in 1968, the article reflected on the peaceful setting of Galilee as it contrasted with the ongoing rumbling of cannon fire between Israeli and Syrian forces in the distance. How little that corner of the world has changed in the intervening years.

I've never had much interest in poetry. Yet on occasion I would try my hand at a small verse, such as this one in 1975:

Untie me, Lord!

Untie my feet that they may go
To places where Thy love can flow.

Untie my hands that they might do
The deed that leads the wanderer through.

Untie my tongue that it might sing
The praises of my Saviour King!

Untie my heart, its bands break loose,
Let all my life be for Thy use!

Untie me, Lord!

The charismatic movement

It was during my years at St. Peter that the charismatic movement began to assert itself in the Lutheran church. Dr. Mark
Hillmer, formerly of the Lutheran Church—Missouri Synod and a
respected Old Testament scholar at Luther Seminary, was known
to be involved with the movement. I invited him to First Lutheran
Church for our Spiritual Emphasis Week. He was being considered for tenure at the seminary at the time. After the event I wrote
to Dr. Hammarberg, president of the synod, to share my views. I
described how Hillmer's presentations had been highly inspiring
and intellectually satisfying. I suggested that he should be given
tenure. I felt certain that in the mix of different personalities and
emphases at a seminary as large as Luther, he would eventually find
his place and make a significant contribution.

> Either he will become so deeply involved in the (charis-
> matic) movement that he will feel uncomfortable in the
> Lutheran church and leave of his own accord, or else he will
> come to the place where he sees that speaking in tongues
> and other such phenomena are a very minor footnote on
> the pages of the Christian life.

Several years later Corinne had Hillmer as a teacher at Luther Seminary and found him to be a superb guide in Old Testament studies.

Vietnam, taxes, the Middle East, and more

The war in Vietnam was raging during my years at First Lutheran. Harvey Enz, a young man from the congregation, had been killed in battle. Ruth and Fred gave a beautiful frontal piece for the pulpit in memory of their son. I felt caught in the middle. I questioned the war but only mentioned my reservations in sermons on rare occasion. I did, however, write to Ancher Nelsen, our representative in Washington, D.C., about the futility of the war. His response in a letter in August of 1973 is interesting from an historical perspective. Pointing out that the U.S. Congress had been assured by the Defense Department that there would be no further engagement in combat activities off the shores of Cambodia, he added:

> Hopefully, we will be able to wind down our military posture in all areas of the world as time goes on. When one thinks of what goes into maintaining our entire defense establishment, we would be prompted to hope that we could abolish the entire Defense Department. This, of course, would not represent realistic thinking. I guess we mere men, though made in the image of our Creator, are not perfect.

We never seem to learn from history. That conflict ended in shame and was an enormous waste of our people and resources.

As I write these lines we are debating the best way to end our debacle in the Middle East. Nelsen's advice that we reduce rather than expand our military involvement around the world never gained much ground. When will we ever learn?

When Gerald Ford took office after Nixon's resignation and pardoned Nixon in September of 1974, I wrote to Ford suggesting that his action

. . . encourages the permissive attitude in this land that "anything goes"—especially in politics. Justice—confession—pardon. To bypass the first and second stages renders pardon meaningless.

I wrote to the U.S. State Department urging them to support the United Nations mandate that the South Africans withdraw their forces from Namibia. Little could I have known that some fifteen years later I would travel to that country and witness firsthand the oppression of the South Africans and the freedom of the Namibians. I find it ironic that the U.S. government was fully in support of using the U.N. to settle that conflict, yet refused to follow that protocol in other parts of the world, notably in the Middle East.

I also wrote to leaders in Washington, D.C., about other matters. In a letter to Minnesota Senator Walter Mondale I suggested that it was time to completely overhaul our tax system and that part of that process should include removing the housing tax shelter that clergy were accorded. Talk about a minority opinion! Churches and church pension boards have argued strenuously that this advantage was necessary for the vitality of the churches in our society. They may be right. But I still think it is a crutch that we could do without. It would mean, of course, that that same benefit would have to be removed from the military, where personnel who live in government housing pay no tax on that benefit. And it would also mean that congregations and other church agencies would have to pick up the full Social Security payment for its ordained employees. I don't expect to ever see any change in that law, at least in my lifetime.

I also wrote to Nelsen urging him to support the anti-abortion Right-to-Life Amendment. I had been reading literature that convinced me that life began at conception and that we must protect it by law. Since then I've come to see it as a more complex issue. Though still leaning toward a cautious and conservative stance, I now believe that we would have a hard time coming up with legislation that would improve on Roe v. Wade. We have had incidents in our own family among relatives and friends that convince me that the decision to end a pregnancy belongs with a woman, her husband/partner, her doctor, and a spiritual counselor.

In 1975 I took my second trip to Israel. The plan had been to combine a group from Trinity and First Lutheran churches. Our itinerary included stops at Rome and Greece. Events in that part of the world became so unsettled that it was virtually impossible to interest very many in the venture. We did combine the two groups and Corinne and I accompanied twelve who wanted to go.

Having been introduced to the Israeli view on my trip with the Bethel Series group in 1969, I was determined to have our contingent gain a broader perspective on political issues and also to see what our Lutheran churches were doing among the Palestinians. Those goals were achieved through our Palestinian guide and our visits to Lutheran World Federation ministries in the area.

While we were there, hostilities broke out among Palestinians and the Israelis. On our last night in Israel a terrorist attacked a hotel in Tel Aviv not far from where we stayed. Oddly enough, it didn't seem all that frightening to us who were there. I have had this same sense of calm on subsequent trips to troubled places in the world. Everything seems more threatening from a distance.

Do I finish my doctorate?

When we moved to St. Peter I had completed all but one course requirement for my doctorate at New York University. And then, of course, there was the dissertation—the mountain beyond the foothills. In the first couple of years at St. Peter I saw no way that I could complete that journey. I was nearly overwhelmed in the parish and was increasingly involved in other activities. I had a family to care for. I had almost concluded that it would be impossible.

Corinne knew all this. She was not eager to push me over the edge. Yet she also knew it was important for me to explore the possibility. Then one day Dr. Clair McRostie, who had chaired the call committee when I came to First Lutheran Church, dropped by my office. Among other things, he asked what I was doing about my doctorate. When I reported that it was on hold he looked at me gravely and said, "You must try to finish it."

That was the nudge I needed to get me off dead center. I had worked on a preliminary draft of a dissertation that was designed to develop a course on marriage and family for use at colleges of the church. My advisor was Dr. Lee Belford, chair of the religious education department at NYU. I sent drafts of materials to him and waited for a response. After no word for several weeks I would call him to see what he thought about the material I had sent. I could hear him put the phone down and split open the envelope I had sent. After some delay he would make some cursory and superficial comments about it. I knew the project was going nowhere. It was dead.

One day in utter frustration I walked from my office to the sanctuary. I sat there alone, thinking and praying. Suddenly an idea came to me. Why not abandon my other effort and move in an entirely new direction? Why not do an analysis of the Bethel Bible Series?

I contacted Harley Swiggum to find out if I could have open access to the address files of the series. He agreed. I set to work on an outline for a dissertation. I sent it to Belford. In the meantime, I decided that the only way for this to work would be for me to convince Belford that Dr. Norma Thompson, one of his colleagues in the department, would be the best person to advise me on this project. But with Belford as chair of the unit, that might be risky. When I called him I lifted up the suggestion about Thompson and held my breath. After a moment of hesitation he said he agreed. What a relief.

From that moment the doors opened wide. I set aside the sacristy at First Lutheran Church for my research center. Every Monday I devoted the entire day to working on the dissertation. When I got to the analysis stage I enlisted the help of my neighbor Milton

Brostrom, professor of mathematics at Gustavus. He introduced me to the computer at Gustavus—a machine that occupied a full room. I learned how to punch cards, feed them into the computer, and push the buttons that would start the innards working and cough out the results. I felt like the Wizard of Oz.

In the midst of the dissertation writing I returned to the East coast in June of 1974 to complete the last class. Mary flew out with me to visit some of her old friends in Teaneck and to go with me for a visit with sister Janet and her family southern New Jersey. It was a memorable bonding time for Mary and me.

I sent Corinne some roses for our anniversary. In a note she wrote:

> I didn't know the roses would last so long. I really appreciate the love that sent them. I appreciate your faithfulness—I pray that it will remain and grow as the years unfold. I'm glad I can look forward to growing older with you!

By early 1976 the dissertation was complete and I was ready to fly out to New York to defend it. This time Chris went with me. In his customary deliberate way he made careful plans in advance of our trip. He arranged to visit a firm on Wall Street to look into the world of high finance. We had lunch at the inn in lower Manhattan where George Washington had once dined. We went to the top of the World Trade Center, never imagining that such structures would one day be ravaged by suicide pilots with the loss of thousands of lives. All in all, it was a very good trip and a time for us to bond more closely.

I felt at ease defending my thesis. The committee was congenial. After it was over I sat with Chris waiting for the outcome. Dr. Thompson emerged from the conference room and announced to Chris, "You can now call your dad 'Dr. Chilstrom.'" It was the grateful end to a long journey.

Family life

As a family we had six good years in St. Peter. We did many things together. There were camping trips, including a memorable hike with our First Lutheran youth group in the Canadian Rockies. I played with the boys in the backyard. We canoed down the Minnesota River both as a family and with others. Our children were all doing well in school. They were all taking music lessons. Mary concentrated on the flute. Besides piano, Chris was also working on the French horn. Andrew also took piano lessons.

Family hikes at Seven Mile Creek and Robard's Creek were like adventures into an unknown world. We made frequent trips to our Lake Lida cabin, often bringing along friends of our children. We often clamored into our boat or pontoon for an evening on the water. Mary read a book while the rest of us competed to see who could catch the most sunfish. Our close connection with nature, as well as water skiing and hikes in Maplewood State Park across the lake, filled our memory banks with recollections that have lasted for a lifetime.

No, we weren't the perfect family by any stretch of the imagination. At one time of particular difficulty we decided that it would be good to seek counseling at Lutheran Social Service in Minneapolis. One of my own issues was that I was not as communicative in our family circle as I should have been. The outcome was that I not only became more involved in disciplinary issues with the children, but also learned to share my feelings more effectively with Corinne.

Time to move?

It was in the fall of 1975 that I began to sense that a move of some kind was in the offing. I was contacted by Messiah Lutheran Church in Fargo, North Dakota. On the surface, it made no sense to even give this possibility a second thought. Two things, however, intrigued me. First, the congregation was broadcasting its Sunday morning service on a major television station that reached most of northern Minnesota, North and South Dakota, and even into Canada. I had always felt comfortable in front of a television camera and the thought of having that kind of ministry, in addition to being pastor of the congregation, stirred my interest.

The second factor was that Fargo was only an hour from our cabin at Lake Lida. I envisioned days when I could sneak out to the lake and enjoy some fishing, hunting, gardening, and other activities.

I wrote to Dr. Hammarberg and alerted him to the situation. He called and asked if Corinne and I would meet him and Mrs. Hammarberg for dinner at Le Sueur, ten miles north of St. Peter. Over dinner he inquired about the call to Fargo. He agreed that there was no call in the Minnesota Synod that offered an opportunity quite like it. He made it clear, however, that he did not want me to leave. Hammarberg had been diagnosed with prostate cancer many months before this time. Though it seemed that he was in remission, he may have already known that the prospects for recovery were not good. After his death I learned from his wife Ruth that Hammarberg was thinking of me as a strong possibility to be his successor. He could not have said that directly to me at the time, of course, because his health condition was not known to the general public and also because it would have been inappropriate for him to give any impression that he had a favorite successor in mind.

In the meantime, I persisted in pursuing the call to Fargo. Corinne and the children were totally turned off by the idea. But they agreed to go to Fargo and take a look at the situation. On the day we left, a fierce blizzard blew in from the northwest. We got as far as Hector, Minnesota, and should have settled in for the night. I was certain, however, that we could drive out of the storm if we pressed on. About four miles north of Hector we hit a snowdrift across the road, followed by sheer ice. We spun off the road and down into the ditch, coming to rest a few feet from a telephone pole. We all drew a deep breath. Mary was sitting in the front seat next to me. Noting that the car was pointing directly back to St.

Peter, she was the first to speak. "Dad, I think God is trying to tell you something."

After spending a miserable night at a crummy motel in Hector, we pressed on the next morning. Mary was right. The visit was less than satisfying. By the time we left Fargo it was clear to me that this would be the wrong move.

I could not have known at that time that the next move would be my election as bishop of the Minnesota Synod of the LCA, the story I will share in the next chapter.

First Lutheran and St. Peter: yes, the right place

In my June 8 letter of resignation to the church council, I said that there simply could not be a congregation that was more supportive of its pastor and family. I noted the variety of talent and ability in the membership. "If we are able to serve the larger church in an effective way," I wrote, "we will give much of the credit to our friends here at First Lutheran who have helped prepare us for this greater task." Little could I have known then that the "larger church" would include leadership of the newly formed ELCA eleven years down the road.

In July 1976 I wrote my last monthly letter to the congregation. I referred to the grief all of us in our family were feeling as we moved away from a church and community we had come to love so dearly. But I also wrote about our hope for the years to come.

> Painful as it is for us to leave this congregation and a beautiful community like St. Peter, we do so in the hope and expectation that God has in store for us experiences that are equally as beautiful and equally as meaningful.

The congregation held a farewell dinner for us at Gustavus on August 15. Along with the tributes came an unexpected and breathtaking gift—a Paul Granlund sculpture. He was well-established by then as one of America's foremost fine artists. The piece we received

is a smaller version of the large one in front of Westminster Presbyterian Church on Nicollet Avenue in Minneapolis. Called "Birth of
Freedom," it is based on Galatians 5:1: "For freedom Christ has set
us free." At the base is a human character that looks dead. On each
side are figures that look as if they are awakening to new life. At the
top stands one who reaches in freedom to the skies. Surrounding
these figures is an abstract representation of the cross of Christ.

In a letter of gratitude to Granlund I mentioned that

> When one of your pieces was presented to Princess Chris-
> tina a couple of years ago, Corinne poked me and asked, "I
> wonder what one has to do to get one of those?" Now she
> knows! Galatians 5:1 has taken on new meaning for us.

The sculpture continues to occupy a prominent place in our
home. We have explained its meaning and made Granlund's witness to hundreds of friends who have visited us.

It was time to take up the next challenge. The twenty years I
dreamed of spending at First Lutheran Church would be abruptly
shortened to only six.

Chapter 9

Call to be a bishop:
the Minnesota Synod years

An inevitable move?

In the early months of 1976 I had the feeling that I was being swept
up in changes that were beyond my control. The call of Messiah
Church in Fargo was like a harbinger of more and larger challenges
to come.

As Hammarberg's condition worsened, buzz about a successor was circulating through the synod. I paid little attention to it,
assuming that I would surely not be involved. After all, I had only
been in the synod for six years and the Twin Cities area pastors
were far more well-known.

Normandale Church—a good next move?

Early in 1976 I was invited to meet with the call committee from
Normandale Lutheran Church in Edina. Events moved rapidly.
Here was one of the larger congregations of the synod, situated in
what was known to be one of the most affluent suburbs of the Twin
Cities. Resources and the potential for ministry and mission were
significant. How could I help but be interested?

Then something rather odd happened. Or so it seemed at the
time. I didn't get the call. Instead it went to Carl Manfred, one of
Hammarberg's assistants. The chair of the call committee, after

informing me by letter that they had called Manfred, went on to add the intriguing comment that "... some members of our call committee are working and praying that you will be our next synod president. Our committee is in agreement that you would be the finest candidate ..."

At about the same time I got an invitation from Hammarberg to be the Bible study leader at the forthcoming synod convention in June. Was that a move on his part to give me a more public face? Taciturn as he was, only he ever knew.

Hammarberg resigns

On the first day of May 1976 Hammarberg resigned from office for reasons of health. Now what everyone had feared was made public. I wrote a note to him the next day:

> Dear Mal, Just before Bible class this morning one of the members told me about the announcement of your resignation. I found it difficult to keep my mind on the subject. This is a keen disappointment to us. Our hope and our prayer are that added rest and freedom from the heavy load will give you the needed boost to regain your vitality. Be assured that you and Ruth will continue to be in our prayers.

A recommitment to First Lutheran Church

In the meantime, I continued to do my work at First Lutheran with the expectation that I would now settle in for a longer ministry. Corinne was completing her work at Mankato State University and the overtures from Gustavus Adolphus regarding a teaching position grew stronger. First Lutheran was at the point where the congregation was ready to call a full-time assistant pastor. John Malzahn, a senior seminary student, accepted the call. There was little doubt in my mind that our coming years would be in St. Peter.

Speculation heats up

About that same time an ad hoc pastors' meeting gathered on May 20 in Minneapolis. The pastors outlined the qualities they felt were important in a new head of synod. At the bottom of the letter they listed the names of fourteen persons they felt should be considered. Only two of us from outside the metropolitan Twin Cities made their cut.

It was on that same day that a group of prominent lay leaders, mostly from Normandale Church, sent a letter to all of the delegates to the June synod convention with detailed information about my background. They urged them to consider giving me their support.

I knew Hammarberg was a dying man, so I wrote to him just days before the convention, thanking him for his ministry to the synod and to me personally. Among other things I noted:

> . . . that day in the late 1940s when you visited my home church at Litchfield. Your words of encouragement to a skinny high school kid were just what I needed at that moment to keep me moving in the direction of the ministry.

The week it all came together

How could more happen in the course of a single week? On *Saturday*, May 29 Corinne received her Bachelor of Science in Nursing degree from Mankato State University. Though I had passed my final oral examination many weeks earlier and had no intention to attend graduation ceremonies, my Doctor of Education degree from New York University was awarded in New York City on *Wednesday*, June 2. And on *Friday*, June 4 I was elected president of the Minnesota Synod. What a week!

The election—an uncertain outcome before strong affirmation

I surely had no sense at the beginning of that week how the election would unfold. More than thirty pastors were nominated on the first ballot.

A strong assumption was abroad in the synod that Paul Werger would be elected. He was the logical choice. Though he was out of ULCA background in a synod that was predominantly Augustana, he had become known and respected for his exceptional ministry at St. Luke Church in Bloomington, Minnesota, and for his stellar service in many capacities in the synod, including chair of a fund drive for Northwestern Seminary.

The process called for the four finalists to give brief addresses to the convention. Each was given five minutes to introduce himself and speak on the subject "The Nature of the Church."

In my comments I began by mentioning that I had just been awarded my Doctor of Education degree from New York University. I added this remark: "For at least three years I dreaded that final oral examination. But I can tell you that it was duck soup compared to what I'm going through right now!" That brought a good laugh from the delegation and eased the tension for me.

As I look back now at that brief address, I realize that my years of teaching at Luther College were critical to my unfolding life as a leader in the church. After referring to the confessional definition of the church, I moved quickly to the scriptural basis for the church. Pointing to illustrations that Jesus, Peter, and Paul used— the vine, the good shepherd, a field, a holy nation, the body, marriage—I suggested that in all of them the servant of the Lord motif emerges and becomes the premier example for what the church should be in the world today.

On the final ballot the margin of my election was substantial and surprising. Our expectations were so minimal that Corinne wasn't even at the convention during the election process. She was at a neighborhood party friends were giving in honor of her graduation from college. When it became apparent that I was running very strong, a friend found her and hustled her over to the college.

In my acceptance speech, written down later from notes I was able to pull together from memory, I began on a lighter note by asking, "Are you sure you know what you've done!" I went on to state that I was ". . . deeply convinced that the Holy Spirit has been at work through the will of the delegation. I accept this challenge with the same assurance and confidence that the Holy Spirit will give me strength and wisdom for the days ahead." I expressed gratitude for those who had shaped my life, including my parents, adding that I felt certain my father was among the "cloud of witnesses" with us that day. I gave thanks for Corinne and our children, noting that they had been of "special strength and support" in the uncertain days leading up to the convention.

I thanked Mal and Ruth Hammarberg, noting that they had created ". . . a deep reservoir of love and respect, not only for you yourselves, but also for the office of the presidency."

I made reference to having made contact with my father's family in Sweden in recent years. I referred to a letter from Professor Sven Kjöllerström, a distant cousin who taught religion at Lund University. Sven inquired whether the family in America, like that in Sweden, was characterized by having "a noble nose and big ears." I said that I sent him a photograph, suggesting that we had no lines of nobility in the United States but that it was plain to see that the genes producing large ears had crossed the Atlantic safely. I concluded with the suggestion that those prominent ears were symbolic of what I considered to be of highest importance—". . . that I listen to the voice of the Holy Spirit, and that I listen to the voice of the Spirit through the people of God in our synod."

One who knew?

At some point either just prior to or after my election, Pastor Arnold Lindgren approached Corinne and handed her a letter. She was too caught up in immediate events to stop and read it. She tucked it into her purse and only discovered it a week later.

Lindgren wrote that he had not been able to sleep during the night prior to my election. He got up at two-thirty in the morning and wrote this letter to me:

> June 4. 1976, 2:30 a.m.
>
> Dear Herb:
>
> Today our Minnesota Synod Convention opens and you will be elected President. When Dr. Hammarberg informed us of his resignation I asked our Lord who he has chosen and a voice to my spirit came loud and clear that you were the man.
>
> Thou art the man! I will pray for you and your dear wife in the coming years.
>
> In Christian love, Arnie

In my response to him more than a week later I wrote:

> I find it a bit overwhelming at this moment to think that so many people have placed such high trust and confidence in my ability to lead the synod in the future. Corinne put it well when she said to me following the election, "If the Lord can take common people and use them, then maybe there is a chance we can serve in this way."

After the election a prominent lay person from the Twin Cities suggested to me that there was some disappointment among pastors in his area over my election. They wondered if someone from a town/gown congregation outside the metropolitan area would have any passion for the mission of the church in the urban setting.

In my response to him I offered my own analysis and strategy:

> One of my first tasks will be to relate in a very direct and personal way to the pastors and try to allay their fears as quickly as possible. I can appreciate fully their reservations about me. If our roles were reversed I'm certain I would have the same reservations about a candidate from the shadows

of Gustavus Adolphus College. I am convinced these pastors will be won over in a very short time when they begin to see that the synod staff shows a genuine concern for the needs of metropolitan pastors and congregations.

A tough blow, a long friendship

There was indeed one person who was deeply hurt by my election, namely, Paul Werger. Though only he knows how strong his hopes were for being president of the synod, reports from others indicated that he was keenly disappointed.

The good news, as I will point out later in some detail, is that this did not make for an irreparable rift between us. Later in the summer, on the first Sunday after we moved to Edina, we attended worship at his church in Bloomington. He and his wife, Dianne, invited Corinne and me to have dinner and conversation a few weeks later. He assured me of his unwavering support. He always lived up to that promise.

Two years later I nominated Werger for the office of bishop in the Iowa Synod. After his experience in Minnesota he was reluctant to get involved in another election. We were together at a meeting at St. John's University, Collegeville, Minnesota. He was wavering. I urged him to stay in the running, suggesting that he should let the Spirit of God work through the folks in Iowa. He was elected and went on to serve both that synod in the LCA and the Southeastern Iowa Synod after the ELCA was formed. He was—and still is—a churchman of the highest order. We became close friends and worked together for years as leaders in the LCA and ELCA.

Reaction to my election

Reports of my election spread rapidly through the secular and church press. I was told that when pastors and leaders of the LCA in other parts of the country heard of my election in one of the church's largest synods their most common reaction was, "Herb *who?*" I was a mostly unknown factor beyond Minnesota.

One of the most thorough reports was a feature article in my hometown newspaper, *The Litchfield Independent Review*, written by my cousin Dorothy (Chillstrom) Harmon, wife of the publisher. Later that year she received the top award in Minnesota for her piece in the category of feature articles in weekly newspapers. She had the advantage, of course, of having known me since my birth. I appreciated her comment that "His worth isn't something that just happened recently; it's been in the making for a long time, beginning with his home and parents."

Dr. Robert J. Marshall, president of the LCA, wrote:

> Your election is a tribute to the respect and confidence that the pastors and lay leaders of the synod have for you. I pray God will strengthen you for the heavy burdens you will be undertaking.

Elmo Agrimson was bishop of the Southeastern Minnesota District of the ALC. He had a penchant for finding exactly the right words for every occasion. He expressed the hope that the Holy Spirit would

> . . . sustain you with courage, patience, theological perception, and a slight tinge of cynicism and humor as you lead your synod in the complexities of contemporary church leadership.

Agrimson thought we had never met. In my reply I reminded him of a time when I was a young pastor, returning by train to Pelican Rapids from Minneapolis. I was reading a theological book of some kind. Agrimson, then bishop of the Western North Dakota Synod, was in the same car. When he caught sight of the book he came and sat next to me, introduced himself, and engaged me in animated conversation for the rest of my trip. "Needless to say," I wrote, "your openness and friendliness made a lasting impression on that young pastor."

Little could I have known on that train ride that Elmo would one day become one of my most trusted and respected friends. Other than his adamant resistance to the growing use of computers and anything that smelled of being high church, we saw eye-to-eye on every theological and social issue. In his gift for expressing himself with exactly the right words, he once talked about a renegade congregation in his district. He said he was grateful for them because they were like ". . .a cesspool where the malcontents in the area could be together in one place!"

Neither could I have dreamed in those early contacts that Mark Hanson, husband of Agrimson's daughter Ione, would be one of my successors as presiding bishop of the ELCA.

Edward Hansen, bishop of the Southwestern Minnesota District of the ALC, reminded me that we had both, at different times, held the same position as dean at the former Lutheran Bible Institute and Luther College in Teaneck, New Jersey. He underscored what I came to learn over the next eleven years—that the fellowship among the seven LCA, ALC, and LCMS bishops/presidents in Minnesota would become one of my greatest sources of encouragement.

Carl and Ruth Segerhammar visited friends in St. Peter shortly after I had been elected. I seized the opportunity to learn from someone who was highly regarded as a synod president on the West Coast for many years. Over coffee at our home I asked Carl for advice on how to be an effective synod president. He replied with naked candor and humor: "Don't worry, Herb. All you need for this job are two things: First, you need a very large bladder to endure long meetings; second, to be able to sleep in any kind of bed." I would soon learn that there was more truth in that comment than I could have imagined.

Farewell to Melvin Hammarberg

Between the end of the synod convention and September 1, 1976, the day I took office, I had two visits with my predecessor. Hammarberg was a man of tall stature with a full head of hair.

He stood out in any crowd. He had been a good athlete in college. He enjoyed superb health all of this life. Now he was emaciated and gaunt, obviously in the last stages of his battle with prostate cancer.

Not long after the convention, we had our first meeting at the Hammarberg home just west of downtown Minneapolis. We sat in the sun on the veranda just outside the kitchen. It was clear to me that I needed to deal only with the most essential issues. First, I moved quickly through the entire roster of pastors, more than five hundred. I shared very briefly what I knew about each of them. He spoke up whenever there was something important he thought I should know about certain ones.

The critical issue for our discussion was building a synod staff. He suggested that I begin with a clean slate in the synod office.

When I asked for suggestions for persons he would recommend for my new staff he offered only one name—Ronald C. Peterson.

My last encounter with Hammarberg was just days before he died. I visited with Ruth before going into the room. She told me that Mal had begun to withdraw even from those closest to him, including her and his children, a very typical pattern for those in the last stages of life. I made my visit very brief. When I asked him how he was doing, he replied in typical Hammarberg fashion, "Fair to middlin." After a brief prayer I was on my way. It was a sad moment for me. He had played such a significant role in my life for almost thirty years. He lingered until the end of August, dying on his final day in office.

At a memorial service for Hammarberg at Orchestra Hall, home of the Minnesota Orchestra, I was invited to give one of the tributes. I began with reference to a comment from a mutual friend: "We carry a mental image of Melvin Hammarberg in this place, and it is the image of a great, gentle, Christ-like servant of the church." I went on to characterize him as a man whose

. . . presence demanded our attention. And when we gave
him our attention, we were rewarded with wise counsel,
sound judgment, patient understanding, and, without fail, a
touch of good humor.

I closed with a reference to the prayer book he co-edited. In it is
a poem by Winfred Ernest Garrison that spoke to our confidence
in God's grace for Hammarberg:

Thy world, O God, so fierce,
    And I so frail,

Yet, though its arrows threaten oft to pierce
    My fragile sail,
Cities of refuge rise where dangers cease,
Sweet silences abound and all is peace.

Building a staff

I moved quickly to form a new staff of assistants. I took Hammarberg's advice and contacted Ronald Peterson. From our first
encounter the rapport was strong. I could not have known at that
first meeting that Ron would become one of the dearest friends
I have ever had. That friendship was deepened when Ron was
involved in a near-fatal accident just north of Duluth less than two
years after joining my staff. His recovery was slow. Eventually he
returned to full capacity and was able to resume his duties.

I had been impressed by Charles Anderson when we worked
together at synod conventions. I offered him a position as an assistant, with a major focus on the town and country congregations of
the synod. I found him to be a wise and consistent partner. Chuck
had moved from Worthington to Golden Valley less than two years
prior to that time. He weighed the offer carefully and eventually
decided that his heart was really in the town and country setting. I had considerable negative reaction from the congregation

at Golden Valley. Besides being responsible for town and country congregations, Chuck also took charge of our work with candidates for ordination, a complex and demanding program.

After the merger in 1987 Chuck joined the staff of the new Southwestern Minnesota Synod and eventually became its bishop, a role for which he was superbly well-suited.

Given the need to send a strong message of support to urban congregations, I thought carefully about a third assistant for that ministry. I knew of the respect and effective work of Peter Erickson, then pastor at Messiah Church on the near south side of downtown Minneapolis. Peter had written to me within days after my election, urging me to make bold moves to affirm the synod's concern for inner city churches.

When I set an appointment to meet with Erickson at his office, he assumed that I was coming to chat about inner city ministry. When I offered him a position on the spot he was nonplussed. After a few days of reflection he agreed to join me.

Because he was a bit older than the rest of us on the professional staff, Erickson assumed a father-figure role among us. Always sensitive and encouraging, he passed a note to my office a bit more than a year after we became colleagues:

> I want to tell you that you have done a tremendous job
> in your first year and a half. You have handled many tasks
> with kindness, forthrightness, patience, and excellent judg-
> ment. In baseball terms, I'd say you are batting over 400.
> May God give you the grace and strength for your impor-
> tant responsibilities.

When I left office in 1987 it was natural for the executive board of the synod to appoint him as interim bishop.

My experience in previous settings convinced me that a competent personal secretary would be as important as any staff I would choose. I cast the net far and wide. Out of the search came Marybeth Peterson. I invited her to fly in from Denver where she was doing social work. She proved to be conscientious, trustworthy, and efficient. She got so good at reading my almost illegible handwriting that there were times when I had to ask her to decipher what I had written!

In time it became evident that Marybeth was overqualified for what she was doing. I invited her to become a program staff person. After the merger in 1987, she went on to the Nebraska Synod where she also proved to be a first-rate assistant to that bishop.

David Jones, a very gifted lay person, took responsibility for several portfolios: Christian education, communications, and the annual assembly. Jones was not intimidated as a layman working with several ordained persons. He more than held his own on the staff and was respected by his colleagues. Jones went on to become a fundraiser for congregations and agencies.

Later Paul Krupinski, an effective parish pastor, joined us as a youth and communications specialist. Krupinski had remarkable skills in the area of video communication, a field that was just emerging at that time. After he returned to the parish several years later Krupinski sent a note in which he said, "Herb . . . you have always been and will continue to be a very special person . . . who believed in me at a time in my life that will forever be cherished. . . ."

One day Paul Graf came to my office. Graf had been director of development for Lutheran Social Service of Minnesota. He volunteered to be an unpaid staff person. After two years Paul suffered a severe and debilitating stroke, leaving him all but speechless. When I visited him he would look at me, exert to the limit trying to say a sentence, and then pound the table as he uttered the only word he could speak: "Damn!" On one visit in 1985 he managed to scratch out a note in shaky letters:

DEAR HERB. HIS GRACE IS SUFFICIENT. PAUL GRAF.

I was not convinced that the Shepherds of the Streets program was the right place for the synod to show its concern for an urban ministry. I was much more inclined to use those funds for aiding congregations in their outreach mission to the Twin Cities. Eventually I brought in Glenn Leaf and Roger Mackey to work directly with congregations in those settings.

The support staff was also of the highest caliber. Helen Bohline, our receptionist, made every visitor feel welcome and important. Katherine Tessien, Fran Forsman, Jean Johnson, Marilyn Erickson, and Carol Robbins were all very capable as secretaries. Harriet Ryberg was unusually competent at keeping accurate and understandable financial records.

Florence Peterson, who succeeded Marybeth Peterson as my personal secretary, was married to Paul, a former LCMS pastor whom I helped get a call to a Minnesota Synod congregation. She wrote a Christmas note to Corinne and me in 1981 in which she expressed thanks for opening that door for Paul and also for giving her a position in my office.

> I don't get so tongue-tied when I see either of you—now that I have found out that you are "ordinary in an extraordinary way."

I have warm memories of our staff mid-morning coffee breaks. All of us came to treasure it as a time when we could let our hair down and enjoy good humor before returning to our desks for more serious matters.

Induction—who lays hands on this man?

My induction into office was set for Sunday, October 17, the date that worked best for Dr. Marshall and the day before I would turn forty-five. Senior staff persons at Gustavus Adolphus College thought it would be good if someone from the Church of Sweden could be present that day. An invitation went to Archbishop

Sundby. He was unable to come but appointed diocesan Bishop Bertil Werkström to represent the Church of Sweden.

I was too inexperienced in ecclesiastical history to realize that this would lead to a rather unpleasant confrontation at the induction. It all had to do with the historic episcopate, an important fixture in Swedish church history, but anathema to Marshall. Werkström came with the full expectation that he would participate in the laying on of hands at the service. Marshall was equally determined that it would not happen.

As we stood in the sacristy at Christ Chapel, Marshall dispassionately but definitively made it clear to Werkström that he was not to lay hands on me. It was an embarrassing moment. I felt Marshall had offended a very important guest. Only later did I learn of the depth of Marshall's conviction that the LCA should never allow for any of its leaders to be installed into office in the tradition of the historic episcopate. It would not be the last time we would disagree over this subject.

The service was the first of many important events in our lives that would be held at Christ Chapel at Gustavus Adolphus College. We processed with the hymn, "Lord Jesus Christ, Be Present Now." We read Psalm 121 as a congregation. The lessons were from Romans 12:1–5 and John 10:1–15. We sang "God's Word Is Our Great Heritage" before Marshall preached the sermon. At the offering the choir sang Handel's "Let Thy Hand Be Strengthened." We sang the hymn, "O Holy Spirit Enter In." The induction began with an anthem written especially for the occasion by Paul Karvonen, based on Psalm 89:20—"I Have Found David, My Servant, With Oil I Have Anointed Him."

Then came what was the most emotional moment in the service. Ruth Hammarberg came forward, bearing the bishop's cross that her husband had worn for more than eleven years. She placed it around my neck. I could feel both the joy and the burden that cross symbolized.

Werkström stood in disappointed silence as Marshall laid on hands.

I began my response by referring to the cross that had been placed on my neck:

> When I was first elected to office I thought of this cross
> as a beautiful ornament, as something to be worn with
> great honor. Now, after several months of preparation and
> some weeks in office, I see this cross from quite a different
> perspective. Certainly it is an honor to bear it. But it is also
> a much heavier cross than I thought. In fact, there are days
> when one might even wish one could be rid of it.

I went on to say that the cross was made bearable by two things. First, that the cross links us inseparably to the cross and resurrection of Jesus Christ. Second, that we never carry the cross alone. I bore it, I said, in the company of those who have promised to help me carry it, who will pray for me.

We recessed with "Guide Me, O Thou Great Jehovah."

A week later Marshall wrote to me, commenting on how impressed he was to see Christ Chapel filled for the service.

> It shows an interest in synod events and support for your
> leadership. Your remarks were very well presented both in
> the chapel and at the dinner. You spoke about fundamental
> things in a poised and frank manner that carried convic-
> tion and should win commitment.

Am I still a pastor?

For some folks, being elected synod bishop, especially if one seeks the office, leaves no regrets. For me, it wasn't quite that way. I had had a wonderful ministry at First Lutheran in St. Peter. I could have stayed on for many years.

Being a synod bishop is a very different experience, especially in the initial period. Yes, I was determined to handle my new responsibilities as a pastor to the congregations and pastors. But they seemed too distant in that first year or two. I would see them only on rare occasion. With more than three hundred and twenty congregations to visit, it would take years to make the rounds.

The first Christmas season, 1976, was especially distressing. Pastors and congregations were very busy in their own bailiwicks. After mid-November it seemed that no one was interested in seeing me. Though I always tried to reserve one Sunday a month to be with my family, attending church with them several Sundays in succession was wonderful. Yet sitting in the pew also had its drawbacks. I had been accustomed to being at the center of all the planning and activities, especially in that season of the year. Now I was on the outer edge of things. Am I still a pastor, I wondered?

What I learned through this experience was that it simply takes time to achieve a feeling of being a pastor when one is in an office such as that of a bishop. By the end of the second year, after numerous contacts with pastors in many settings, after getting to know some of the lay folks in leadership roles, and after visiting scores and scores of congregations, I began to feel like a pastor again.

The other lesson I learned is that one should be grateful for a relaxed schedule at holiday times. I actually began to look forward to the break.

As I got more and more involved in the lives of pastors and congregations, the sense of being a pastor was reinforced. Installations, anniversaries, conflicts between pastors and their congregations, the death of pastors and members of their families, the annual pastors' retreat at Madden's Resort at Brainerd, an annual gathering where I led the pastors in Bible study—these and many other contacts built a strong bond with almost every pastor and with most of the congregations over the eleven years I was bishop in Minnesota.

Having Corinne along on some of these occasions was always beneficial for both of us. It gave her a chance to engage with people around the synod. And, just as important, it was a time for deep conversation as we spent hours together sharing our thoughts and concerns. Our car became almost like a small mobile sanctuary.

It always helped, of course, if I got a report from a pastor that something I said on a visit to a congregation made a difference to someone. Though removed from the local scene, I realized that I was still a pastor in a larger arena.

I also urged pastors to learn to be candid with me whenever they had concerns about something I had said or done that bothered them. In the July 1981 "Update" I wrote to pastors that

> You can call me "Herb" and you can call me "Chilstrom" and you can call me "President" and you can call me "Bishop"—but please don't call me "Synod."
>
> As I read through [pastors' annual reports], I occasionally come across a comment aimed at some unhappiness related to "synod." As I reflect on the comment . . . it is clear that the writer really doesn't have the synod in mind but, rather, the bishop of the synod.
>
> My dear brothers and sisters, I have a name. And I ask you to use my name, even when you feel angry or upset with me because of something I have said or done that does not meet with your approval or that makes life difficult for you. Better yet, sit down with me and speak frankly about the differences we may have.

A few poignant memories and words of encouragement:

A couple of years after I took office Pastor Gary Langness wrote following my visit to his congregation in West St. Paul that

> One young man who has always come to church, but never too excited about anything, was turned on by your presentation. He listened closely and the words of your message spoke to him. Nothing miraculous, but the seeds have been planted and we have had a super meaningful conversation about what is important in life. Thanks for making a difference in his life!!

A pastor who was most adamantly and publicly opposed to any discussion of the homosexual issue came in for a visit. It was not our first exchange on his matter. I finally came to the conclusion that "me thinks thou protesteth too loudly." On one of those occasions I asked if he himself were gay. He looked stunned. After a moment he admitted that, yes, he had those tendencies. But he was certain that God would change him. I suggested that possibly he needed to accept himself as God had created him. Sometimes a pastor needs to be blunt.

Steven McKinley came to the Minnesota Synod when I was bishop. He went on to serve one of our larger congregations and then became known across the ELCA for his "Pastor Loci" series of articles in *Lutheran Partners* magazine. More than twenty-five years later he sent a note of appreciation:

> I don't want to be one of those guys who always believe that yesterday was better because it wasn't. But I do believe that the Minnesota Synod with you as our bishop was the best judicatory I was ever part of. Large and diverse, but also coherent and a place where all of us as pastors trusted our bishop and relied on the bishop and the bishop's staff for support and encouragement. When I was in real trouble at Grace in Andover you came out on notice of a few hours to meet with those who were my antagonists at the time and saved my bacon. It tells them something about how a real bishop worked. . . .
>
> I treasured you as bishop then and I will always think of you that way, though now I am working at thinking of you as friend as well!

A look at some excerpts from my 1980 journal gives a glimpse into what my life was like as pastor/synod president:

> Jan. 1—Last of three days at Lake Lida. Very beautiful— trees covered with heavy frost—a winter wonderland. Slept 11 hours on Mon night.

Jan. 2—Went to see Roy Lund. Still in coma. Pessimistic that he can make it.

Jan. 3—Session with pastor and three members from (St. Paul area) congregation. He's very bright—but very authoritarian & in my judgment, paranoid. His detractors will no doubt leave & go to other churches, as has been the case for years.

Jan. 4—In office all morning. Seems there is no end of phone calls to make to various people about one troubled situation or another. Went to see Roy Lund. Outlook not good.

Jan. 5—Staff retreat at Shores of St. Andrew. [Sem prof] and wife leaders. Accent on growth as spiritual persons. Not outstanding, but good. Found the wife to be a bit overbearing at times. Into Willmar for dinner and back for games.

Jan. 6—Reviewed past three and one-half years and projected our priorities for the future. I outlined five areas as highest priority: Word & Witness program; Stewardship; World missions; Urban & rural strategies; Support for ordained and lay professionals.

In July 1982 I lectured at the St. Olaf College Summer Theological Conference. My thesis focused on the seven crises that pastors have to deal with most commonly: doubt about one's call; marital and family stress; the two-career family; insufficient gifts for ministry; stress among staff personnel; inability to deal with strife in the congregation; poor administration. Bill Thorkelson, writing for the *Sun* newspapers titled his press release on my lecture, "He's a pastor to pastors."

I didn't think what I said was all that noteworthy. Nevertheless, it seemed to strike a responsive chord and took wings. It made *The Lutheran* magazine. *Interchange,* a publication of the Lutheran Council in the U.S.A, reported on it in December 1982. Following the event I had a postcard from Carroll Hinderlie, former director at Holden Village and a national staff person for the ALC. "All pastors agreed," he wrote, "the most healing sessions were yours. There is a special KARISMA from a bishop who is a bishop. As Lilje used to say, not many bishops are bishops! Thanks for accepting that calling, no matter how lonely, and making it a ministry of healing for many." Needless to say, notes like that from people of Hinderlie's stature were most encouraging. It assured me that one *can* be both bishop and pastor.

Like many pastors I could be sharp-tongued at times. One thing that irritated me was that some pastors failed to send me their annual reports. In the April 1985 "Update" I castigated them.

> There are several score inept, disorganized, and careless pastors out there who have failed to send in their "Confidential to the Bishop" report for 1984. If you are one of these "chosen ones" and have a different excuse, please let me know what it is.

Realizing that I had come on much too strong, I apologized in the next "Update."

Gleaning these reflections and comments and including a sampling of them in my autobiography makes me feel a tad embarrassed. I do so in the hope that they will accent the importance of the pastoral role of a bishop and convey to others how much a person in that role needs encouragement from those he or she serves.

The Conference of Bishops

I looked forward to my first meeting with the other thirty-two synod bishops of the LCA. It was held before I officially took office. I was acutely aware of being the youngest among them. Being head of what was then the second largest synod did not impress them—or me. I needed to learn everything I could from the veterans in the circle.

At one session I sat next to Herman W. Cauble, president of the South Carolina Synod. He had been in office for many years, I was certain he would have some sage advice. When I asked him how one does this job, he, like Segerhammar, was disarmingly straight-forward. "Don't worry, Herb. As soon as you take office someone will bring a pile of mail to your desk and the phone will start ringing. From then on you won't wonder what to do." I would soon learn that there was much wisdom in those words.

At that same meeting the bishops discussed program budgeting. This was a method of setting a budget by focusing on program priorities of the church, in contrast to the line item budget configuration that identified budget figures according to various administrative units of the church. I found the latter much easier to comprehend.

During discussion of the budget I spoke for the first time. As I expressed my reservations about program budgeting I realized that a deathly silence was settling over the room. What I didn't know, and what everyone else knew, was that program budgeting was being promoted by LCA President Marshall at every level of the national church organization. I felt myself flushing with embarrassment and quickly concluded my remarks. Silence prevailed until Marshall looked over the heads of the group and to the back wall. Then in measured tones he said, "Well, Herb, some people *just don't understand.*" Though we eventually became good friends, that encounter with Marshall was totally disquieting for me. I didn't speak up again for several meetings, and then only when I was certain I knew all my ducks were in order.

What I learned from that experience about Marshall was that he was ambiguous about authority in the church. He eschewed church structures that were in any way authoritarian. Yet he was personally quite autocratic, finding it difficult to brook disagreement with his views.

Over the next eleven years I would come to treasure the meetings with the other synod bishops. No matter how much I valued my own assistants, it was here with other bishops that I met those who really understood what it was like to have the last buck stop at my desk. Here I found colleagues who could listen with complete understanding and here I could bare my soul.

There were geographical sub-groups within the conference. I was part of the Great Lakes contingent—bishops whose synods touched on one of the Great Lakes—Robert Wilch of Wisconsin, Howard Christensen of Michigan, Kenneth Sauer of Ohio, Walter Wick of Indiana/Kentucky, and Paul Erickson of Illinois. In that group Erickson became a special friend and confidant. As some of these left office and others took their place that spirit continued.

Is there no end to meetings?

Sitting through meeting after meeting was part of my lot as a bishop. Yes, there were more than enough of them in the parish. But that was nothing like the seemingly endless meetings a bishop was expected to attend. And it was a pattern that I would have to deal with for almost twenty years.

I did fairly well with them most of the time. Some, in fact, were quite fascinating, especially when a process developed during a meeting resulted in a productive new initiative.

Having said that, many meetings were almost impossible to tolerate. I confess that I found ways to avoid boredom in those confined settings. Sometimes it was by keeping a crossword puzzle inside a folder and working on it clandestinely when others did not notice. At other times I faked listening while doing something more interesting. A letter to two of my sisters in early 1983 illustrates my point:

> This is being written during a meeting. The lecturer sees me writing. He thinks I am taking notes on his brilliant comments. He thinks I am intensely interested in what he is saying because every now and then I look at him. He is wrong.

I went on: *(Pause. I must look at the speaker intelligently for two minutes.)*

> The lecturer is now winding down. He thinks I have a detailed outline of what he has said. He thinks I will go around talking about what a brilliant talk he gave. He is wrong. I'm surely glad to know that no one does this to me!

Growth in membership and in stewardship

In contrast to the rest of the LCA, the Minnesota Synod continued to grow in numbers. Much of that growth came in the new congregations in the greater Twin Cities area. I reminded the 1979 convention, however, that

> Contrary to what some may think, a new Lutheran mission does not get off to such an impressive start only because we have a large pool of Lutheran prospects. In fact, more than half of the new members at the time of organization are of non-Lutheran background ("Facing Forward," page 95).

Between 1962 and 1980 the LCA grew by some eighty-five thousand members. Forty-one thousand of that growth, almost half, occurred in the Minnesota Synod.

I attribute much of the credit for that growth to Dr. Thomas Wersell, former Minnesota Synod staff member, and Dr. Frederick Marks, a regional staff person for the LCA's Division for Mission in North America. Wersell chose good sites for planting new mission congregations. Marks did the same. Marks not only got the mission congregations off to a good start but also formed a close bond with our synod staff and the pastors in those new settings. I often said that Marks was like another member of our staff.

Stewardship was another matter. I didn't realize until I took office that the Minnesota Synod had one of the poorest per capita giving records of all of the thirty-three synods in its support of the churchwide mission of the LCA. I was determined to change that pattern. I give Ronald Peterson major credit for bringing change.

Over the years I was in office the synod moved up to the middle range of support for that work, a major accomplishment for a synod as large as ours. In some years our income from congregations increased by anywhere from six to nearly ten percent per year. In my first four years in office our support for the LCA mission increased by more than twenty percent. Yet in spite of that improvement, I was never satisfied with our record.

Pastoral letters

It became my custom to write occasional "pastoral letters" to the ordained ministers in the synod. The pastors seemed to appreciate my efforts. John Kendall, an ordained pastor who served as president of Gustavus Adolphus College, wrote that he was

> . . . very happy to have a bishop who takes the time to carefully review issues . . . and then write papers on them. I don't believe this is a common occurrence and I also know how difficult it is to find the time for such activity. You are to be commended.

Some of the subjects I addressed:

1976—Evangelism

At the time I was moving to Minneapolis in the fall of 1976 the LCA was engaged in a program called Evangelical Outreach. That brought an invitation to lecture at a workshop in Chicago in September. The timing could not have been worse, given the complete overhaul of the synod office and staff. Yet it was a choice opportunity for me to share my convictions about evangelism.

Once more I was indebted to my teaching days at Luther College. There I had come to understand more fully the role of the Holy Spirit in the life of the church and especially in our evangelism efforts. I pointed out the high place Martin Luther gave to the work of the Spirit in the life of the church. I pointed to our tendency in the church to work for results rather than to depend on the Spirit to take our witness and work and give them life in the hearts of those who hear it. "The Lutheran church," I declared, "is not the place to count stereotyped 'decisions for Christ.' I don't believe the Spirit works in ways that can be so neatly catalogued." I referred to those places where Paul speaks of the "mystery" of our relationship with Christ. "Your encounter with God is *your* encounter," I said.

> It is the Spirit's special gift to you. It may come as a dramatic experience, or it may come as a "still, small voice." In either case, we cannot describe adequately what has happened. We can only affirm that at the deepest level of life, Spirit has touched spirit and life is new. . . .

If we can accept this good news, then witnessing and evangelism are simply letting the good news flow through us. I concluded by stating that whenever we speak about "making a decision for Christ," it must be seen in terms of:

> . . . our surrender to God's decision for us. It is not a once and for all decision. Rather, it is a matter of many decisions in the course of a lifetime. In fact, we can even think of it in terms of the daily decision and renewal that Luther speaks of in the explanation of the Fifth Petition of the Lord's Prayer.

Later in the fall I sent my lecture to the pastors of the synod as a pastoral letter. It would be the first of many such letters to them on a variety of subjects.

1977—The ordained ministry

A request from the North Minneapolis District pastors to discuss ordained ministry gave me the occasion to develop this letter. I accented what I considered to be the central questions:

- Is the church for the ministry or is the ministry for the church? I pointed to Christ as the model, the one who came ". . . not to be served, but to serve. . . ." The Suffering Servant is the motif that best describes what ministry should be. I cited the words of Luther: "My office is merely a service which I am to give to everyone freely and gratuitously, nor should I seek from it either money or goods, either honor or anything else." This does not free a congregation of its obligation to support its pastor. Again I cited Luther: ". . . if I do this service, it, in turn, is your obligation to support me. For since I am to serve you . . . I cannot at the same time attend to earning my support."

• Is the ordained ministry an *order* or an *office*? Here churches go in two directions—Episcopal or congregational. In the first group ordained ministers are part of an *order*, ordained for life. They are the channels through which Christ, the Head of the church, does his work. For most Protestants, including Lutherans, ministry is an *office,* with the accent on the *function* of the minister. In these churches, all are ministers; only their function differs. The source of one's call to the office is two-fold: the minister's own sense that God has called one and the call from a gathering of believers to serve them.

I cautioned the readers to remember that the line is sometimes drawn too sharply between these two traditions. Alluding to changes in the Roman Catholic Church resulting from Vatican II, I noted that even in that hierarchical church there was now a more collegial spirit. (And, of course, in a debate that came almost two decades later when Lutherans and Episcopalians affirmed "Called to Common Mission" [CCM], that debate became very complex and intense.) In the end, as Luther taught, the authority rests not in the office, but in the Word of God. I suggested that on this question even the Confessions of the Lutheran church were somewhat ambiguous and that we would need to live with some lack of absolute clarity. (Our discussions since then bear witness to what I wrote.)

• What happened when the role of the pastor is in jeopardy because of dissention or division in a congregation? It is assumed that the bishop's role is to be pastor to pastors. But the constitution of the synod also underscores the bishop's responsibility to the laity of the congregations. How can one do both? "At no point," I suggested, "is [the synod president] more vulnerable for criticism and at no point is he more likely to make mistakes." No president/bishop, I averred, has "immaculate perception." One must work for reconciliation. If that fails, the wisdom of a larger group, an investigative committee, is the next step. And in all such situations, due process must be available to an accused ordained minister.

I closed with a quotation from Swedish Bishop Bo Giertz's book *The Hammer of God* in which a pastor is in prayer:

> For himself, he prayed that he might be given grace to be
> a true pastor, himself saved for Christ's sake, rooted in the
> old message, and equipped to care for souls and one rightly
> dividing the unadulterated Word of God. Finally, he prayed
> for his own Church, as one prays for a beloved mother. He
> prayed that she might always be truly apostolic, built on
> the age-long foundation, and always just as vigorous and
> youthful, filled with the renewing impulses of the life.

1978—The church and homosexuality

In 1974 the city of St. Paul passed an amendment to its human rights ordinance banning discrimination against homosexual persons in housing, jobs, education, and public accommodations. A petition drive early in 1978 called for repeal of that action. I was asked to give my opinion. After checking with ALC Bishop Elmo Agrimson and Roman Catholic Archbishop John Roach and learning that they planned to oppose any repeal, I decided to join them. Six leaders of Protestant churches in Minnesota—Lutheran, Episcopal, Methodist, American Baptist, and UCC—joined in issuing a statement opposing repeal of the ordinance.

I wrote to our LCA pastors in St. Paul stating that giving equal rights to homosexual persons was

. . . consistent with the support of our church for the basic rights of all people. We do not pretend to understand the complexities of homosexuality. While as a church we reject the practice of homosexuality in sexual relations, we recognize the gay person as one who, like all others, needs the full ministry of the church.

I hoped that my letter would be the end of my involvement in the issue. What I could not have known at that moment was that this was only the first very small trickle of what would become a wide stream in my ministry for the next several decades.

Shortly after my letter was released I got a call from a young gay man inviting Corinne and me to meet with him and other gay men in St. Paul. I was not eager to go. But when he kept asking for an open date I realized I had no excuse. These were members of our churches. I was their bishop.

The meeting was held at a large, elegant older home on Summit Avenue in St. Paul. There were about twenty in the group. They were as nervous as we were. In the course of the evening they shared stories that we have heard hundreds of times since then:

No, they had not chosen to be gay; it was simply who they were.

No, they had not been abused as young boys; nor did they have domineering mothers.

Yes, some had tried marriage as a "cure" for their homosexuality. It had not worked. Not only did it leave them feeling miserable; they felt they had also done damage to their straight marriage partners.

Yes, they had tried reparative therapy, spending thousands of dollars on counseling. It had not worked.

Yes, they loved our Lord as much as we did. Yes, they wanted to be accepted as full believing brothers-in-Christ in our churches.

It was, to say the least, a life-changing evening for Corinne and me.

Several days later I got a call from a woman in Minneapolis. Having heard about our St. Paul meeting, she asked if I would spend some time with a group of both men and women who were homosexual. Now I felt a bit more comfortable and was eager to chat with them.

When they walked into the room I was stunned. Among them was David Lein. I had known David since he was four years old. His father had been one of my mentors, a man I respected highly as an ideal parish pastor. This was not supposed to happen. Children brought up in a home like that could not turn out to be gay. Or so I had thought. I learned that David had been living in a loving and committed relationship for many years and that he and his partner were active members of one of our LCA congregations.

I was beginning to realize that the issue had repercussions far beyond simple human rights. This was a question the church was going to have to deal with from the standpoint of the Bible and Christian ethics as well.

In the meantime, the voters in St. Paul encouraged by such luminaries as the popular singer Anita Bryant, did in fact repeal the amendment to their human rights ordinance. Now the community was free again to discriminate against homosexual persons.

This action was a wake-up call for those concerned about preserving fundamental rights for gay and lesbian persons. No less than fourteen resolutions came to our synod convention when we met at St. Peter in early June. In what the *Minneapolis Star Tribune* reported as "an unusual move," I left the presiding chair and read a prepared statement to the convention before debate on any of the resolutions ensued. I expressed my

> . . . adamant opposition to immorality of any kind, be it heterosexual or homosexual in nature. I firmly support

legislation that protects us and our children from perversion of any kind.

I went on to forewarn gay persons not to use their civil rights ". . . to flaunt a form of sexual practice that our LCA has declared unacceptable." I added, however, that

> . . . there is an even greater and far more insidious danger. It is the danger inherent in the attitude of a majority to suppress the rights of a minority. It becomes even more dangerous when it is done in what I feel is a strident and unevangelical use of the Scripture.

I concluded by stating that I was in the process of developing a "lengthy statement" on the subject that would be released later in the year.

The resolution that prevailed at the convention named the St. Paul vote an injustice and called on state and city governments to ". . . take measures to assure that the human rights of all people are protected. . . ." The resolution, no doubt following the lead I had set in my opening statement, went on to make a careful distinction between rights and behavior. It read: "In supporting the civil and human rights of homosexual persons, we are not condoning the life style of such persons."

Now there was no turning back. I had taken a bold step into an arena that would consume a good deal of my time and effort over the coming years. And in those years I was destined to change my views in several critical areas of the issue.

The pastoral letter that appeared in the fall of 1978 addressed a number of what I considered crucial issues in the discussion:

What does the Bible say on the subject?

Is our sexual orientation given or chosen?

What is the stance of our church?

What behavior is to be expected of homosexual persons in the church?

Can we ordain gay persons?

I urged congregations to give pastoral care to gay and lesbian persons. I stated that I did not think we should ordain persons in same-gender relationships.

Then I added a comment I would live to regret: "Let us hate the sin, but love the sinner." That was the sentence that was remembered more than any other. And it is the sentence I came to wish I could forever delete from that paper.

What then, I asked, should we say to one who insists that being homosexual is not a choice? Here I took an interesting tack. I wrote that I had come to the conclusion that

> . . . it may not be wrong for some individuals to live together in a covenant of fidelity between two persons. Much as some would want to dwell on the specific sexual activity of such persons, we would rather focus on the LCA statement's insistence that the private lives of consenting adults—heterosexual and homosexual—are not to be the object of our intrusion.

As for ordination of such persons, I came down on the side of the position reinforced by the LCA, namely, that "Only those homosexual persons who maintain a celibate life may be ordained, assuming they qualify on all other grounds." I pleaded for allowance for differences of opinion in the church while our discussions were proceeding.

The letter reflected where I was at the time. And though I now look back and see many areas where I have changed my mind, at the time I was far out in front of most church leaders.

Responses to the letter were mostly positive.

Paul Lindberg, who had been one of my seminary professors and then my assistant at St. Peter, called it ". . . one of the fairest studies

I have seen yet. You have not spared the truth by minimizing the issue as so many are doing today. . . . You have not cheapened the office of the ministry or thrown it wide open to avowed practices that defy our traditional and Scriptural positions."

Martin Carlson, a former officer of the LCA who had been involved in arranging treatment programs for homosexual pastors, predicted that I would get come flak on the "letter," but urged me to "Hang in there. Your position seems to be absolutely sound."

Paul Knutson, chaplain at Luther Seminary in St. Paul, said he found the "letter . . . helpful in my work as I'm trying to formulate my thoughts on this subject."

Robert Roth, professor of systematic theology at Luther Seminary, said, "This is a scholarly piece of work, which is enough to commend it, but in addition you have combined bold courage with sound and compassionate judgment. I will be able to use this treatise in my course on Christian ethics."

1979 and 1981—Abortion
When the Bethesda Lutheran Medical Center Board approved a policy on abortion that I felt was too restrictive I protested to Gustav Larson, a prominent attorney who chaired the board.

> This matter is all the more distressing to me because of the conservative stance I take regarding abortion. I believe life must be guarded with utmost care. But I recognize that even a conservative person cannot avoid difficult decisions. If our present policy stands, it may mean that one day a young girl, made pregnant by her father or an older brother, will appear at Bethesda. Too frightened to tell her story sooner, she may be several weeks pregnant. She will have to be told, "I'm sorry, you'll have to go over to Ramsey County Hospital. We don't deal with people like you at a church hospital." Let this letter be my strong protest to a policy I believe is contrary to the theology and practice of the church I serve.

In the fall of 1981 George Hulstrand, a well-known LCA layman and prominent attorney from Willmar, Minnesota, wrote a
strident letter to most of the LCA and ALC pastors in Minnesota
criticizing the churches for failing to address the issue of abortion. His thinly veiled reference to "little guidance from the top"
was clearly aimed at me.

I responded to Hulstrand with an "open letter" to the pastors and
lay leaders of the synod. I reminded him that both the LCA and
the ALC had adopted social statements on abortion and that I had
little to add. I wrote forthrightly about my personal stance, framing
it in the context of my experience as one who had a brother who
is developmentally disabled and three adopted children. I affirmed
their right to life, giving thanks they had not been denied this gift
because of physical impairment or conception "out of wedlock."
I went on to state that I saw only three circumstances that could
justify abortion: rape, incest, or the health and life of the mother.

Having said that, I reminded Hulstrand that the issue is rooted
in the tension between belief and certainty.

> No matter how convincing your case may be, let's face it,
> George, neither you nor I *know* when human life begins.
> We *believe* it begins with the single cell of a fertilized egg.
> But we don't *know*. And neither does anyone else. This is
> what scares me about strident pro-lifers. They don't *know*
> either. Yet, they want to base public law, even a constitu-
> tional amendment, on the unproved belief that human life
> begins at conception. I, for one, will continue to hold to a
> conservative position, urging others to do the same. But
> I will not insist that other responsible and conscientious
> Christians must come out exactly where I do.

I took some heat for what some regarded as a "pro-choice"
stance. Yet even Richard John Neuhaus commended me for what I
had written:

To be sure, when it comes to public policy, Chilstrom collapses into a pro-choice, I-don't-want-to-impose-my-values position. But he does raise some of the agonizing moral questions for *Christians and for the Church*. He does urge a more honest and no doubt painful reexamination of these questions by the LCA. That is no little contribution and for that, it seems to us, he should be commended (*Forum Letter*, April 30, 1982).

Other social, theological, and ethical issues
Some may have thought that I was so deeply enmeshed in the sexuality issues that I gave little thought to other equally important social, theological, and ethical questions. That was hardly the case.

Baby formula
I supported the Nestle boycott in 1979, aimed at encouraging people to stop that company's attempts to sell its baby formula in third world countries.

Holy Communion for younger believers
Questions about giving the Sacrament of Holy Communion to young children, including infants, surfaced when Professor Eric Gritsch from Gettysburg Seminary decided to do so in early 1970. I sided with him, believing that our theology of the sacraments gave us good reason to do so. In a letter to me Gritsch expressed his hope that the phrase "Thus infant communion is precluded" would be deleted from church statements on communion practices.

The charismatic movement
It was gaining strength across the country and in some corners of the synod. I had to deal with it gently. I found some elements of the movement wholesome for the church. But I also had reservations.

Fundamentalism
In 1979 I voiced public concern over the inroads of fundamentalism in our LCA congregations. *The Lutheran* magazine ran

a major news story on a statement I had released on the issue. I pointed to three sources for the invasion of this alien theology into our churches: the impact of the electronic church; our failure to teach our adult members about our faith tradition; our reluctance to confront fundamentalism for fear of "rocking the boat." Further I said, ". . . changing the theological climate of a congregation is not the work of a day or two . . . we must be at it constantly, especially in an age when our people are bombarded with a theology at odds with our own traditions. For a refreshing renewal of your faith, may I suggest that you dust off your old catechism and use it as a resource for personal, family, and congregational renewal" (3/7/79).

The ordination of women

I became an advocate for the rights of women, including ordination of women. Though it has been approved for more than a decade, many still wondered if the churches had made a proper decision. At a forum at the 1982 LCA convention in Louisville I reviewed my journey. The convention summary reported on my comments:

> If he had been forced 20 years ago to state his attitude
> toward women entering the ministry . . . even an unambiguous answer could scarcely have masked his negativity. This
> was changed when he became a synod president, where he
> found it necessary to place women in congregations. This
> he found rewarding . . . now . . . he and his wife are looking
> forward to her joining the ranks of the clergy.

Peacemaking

On several occasions I addressed the issue of peacemaking. In the late 1970s I supported a ceasefire in Lebanon. On another occasion I wrote to the synod pastors that "basic and common among us must be our First Article affirmation that this is God's world and that (God) made us responsible caretakers of it." I went on to

cite approvingly the position of Mikko Juva, head of the Church of
Finland, who distinguished between "peace work" and pacifism. I
suggested that

> . . . it is possible to work for the reduction of arms produc-
> tion and the reduction of tensions in the world without
> withdrawing from the real world where nations will always
> justify some degree of military defense. I side with those
> who will work for reasonable military defense in a climate
> of open communication between East and West. I urge all
> of you to join me in a search for any and all ways in which
> we can contribute to a more peaceful world. Do we have a
> choice? ("Update," August 1981).

Just prior to Christmas 1981 I spearheaded an effort to coordinate *a plea for peace* that was signed by more than twenty judica-
tory leaders in Minnesota, ranging from all LCA and ALC bishops
to Roman Catholic, Lutheran Brethren, Seventh Day Adventist, and
many more. The plea called for citizens to write to President Reagan and those in congress, urging them to support disarmament,
and particularly that of nuclear weapons.

When the U.S. Roman Catholic bishops issued a pastoral letter on the use of nuclear weapons, calling it immoral, I supported
them, pointing out that in areas such as abortion and support for
private schools we had differences, but on this issue we were of one
mind (*Minneapolis Star Tribune,* 11/14/82).

At the 1982 LCA convention in Louisville I was asked to speak
in support of the church's global mission study document on our
responsibility as peacemakers. The U.S. was making a dramatic
upgrade in its stockpile of nuclear weapons. I spoke of three things
the church must do:

> 1. Pray. "Is there a Christian church anywhere in the world
> where prayers for peace should not be part of every wor-
> ship experience?"

2. Link with other Christian churches and other world religions in advocating for peace. "Scripture assures us that 'God has not left himself without witnesses anywhere in the world.' Is this not sufficient basis for us to band together with all persons of good will who want to be peacemakers?"

3. Look especially at our own country where we are spending an increasing amount of our dwindling resources "beating plowshares into swords."

Energy conservation

In November 1982 I wrote a lengthy pastoral letter regarding the energy crisis. With advice from a lay leader who had a sense of calling to aid churches in this regard, I suggested numerous steps every church could take to conserve energy and help in the preservation of the environment.

The lottery

In 1984 I voiced opposition to the establishment of a lottery in Minnesota, even though surveys showed that seventy percent of Minnesotans favored it. In that same year I recommended to pastors that they speak out against the establishment of a state lottery.

Agriculture

In 1985 I joined ten other Lutheran and Roman Catholic bishops in Minnesota to urge Congress to effect farm legislation that would ". . . guarantee a just price, promote protection of the land and regenerative agriculture, and strongly support more, not fewer, farmers on the land."

Confidentiality

Acknowledging that it is a complex question, I addressed a major letter to the pastors of the synod on the subject in March 1978. I concluded that the only alternative was to exercise careful discretion, recognizing that it was important for the church to keep sacred the confessional office, yet also distinguishing that there may be times—threats of murder, suicide, abuse—when a pastor may have to make an exception to the rule.

The Iran-Contra Affair

In 1986 I wrote to Minnesota Republican Senator Rudy Boschwitz expressing my disagreement with our nation's policy in Central America. In a strongly worded handwritten response Boschwitz castigated me for comparing our involvement with the actions of Russians, Libyans, and Cubans in other parts of the globe. "History," he wrote, "is unfortunately a recitation of tyranny emboldened by the inaction of responsible and free societies."

In this instance Boschwitz would be proven wrong. As the seamy side of the affair began to come to light later that year I wrote to Boschwitz again. This time I got no response from him.

The other Minnesota Republican senator, David Durenberger, questioned our involvement. In a letter I thanked him for upholding the system of checks and balances that made it possible for Congress to investigate the CIA's clandestine operations in Central America.

After I became presiding bishop and traveled to Central America I saw with my own eyes the mistake our country had made in its support of the tyranny of the Contras.

HIV/AIDS

As we moved through the decade of the 1980s the AIDS pandemic was coming to the attention of the world. At first it was thought that this was a plague on the homosexual community. Before long, however, it became clear that this was common to persons of every sexual orientation. In April 1987, just prior to the merger, I initiated an effort on the part of LCA, ALC, and AELC bishops in Minnesota in issuing a position statement. It began with a reminder to the readers that the traditional sexual mores of the church made most sense.

> What seemed so passé, so mundane, so dull to so many,
> a commitment of trust to one other person, now emerges
> again not only as the ideal, but as an absolute necessity.

On that basis, we suggested, we could wash our hands of any concern over the issue, looking at the victims as deserving of their fate. In the spirit of Christ, however, the church can never react in that way. Our statement said, "We need not add to (victims') feelings of condemnation. Instead, because of a loving Christ who gave his life that undeserving sinners (which includes all of us) might be made whole, we too should do everything to bring wholeness to others."

We outlined several ways to address the situation:

We should uphold the sanctity and joy of monogamy.

We must take responsibility for providing sex education to our youth.

We should not be naïve. Even members of our churches do not necessarily adhere to our sexual behavior ideals. "It is in the interest of the entire community to make certain that these persons have the information needed to keep AIDS from spreading."

We also affirmed the advice of the U.S. Surgeon General, urging the use of condoms by those who chose to be sexually active.

We added that we should remind people that AIDS is also spread through means other than genital sex, such as blood transfusions and legitimate sexual contact with someone who may have AIDS.

The statement concluded with a plea for compassion. "When the story of these times is written, the truest saints will undoubtedly be those who, like Jesus, dared to touch the untouchables."

The thread that links all the issues

In all of the matters I've mentioned—the pastoral letters and statements on other issues—it seemed natural for me to do so. It never occurred to me that a bishop would not confront these things. Yes, it got me into hot water at times. Pastors and laity who did not like the church to be dabbling in controversial questions got upset with me and reacted in anger. But I persisted because I thought it right.

In a lecture at the Lutheran School of Theology at Chicago in May 1984 I wrestled with the question of why it seems that on social issues clergy and laity are often at odds. Rather than deplore this gap, I suggested that we should actually expect it.

> If the pastor is faithful in the study of Scripture; if the pastor is in tune with the world with its war, poverty, and prejudice; if the pastor has a deep sense of being called for a life of servanthood, is it not inevitable that there will be a gap?

> The pastor has a prophetic calling. As she or he probes the depth of the biblical material, it is inevitable that one will find oneself going to the pulpit or podium with a word that will not necessarily be received with receptive hearts and minds by the hearers.

In the midst of these kinds of conflict it was reassuring to receive affirming letters such as the one that came from Joseph Wagner, assistant executive director of the LCA Division for Professional Leadership and later the executive director for the ELCA Division for Ministry.

> Minnesota is a healthy and upbeat synod and I believe much of the reason for that is related to the style in which you provide leadership. It is a style that is both strong and authentic, but at the same time you are willing to explore new possibilities and even very sensitive issues in a very public way and to share your struggles with your pastors. First, they see that you are willing to struggle with emerging and unclear

matters—the same sorts of struggles they engage in. Second, they see that you are able and willing to do this in a public arena, sharing some of your uncertainties and vulnerabilities. Third, they share with you in your struggles and observe that you are listening and learning and willing to change a position.

A taste of the international church

Europe

In 1977 I applied for and was chosen to attend an interchurch dialogue for American pastors and church leaders and spouses with a counterpart group from Germany. The event was held near Munich. The purpose was to share ideas and information about our respective churches.

My major assignment was to deliver a paper on "An Overview of American Lutheranism." Again my experience at Luther College proved invaluable. I traced the history of the Lutheran church in the United States, beginning with the early colonies of Dutch, Swedish, and German Lutherans on the eastern seaboard and following the story to the present day. The Germans took delight in my quotations from Henry Muhlenberg's journal where that early leader writes derisively about the character of the immigrants from Germany:

> It is almost impossible to describe how few good and how many exceptionally godless, wicked people have come into this country every year. The whole country is being flooded with ordinary, extraordinary, and unprecedented wickedness and crimes. Surely the rod of God cannot be spared much longer. Our old residents are mere stupid children in sin when compared with the new arrivals! Oh, what a fearful thing it is to have so many thousands of unruly and brazen sinners come into this free air and unfenced country!

I concluded the paper with a rather dim view of the current cooperative situation in the Lutheran churches in the United States. I pictured the Lutheran Church—Missouri Synod as a church body in disarray. As for the Lutheran Church in America and the American Lutheran Church, I suggested:

> One might think that this would be a time for them to ignore the Missouri Synod and proceed with haste to form a new Lutheran church. For reasons about which we can only speculate, that is not the case. Each is looking at the other and saying quite politely, "I love you. Someday I may even marry you. But not yet."

That would change, of course, in the next few years as those two churches moved toward merger.

The Far East

In the spring of 1981 Corinne and I traveled to the Far East to visit missionaries who had a connection with the Minnesota Synod. Our travel companions were Del and Betty Anderson. Del, a classmate from seminary, was then secretary for Asia for the LCA Division for Global Mission. We started in Hokkaido in the north of Japan, stopped for several days at Tokyo and Kumomoto, then on to Taiwan, Hong Kong, Malaysia, and Indonesia.

Possibly the most sobering moment in the trip was our time in Nagasaki, site of the atomic bomb holocaust near the end of World War II. In my travel journal I wrote:

> I came away from this experience with a sick feeling in the pit of my stomach. Among many thoughts that race through my mind are two that predominate. First, there is the absolutely distressful thought that the bomb dropped on Nagasaki was only a minor explosion compared to the awesome nuclear weapons that are poised for an unthinkable holocaust. How can we go on building ever more powerful weapons? Second, there comes an even deeper and

more determined conviction that I must do everything I can to bring peace and understanding to that corner of the world, however small, where I may have some influence.

This was a time when the United States was trying to persuade Japan to begin rebuilding its military forces. To a person, both clergy and lay, the Japanese churches resisted that idea. They had the feeling that the United States was trying to make them a buffer between our country and the Soviet Union.

A visit to a refugee camp for the Vietnamese in Hong Kong evoked similar convictions.

> The tragedy of Vietnam is before our eyes. As with all wars, everyone has lost—especially those who can do least to defend themselves.

At our last stop in Indonesia it was fitting that Corinne and I should be called forward for a special gift.

> Words of welcome are spoken by the president of the congregation, an elderly man with distinguishing strands of grey hair, a handsome mustache, and high cheekbones. He unveils a beautiful handwoven ulos, a shawl-like cloth, which he wraps around Corinne and me as a welcome and for good wishes for safety, peace, and good health. Then, on signal from this man, the congregation shouts, *"Huras, Huras, Huras."* Huras is an abbreviated phrase that means, "May your body and soul be kept together and may your spirit always be warm."

> The leader of the congregation invites everyone to come forward to shake our hand. I notice that each one touches their hand to their breast after shaking hands with us. I leaned that it is the Batak custom by which the person receives to himself or herself the spirit of the one with whom they have shaken hands.

I summarized the impact of the trip with these words:

One thing that stands out more clearly than ever is that the gospel really does have power and that the Holy Spirit continues to build the church. We have met some of the people God has been using—missionaries and their families, and leaders in the churches in the Far East—and we thank God for each of them!

President of the Lutheran Church in America?

Early in 1978 Dr. Robert Marshall shocked the LCA by announcing that he was resigning from office, effective at the forthcoming churchwide convention in Chicago in late July. He was still in his late 50s. Everyone, apparently including his wife Alice, was caught by surprise. To this day no one knows for certain what precipitated his action. Was it asthma? Not likely, since he had been troubled with that for many years and it didn't seem to hamper his work. When I visited Marshall in Allentown, Pennsylvania, more than twenty-five years after his resignation, I left the door open for him to share his reasoning. He remained taciturn.

Speculation about Marshall's successor ran wild. In the *Forum Letter*, an independent publication of the American Lutheran Publicity Bureau (ALPB), editor Richard John Neuhaus opined that it would come down to two persons, H. George Anderson and Franklin D. Fry, ". . . with Anderson having the edge." As we will see—and as was often the case with Neuhaus' speculations over the years—he was half right. Going on to note that Anderson would not likely stand for election, Neuhaus suggested that if Anderson withdrew and no other strong candidate became apparent, the convention might give the nod to James R. Crumley, Jr. Then he added what was for me a rather unsettling word: ". . . some knowing types suggest we keep an eye on Herbert Chilstrom, president of the Minnesota Synod."

Because it was one of the most fascinating elections I have ever witnessed, I want to lay it out in some detail.

I came to the convention with no clue as to what might happen. As was my pattern in every election, I asked no one to vote for me or promote my candidacy. I was open to whatever might happen. On the first ballot seventy names emerged. The top vote getters were:

H. George Anderson	244
William Lazareth	48
Kenneth Sauer	38
Herbert Chilstrom	37
James Crumley	29
Howard McCarney	27
Reuben Swanson	25

It was clear that H. George Anderson could have been easily elected on the next ballot. As some had speculated, Anderson went to the microphone immediately after the vote was announced and withdrew his name from consideration. He gave as his reason for withdrawal that he felt called to his current responsibilities. I encountered George in the hall a bit later and expressed my disappointment that he had withdrawn and then added, "You have just made my life more difficult."

The report on the second ballot stunned me. I was at the top of the list:

Herbert Chilstrom	136
William Lazareth	107
H. George Anderson	92
James Crumley	87

I was nervous. Having had only two years experience as bishop in Minnesota, I felt totally unprepared for this office.

Maybe I too should have withdrawn. Yet my understanding of call to ministry, wherever it leads, kept me from stepping aside. I remember attending the early morning Eucharist with Corinne the next day and praying earnestly that God's will would be evident to the delegates that day.

On the third ballot Lazareth emerged as the top candidate.

Now I breathed a bit easier. I could not imagine, given the broad churchwide experience of the other finalists, that I would survive another vote.

On the next ballot Lazareth extended his lead, but I was still running strong:

William Lazareth	214
Herbert Chilstrom	160
James Crumley	158

Now I was certain I was out of the running. Given Lazareth's lead and his stature in the church, it seemed safe to assume he would be elected.

What happened on the fifth ballot was fascinating. All three of us picked up some support: But the vote also eliminated me. The "Summary of the 9th Biennial Convention" noted: "Immediately, members of [Chilstrom's] synodical delegation presented him and his wife with flowers signed, 'Welcome back to the Minnesota Synod!'"

Now the big question was where "my" votes would go, to Lazareth or to Crumley? When the sixth and final ballot results were reported, the chair of the elections committee stated that 336 votes were necessary for election.

James Crumley	337
William Lazareth	330

Stunned silence fell over the convention before it was announced that James Crumley was our new president. Only later did we learn that a number of Lazareth's friends, assuming he would be elected, had gone out for dinner. History's door does indeed swing on small hinges.

Neuhaus was probably right. It was, more or less, an election by default. Lazareth frightened many folks. His style was so assertive and aggressive that many wondered if he could lead us as a pastor and shepherd. There were also those who, after hearing him a number of times, found themselves impressed when he spoke, but woke up the next morning wondering what he had actually said.

Crumley, in contrast, came across as warm, pastoral, and gentle. One news report described him as a "Folksy Tennessee pastor . . ." (*Minneapolis Star Tribune*, 7/16/78).

Following the convention many kind notes came to us.

Bill Lazareth showed his pastoral side, not often seen in public, when he wrote:

> I want to express my thanks again for your genial spirit and pious dignity in our association during the LCA presidential election process. I'm grateful that nothing emerged to mar our developing friendship. We will all provide Jim Crumley with the support he deserves as a committed churchman. May the Holy Spirit bless you with his incomparable gifts.

Eric Wahlstrom, my beloved New Testament professor at Rock Island, said that it was particularly gratifying that Reuben Swanson and I were among the four final candidates.

> I extend to you my cordial congratulations to your capturing such a great support. But you are young yet, and there will be more changes later on. I am sure you understand how proud it makes an old professor to see that his former students are enjoying their ministry and receive due recognition. I pray that God may continue to bless you in your ministry now in the Minnesota Synod and in whatever new field may be opened to you.

Election to the LCA Executive Council

Later in the 1978 Chicago convention I was one of several elected to the national LCA Executive Council. At my initial meeting I expressed my hopes for the years ahead:

Through my service . . . I want to accomplish at least two
objectives. First . . . to be a useful servant to the national
church by helping to shape its life in the form that I believe
to be in keeping with the biblical witness and the living guidance of the Holy Spirit. Second . . . to bring to the . . . council
the concerns, hopes, and dreams of the people I serve in the
Minnesota Synod.

Lutheran unity

In the late 1970s my expectation for Lutheran unity was rather
dim. In the February 9, 1979, issue of *The Concord,* a publication of
Luther Northwestern Seminary, I wrote of my dismay:

> The ALC worries about the LCA being too liberal and the
> LCA worries about the ALC being too conservative. I don't
> think that holds true. If you take a crosscut, you'll find
> practically every element in both churches.

Speaking to the fear of some that one church would lead to
centralization and top-down administration, I suggested it was not
a legitimate fear.

> We have the prerogative to choose what the nature of
> the church would be. A safeguard is that in our system
> those who lead the church are subject to election periodi-
> cally. Our doctrine of the ministry saves us from fear of
> centralization.

Unification, I suggested, could come about quickly if we had
more enthusiasm and encouragement. "Otherwise it could be a
very long time."

My comments were clearly directed at both David Preus and
James Crumley.

Preus, presiding bishop of the ALC, had obviously been dragging
his feet. In 1980 I wrote to Preus expressing my concern that he had
unfairly characterized LCA synod presidents as acting aloof and as

though we thought some of our ALC counterparts were behind the times. I assured him that this was not the case with most of us. In his response Preus again underscored his theme. Pointing to the many ways in which the three churches were cooperating, he stated, ". . . the question may remain 'why' instead of 'why not.'" In other words, he was saying that there was still no compelling reason for merger. ". . . there are a variety of ways to express the unity of the church." He asked for more time "for at least some of us . . . until we get to know each other better" (*The Lutheran*, 4/2/80). When he greeted the LCA convention in Seattle in July, Preus again ". . . reiterated his belief that developing strong congregations and expanding mission outreach are more important than moves toward consolidation" (*Minneapolis Star Tribune*, 7/4/80).

A bit earlier, in the spring of 1980, I was delegated by the LCA synod presidents to present a statement to the ALC leaders urging them to move ahead with ". . . gathering of opinions regarding merger" (*The Lutheran*, 4/2/80).

In the midst of those early discussions about Lutheran unity Bill Thorkelson, religion editor of the *Minneapolis Star Tribune*, shocked me one day in late 1980 when he did some speculating about the leadership of a merged church. He wrote:

> If merger comes, two Minnesotans probably will be leading contenders to head the united church of more than 5 million members: Bishop Herbert W. Chilstrom of the LCA's Minnesota Synod and Lloyd Svendsbye, president of Luther Northwestern Seminaries, St. Paul (10/10/80).

That was the first time I had seen any conjecture of that kind. At that point it seemed like a bit of Midwestern hubris on the part of Thorkelson.

In an article in *dialog* magazine (Spring 1981) I tried to get the readers' attention by suggesting that Lutheran merger was not "desirable." That made it seem that I was agreeing with Preus. I pointed out that there were many things about the Minnesota

Synod and the LCA that I would miss if we merged with the other two churches.

But I moved on quickly to say that in spite of my longing to keep things as they were, it was "imperative" that we move toward merger.

> Much as I enjoy my identity with the LCA and the Minnesota Synod, and much as I fear a loss of momentum during a decade of merger discussions and structural changes, I read in the Bible and the confessions of the church a more basic mandate. It is the mandate that calls to unity those who are already bound together in a common faith and confession (page 150).

As for the structure of a merged church, I advocated in the article for certain elements: a strong sense of being one national church, one that could speak for the majority of Lutherans in the United States; regional entities with about one hundred and fifty congregations that would give members a feeling of being part of a family of Lutherans in an area, linked by a common geographical identity. I wrote:

> I do not accept the assumed notion that we must choose between a strong national church and a strong regional church. I believe we have the creative genius and commitment to give us the best of both worlds (page 152).

I concluded with a note of realism.

> Our best efforts to bring about a new church will surely fall far short of God's, and our own expectations. But we are also a church that believes in grace. And it will be grace that will keep reminding us in the midst of organizational turmoil that our calling, first and foremost, is to simply be the church, the Body of Christ (page152).

In retrospect, it is interesting to note that the structure that evolved in the ELCA was remarkably similar to what I had envisioned in that 1982 *dialog* article.

"Those Catholics"

I grew up calling them "those Catholics." We Lutherans had little
to do with them. But Vatican II changed all that, and I was one of
the happy revelers in that change. Thanks to the initiative of Bishop
Elmo Agrimson of the ALC and Archbishop John Roach, who had
formed a strong bond in their St. Paul bailiwick, the Lutheran and
Catholic presidents and bishops agreed to meet in retreat for a
full day each year. I have wonderful memories of those occasions.
We spoke openly and freely of our likenesses and differences. We
worshipped together, though never in a sacramental mode. We ate
together. We shared our joys and disappointments.

Bishop Ray Lucker of the New Elm Diocese became a special
friend. He and I had taken office at about the same time. Through
the initiation of Father Gene Hackert, my friend from St. Peter
days, we met shortly after coming into office. The chemistry was
good. We always enjoyed each other's company. To a somewhat
lesser degree, I also enjoyed fellowship with Roach. Years later
when I retired from office as presiding bishop of the ELCA,
Roach attended my farewell party at the Minneapolis Convention
Center plaza. I could not have believed in my days of youth that I
would ever see the time when such a close bond could be forged
with "those Catholics."

In late October of 1980 and not long after John Paul II had
become pope, I shared the platform with Bishop William Bullock
of the St. Paul Archdiocese. We each presented our perspective on
Lutheran-Roman Catholic relationships. I focused on the Augsburg
Confession, pointing out that on the Sacraments of Baptism and
the Lord's Supper we were in virtual common understanding. As
for ordained ministry, I saw no hope that our differences would
ever be resolved. I did point out, however, our Lutheran inconsis-
tency in asserting that in order to be in the office of ordained ministry one must have a legitimate call to a community of faith. Yet at
the same time, we allowed retired pastors without a call to remain

on our rosters. Neither did we re-ordain those who resigned from the ministry and then accepted a call again. And we allowed pastors to remain "on leave from call" for three years when they did not have a call. On the question of justification by faith, I predicted that one day we would resolve those differences, as we did some twenty years later. I concluded by noting that the air had chilled a bit with the arrival of John Paul II. But . . .

> We ought not to be discouraged. We must take the longer look. My heart was warmed when a Roman Catholic bishop spoke to me privately at a recent meeting and said in effect, "I feel bad that there is some cooling right now in our relationships with other churches, including yours. But some of us have known the joy of our earlier relationship and we will move on in the hope and expectation that it will be renewed again with even greater rigor."

A look at the '80s—the perils of prophecy

I decided that a word of prophecy from the president of the synod might be in order as we moved toward the decade of the 1980s. I began by acknowledging that church leaders far more eminent and well qualified than I had tried and failed to predict what the 70s would be like. I decided to go ahead anyway.

> In spite of the rise of fundamentalist churches accenting personal experience at the expense of our own emphasis on Word and Sacraments, I predicted that these movements would begin to wane. Wishful thinking. I was wrong.
>
> I expected that progress in our discussions with Roman Catholics would continue to bear fruit. My prognosis was, at best, too optimistic. Of course, we did not know at that time how John Paul II would be responding to earlier initiatives. As it turned out, progress slowed considerably during his time as pontiff.

Recognizing that there is a wide gap between the way pastors and laity interpret the Bible, I ventured the hope that our pastors would take their teaching role seriously and help our laity understand our theological traditions. Though many made bold attempts at that task, the decade saw little change in that gap.

On my fourth point I was right. In spite of the insistence of some that merger of Lutherans was not a necessity, I stated forthrightly that "My firm hope and expectation is that another ten years will see us—the ALC, LCA, AELC—as one church."

Maybe one and a half out of three wasn't so bad after all.

What's in a name? Shall we call them "bishop"?

The LCA 1980 convention was held in Seattle. The hot-button issue was whether we, as the ALC had done several years earlier, should start calling our LCA churchwide and synod presidents by the title "bishop." Synod presidents were reluctant to speak on the issue since it involved them personally. LCA President Crumley had made it clear that he was strongly opposed to the change in the way it had been proposed. When the vote passed, there was a spontaneous outburst of applause. Crumley reacted with passion, pounding his gavel and bringing the convention back to order. In somber tones he reminded us that this change was in title only and did not vest any added authority in the office.

I was at the microphone prepared to speak in favor of the change when the question was called. I felt free to do so since I had openly favored such a change for several years. I was ready to make two points: first, our LCA polity protected us from the abuse of power by bishops who might let the title go to their heads. We could simply vote such autocrats out of office. Second, there was the practical matter of helping those outside our church understand what those of us in those offices actually did. When I would explain to someone that a synod president was like a bishop they understood immediately the nature of my work.

Holden Village—a time for reflection and renewal

On our way back to Minnesota from the Seattle convention, we stopped at Holden Village in the eastern Cascade Mountains of Washington for two weeks. I was on the teaching faculty. Once more my days at Teaneck were a lifesaver. I taught the prophecy of Amos, a book I had learned to love during those years. All three of our children were with us. It was good family time: hiking, talking, working in the camp kitchen, and getting to know folks from across the country.

Most important, it was a time for quiet reflection. I was approaching my forty-ninth birthday. One day I went to the library, took a sheet of hand towel paper from the bathroom and scribbled out my hopes for the decade of my 50s. I wrote about my tendency toward being an introvert, yet entrenched in the job of an extrovert. I felt I was moving into a stage of my life where I must move out of self-doubt and "let the chips fall where they will." Even so, I cautioned myself to ". . . do so with the earnest prayer that God will save me from pride—that the motivation will be for the good of others and for the satisfaction of my own need to use the gifts I have from God."

I reflected on the urgency of developing a pattern of physical exercise that would fit what I was doing: ". . . a balance by which one can maintain a reasonable sense of vitality without feeling exhausted."

I was getting more and more invitations to speak in other parts of the country. "My first duty must be to family and the MN Synod. To choose carefully what I do beyond those basic responsibilities will grow in importance."

I looked ahead to the time beyond the decade of my 50s. I had met some retired pastors at Seattle who seemed ". . . lost and forlorn, grasping at the past for some small wisp of significance because the present seemed to have none for them." I outlined four areas for cultivation:

1. Deepen new friendships and nourish old ones.

2. Maintain old hobbies and develop new ones. I wrote, "When I walk through a flower garden the old feeling surges back. I can lay that hobby aside for now, but I know it will quickly emerge again when time and situation permits." I added comments about encouraging Corinne to do likewise, and noted her ". . . obvious delight in handwork of so many kinds. . . ." In parenthesis I added: "(If she can now find a meaningful vocational outlet it would be so very good!)" I chided myself for being niggardly in spending money on hobbies and personal interests.

3. Use the Lida cottage more than ever as a place for retreat and renewal. I wrote that "As the demands grow, it will be more important to have these times for renewal."

4. I concluded my Holden paper towel comments by suggesting that, "Possibly most important of all is to nurture a feeling that has been growing in me . . . to just be myself—to relax in the acceptance of God's acceptance of me as I am—sinner and saint—and to move forward in every area of life in this basic confidence of life as gift to be enjoyed and shared. . . ."

Challenge James Crumley? Succeed David Vikner?

In June 1981 I was in New York City at the LCA headquarters for a meeting. At the intersection of 37th and Park I ran into Pastor LaVern "Deke" Grosc, a fellow member of the Church Council. An affable man who had held important positions as a pastor in large congregations and former editor with the Lutheran World Federation, Deke was always ready to engage in conversations involving church politics. He told me that he was disappointed with Crumley's leadership of the LCA. He inquired whether I might be willing to challenge him when he came up for reelection in 1982. I gave him what was probably a flip, superficial response.

After I returned to Minnesota, however, I thought that I should take his suggestion more seriously and give him a more complete and decisive answer in case he and others were thinking of promoting my candidacy. My letter to Grosc outlined a pattern that was typical in all such situations.

> First, there is the very normal, human response to a high compliment. I have enough ego to feel very good about the fact that anyone should have such an elevated opinion of me.
>
> The reaction that sets in next, however, is anything but pleasant. The reality of the demands of such an office is all but overwhelming. Coupled with that is the thought of moving one's family, living and working in New York rather than Minneapolis, constant travel rather than occasional travel. . . . I can only say, "God forbid."
>
> After passing through that phase I come to the third and most important phase where I simply find myself wanting to live out the will of God for my life, whatever and wherever that may be. Like you, I have long since learned that a sense of being in God's will and in the will of those I serve, is most important.
>
> To put it simply, I have no personal designs on that office and my preference would be to stay right where I am for a few more years before returning to a parish or teaching setting. Thus, I will not knowingly do anything to promote my candidacy for a national office.

I went on in the letter to question the wisdom of trying to change the leadership of the LCA at such a critical time in the move toward Lutheran unity. Furthermore, I assured Grosc that Crumley's support in Minnesota was strong. I felt it was the same in other parts of the church.

Then in November of 1981 I received a letter from Crumley informing me that "Your name has been suggested as a person qualified" to succeed David Vikner as executive director of the LCA Division for World Mission. Had I been open to such a move, I have no idea what my chances would have been for selection. This, however, was a no-brainer. Much as I might have loved to do this at some other point in my ministry, our family situation was such that I simply could not have given it consideration. My response was thanks, but no thanks.

Another wake-up call?

In spite of my determination to keep my work schedule under control, there were times when it seemed impossible. It came to a head at the Summer Theological Conference at St. Olaf College, Northfield, Minnesota, in mid-July 1982. I delivered the major paper noted earlier on "Ministry as Gift." I was just recovering from an attack of diverticulitis. In my journal I poured out my dilemma:

> I really wanted to do this. Having given considerable thought to the subject . . . I wanted to go & deliver it. Corinne was also scheduled to lead a workshop on wholeness—so we both looked on it as something with top priority.

> So we went & I gave the opening lecture in an auditorium seating some 700—and a very difficult setting requiring intense vocal projection.

> About half way through the lecture I felt very, very weak & exhausted. But instead of quitting, I reached for the very last ounce of energy I could muster & got through it. I was totally spent at the end. That night I awakened at about three a.m. with an intense pain in my lower left back, just under the rib cage. That pain proved to be a distress that would go on for weeks & months.

I sought more medical attention. I was tested for all kinds of maladies. Getting a good night's sleep became a problem. During the day I struggled to get through the schedule. My staff, led by

Pete Erickson, took me out for lunch one day to express their concern. They said I seemed distant and detached. There were some complaints from others that I didn't seem interested in greeting them or talking to them. They were right on target. That's how I was feeling at the time, so tired that I struggled to relate to others.

Finally, my own self-diagnosis was confirmed: a strained diaphragm muscle from preaching and lecturing too often when I was fatigued. That, combined with lack of sleep, had done me in.

Fortunately, I had a break over the Advent and Christmas seasons. I rested as much as I could. In my journal I wrote:

> By the end of Jan. '83 I was sleeping through the night
> again & was feeling new vitality.

The next line in my journal now leaps from the page:

> *In the meantime I . . . started walking in the mornings, at
> first a mile & gradually more.* That decision to walk in the
> mornings changed my life. We lived across the street from
> a wooded, quiet neighborhood. No matter what my schedule was for the day, I rose a half hour earlier than usual
> and hiked the hills. My main goal was to get some exercise.
> What I soon learned, however, was that this was only a
> small part of the benefit of that early regimen. I discovered
> that it was a marvelous time to meditate, to pray, to process
> the activities of the previous day, and to set the affairs of the
> new day in order. After a time I memorized three morning
> hymns and used them as my prayer mantra:
>
> "Awake, My Soul, and with the Sun"
> "Father We Praise You Now the Night Is Over"
> "God of Our Life, All Glorious Lord"
>
> Years later, after I retired, I added a fourth, the lovely
> Swedish hymn:
>
> "Again Thy Glorious Sun Doth Rise"

I learned that walking was an exercise program I could pursue any place in the country and the world. And that is exactly what happened for the rest of my ministry as synod and presiding bishop—and on into retirement. Once I got disciplined into that routine, I had no problems with fatigue. The load of responsibilities got heavier and heavier. But I was able to handle them because of this wise decision about healthy exercise. Corinne, of course, sometimes joined me on those morning walks and it became an important bonding time for us as a couple.

A harbinger of things to come: a fiery debate on homosexuality

Though it is now ancient history, I need to write at some length about the most taxing time in my eleven years as Minnesota Synod bishop. The events that unfolded in 1982 were a harbinger of what we have faced in the whole ELCA since then.

Minnesota Council of Churches

It began in late 1982 when the Minnesota Council of Churches issued a statement on the need to deal with the questions surrounding homosexuality. By today's standards it was a very mild document. I supported it. As correspondent Kay Miller wrote in the *Minneapolis Star Tribune,* it ". . . urged congregations to accept and welcome gay and lesbian persons into their folds and to fight for legislation protecting their rights." In the same article and in defense of the MCC statement I was quoted as saying, ". . . there is a growing sense in the church and in the community of the fact that . . . a significant number of fine people . . . happen to be homosexual through no design of their own" (11/12/82).

In strong opposition, fifteen pastors from our Minnesota Synod, along with even more from the ALC Southeastern Minnesota District, signed a public statement in which they declared that ". . . we publicly disassociate ourselves from the Minnesota Council of Churches on this issue and deny that they represent us." The newspaper editorialized that "The issue is considerably more complex than that. Fortunately, many people appear willing to consider those complexities; Herbert Chilstrom . . . says his mail is running 2–1 in favor of the council" (*Minneapolis Star Tribune*, 11/18/82).

Among those opposed to the MCC action was one from a man who wrote that a friend of his had been a student at the Lutheran Bible Institute when I was there. "He openly wept . . . because of you. He felt you were a *giant* at that time. But now your biblical stance on homosexuality—it really ripped him apart." Every letter of this kind got an answer. I tried to help each one understand the harm the church had done by its cruel and unjust treatment of homosexual persons. I wrote that "I have come to the conclusion that a deeper and more comprehensive understanding of homosexuality calls for us in the church to stop calling 'unclean' those who happen to by gay or lesbian through no fault of their own."

Just when the MCC upheaval began to abate I was faced with yet another controversy that would evolve into an even thornier problem.

Lutheran Social Service and FELLP

It started when a therapy program for juvenile sex abusers at Lutheran Social Service of Minnesota came to the attention of several conservative Lutheran pastors. Called "Personal/Social Awareness," it was based on the theory, among other things, that the best way to work with these youth was to employ explicit sexual films and to discuss issues like masturbation and homosexuality. The entire family of the offender was required to be involved in some way.

Nine Lutheran pastors, especially David Barnhart at Trinity Lutheran Church of Minnehaha Falls in south Minneapolis, decided to launch a public campaign against it.

I had investigated the program enough to be convinced that I should defend it. Hennepin County court and health officials had lauded it. Parents of the boys involved in therapy had overwhelmingly commended it.

Other Lutheran leaders were not as supportive. In fact, one Missouri Synod district in Minnesota threatened to put its funding support for LSS in escrow until it could evaluate the program itself. Parish pastors were understandably reluctant to step forward, fearing that it might divide their congregations. Outside of the LSS staff I stood virtually alone.

The brouhaha hit the local press, as one might expect with any subject that had to do with sex. Barnhart dubbed the program ". . . slime, unadulterated slime from the pits of hell" (*Minneapolis Star Tribune*, 3/13/83). Several congregations in the Minnesota Synod threatened to withhold funds. Nine pastors, three each from ALC, LCA, and LCMS congregations, met with LSS administrators, Lowell Erdahl, the LCMS district president, and me. James Raun, the head of LSS, reported that the meeting produced ". . . lots of accusations and allegations, but no conclusions." I stated that ". . . no minds were changed but dialogue is always important" (*The Lutheran*, 3/2/83).

In the meantime a new organization sprang up to unite those who were opposed to the LSS program. In time it became apparent that their larger agenda was to address the homosexuality issue. Called Fellowship of Lutheran Laity and Pastors (FELLP), its aim was to turn the church back from any change in its stance regarding homosexuality and inclusion of homosexual persons in leadership positions in the church.

In early April I agreed to be part of a forum at Normandale Lutheran Church in Edina. The panel would consist of Howard Paulson, staff person from LSS, David Barnhart, and me. Barnhart made certain that his supporters came early and filled the basement auditorium to capacity. Paulson, though a wonderful man and effective administrator, was inept as a public communicator. It was entirely on my shoulders to carry the freight for the LSS program. The evening turned ugly. After the session one man was so aggressive that he repeatedly thrust his finger into my chest to make his point.

Because of all the confusion over the issues, and in response to a mailing that FELLP had sent to all Lutheran congregations in the area, I decided to draft a substantial letter (4/12/83) to the pastors of our synod, seeking to put into perspective what was going on. I began by affirming the right of FELLP to organize and attempt to make an impact on the church. I went on to make what turned into a prophetic statement: "Much as some might like for [homosexual persons] to 'go back into the closet,' you can be certain that will not happen."

The letter went on to discuss the use of Scripture in dealing with thorny questions. I lifted up the difference between a *prescriptive* and a *descriptive* methodology. The former, *prescriptive*, looks to the Bible for final answers, often amassing texts that seem to address a question and then declaring that "God has said." The assumption in this school of thought is that the Bible has an ultimate answer for every question.

The other possibility, *descriptive*, also uses the Bible as a "norm," but in the sense that it is a "guide" along the way. In this methodology one also looks to other sources for wisdom in understanding a question. In this scenario one must continually ask questions about what God is saying to us in today's context. We must be ready for surprises—". . . the kind of surprises we will discover in the witness of some brothers and sisters in Christ who happen to be gay or lesbian through no choice of their own."

I went on in the letter to make statements that I have long since discarded. I referred to homosexuality as "a handicap." I affirmed the LCA posture then in effect, which called homosexuality ". . . a departure from the heterosexual structure of God's creation." I also insisted, however, that homosexual persons are not sinners in some unusual way. "Everyone is to repent and everyone is to seek healing, no matter what their brokenness may be."

Noting that the FELLP organization was working hard to make certain that delegates to the forthcoming synod convention were, by its own definition, "evangelical," I asserted that such a magnificent term must not be subjected to a narrow definition, namely, to persons who had a particular view of homosexuality.

I concluded with words of hope

> . . . that we can show the world that the church is a place where people can disagree openly, where they can come to decisions in an orderly way, and where they can live and work together in harmony even when the decisions are not to everyone's liking. May God grant that we may be able to witness to the true unity of the Body of Christ.

At about the same time that the letter went out, both major newspapers in the Twin Cities gave me space for a major article. It was a way of informing the general public of what was going on in the halls of area Lutheranism (*Minneapolis Star Tribune*, 4/17/83; *St. Paul Pioneer Press*, 4/27/83).

Reports of the turmoil in Minnesota spread far and wide. The *National Catholic Reporter* carried a full-page story. The *Lutheran Perspective*, the national organ for the AELC, had an account. As did *The Lutheran* magazine. I was invited to appear on John Gallo's Sunday morning religion telecast on WCCO-TV, the major station in the Twin Cities. If FELPP wanted notice, they surely got it.

Response to the letter and the public discussion was mixed, but overwhelmingly positive.

> One pastor was so distressed that he wrote a letter full of scriptural judgment on me, printing the biblical texts in red. "You have abandoned your first love—love for Christ and the lost." He concluded by assuring me that "we are praying for you, brother, that the Lord will grant you divine wisdom. . . ." It wasn't difficult to guess what kind of wisdom he had in mind.

An anonymous post card chastised me: "Shame on you! Wake up! We hope that all churches won't get caught in your filthy communist satanic anti-God net, but that they will pull away from the synod and become free. You are accountable to God! Better shape up and ship out. . . . You've been warned!" (8/16/84).

Those were the exception. The attention in the press brought dozens of letters, especially from pastors, heralding what I had written and offering encouragement.

Ronald Clark, editorial page editor of the *St. Paul Pioneer Press* and a member of one of our LCA congregations, wrote that "It takes a strong man to handle with calm and reserve and dignity the problems that have been foisted on you recently . . . it must be taking a personal toll. I hope you find the strength to continue in your important work."

Pastor Richard Borgstrom reflected on the core issues in the dispute: "It seems we are in a confrontation regarding biblical authority. Some of God's messengers seem they must mount the ramparts to protect the Almighty, as if he has a problem on his hands beyond his ability. Such an attitude I find bewildering, to say the least. Stay the course. These enthusiasts tend to shoot themselves in the foot.

St. Olaf College religion professor Chuck Kammer suggested that "What is most disturbing about the position taken by the [FELLP pastors] is their unwillingness to be open to persons who are 'different' and their refusal to engage in open dialogue and discussion. This attitude is frightening."

One thoughtful pastor, Judith Mattison, wrote a special note to Corinne, knowing that she was surely bearing some of the brunt of this controversy. "Oh, it is a hard time for you. [Herb's] doing a magnificent job in the heat of criticism. But I also pray for you. Oh, Corinne, don't worry that people believe some of the nonsense about Herb, we know better. And somehow I know that that sturdy of a man can withstand these pressures and taxing times."

Later in the spring of 1983 LSS agreed to stop using the films until their effectiveness had been evaluated. The program, however, continued for several years until it was transferred to the University of Minnesota. I was told as recently as 2006 that it continues to be effective in treating juvenile sex offenders.

Unfortunately, the leadership of FELLP decided to continue its fight. They announced that they intended to found a national organization to ". . . affect the nature of the new Lutheran church . . ." (*Minneapolis Star Tribune*, 6/9/83).

FELLP's next move was to try to do an end run on me by appealing directly to Bishop James Crumley. Fortunately and wisely, he refused to meet with them without me being present. They yielded and agreed to a meeting. I insisted that it be in the board room at the synod office. They agreed reluctantly. But on the day of the meeting they tried again to meet separately with Crumley in the chapel of the Church Center. Again we resisted. I told them we would be waiting for them in the board room if they wanted to meet. After much delay, and the departure of Pastor Thomas Basich in protest, we held the meeting. Surely no minds were changed. I concluded the meeting by assuring them that my door would be open for further discussion.

Later in the summer of 1983 I wrote a note to myself:

> I'm recalling today a comment that Charles Anderson from Beckville Church, Litchfield, made to me several months ago. . . . Charles recalled the comments of a U of M Ag professor to his class years ago—that one can go through almost anything so long as one maintained one's integrity.
>
> In all of these months of struggle, turmoil, misunderstanding, false accusations, etc., my integrity has remained

intact. I may have made mistakes; I may have erred in judgment at times. I may not always have expressed my thoughts clearly. I may have reacted unfairly or hastily at times. But I can say without hesitation that I have never been deliberately and knowingly deceptive or dishonest. . . . My integrity has been preserved.

Putting things into perspective

It is interesting to note that in my April 12, 1983, pastoral letter I suggested that one of three things happens to so-called free movements: Some prosper, often integrating themselves later into the life of a church body; others serve a good purpose for a time and then gracefully end their ministry; others fail almost as soon as they are born. For FELLP, which seemed so threatening at the time, the last scenario proved to be their story. While a few congregations withheld or reduced their support for the mission of the synod, the overall effect was minimal.

The passage of time brings interesting changes.

Paul Swedberg, one of the key organizers of FELLP, wrote to me in 1990 and apologized. "I need to ask your forgiveness for the spirit of fault finding that sometimes characterized the FELLP organization," he confessed. "I should have spoken out more forcefully to the brothers on the danger of judgment without love and without the desire for restoration and health for the body of Christ."

Morris Vaagness, co-leader with Swedberg of the FELLP organization, built a large congregation in the St. Paul area. But years later, against his wishes, the congregation left the ELCA.

Barnhart split Trinity Church and led a remnant into another church body.

Thomas Basich took his Roseville church out of the ELCA and formed a separate denomination. The last I heard it was the only congregation in that church body.

The granddaughter of another signer of the newspaper ad railing against LSS came out of the closet in 2007 to declare to the public that she is a lesbian. I have met her. Her grandfather's brother was a well-known New Testament professor at Luther Seminary. She is a beautiful, talented, and responsible woman. Today she is on the staff of one of our ELCA seminaries, assisting future pastors in honing their writing skills. I wrote to her, congratulating her on her appointment and suggesting that this is further evidence that God is full of surprises and good humor.

One of the puzzling aspects of this conflict was the fact that several of the leaders and supporters of FELLP were pastors who had received their theological training at Augustana Seminary. They sat under the same professors as I. How could they have held such different views on the interpretation and use of the Bible? Though not referring to them directly, I tried to answer that question in a more general way in the lecture at the Lutheran School of Theology in Chicago that I referred to earlier (May 2, 1984):

> I find myself baffled . . . by pastors who reflect a theology alien to their denomination. I have no easy answer. One possibility, of course, is that a person may go through the seminary "unscathed." I can appreciate how this can happen. Had I refused to deal with some theological issues, I suppose I could have moved through seminary and into parish ministry with an almost fundamentalistic theology.

> Another possibility, of course, is that a person may go through a genuine metamorphosis from liberal to moderate or from moderate to conservative. Life is ever-changing and nothing says that a move in one direction precludes a move back in the opposite direction.

> Having acknowledged these two possibilities, I am convinced that the reason for division within the church has more to do with power than with theological issues. The greater problem is with congregations where dialogue is not even allowed.

Through these times of turmoil the synod continued to grow in membership. *The Lutheran* magazine reported that "Minnesota has had an increase almost every year since the LCA was formed. It is the fastest growing denomination in Minnesota" (6/20/84).

What can one say about conflicts of this kind other than, "This too will pass." Indeed, in a report to the synod as the dust began to settle on that time of stress in the church, I wrote:

> I believe that something good has emerged from all of this. . . . many in our congregations have come to a new sense of who we are as a church and how we in the LCA go about grappling with these issues. We have learned that we are not a church that is content with easy answers or long lists of provisions for every conceivable problem. Our LCA is a church that takes Scripture seriously, that provides us with statements for guidance, but that refuses to let us get by with simple solutions. We have learned that we are a church whose foundation is in the Word and the Sacraments. Within that broad but very firm circle of doctrine most of us have come to realize that there is room for some dis- agreement, disagreement that does not separate us because we are bound by the larger circle of Word and Sacrament. We have also learned that trust for one another is basic to the unity of the church ("Facing Forward," page 107).

Have I had enough?

Although I have long since forgotten it, I apparently had some res- ervations in late 1983 about continuing in office when my second term expired in mid-1984. This does not surprise me. Battling with the FELLP group and those who were upset about the sexuality and other hot-button issues took its toll. And given my love for parish ministry and the sense that my time in those settings had been too short, I'm sure that longing must have surfaced from time to time.

In any event, I found a letter in my 1984 file from Greg Raymond, a highly-regarded member of the synod executive board from Duluth:

It appears that the idea of your not running for office again may have been resolved, at least I hope so. You have given us strong, well-balanced leadership over these past years & we desperately need that in the next few years as we move into the new church. In my opinion, you're not running would cause a terrible rift that could not be healed. I am sorry, but as a layman I can see this as only a political struggle by those people & it looks like they are willing to use all the tricks in the book. A lot of us would like to fight back, but I'm sure that's exactly what they want. We need a cool head and you're it.

At the convention in June 1984 I was reelected on the first ballot by a vote of 677 out of 723 ballots cast. That seemed to be evidence of solid support from the synod pastors and laity as well as a strong message to those who had advocated for change.

Authorship

In 1983 I decided to try my hand at book authorship. Again I was leaning on my Teaneck years. In spite of Luther's dim view of it, I had come to appreciate the Letter to the Hebrews. I realized that there was little on that book of the Bible that was available to a lay readership.

Out of my efforts came the book *Hebrews—A New and Better Way*. In a review of the book Martin E. Marty wrote:

Lay people . . . are often put off by books on the Bible, which are too long, too technical, too remote. Let me help stock the satchel for hammock reading with a short and direct book, Herbert W. Chilstrom's, *Hebrews: A New and Better Way*. Chilstrom aims for the heart as he chops the book of Hebrews into 40 day-sized chunks, always having as his goal the lifting up of the glory of God in Christ (*The Lutheran*, 6/6/84).

That same year, 1983, I collaborated with others in writing *Faith and Ferment*, a project of the Institute for Ecumenical and Cultural

Research at Collegeville, Minnesota. The volume was based on an in-depth study of religious attitudes in Minnesota. Out of the study came both affirmation and concern. At the public forum when the book was released I suggested that the findings showed that those who preach and teach appear to be too far removed from the workaday world of the laity (*St. Paul Pioneer Press,* 9/24/83). Others came to similar conclusions. In a report in *Newsweek* magazine (9/19/83) Martin Marty stated that if the findings were consonant with the rest of the country, they show that Americans were drifting away from a sense of community to a pick and choose mentality regarding the church. Most everything we have witnessed in the last three decades confirms those conclusions.

For the January 1986 issue of *The Lutheran* I was invited to write the lead article on the subject, "God's Will for My Life." I began by emphasizing that there is no easy climb to certainty. I wrote about Luther's idea of "the hidden God," suggesting that "within the richness and mystery and complexity of our relationship with God we are invited to search out God's will and purpose for our lives."

The article earned an Award of Merit from the Associated Church Press in 1986 in the category of "Theological Reflection."

Honors along the way

In 1979 the honorary doctorate from Luther Northwestern Seminary would be the first of such awards that would come over the next fifteen years. I have to confess to a bit of wariness in relationship to these kinds of honors. Were they given because of the office I held? Or because the institution wanted to make certain they remained in the financial pipeline of the entity I headed? Or because I really did live up to the lofty words of praise they showered on me? Maybe it was a mix of all of the above. In any event, the citation from Luther Northwestern Seminary was typical of what was said on such occasions. It read, in part:

Herbert W. Chilstrom would have honored any calling that
he might have entered. His range of abilities, his capacity
for friendship, patience, and understanding, as well as his
conscientious dedication to every assignment given him,
would ensure very high levels of performance and achievement in a wide range of professions. All who are committed
to the church and concerned about its future are grateful
that he has felt called to exercise his exceptional leadership
within the church.

In my response I suggested, only in slight jest, that after the ceremony I might find a scissors and cut the hood into many pieces,
not out of disrespect, but in order to share it with many others,
including Corinne and the synod staff.

A family in transition

This may be a good point to put in a word about our family and
the impact all of these changes had on us. Backing up to 1976, our
decision to look for a home in the Minneapolis suburb of Edina
was driven in large part by choice of schools for our children. Dr.
Filip Vikner, head of the education department at Gustavus Adolphus College, suggested that the Edina system was the finest in the
Twin Cities area.

Corinne

I've written a bit earlier about Corinne's hopes following her graduation from Mankato State University. When we moved to Minneapolis it seemed that those kinds of job opportunities in nursing were
filled. In one sense, this was a blessing. This gave her time to give
her undivided attention to our children through their time of transition, to settle our home, to get involved at Normandale Church,
and to be with me at important synod events. A good example of
the respect she was gaining around the synod came in a letter written in June 1977 from David Pearson, pastor at Brainerd:

I must . . . share with you the deep appreciation and gratitude
we have for your wife Coreen *(sic)*. Her personal interest
and concern for Judy and me come not from her role as our
bishop's wife, but from her own sense of compassion. I feel
our synod has indeed been doubly blessed with both of you.

One day Corinne said to me that she was thinking about taking
a class at Luther Seminary in St. Paul. She had always had an avid
interest in and curiosity about systematic theology. I encouraged
her to do so. She thrived. One class led to another. When questions
about ordination surfaced, she adamantly turned them aside. She
was the wife of the synod bishop; she was a woman; she had grown
up in a church culture that took a negative view of most clergy, to
say nothing about women pastors. Others, however, saw it differ-
ently. One day after class, Dr. Warren Quanbeck stopped her at
the door of the classroom. "Corinne," he said, "you should become
ordained." She felt moved to the core of her being by his comment.
When she reached her car in the parking lot she sat and wept for
a long time. Something deep inside told her that Quanbeck was
right. But she continued to feel that it could not be for her. She
completed her work for a master's degree in systematic theology.

Corinne's graduation from the seminary in June 1980 was a
proud day for all of us. Her father, Jens, a widower by then and in
his eighty-second year, decided to come from South Dakota for the
ceremony at Central Lutheran in Minneapolis. Though he had once
refused to support her longing to go to college, it was apparent
that he was now immensely proud that his youngest child had not
only done that, but was now graduating as an honor student from
the seminary. He loved having his picture taken with her that day,
beaming from ear to ear. Who could have believed that this crusty
old Hauge Lutheran could have come so far?

For a year Corinne worked in a hospice setting. Before long,
however, it became clear that this was not satisfying her deepest
longings. Through career counseling her profound inner call to

ordained ministry became clear. One day we were together at our beloved Lake Lida. Here at that place we had often stepped back from the wild rides of our life to reflect and take stock of what was going on. This was such a time. I could see that she was deeply troubled. Neither of us could sleep. We got up in the middle of the night and went to the living room. I stoked the fireplace. We talked. Finally, I looked at her and asked, "Corinne, if I died today what would you do?"

That question opened the door. It helped her to drop her guard long enough to say, "I would go back to seminary, get ordained, and serve a little white church in the country." I looked at her and said, "Then that's what you must do while I'm *living*."

She returned to the seminary and worked for her Master of Divinity degree. In a birthday card in December 1983 Mary affirmed her mother's decision:

> I love you Mom, and it seems my love and appreciation
> for you grow every day. I thank God he gave me to you.
> I am proud of you and happy too as I see you involved in
> a quest that has burned in you for so long and seems so
> right. I love you.

Corinne spent two years on a part-time internship at Prince of Peace Lutheran Church in St. Louis Park, a suburb of Minneapolis. Her association with Pastor Lynn Strand was exactly the right combination. He was unusually sensitive to the needs of women in ministry and gave her the freedom to hone her already remarkable pastoral skills. Corinne and Lynn became fast friends and worked well as colleagues. The friendship continues to this day.

Along the way she continued to be affirmed by others. In a note left for me when she was gone one day (which included detailed instructions for what I should eat for dinner!), she added this comment:

> Finished my course with Dr. (Paul) Sonnack this a.m. He
> gave me a nice gift. . . . Wanted to tell me that he feels I am

very intelligent, articulate and . . . sees me as particularly gifted for ministry! What a nice gift!

In my journal on March 31, 1982, I wrote:

Corinne finds much joy and contentment in being back at the seminary working toward ordination. She had three obstacles to overcome: 1. Having been raised in the old "Hauge Synod" atmosphere of her childhood church, she had to deal with the anti-clergy attitude that prevailed in that part of our Lutheran heritage. 2. Being a woman, even though it has been twelve years since the LCA approved ordination for women, there is still residual resistance. 3. Being wife of a bishop, maybe the biggest obstacle. But it seems that she has encountered surprisingly little resistance. In short, I think people are genuinely happy to see that she has taken this step.

During this time Corinne continued to serve on the Bethesda Lutheran Medical Center board. For a time she was chair of the Quality Assurance Committee. Under her leadership more physicians became involved in the peer review process. In her last three-year term she was vice chairman of the board.

On a broader scale, she was appointed a member of a LCA committee that developed a pace-setting *Statement on Death and Dying* that was adopted by the LCA Churchwide Convention at its 1982 Louisville gathering. It became a model for other denominations.

She finished the seminary the second time in 1984. More about this later.

Our goal was always to be good parents for our children. We had traveled and camped with them in all corners of the country. We encouraged them to take music lessons, to be involved in church and school events, to bring their friends to our home. My journals are filled with happy memories of their early childhood. We attended when they were involved in an event. Choral concerts, honors convocations, sporting events—we made it a point to clear our calendars for them whenever possible. On one occasion Andrew suggested to me that I came to more wrestling matches than any other dad. He thought that maybe it would be all right if I missed one now and then.

Mary

Mary made a good transition to life in our new setting in Edina. I still recall how she marched off to a football game a few weeks after our move, determined to get to know other teens her age. She got involved at Normandale Church, singing in the youth choir and giving her witness at concerts when they traveled. In school she was in plays and choir. She sang as one of the villagers in the production of "Fiddler on the Roof." On her junior year PSAT tests she emerged as one of only seventeen in her class in the "commended" category. In a system as competitive as it was at Edina, that was a singular achievement. Her score placed her among the top two percent of the total number of students in her class in the nation. She graduated with high honors.

Mary's choice of Concordia College, Moorhead, Minnesota, pleased us. We knew it to be a fine Lutheran college with high academic standards, a place where she could blossom as a whole person. She decided to major in social work and English. She spent one year at Arizona State University, known for its excellent social work curriculum. She graduated with honors and a double major in her chosen fields.

During her senior year at Concordia, Mary decided to try to make contact with her birth mother. Just before Christmas she got a call from LSS, informing her that they had located her birthmother and that she indicated openness to meeting Mary.

Then in early January came the fateful call from the social worker. Her birthmother had changed her mind. She wanted never to see Mary. In an article published by *The Lutheran* magazine she expressed her intense disappointment:

> My own mother doesn't want me. She has just shoved me
> out the door . . . again . . . out of her life . . . like she did
> before . . . her decision was final . . . no more contact ever!
> I will never know if I've got her nose . . . or if her eyes can
> sparkle like mine . . . or if she talks like me. . . .

In the wake of her rejection Mary felt as though she were living in a trance, ". . . empty inside, devoid of feeling."

She remembered me saying to her:

> We are thankful that one woman's loss has been our gain
> and that one woman's sorrow for twenty-one years has been
> the cause of our love and joy for twenty-one years. . . .

Important words, yes, but they could hardly make up for her intense disappointment and anger over what had happened.

The years that followed were difficult for Mary. Fortunately, she is a survivor and somehow came through it. Eventually, and very gradually, she emerged as a stable, responsible person.

Today she is using her education and skills as a program manager for the American Academy of Neurology in St. Paul.

Christopher

I have positive memories of Chris from his early years. He smiled so easily and was loved by everyone. He was diligent in school and in his part-time jobs, the first being a paper route in our St. Peter neighborhood. His customers loved him and years later commented to us about what a gentleman he was.

Chris and I enjoyed our times at the cabin. He was an avid and a good fisherman. Never without a hobby to pursue, he built racing cars for scout events, sent up small rockets in the gravel pit next to our St. Peter home, and engaged in all sorts of craft projects. His excellent musical gifts expressed themselves in the high school chorus.

Unlike Mary and Andrew, Chris showed no apparent interest

in searching for his biological roots. Then something happened that changed the course of his life forever. He was planning a trip to Europe. He needed his birth certificate to get a passport. He went to LSS in Minneapolis to get the information he needed. While there he discovered by sheer chance the name of his birth mother. After a brief but intense search he found both her and her family, including his grandparents who lived only minutes from our home in Edina. Chris found them to be loving, caring persons.

He enrolled at the University of Wisconsin-Madison, and did very well in his studies, majoring in international relations and political science. After a time Corinne and I were eager to meet his grandparents. When he learned that we had invited them to our home one evening, he drove to Minnesota so that he could be there at the door to introduce them to us.

Then he discovered law as a career goal. It was, as he would say, his "calling." He thrived at William Mitchell School of Law in St. Paul and graduated near the top of his class. He was also chosen to be on the coveted editorial board of the school's Law Review. That earned him a fine internship and later a position at a prestigious law firm in Minneapolis. After several years in litigation practice he decided to move into the field of tax law.

Chris is incredibly talented with his hands—a trait, as I noted, that we saw in him from early childhood. After he completed law school he purchased an old house that was nearly ready to be razed. He fixed it up and sold it for a premium price. Since then he has rehabbed three more houses, including one only a short distance from where he grew up in Edina. He made the comment to us when he moved into that home that he liked it so much "they'll have to carry me out."

Little did he realize that his life would take a sudden turn after only a couple of years. His company consolidated its offices and he was transferred to corporate offices at Dallas, Texas.

Andrew

Andrew was our dreamer boy. He loved to have Corinne read from C.S. Lewis and J.R.R. Tolkein. He treasured *The Tales of Narnia*. He told Corinne that when he grew up to be a father he would read those tales to his children, too.

In the early days of my time in office as synod bishop Andrew and I developed a very special relationship. On several occasions I took him along on weekend trips when I visited congregations around the state. Because he was such a handsome young fellow, it became routine that a letter would arrive some days later from a young girl in one of those congregations. I kidded him, suggesting that he was like the sailors who boasted about having a gal in every port. Those were wonderful times of father/son bonding for us.

Unlike Mary and Chris, who were always industrious and reliable in their part-time jobs, Andrew could not seem to get his act together. He struggled with the adoption issue. When his class in school was doing a family tree project, he came home and slammed the papers on the table. "I'm German. And I've never seen anyone who looks like me!" It was his way of telling us that being adopted made him feel alone in the world.

Andrew was fascinated by war gaming and spent many happy hours painting miniature soldier figures from Napoleonic times. After a Saturday of intense strategizing with war-gaming friends of all ages he would say to us, "That was so much fun! But I have such a headache!" I took him along on a trip to Gettysburg, Pennsylvania, when I was there to deliver a lecture. We enjoyed touring the battlefield with Dr. Eric Gritsch from the seminary as our guide.

He was also a fine athlete and participated in soccer, football, and wrestling in junior high school. I recall vividly the first time I took him along for a round of golf. I had dabbled at the sport for several years. After five holes he was leading by a stroke or two. After nine I finally edged him out. But that was the last time. Without ever having taken a lesson, he easily topped me on subsequent outings.

Like our other two children, Andrew was a very promising child. On the basis of his test scores he was ranked in the top five percent of students in his age group in the United States. (Ironically, the letter was posted on the day he died.) His special love was German. In tenth grade he scored with the highest in his German class. For three summers he spent several weeks at the Concordia German Language Camp in northern Minnesota.

He seemed to be sensitive spiritually. After Bible camp in the summer of 1979 Corinne wrote a note to our pastor:

> A special thanks for another week of camp this summer! When I asked him what was the very best part of camp, he thought a minute and then said, "Getting to know Christ better . . . and then all the love . . . and the FUN." I can't imagine a better recipe for Bible camp!

Corinne remembers the day Andrew came home from school and sat by the kitchen table munching on a cookie and downing a glass of milk, a regular routine. They were talking about the future. Andrew said, "When I'm at the seminary . . ." Realizing that he didn't intend to reveal those inner thoughts, he quickly changed the subject. He never spoke about it again. It was obvious, however, that he harbored such hopes for this future.

When he expressed a desire to know more about his biological roots, I helped Andrew write a letter to the adoption agency in New Jersey. When they replied, he took the letter to his room. Several days later he brought it to the family room and shared it with us. It told of a birthmother who came from a well-educated family. She was interested in literature. She said she gave him up because she felt it would be better for him and she wanted to get on with her college career. His father, the letter said, was already married and had children. He was of blue-collar background, aggressive, and into weight lifting and body-building. Andrew never spoke of it again and we never found the letter after he died.

If I ever doubted that our genetic make-up has a strong bearing on how we eventually develop as teenagers and mature adults, those doubts evaporated as Andrew read us the letter. From birth Andrew showed all the signs of the streams that flowed into his life from those two persons. Tender, poetic, and philosophical—strong as an ox and aggressive. Fascinated with great literature; equally fascinated with dark and pessimistic writing. Showing signs of remorse when he shot a pheasant or rabbit; an intense competitor and hard-hitting participant in contact sports. Gently caressing a baby—vigorously lifting weights.

After his death we found poems, apparently written by him and with his mother in mind. In one he wrote:

BIRTH

Surging torrents of glory
Flow through my soul,
Blood rushing through my mother's womb
Sparks my heart to fire,
Drops of purest love
Dance burning on my tongue,
The dark warmth of heaven
Plunged into the cold blinding light of day.

I found other things he had written sometime during high school, all exuding a grim fatalism.

PURPOSE

When I think of what I dream
And compare it to
The worthless
Occupations
People spend their lives
Perfecting
I become depressed.
Somewhere

Along the line
We lost the purpose
Of existence.
I believe
In things no one can feel anymore.
They hurt
Or they provoke
Sensuality.
I love till I'm afraid to care.
I become excited and destroy
All that matters to me.

Andrew tried his hand at a variety of part-time jobs, but none lasted long. When it came time to graduate from high school, we felt certain he would not finish his course work. Somehow, possibly by the sheer goodness of some teachers, he managed to make it.

Andrew was determined to go to college. Even though we doubted his readiness, we supported him when he enrolled at Gustavus Adolphus College.

The story of his plunge into chaos and his decision to end his life changed our family forever. Corinne and I agreed that we would not retreat from the ministries to which we had been called. We believed we must be open and forthright about what had happened to our family.

Corinne began to speak in various places about Andrew's death, focusing on his struggle with issues related to his adoption. When Roland Sebolt at Augsburg Fortress, Publishers became aware of her work he encouraged her to write an account that could be published as a book. It took several years until she was ready to do so. But when the moment came she wrote almost non-stop until the book *Andrew You Died Too Soon* was complete. Now, almost twenty years later, and after many printings, it remains in strong demand. A week rarely goes by without someone calling or writing to thank her for that effort. The most recent was a woman who had lived in Japan for several years and discovered it in a church library while living there.

Cancer is for others

Now I need to back up a step. In the spring of 1985, about five months after Andrew's death, I began to feel some uneasiness in my lower abdomen. Our family physician thought it was simply a bladder infection and prescribed an antibiotic.

When that didn't help; I sought still another opinion. This time it was confirmed that there was indeed a small growth on the prostate gland. A biopsy was done. A day or two later I was sitting at my desk at the synod office when the specialist called. "Herb, I'm afraid I have bad news. We definitely have cancer." He went on to speak about other matters related to the test results. All I heard was, "We have cancer." I couldn't believe my ears. Cancer, I thought was for *other* people, not for me.

In the last twenty-five years there have been major advances in the treatment of prostate cancer. At that time for a male in his early 50s there was only one option—radical, major surgery.

We called Richard Preis, our pastor, and asked him to come to our home to conduct the church's "Service of Healing for the Sick." It was a reassuring evening. Yet the uncertainty hung heavy. When we fell exhausted into bed that night, we could not find words for prayer. We leaned on the promise from Romans 8 that the Spirit would pray for us when our own words fail. I did manage, however, to utter a five-word prayer: "Lord, give me a dream."

God answered with several dreams over the next nights. In one, dawn was beginning to break on the horizon. I could see huge trees lining the street. My attention was drawn to an unusually large one. In the middle of its trunk I noted a place had been hollowed out. Yet, it did not fall. It stood because other trees around it were supporting it. Their branches were so intertwined with its boughs that it could not fall.

As I continued walking down the street in the dream, I came to a place where the road dipped far down into a deep, dark valley before rising again on the other side. I stopped, afraid to go through the cleft because I could not see off to the sides at the bottom. There was no choice. I had to go on. I ran. When I got to the bottom I looked in both directions and saw nothing. I ran on up the hill with a great sense of relief and exhilaration.

All of this was happening just prior to the annual synod convention in early June 1985. Only Corinne, our children, our pastor, and our dear friend Flossie knew what was going on. Until we had a clear picture of my medical condition, we felt it wise not to tell others.

In spite of the encouragement of the dreams, I felt dread. As I walked down the aisle at Christ Chapel for the opening service, I remembered walking that same way just seven months earlier, following Andrew's casket. Now, I wondered, will it soon be my turn to be wheeled down this same aisle at my own funeral service? As I looked out over the congregation I noted the face of Ruth Hammarberg, my predecessor's wife. I thought to myself, "How ironic. His cancer started in the same way. Is history going to repeat itself? Will Corinne be sitting here one day, like Ruth, thinking about the time when I was bishop of the synod?"

After one of the sessions, one of my assistants informed me that I should call my doctor. I rushed to a phone. "Good news," my doctor said. "The cancer has not spread beyond the prostate."

In the August 1985 "Update" I described what the experience had been like. I began by reflecting on the sense of authority one might have as bishop of a large synod. Now, however, it was time to surrender all of that and own my weakness and vulnerability.

> For one with such authority to submit to the helplessness
> of major surgery is an experience of surrender. At that
> moment before going to sleep there was no choice but to
> empty my hands of everything over which I thought I had
> control.

In the days that followed there welled up within me a
profound sense of gratitude for the smallest of blessings:
a hypo to relieve pain, a dry gown after a sweaty struggle
with pain, a warm blanket, a few chips of ice in the black
of the night, the first rays of light after a seemingly endless
night, a phone call from another "prostate pilgrim" who
had walked the road before me, a gift from a young man
I hadn't seen for years. In the depths of an awful sense of
weakness came an awesome sense of strength.

Now that vitality is returning with each new day I wonder
if I will lose that gift of strength that came in weakness.
As I begin making decisions again, as I give my opinion
about one thing and another, as I ask others to do this or
that—will I revert to that subtle deceptive thought that the
strength is in me?

Thanks for your prayers. For the sake of the church and
of this office, keep praying. Pray that you and I might not
forget: "When I am weak, then I am strong."

Seven years later I pondered on whether I had lost something,
if something out of the depth of those two overwhelming blows—
Andrew's death and my bout with cancer—had slipped away.

I wonder sometimes if I have lost touch with my mortal-
ity. It was so fresh when Andrew died. So painful that it
hurt. So crushing that I wondered if I would ever really
live again.

When I was told I had cancer it was the same—especially
in those days between the diagnosis and the surgery. I was
so shattered. Yet, I was so deeply in touch with myself as a
fragile human being.

No, I don't want to go back. I don't want to deal with
another devastating death in our family circle—Corinne,
Mary, or Chris. That is too awful, too crushing. But there

was, along with the pain, a spiritual sensitivity that I wonder if I have lost. Is it not possible to retain that quality without the grief and without being cast out to the edge of existence?

. . . there must be a golden mean—some point of balance between an awareness of the possibility of death and a healthy hope that one may have many more years to enjoy this life.

At long last, Corinne is ordained!

Again let me move back a bit and pick up the story of Corinne's graduation from seminary and her ordination. As I wrote earlier, she finished Luther Northwestern Seminary in May 1984. No one could have been more proud than I when she was ready to be ordained. I had walked with her through this arduous journey. I had seen how diligent she had been in her studies while, at the same time, holding up faithfully her calling as wife, mother, and worker in the church. Now she was ready for a call to a congregation.

But we were faced with an impossible dilemma. As bishop of the LCA Minnesota Synod, I was the one who recommended candidates to congregations. In my office were huge piles of applications from pastors all over the country who wanted to move to Minnesota. And not just to Minnesota. They wanted a call in the Twin Cities area, the only setting where it was feasible for Corinne to serve.

My hands were tied. Even offering her name for consideration would have smacked of nepotism. We wondered, after that long and arduous journey, if she would ever be an ordained pastor.

It was in the midst of my prostate cancer tests in the spring of 1985 that Pastor Hubert Nelson called Corinne. He said he wanted to speak to her about serving on his staff at Bethlehem, an ALC congregation in south Minneapolis. When Corinne inquired about others he was considering for the position Hub replied, "No one. I want you." That opened the door. I, of course, had no jurisdiction in ALC congregations.

A few weeks later—June 16, 1985—and just before I had surgery, she was ordained by Bishop Lowell Erdahl of the Southeastern Minnesota District of the ALC. I was proud beyond words to be her ordination sponsor.

On the first Sunday Corinne preached at Bethlehem, I was at home for the weekend. I was still recovering from surgery so was free to go to church with her. I knew, however, that my presence might add pressure to her day. Being the first female pastor they had ever had at Bethlehem was enough of a challenge. Having her bishop husband in the congregation that morning might be a bit much.

I dressed in old clothes and settled down with the Sunday newspaper as she went out the door. Within minutes I went to the bedroom and changed clothes and drove to Bethlehem Church. Since folks there did not know me, it was easy to slip into the church incognito. I found a place in the nave behind a huge pillar where I would not be seen from the pulpit. I, however, could peek around the edge of the pillar and see her plainly. As I expected, her sermon was superb.

I slipped out during the last hymn and returned home. When she arrived, I asked about the service. She thought it had gone well. Then I began dropping little hints about several things that had happened during the service. Eventually, she got curious and started asking, "How did you know that? Who told you about that?" The truth came out and we had a good laugh.

As affirmative as the general reaction was to her first sermon, she learned later that one chauvinistic male board member had commented that it was a fine sermon, ". . . but I wonder if she can do it again." He was to learn that indeed she could. Another asked if her husband may have helped her write the sermon. If he knew us better he would have realized that in all of our teaching, preaching, and writing we have always worked independently.

A long and difficult recovery from surgery

The surgical procedure in mid-June 1985 went as expected. On direct examination it was confirmed that cancer had not spread to the lymph nodes. That was a huge relief. About two months after prostate surgery I developed an inguinal hernia on one side of the abdomen, requiring surgical repair. Six months later, March of 1986, a hernia on the other side again called for surgery. Now within a few months I had had three surgeries involving the abdominal muscles.

As soon as I was able to move about somewhat freely, Corinne and I went to our rustic cabin at Lake Lida. She returned to Minneapolis after a few days and I remained by myself for another two weeks. On the first days I could walk only a block up the county road. By the time I reached home I was completely depleted. Each day I walked a few steps farther. Day by day, stride by stride, I began to recover some physical stamina. I was slowly on my way back.

An evangelical conservative

Just before the end of 1985 I was invited to give a major address at The Lutheran Seminary at Philadelphia at its Seminary Day event. It was a gathering for faculty, student body, and friends of the school.

I decided that it would be a good setting to speak about my self-definition: "An evangelical conservative, with a radical social conscience." Among other things I said:

> An evangelical is simply one who believes the good news about Jesus Christ and becomes a bearer of that message of hope. The moment you get beyond that core by adding requirements about lifestyle or demands about how one is to interpret the Bible on this or that issue—at that moment you begin to drift from the center.
>
> . . . it's important for me to be a conservative. I'm a trinitarian Christian—that's conservative. I believe God reveals

himself to us in Jesus Christ—that's conservative. I believe
that the Bible is the Word of God whose purpose is to lead
us to faith in Jesus Christ—that's conservative. I accept the
Christian Creeds—that's conservative. I believe we have an
important treasure in . . . the Lutheran Confessions—that's
conservative. I believe we are justified by grace through
faith—that's conservative. I believe that the church is the
creation of the Holy Spirit—that's conservative.

I also found it important to go on and say that being an evangelical conservative moves one to become radical.

The prophetic word can only be spoken by those who
have a radical social conscience. . . . the most radical word
we can speak is a word of hope. Let it be . . . a message of
hope for the earth. To say that we believe in life when we
are surrounded by death is a very radical idea. To face the
possibility of the ultimate destruction of life as we know it
and say that God still has a word to speak—that is radical.
A radical social conscience will . . . call for pastors who will
speak out courageously on human justice issues.

During all this time as synod bishop momentum was building
for the union three Lutheran churches: The Association of Evangelical Lutheran Churches, the American Lutheran Church, and the
Lutheran Church in America. Though I was on record as a strong
supporter of this process, I had no idea I would be called to play a
role in it. In the next chapter I will try to review that process.

Chapter 10

In the shipyard:
building a new Lutheran church

Louisville and Lutheran merger

Do you hear those wedding bells?

My earlier pessimism about Lutheran unity changed as the decade of the 1970s unfolded. By 1972 the three churches decided to put these sentiments to the test. It was agreed that the churches would meet in simultaneous conventions in August 1982: the LCA in Louisville, the ALC in San Diego, and the AELC in Cleveland. The major issue, of course, was whether to merge.

There was little doubt about where the AELC and the LCA would come out. The AELC had already played a large role by being committed to merger from the day it formed. It was assumed that the LCA would vote positively.

The question mark was the ALC. A two-thirds vote was needed. Given the reluctance of David Preus to show anything other than lukewarm interest in merger, many wondered if that church would reflect the sentiment of its leader.

The three conventions were linked by telephone so that the results of the vote could be announced simultaneously at all three sites. Martin Marty was the moderator. When he asked James Crumley for the LCA vote, the results were even better than expected—ninety-eight percent in favor. There was a strong response of affirmation in the Louisville convention hall. When Marty asked William Kohn for the response from Cleveland, no one was surprised to hear that the AELC had given unanimous affirmation for merger.

Then a hush fell over the three conventions. We waited for word from Preus on the West Coast. There was a brief interruption in the telephone link, heightening the tension even further. Finally Preus came on the line. "Votes cast," he said, "987 for . . ." No one in Louisville heard the negative count. It was drowned out by shouts of acclamation. Everyone knew that the positive vote was far above the necessary two-thirds. As it turned out, the negative votes were ninety. It had passed by ninety-one percent.

All three conventions exploded in sustained applause. It was a delirious, unforgettable moment. Old friends embraced, strangers hugged. As the *Louisville Courier-Journal* put it: "They were on their feet, clapping and cheering. Some literally leaped for joy" (9/9/82).

Several years later in an interview with Clark Morphew of the *St. Paul Pioneer Press*, Corinne remembered that moment:

> I was sitting in the back of the auditorium, in the observers' section. When the . . . vote was announced, I saw Herb get out of his chair in the delegates' section and start walking to the back of the room. We hugged and wept together, and then I knew how deeply we both wanted Lutheran unity (4/26/87).

When the three conventions settled down Martin Marty led us in our first joint prayer: "O Holy Spirit . . . call us now to ever deeper levels of unity, gather us as long dispersed Lutherans into richer communion." Later Marty said that it was "the most decisive" day in the three hundred-year history of Lutheranism in America.

The Commission for a New Lutheran Church (CNLC)

Prior to the vote on merger, the churches had wrestled with the question, "Who will guide us if the vote is affirmative?" They made provision for a Commission for a New Lutheran Church (CNLC) to oversee that process. The commission would have seventy members: thirty-one each from the ALC and LCA, and eight from the AELC. They agreed that the process would span six years. A so-called "quota system" for the CNLC was agreed to by all three churches: sixty percent lay, forty percent clergy; fifty percent male, fifty percent female; ten percent persons of color or whose primary language is other than English.

I came to the convention assuming that I would not be part of that planning group. Howard McCarney had been nominated by the LCA Executive Council and I concluded that he would be the only LCA synodical bishop elected to the CNLC.

The assembled delegates decided, however, to make a small exception to the quotas. They would leave four slots open where there would be no limitations to election. Anyone—male, female, ordained, lay, majority, minority—could be nominated. The nominating ballot produced fifty-three names, forty-eight of them male. The top six included:

William Lazareth	229
Robert Marshall	197
John Reumann	168
Herbert Chilstrom	101
David Vikner	85
Kenneth Sauer	82

On subsequent ballots the top four retained their places and were elected.

Having attended the ALC convention in San Diego, Richard John Neuhaus offered the post-conventions observation that "The ALC voice will be countered by some LCA heavyweights . . . Robert

Marshall, former LCA president; Herbert Chilstrom, bishop in
Minnesota; William Lazareth, head of Faith and Order; H. George
Anderson, of Luther College." He went on to mention that the
last three ". . . are regularly mentioned as 'very possibles' for presiding bishop of the new body" (*Forum Letter*, 10/22/82). I have
no idea why he did not include Reumann among the so-called
"heavyweights."

Though I often questioned the judgment of Neuhaus, he made
what proved to be, at least to a degree, a prophetic observation of
how the CNLC would function:

> A contrived inclusiveness ends up with people who do not
> have the confidence of significant constituencies, who do
> not know what is happening, and who are therefore prime
> candidates for the manipulation of bureaucrats who know
> how to play the relevant games. At the same time, although
> recognized leaders can be held more accountable, there is a
> sincere determination to get the broadest possible partici-
> pation in this merger process.

Speculation about leadership

It was inevitable, of course, that speculation about a leader for the
new church would begin to spring up as soon as the decision to
move forward was made. Neuhaus was not the only one who was
pondering that question.

When asked for his opinion, Elmo Agrimson simply stated that
he was certain none of the current leaders—Crumley, Preus, or
Kohn—". . . would be a viable candidate for president of the new
church. I think in establishing a new church they're . . . looking for
new leadership" (*Minneapolis Star Tribune*, 11/9/82).

Prior to the Louisville convention, my staff colleague Charles
D. Anderson had visited with Lyle Schaller about merger issues.
Schaller, along with researcher George Barna, were regarded as the
country's chief "gurus" on matters of Protestant church life. Among

other things, Schaller shared his perception about leadership of the merged church. Anderson's notes stated:

> I am sure you are Lyle's favorite candidate for bishop of the new church. He feels that you have one liability and that is that you do not come out of the ALC. However, when I explained your roots at Augsburg [College] and that you had gone to Augustana [Seminary] . . . he felt that that would reduce the liability. He knows that you have high credibility with the ALC in the North Central Region—a powerful area in the ALC. Nonetheless, he feels that an ALC bishop would stand a better chance of pulling the church together. He agreed that even more important was that the new bishop come from the Midwest (5/31/83).

The *Forum Letter* opined in November 1982 that three persons seemed the most likely candidates for leadership of the new church: H. George Anderson, William Lazareth, and me. A few days later in a letter to my daughter Mary and son Chris I wrote:

> I would like to bury my head and pretend it isn't being said, but that would be very naïve. . . . it's a heavy burden to live with. And to live with it for another five years is something I don't relish. I find that I have to come back again and again to the basics and pray, "Thy will be done"—and to go on simply doing my best to accomplish the job I have been given—and not worry about the future. I know that's idealistic, but I also know that it can eat a person up with anxiety if you let it preoccupy your mind at all times. The words of Jesus, "Be not anxious for the morrow" make a lot of good sense.

Continue on the LCA Executive Council?

Later in the convention I was reelected to the LCA Executive Council by a strong vote. Now I would have to wrestle with the question of whether I could serve in both arenas, the council and the CNLC, and still give effective leadership for the Minnesota Synod.

Not many days after the convention I received a long letter from Paul Werger, bishop of the LCA Iowa Synod. It was a kind and wise letter from a brother in Christ. After telling me that he had asked the Iowa delegates to vote for me for membership on the CNLC, he went on to say,

> I have believed for some time that God has his hand on you in a special way. You have *the* significant place in the new church in 1988. I want to do everything I can to support you because I believe in the direction you give to the ministry in the new church. We are not only friends but we are of a kindred spirit and it feels good to see that succeed.

Werger went on to counsel me to take care of myself and to think seriously about relinquishing my membership on the LCA Executive Council. "You give great leadership to the church, but you must ask yourself if you aren't stretching yourself too thin."

I don't recall whether I had already decided to do exactly as he suggested. In any event, it was wise counsel from a trusted friend. I resigned from the Executive Council. Though it was the right decision, it was not an easy one. I felt I was just beginning to come into my own on the council. I thoroughly enjoyed the companionship of others in that leadership group. Nevertheless, it was the right choice. My hands were more than full.

The CNLC—Initial stages of its work

It was agreed that the CNLC would meet ten times over a four- to five-year period. Meetings would range from three to five days in length. Commissioners were also assigned to a variety of sub-committees for work in specific areas, such as constitution and bylaws, purpose, synodical boundaries, legal matters, headquarters site, and constituting convention. In short, the time commitment for each member of the commission was substantial.

All sessions were to be open to visitors. Equally as important, the CNLC decided to meet in a variety of locations across the country so that visitors might have access to at least one or two of the meetings in a given area.

The first meeting of the CNLC was held at the St. Benedict's Center near Madison, Wisconsin. I soon learned that one of the qualifications for being named to the CNLC belonged at the top of the list—"good humor and patience in fulfilling demanding tasks." It was not a pleasant meeting. Arnold Mickelson, executive for the CNLC, had done his homework. But it soon became apparent that it would take a Herculean effort to bring all of the disparate parts of the commission together.

Early in the process it was clear that certain issues would be most formidable for the CNLC. In my journal in mid May 1983 I noted:

> There are some elements that could be disruptive. For example, the status of clergy in the new church could be a problem for us. In the LCA we have tended to give more recognition to clergy—delegates to synod convention, e.g., whereas in the ALC clergy do not necessarily have that privilege—especially non-parish pastors. There is also an element of congregationalism in the ALC and in certain parts of the LCA—PA, e.g.,—that could prove troublesome. These people like to speak of the *congregations* as being the base & foundation of the church. I don't question the importance of the congregation. But it seems to me that the N.T. does not give us much evidence that the congregational entity should be elevated above other expressions of the church—the region or the church in all the world. The same Greek term "ecclesia" is used to describe all three.

> If some division develops I don't really think it will split off ALC from LCA & AELC. I think it more likely that some congregations & some members of congregations will pull out and go elsewhere.

Now, writing nearly twenty-five years later, and as we witness the formation of new splinter churches like the North American Lutheran Church (NALC) and Lutheran Churches in Mission for Christ (LCMC), I could hardly have been more prophetic.

In that same journal entry I speculated a bit on interactions within the CNLC and on those who appeared to be emerging as leaders.

> It is interesting to watch the dynamics at work at our meetings. It's difficult to say at this time which persons will have the most influence on the process. It looks like Frank Fry and Al Anderson are out to muscle their way into positions of leadership. They seem determined to be in places where they can throw their weight around. (And both have considerable physical weight to back up their moves!) But in the long run I don't see either of these men as bearing a major role in the formation of a new church. Neither, in my judgment, has the deep respect that one must have to play such a role.
>
> I see the major forces as residing with Bob Marshall, John Tietjen, Bill Lazareth—possibly David Preus. I expect that Bill and Dave will not hit it off well as this thing unfolds. In fact, I fear that either or both could slow the process or even thwart it.

I went on to observe that David Hardy seemed too eager to speak and wondered about the long-term effectiveness of his role on the commission.

Those early speculations proved to be interesting, but hardly accurate. Hardy and Anderson soon emerged as strong and important leaders on the commission. Without their initiative and acumen I doubt we would have kept to our deadline for merger. Others who came to the fore and became significant players in the early meetings were Reuben Swanson, Dorothy Jacobs, and Molly Shannon. Shannon, strong but not offensive, made certain that the role of women in the new church would be assured. Jacobs, a diminutive, soft-spoken Texan, was probably the key behind-the-scenes member of the CNLC. Swanson, always a churchman of the highest order and a competent administrator, gave skill and energy to the process. Hardy, outwardly a grizzly bear but inwardly a teddy bear, asked hard questions but never with the thought of slowing the process.

Meetings of the CNLC were what one might expect. We paid attention to crucial issues, including the doctrinal questions related to forming a new constitution. We cared for mundane matters. But in the midst of the ordinary, there was always a sense of prayerful dependence on the Spirit of God to be our guide and helper. After the spring 1982 meeting of the commission I reported to the Minnesota Synod that

> This meeting was characterized by a spirit of prayer and
> a sense of community that grows with each subsequent
> session. I found it most moving to kneel with the other
> seventy commissioners at the beginning of the meeting to
> implore the grace and wisdom of God as we undertook our
> task. On another occasion we took time to exchange the
> peace of God when we had passed through a particularly
> intense time of discussion ("Update," March 1982).

Yet having said all that, I have to admit that the observation of Eric Gritsch about decision-making bodies proved to be true of the CNLC as well: "Non-theological factors always enhance theological dialogue, be it a cocktail hour or a worship experience" (*The Boy from the Burgenland*, page 81).

Where am I headed?

On March 31, 1982, midway through my service as Minnesota Synod bishop, I sat down to reflect on where my life seemed to be heading:

The struggle is to find balance. Balance in work, home, family, rest, recreation. I suppose these struggles will last as long as I live. Sometimes as I drive down the highway on my way to yet another service or meeting I find myself asking, "Why me?" I think of my very ordinary home background as a child & youth & wonder what it is in me that keeps bringing greater & greater responsibility. And what is it that drives me on to accept more & more? That will remain a mystery. I only want to *be* what I was made to *be*. And that can get so easily distorted because of sin, etc. I'm reading *The Cardinal Sins* right now—a book about the R. Catholic Church—actually a novel, risqué in some ways, but very sobering in other ways. It raises questions about politics in the church, about how easily one gets caught in the web of things, how quickly perspective is lost. After nearly six years in office, am I the kind of person who should be a bishop in the church? Am I so caught in the web that I've lost perspective? How much integrity is there in me? How pure are my motives? How fair? How coura- geous? How wise? How kind? How effective? I need grace more than ever—but oh how easily that is forgotten!

On the road for the new church

It was expected that members of the CNLC would be available to interpret the actions of the commission and advocate for the formation of a merged church. In my presentations I tried to make the case for a church that would give equal weight to three entities: the local congregation, the synod, and the churchwide organiza- tion. This was particularly important in view of the suspicion of former ALC congregations that there might be an intrusion into their local autonomy. At a clergy/laity gathering at the Lutheran Theological Seminary at Gettysburg, I said that "I would hope that most of the Lutheran churches have matured enough to see that the local congregation is only one of several expressions of the church."

I also argued for the importance of remembering our past while, at the same time, thinking creatively about what a new expression of that heritage might mean.

In September 1983 I probably did one of the more courageous acts of that era when I went to Waldorf College in Forest City, Iowa, to speak to a group of mostly ALC clergy. It was expected that one of the hot-button issues in the merger would be whether the terms "inerrant" and "infallible" would be used in governing documents to describe the Bible. The ALC had used them in its constitution. The LCA and AELC had not.

I waded in at Waldorf, trying to make the case for not using them. The audience was kind. But it seemed clear to me that there were some who were suspicious of this LCA "liberal" who had invaded their territory. If I had had any thought about collecting points for a campaign to head the new church, this strategy would have been anathema. My feeling was that there was no way to avoid this confrontation, and one might as well do it in Iowa as in any other place.

Among other things, I used a reference from Frederick Schiotz's book *One Man's Story* to make my point. Schiotz, former president of the ALC and highly respected in his own church and beyond, insisted that when the ALC incorporated those terms into its constitution it was not referring to the *text* of Scripture, but rather to the idea that the Bible leads us *inerrantly* and *infallibly* to faith in Christ. I also mentioned that I knew that there were many in the ALC, especially among pastors and theologians, who would be happy to be rid of these terms.

> The Bible is the Word of God when it is the means by which we come to know the living God through the cruci-fied Son. When we allow ourselves to get hung up on theories of inspiration or descriptive terms to tell us what the Bible is or is not, we miss the deepest utterances of the biblical speech. . . .

... the formation of a new church gives us the opportunity
to bring new life to the church by recapturing the dynamic
force of the confessional understanding of "the Word of
God."

After my lecture H. George Anderson, another lecturer at the
event and a fellow member of the CNLC, approached me and said,
"Herb, you certainly were courageous!" He was president of Luther
College in Decorah, Iowa, at the time and knew well the climate in
that part of the church.

At a convention of the Southwestern Minnesota District of the
ALC, I waded in on this subject again. In a letter to an editor one
person reacted against what I had said:

The holiness of Scripture involves God and the Holy Spirit,
yet it appears that Chilstrom is conveying the idea of reason
over the absolute will of God. Is not Chilstrom knowledge-
able enough to lead other men as God would have him lead
them? It was sickening to hear from Chilstrom that the
LCA does not accept the inerrancy and infallibility of the
Scriptures.

The issue of use of these terms got resolved later by the CNLC,
largely through the leadership of David Preus. He urged the commission not to include them in the definition of Scripture, pointing out
that they had been the source of "endless nitpicking" in the ALC.

In 1985 I got caught in the crossfire of the argument over control
of local property. Coming out of LCA background, I felt strongly
that when a congregation voted to leave the denomination the
property should go to those who agreed to remain with the church
body. I advocated that this should be a provision in the constituting
documents of the new church.

This put me in direct opposition, of course, to folks in the AELC
who had broken from the LCMS. AELC members of the commission argued that their experience with Missouri had been just the

opposite; namely, that it was the national body that had forsaken the historic Lutheran understanding of the faith. They insisted that in these instances the property should be ceded to the group that remained faithful to those confessions.

The discussion reflected the polity of the merging churches and would remain a sticking point even after the new church came into being.

As much as time permitted, I went to other places to make the case for the new church.

Throughout this process I kept reminding folks in the Minnesota Synod that Lutheran unity would not come without some painful changes in our synod. In 1982 I wrote:

> Although we are the largest synod in the LCA, we number only half the size of the ALC in Minnesota. Unlike the LCA on the East coast where there are virtually no ALC congregations, and where there will be little impact on the regional level, we will no longer have any sense whatever of what was once the Minnesota Synod. There is some grief in that, to be sure. But if we recall our Lord's words about the seed dying in order to bring new life, then we can look forward with excitement and enthusiasm to the development of our new church in our area. ("Facing Forward," page 102)

Issues confronting the CNLC

What's in a name?

The February 1986 meeting of the CNLC in Minneapolis would prove to be one of the most critical in the entire process of bringing the new church to reality. Contrary to the expectations of some, the commission came together quickly and solidly in designing most of the elements of the "Statement of Faith" for the new constitution. Much more taxing would be the decision on the name and the site for the headquarters for the new church.

A subpanel of the commission had narrowed the field of names to "Lutheran Church in the United States of America" and "Evangelical Lutheran Church in the USA."

I was not at peace with either name. I wrestled with this question right up until the CNLC began its sessions on February 15, 1986. I concluded that the name should be: "Evangelical Lutheran Church in America."

Before taking my proposal to the commission I knew I had to do certain groundwork. Some had opposed the use of the term "America" in the name out of deference to other churches in the Western Hemisphere who were also Americans—and especially our sister church in Canada. I decided to test that objection. I called three of my Canadian bishop friends—men who had been synod bishops in Canada prior to the formation of the Evangelical Lutheran Church in Canada in 1986. Don Sjoberg, president of the ELCIC, was not enthusiastic about the idea, but said he would raise no loud cry against it. Lee Luetkehoelter and Bill Huras had no objection whatever. "That's what we call your country—America—and what we call you—Americans."

I also needed the support of the commissioner from the Caribbean Synod, Josefina Nieves Libran. I knew she did not like the use of "USA" in the name because Puerto Rico and the Virgin Islands are not states. I informed her of what I intended to do. She liked it and agreed to speak in favor of my recommendation.

At the appropriate moment I rose and presented my recommendation: "I move that the name of the new Lutheran church be: Evangelical Lutheran Church in America."

In my remarks in support of my recommendation I covered several important points:

> I reviewed my conversations with leaders of the Lutheran church in Canada, indicating that they had no strong opposition to the use of "America" in our name.

For the people in the Caribbean, I suggested, ". . . the 'Lutheran Church in the USA' means *their* church. But if you say 'Evangelical Lutheran Church in America' it means *our* church. The use of America would be seen as more inclusive."

I concluded that "We will be happier in the long run with Evangelical Lutheran Church in America."

When I sat down a strange an almost eerie silence fell over the room for a few moments. John Tietjen, who was sitting directly in front of me, turned around and said reflectively, "I like that. I really like that."

Nieves gave a strong pitch in favor of the name, citing the reasons already mentioned. George Villas, a Hispanic commissioner from the Pacific Southwest, reinforced her points.

Soon others got up and spoke in support of my recommendation. Lloyd Svendsbye reminded us that most national Lutheran churches around the world use the term "evangelical" in their name. He also liked the idea that this would accent that we are evangelical, strongly identifying with our confessional heritage.

Albert Anderson looked back at Lutheran history in the United States and pointed out the obvious; namely, that many of our predecessor church bodies prior to the mergers in the early 1960s incorporated "evangelical" in their names: Evangelical Lutheran Church, United Evangelical Lutheran Church, Association of Evangelical Lutheran Churches, Augustana Evangelical Lutheran Church, and others.

I waited for opposing voices. Surely in this group there would be some. There were none. It was as though we were all in solid agreement, a rare moment after debates about quotas and other incendiary issues. After only thirteen minutes of discussion, the chair noted that there were no more speakers at microphones. He called for a voice vote. According to reporters, it passed without any "audible dissent."

No one was more stunned than I at the outcome. And no one could have been more pleased.

As Edgar Trexler pointed out in his book on the formation and early years of the ELCA *(High Expectations)*, it may have been the only time in history when the name of a Lutheran church body was recommended by the one who eventually became its first leader.

Where should our headquarters be located?
If there were any members of the CNLC who thought our relatively easy choice of a name would carry over into our choice of a location for the headquarters of the new church, they would soon be disillusioned.

A subpanel had been working on the question and a straw vote had seemed to favor Chicago. I was among those who were leaning in that direction. We all waited, however, for the results of a feasibility study that would give us some indication of the cost of office space in various locations, especially in New York, Chicago, and Minneapolis. That report came out just prior to our meeting in Minneapolis in February 1986. When those figures showed that operating costs in Minneapolis would be from $500,000 to $2 million less than in Chicago, I shifted my preference to Minneapolis.

I had reasoned earlier that locating in Chicago with its larger minority population would be expedient and wise. But in reflecting on church history—as seen through the eyes of Lloyd Svendsbye who had studied the record of predecessor church bodies and concluded that the ULCA and Augustana church bodies had been, among all Lutheran churches, the most engaged in social justice issues—I decided that this factor need not weigh so heavily in this decision. This was further reinforced when I also noted that in more recent history both the LCA and the ALC, with headquarters in New York City and Minneapolis, had been equally involved in such matters.

I also observed that when the staff for the new church was selected there would no doubt be many from the current ALC national staff in Minneapolis who would be chosen to serve. It made sense to me that moving as few people as possible during the formation of the new church would be an act of kindness on our part. Fewer families would be disrupted. I also noted that international flights out of the Twin Cities were becoming more and more common. This was an important factor for global mission and ecumenical work and for staff who travel abroad.

At the commission meeting the battle raged between Chicago and Minneapolis. The *Minneapolis Star Tribune* reported that the one-and-one-half day debate was "emotional and sometimes testy" (2/18/85). Support for each seemed about equal. When it became apparent that there was not enough support for Minneapolis, some recommended that the churchwide offices be scattered to several locations for the first years in the new church. That proposal got little consideration.

In the midst of the debate and when patience was wearing thin, William Kohn, head of the AELC, offered what he thought was a worthy compromise: Milwaukee. Later he admitted it was a "shot in the dark." The impasse between Chicago and Minneapolis led some commissioners to the conclusion that Milwaukee might be a worthy option. It was argued that Milwaukee offered the ethnic diversity of Chicago and the affordability of Minneapolis. After no less than seven votes, Milwaukee finally prevailed by a margin of fifty-nine to nine.

> With the decision finally at hand, the tired adversaries prayed together, shook hands, hugged and thanked God and one another for patience (*Minneapolis Star Tribune*, 2/18/85).

Not everyone was happy. Robert Marshall let it be known that he was "completely negative" about the decision. I, too, was keenly disappointed. I was one of the nine who voted against Milwaukee. When asked by the press about our decision, I tried to put a positive spin on it. I thought our decision was final and that we needed to begin to get used to the prospect of Milwaukee being our headquarters.

Others were of the same opinion. When interviewed by the AELC's *Lutheran Perspective* (3/3/86), both Bill Kinnison and Dave Preus stated that there was no turning back. Kinnison called any such attempt "unlikely to succeed." Preus called reopening the debate "highly unlikely." He went on to say that there would have to be ". . . a great groundswell of objection . . . in order for the commission to reconsider its action."

That is exactly what happened. There was a "great groundswell of objection" to the Milwaukee selection. Martha Sawyer Allen, writer for the *Minneapolis Star Tribune* reported:

> The commission's February decision to put the headquarters in Milwaukee . . . has been roundly scoffed at by all sides of the Lutheran power structure and appears to be dead. Although most don't complain about the city itself, they said it simply isn't convenient for travel (4/6/86).

In the weeks that followed I was asked over and over, "Why Milwaukee?" I had no good answer. In the interim a chorus of objections to Milwaukee continued to surface.

While that decision hung in the balance a more sobering challenge emerged.

A serious threat to merger and an unexpected role
What happened next probably should have been anticipated. But hindsight is always perfect; foresight is a bit more complicated.

While we were engaged in intense discussions about other matters, the commission had been making decisions about fundamental issues such as a statement of faith, the definition of the church, and other elements of the constitution for the new church. But we had not, in the judgment of some, come to complete clarity on several critical issues, and especially about the ministry, quotas, the relationship of congregations to the larger church, and pensions for clergy and other church workers.

At a meeting of the LCA Conference of Bishops in New York City in early April 1986—and just prior to the meeting of the Executive Council of the LCA—the bishops discussed these issues. They worried that the proposed definition of the nature of the church leaned too far in the direction of emphasizing the local congregation as the locus of the church and did not place enough accent on the role of ordained ministers and the importance of the synod and the churchwide organization. LCA Bishops were also hearing more and more complaints from white male clergy about feeling disenfranchised.

The bishops recommended to the LCA Executive Council that several changes be made. The council agreed (with the exception of the CNLC recommendation on quotas) and issued a statement underscoring that if its demands were not met by the CNLC at its June meeting in Seattle the council would recommend to the LCA convention in August that delegates vote *not* to merge. Bishop Crumley reinforced the action of the council by stating that though he was still in favor of the new church, he wondered if the constitution in its current form ". . . is the kind of thing the LCA could adopt . . ." (*Minneapolis Star Tribune*, 4/6/86).

The press reported that the LCA ". . . appears to be reneging on its desire to join the new church" (*Minneapolis Star Tribune*, 4/6/86).

It was at this juncture that I stepped into my role as mediator, a function I had played out in many settings throughout my ministry. It happened by sheer coincidence that I stayed on in New York City after the bishops' meeting to make a presentation to the LCA Executive Council. Also by sheer coincidence Lloyd Svendsbye, president of Luther Northwestern Seminary and a member of the CNLC, was in New York City to meet with the Executive Council

on matters related to the seminary—not at all to CNLC matters. I
learned that Lloyd and I were flying back to Minnesota on the same
flight. I suggested that we try to arrange for seats together on the
flight so that we could discuss what had just happened at the Conference of Bishops and LCA Executive Council meeting.

From the time Svendsbye and I were installed into our respective offices in 1976, he as president of the seminary and I as synod
president/bishop, the chemistry between us had been excellent. We
were accustomed to speaking openly and frankly about any subject.
Thus, on this occasion we were able to go to the quick on the questions raised by the LCA leadership. Our conversation on the flight
was intense. Both of us were totally committed to Lutheran unity and
believed that a way simply must be found to get through this impasse.

Before we landed in Minneapolis we agreed to bring together
CNLC members from the Twin Cities as an ad hoc group to see if
we could work out some compromises on the issues. I happened to
know that Reuben Swanson would be in Minnesota for other meetings and agreed to contact him and invite him to attend. I knew
that Swanson, like Svendsbye, was also totally committed to merger
and was experienced in working for reasonable compromises.

Meanwhile Crumley continued to express reservations about
merger. He kept insisting that we needed to be clear about "ecclesiology" before proceeding with merger. When pressed, he found
it difficult to explain exactly what he meant by that term. The
Lutheran Standard reported him as saying (5/14/86) that ". . . the
solid embodiment . . . of our self-understanding and self-identity as
Lutherans" was more important than focusing only on merging our
three churches.

The reaction to the LCA actions was greeted with surprise and
thinly disguised disdain by the leadership of the AELC and the
ALC. Though no public statements were issued, leaders in those
churches wondered privately why the LCA leadership had waited
so long to air its concerns.

Kinnison, chair of the CNLC and out of LCA background, was less charitable about the actions of the LCA bishops. He minced no words: "The bishops of the (LCA) have given no vision for four years," he railed. He called their recommendations ". . . a pathetic display of false leadership. We have an opportunity for unity but we don't trust the people who are coming together to decide on it" (*Minneapolis Star Tribune*, 4/6/86).

Meanwhile our Twin Cities ad hoc group came together for two evenings of meetings at Luther Northwestern Seminary. Unfortunately I do not have a record of exactly who was in attendance. To the best of my recollection, in addition to Svendsbye, Swanson, and me, there was Kay Baerwald, Albert Anderson, Darold Beekmann, and Gerhart Forde. I am quite certain that Arnold Mickelson, executive director of the CNLC, was also at the meetings. I also seem to recall that David Preus was out of town and unable to attend. Or it may have been our judgment that having only one of the three church heads in attendance would not be wise.

We made good progress on the issues.

> We emphasized the interdependence of congregation, synod, and churchwide organization in the new church.

> We suggested refinements on the definition of ordained ministry.

> Recognizing that the LCA had accented conversations with Roman Catholic and Orthodox churches and the ALC had leaned more in the direction of partnership with Reformed churches, we saw the new church as a forum for looking in both directions.

> We suggested that we needed to trust the churches to resolve the questions surrounding the so-called quota system.

> We stressed that compromise regarding the pension program could be resolved.

When I learned that other members of the CNLC would be in the Twin Cities the next day, April 17, I arranged to meet with them to share what our ad hoc group had done and to invite their suggestions. Included in that group were Darold Beekmann, David Hardy, Paul Dovre, Carl Johnson, and H. George Anderson. Some of these were very strong players on the CNLC. They gave good suggestions, which our ad hoc group incorporated into our work.

Reports from our meetings went with Mickelson to the CNLC and to Kinnison. In a personal letter to me Kinnison affirmed what we had done.

> Your participation in an informal group in the Twin Cities
> area is a positive step. . . . This is what needs to happen in
> a number of places. I do not believe the issues are so great
> that a resolution cannot be found. However, I fear that
> some do not really want resolution.

Kinnison was especially angry at some members of the LCA Executive Council.

> We are missing leadership . . . and its absence is not easily
> provided for. Those who should be providing it shrink from
> the responsibility.

He went on to say that in spite of the bump in the road, he felt optimistic about the prospects for Lutheran unity. He said he believed that the lay members of the church were so fully committed to unity that the process could not be sidetracked. He concluded by thanking me for my efforts.

> You do not need a heavier burden, but many of us welcome
> all of your efforts in the past and in the future.

In the Minnesota Synod I continued to work for Lutheran unity. In a press report distributed by Religious New Service out of New York City (4/15/86) I characterized the differences as "a lover's quarrel" before marriage. Aborting the merger at this time would be "a total disaster."

In a letter to the pastors of the synod I assured them that I remained "unequivocally" committed to Lutheran unity. "The questions raised by the LCA bishops . . . can be resolved. I am confident we will have a new church January 1, 1988."

As time permitted I continued to speak at various events about the CNLC process. I tried to be careful not to underestimate the seriousness of the issues. I also emphasized in public comments that the Lutheran leaders in Minnesota had learned to trust each other over the years and that this kind of relationship would auger well for us in our quest for unity.

In one place (*Metro Lutheran*, May 1986) I conjectured that there may have been similar groups meeting in other parts of the country, working to find resolution to the issues. I learned later that Bishop Kenneth Sauer had been doing similar behind-the-scenes work in Ohio. Other than that, however, I heard nothing. Little wonder that Svendsbye and I got so much credit for "saving the merger." In the broader scheme of things that was probably more credit than we deserved.

Strong reactions from some LCA colleagues

My comments about a "lover's quarrel" put me on a collision course with Franklin D. Fry, another member of the commission.

The next time we were together at a meeting Fry invited me to his hotel room. He proceeded to rake me over the coals for disagreeing with him and underestimating the gravity of the situation. I choose my battles carefully. I engaged in no argumentation with him. I simply apologized if I had offended him and went on my way.

My comment about "a lover's quarrel" also brought intense reactions from some fellow LCA bishops. In a strongly worded letter my close friend Paul Werger, bishop of the LCA Iowa Synod, stated that my actions gave the impression that the LCA bishops, contrary to the statement that came out of our New York City meeting, were actually divided on those issues. He feared that we might "give away the store" if we did not adhere strictly to our bishops' statement. He appealed to the need to abide by the "... solid theological and ecclesiological precepts that motivated us to take the firm actions we did."

Ralph Kempski, bishop of the Indiana-Kentucky Synod, took a similar stance. He felt that the effect of my comment was to "trivialize the difference" between the LCA's "ecclesiology" and that of the other churches.

In my responses to Werger and Kempski I began by stating that I had no need to come off sounding apologetic or defensive. As for the "lover's quarrel" comment, I reminded them of what I had stated at our meeting in New York City, namely, that

> I saw the recommendations . . . as serious points of discussion that needed to be ironed out between the three churches. I made my pledge to (the LCA bishops)—publicly—that I would go back to Minnesota and do my part in that corner of the church to bring about resolution. That is exactly what I have done.

I went on to insist that the issues we raised in New York City were not just matters that divided our three churches; they were also issues of division *within* our churches.

I pointed to places in our LCA constitution where congregations had large measures of autonomy.

I noted that the LCA Executive Council had rejected our recommendation regarding quotas.

On pension issues, I reminded them that Howard McCarney and Reuben Swanson, prominent LCA members of the CNLC, had joined me in voting in favor of the compromise recommended by the CNLC.

I noted that even James Crumley had apparently softened his resistance to merger since our New York City meeting and was now being quoted as saying that "We'll make it. Even though I am concerned about the transit-issues and how much has to be done in that regard" (*Texas-Louisiana Lutheran*, May 1986).

I ended my letter to Kempski with an appeal to Joseph Sittler, a respected "godfather" LCA theologian. I had just heard Sittler give an address at an LSTC event at which he gave what I termed a "not-so-gentle rap on the fingers" to our LCA bishops for our preoccupation with polity. Sittler pointed out that LCA polity had been influenced by the tradition of the Pennsylvania Ministerium of the old ULCA. Clergy played a dominant role in that tradition. In contrast, Midwestern Lutherans came with sparse pastoral leadership. It was lay-driven in most places. Here, too, Sittler insisted, the gospel was preached and the sacraments administered. He concluded by wondering out loud when we would get beyond talking about polity and focus on the mission of this new church.

When I was elected bishop of the ELCA more than a year later I put the whole episode into perspective (*The Spirit*, 5/2/87) by suggesting to reporter Daniel Cattau that:

> I don't feel as if I broke any ranks. If the documents were
> not for the purpose of negotiation and discussion, then I
> don't know what we were doing.

A retrospective on the spring of 1986

What can one say about the events of the spring of 1986? In my judgment, the substance of the meetings Svendsbye and I set up in Minnesota was not all that consequential. We did come up with some important recommendations related to procedural matters. But I'm convinced that the recommendations we made might have come from other places had we not made them. There was simply too much momentum for merger to stop it. The major impact of those Minnesota meetings was essentially that we *had* them. As word got out that we had met and that we were working on resolution as an inter-Lutheran ad hoc group, it gave hope to others to think positively about the merger.

It is also my strong conviction that had not both Reuben Swanson and Albert Anderson attended the Minnesota meetings, little would have come of them. Throughout the process they were key players. Their participation carried enormous weight.

It also needs to be said that the ALC Church Council, under the leadership of David Preus, played a key role during this time. Had it chosen to counter point by point the strong recommendations coming from the LCA bishops and Church Council, an acrimonious atmosphere would have resulted that would surely have delayed the merger. ALC Bishop Darold Beekmann wisely noted that had the ALC ". . . postured against the LCA with the commission in the middle," it would have been disastrous. Instead, ". . . with a strong ALC endorsement and the strong support from major segments of the LCA," he could be optimistic about progress toward merger.

Can we keep this name?

My plate was full during these months. I didn't need another stress point. But one came very unexpectedly. A seminary student, probably working on a church history project, informed the CNLC that the name "Evangelical Lutheran Church in America" was already in use. It seemed that the tiny church body known popularly as "The Eielsen Synod" actually had "Evangelical Lutheran Church in America" as its official name. Founded in the 1800s by an itinerant Lutheran minister named Elling Eielsen, the church body had dwindled to only two congregations and had no living clergy. Yet it was still in existence.

This set off a flurry of legal activity. After a thorough search, attorneys determined that the Eielsen church had never bothered to register its name. This seemed to clear the way for the new church to use that name. There were some, however, including James Crumley and Reuben Swanson, who felt that an ethical issue was involved. Even though they had not registered the name and were scarcely alive, it was felt that we should respect them by not taking the name.

This is where Corinne's roots in the Hauge tradition came into play. The Hauge Synod merged into the Norwegian Lutheran

Church (later the Evangelical Lutheran Church—ELC) in 1917. But the Hauge tradition continued to run strong in some places, including South Dakota. There was a close affinity between the Hauge and the Eielsen folks. Both accented the importance of personal conversion, lay leadership, and public testimony of one's faith. The two small groups often had joint gatherings, usually referred to as "testimony meetings."

The head of the tiny Eielsen Synod was a layman by the name of Truman Larson, the son of the last surviving pastor of that church. We learned that he lived on a farm with his widowed mother near Jackson, Minnesota.

I called Larson and asked if Corinne and I might visit with him about the name issue. When he learned that I was married to the daughter of Jens Hansen from Vermillion, South Dakota he warmed considerably to the idea and agreed to the meeting. Prior to our visit one Sunday afternoon, I wrote a long letter to him giving him some personal background and outlining the name issue as I understood it.

In my journal I described our visit:

> We drove up to the Larson farm between Windom and Jackson (Minn.) exactly at 5 p.m. It was an impressive-looking farm—good land, fine buildings, a well-kept farm house. As we walked up to the door everything was very quiet. No one to meet us or greet us. I pressed the doorbell and we waited. After a couple of minutes Truman appeared at the door—dressed in a long-sleeved shirt and tie with a wide belt and large buckle. He invited us in. We entered through the kitchen. I noticed that a large well-preserved cookstove was covered with a single layer of newspapers.
>
> Truman was quiet, obviously very uneasy with these visitors from Mpls. I asked about his mother. He pointed to the living room and said she was waiting for us. We walked though the dining room area and into the room where

> Mrs. Larson was sitting in a high rocker by a bay window. Behind her was an organ. Next to her was a small stand with a Bible and writing tablet.

> It took only a moment to realize that this was "not my show." I seated myself off to the side while Corinne took the chair immediately in front of Mrs. Larson. Truman sat across the room on the davenport. Within moments we knew we had met the matriarch of the Eielsen Synod!

For well over an hour Corinne and Mrs. Larson engaged in animated conversation about mutual family ties and common acquaintances. It turned out, for example, that Mrs. Larson and her late husband had been at Corinne's dad's home for his eightieth birthday. She recalled meeting Corinne on that occasion. That was just one of many connections.

I began to wonder if we would ever get around to the primary business of the day. This conversation between the two women, however, was absolutely critical in establishing good rapport.

When we moved to the subject of our visit, one of the first things Mrs. Larson said was that she recalled how incensed Pastor Blennis, the president of the Eielsen Synod, was back in 1946 when the former Norwegian Lutheran Church changed its name to Evangelical Lutheran Church. She said that Blennis had accused them of "taking our name." That was my first clue. Why would Blennis have been so upset if the official name of the Eielsen Synod was "Evangelical Lutheran Church in America"?

At that point Truman suggested that I might like to see a copy of the Eielsen Synod constitution. Indeed I would.

> First, he brought me an English translation. Then he produced the original Norwegian version. As I studied them suddenly my eye fell on something quite astonishing. I noticed that in both versions there were quotation marks placed strategically around the words "Evangelical Lutheran Church." The Norwegian read:

Den uforandrede Kirke-Konstitution for den "Evangelist lutherste Kirke" i Nord America.

The English read:

The original (translated from Norwegian) Constitution of the "Evangelical Lutheran Church" in America.

Suddenly it dawned on me that this was why Pastor Blennis was so upset when the former ELC took that name. This was identical with their constituted name! This church's (the Eielsen Synod) name was "Evangelical Lutheran Church" after all and not "Evangelical Lutheran Church in America" as they . . . seem to have thought.

With this information in hand, the CNLC had no difficulty moving ahead and keeping the name for our new church.

Final Minnesota Synod Convention

In June 1986 we held our last Minnesota Synod convention at Gustavus Adolphus College. This would be my tenth.

As expected, the synod accepted the recommendation of the executive board and enthusiastically affirmed Lutheran merger. This was in contrast to the two other large synods of the LCA—Illinois and Central Pennsylvania—which voted for a delay of the merger if issues could not be resolved.

I had started off wondering if one could be both a pastor and a bishop. Now as we began to move into our final year I realized that I had, indeed, been both. My bond with pastors and lay persons across the synod was deep and pastoral.

Seattle: the CNLC resolves differences

Sensing that there was strong momentum in the three churches to get on with the merger, the commissioners made enormous progress at our meeting in Seattle, June 23–25, 1986.

The LCA backed down on its demand for a higher rate for clergy pensions.

The quotas recommended earlier were affirmed.

The recommended boundaries for the sixty-five synods were accepted.

On ecumenical affairs, the LCA's strong constitutional stance was approved for inclusion in the new church documents.

The LCA's insistence on defining the nature of the church as the interdependence of congregation, synod, and church-wide organization won approval.

It was agreed that rosters of "ordained ministers" and "associates in ministry" would be maintained in separate categories.

In less than thirty minutes (in contrast to the eight hours of debate in February in Minneapolis) the commission rescinded its decision on Milwaukee and chose Chicago as the site for the headquarters of the church.

Regarding local autonomy, congregations with historic ties to the LCA would have to have synod approval in the new church if they wanted to leave it; congregations with ties to the ALC and AELC would not.

In retrospect, I think John Tietjen was right regarding that last point when he noted that in a few years distinctions would be blurred and it would be a moot point.

Prior to the Seattle meeting I changed my mind about working for Minneapolis as a substitute for Milwaukee. I came to believe that Chicago was the preferred site.

Knowing his strong preference for Chicago, I informed Robert Marshall of my conversion. In a reply written several weeks prior to our Seattle meeting, Marshall expressed doubt that the decision about Milwaukee could be changed. He felt there was simply too much resistance to Chicago. He expected that the agenda at Seattle would be too crowded to accommodate another discussion about site. And he thought that the fact that the ALC Church Council had approved Milwaukee was enough to defeat a motion to rescind. He was also dismayed by the decision of the LCA Executive Council to make no decision, but to allow for multiple temporary centers and let the matter be resolved by the new church. All of this obviously dismayed Marshall. In spite of my switch to Chicago, I had little hope that the Milwaukee decision would be rescinded. Neither Marshall nor I could have anticipated what happened at Seattle. During the debate the commission tested its sentiments with three straw votes:

> On the first, Chicago was favored over Milwaukee by 39–38.
>
> On the second, Milwaukee was favored over a three-city plan by 38–29.
>
> On the third, Milwaukee was favored by 35–34.

It seemed that we were back where we started at the previous meeting. In the ensuing debate commissioners from the AELC took the lead and argued strenuously for Chicago. One of them made a motion to substitute Chicago for Milwaukee. I spoke in support of it, stressing again the importance of a site that was easily accessible for international travel. David Preus, in a surprise and unexpected move that appeared to be in opposition to his own ALC Church Council, announced his support for Chicago. Martha Sawyer Allen reported that after Preus' remarks ". . . a sigh went through the room as commissioners prepared to vote . . ." (*Minneapolis Star Tribune*, 6/26/86).

The vote was 41–25 in favor of Chicago. At long last the decision was final. Chicago it would be. Little could I have known that day how consequential that decision would be for Corinne and me.

The Seattle meeting had indeed been a remarkable event in the long journey for the CNLC. At the outset some commissioners spoke openly of delay because of uncertainty about unresolved issues. At the end John Tietjen from the AELC declared, "There's a feeling of cordiality and harmony here. No one dares upset the apple cart now" (*Minneapolis Star Tribune*, 6/26/86).

There were cynics, of course, who wondered if David Preus's change represented a genuine desire for Lutheran merger or if he was simply positioning himself for leadership of the new church. Having been the object of much speculation about why I did one thing or another, I gave Preus the benefit of the doubt.

In this connection, another issue the CNLC dealt with was the title for the head of the new church. The ALC had called this person the "presiding bishop." The LCA used "bishop," often appending "of the church." On this matter Crumley, for reasons I never understood, was adamant. He argued that "presiding" implied chairing an assembly of the church and that this person does much more than that. Yet the Episcopal Church had used "presiding bishop" without that implication. Had I known that I would be elected the first head of the new church and how much confusion this would precipitate I might have argued for the ALC usage. But that might have given the impression that I was think- ing of myself in that office and I was surely not going to step into that morass.

Crucial leaders

This may be a good point in this narrative to set down a word about those who, in my judgment, played the most crucial roles in the CNLC process. As you will see, some of my impressions at the first meeting of the commission held true. Others were com- pletely wrong. At all of the meetings I found myself surrounded by a remarkable group of persons with incredible skills, each bringing the strength of his or her peculiar background.

Let me, in spite of the risk, single out a few and suggest why they played such significant roles.

Molly Shannon, a lifelong educator and administrator, was one of those women, as I observed earlier, who didn't demand your attention, but got it by the sheer force of her personality and leadership skills. She had spent her life in administrative positions. The key role she played was to always remind the CNLC that we must be a church where both women and men would be given equal opportunity to serve. She was never obnoxious in stating her position. I can't imagine anyone on the CNLC who did not respect her.

David Hardy was a high-powered Chicago attorney. When you first hear him speak you are certain he must be mad at someone, and especially those to whom he is speaking. But in a very short time you come to know him in a more personal way and realize, as I observed, that this bear is a teddy bear. He was clearly a man with a deep love for the church. For decades Hardy had attended church conventions and other church-related gatherings, at times as an official delegate but usually on his personal vacation time. He was one of the most well-informed lay persons I had ever known. It is hard to imagine how the CNLC could have maneuvered its way through the legal aspects of the merger without Hardy's astute hand in the process.

Reuben Swanson was the secretary of the Lutheran Church in America prior to the merger. Swanson had been a parish pastor and synod president (bishop) prior to becoming an officer in the LCA. His administrative skills were legendary. He would often come to a meeting with ideas that he had thoroughly refined to the point where the group found it reasonable to follow his lead. He was a master at crafting resolutions and bringing them into a form that could be used by the larger group. He was personable and easy to like.

William Ellis was a black attorney from New York City. Though not as ebullient as Hardy, he was skilled in aiding the commission to frame the constitution and other legal documents in such a way that there would be no hitches when it came time for the constituting convention. The fact that things went so smoothly was in large part due to the exceptional work of Hardy and Ellis. I recall vividly the speech Ellis made in the heat of the discussion about quotas for the new church: "I do not ever want to be elected to anything on the basis of my race. I want to be elected because I am capable of serving and can make a significant contribution to the church. However, there are times in history when the church must be very deliberate about the way it goes on with its business. It is not legalistic for the church to say to itself that we must find appropriate ways for minority persons and others whose voices are not normally heard to have visibility in the decision-making process."

Dorothy Jacobs, a diminutive woman with a soft-spoken Texas accent, was both quiet and forceful at the same time. She never raised her voice, never showed any sign of being upset about anything, yet had convictions as strong as steel. She chaired the Design Committee, through all of the stages of drafting and designing what the structure of the new church would be. This proved to be far more taxing than the work of the committee on theology. Jacobs often worked behind the scenes, doing the kinds of seemingly mundane tasks that more prominent leaders would have tried to avoid because they considered it beneath their dignity. Jacobs was the kind of person a group like the CNLC needed to carry the process forward from meeting to meeting.

Albert Anderson can best be described as "dumb like a fox." He was so "old shoe" that he could relate to anyone, high or low or middle. He was comfortable in any setting. He had headed Augsburg Publishing House of the ALC for many years and built it into one of the leading church publishing enterprises in the country. Endowed with an ample girth that lapped over his trousers, Al's first move when he stood to speak was to hitch up his pants, and to repeat the gesture many times as he spoke. Those sitting behind him often wondered when they might slip to the floor. (They never did!) I sometimes described him as the only person I knew who could reach for a dime in his pocket and scratch his knee at the same time. Back of all that low-key demeanor, however, was a person who could get things done by his persuasive remarks and hard work behind the scenes. Again, Swanson and Anderson, one from the LCA and the other from the ALC, were probably the most important pair of persons through the merger process. It's difficult for me to imagine how we could have had a new church without the joint work of these two men.

John Reumann was professor of New Testament and Greek at Philadelphia Seminary. When he spoke we listened. His words were always carefully chiseled and honed to perfection. He was that valued professor whose skill as a biblical theologian was matched by his love for the church.

William Kinnison, chair of the commission and president of Wittenberg University, kept the group's nose to the grindstone. When the CNLC got bogged down in minutiae, Kinnison would remind us of the larger picture and cajole us into action. Though his red hair made one think that he might lose his cool, I only recall one instance when he did. That was when the LCA bishops gave signals that they thought the process toward merger should be slowed or halted.

Arnold Mickelson was not a member of the commission. In his role as executive director, however, he and his staff handled with skill and efficiency the mountains of materials that had to be produced and reproduced. I don't ever recall hearing anyone criticize him for doing less than what was expected of him. It was always more. His background as a businessman and then longtime secretary of the ALC were invaluable experience in carrying out his task. It needs to be added that his chief assistant, Lori Bergquist, also deserves high praise for her high dedication to the vision of the CNLC.

Let me repeat what I suggested earlier. Were someone else on the CNLC writing these lines they might well choose an entirely different set of key leaders of that group. Surely the parish pastors, theologians, other lay persons, synod bishops, church staff persons, and others brought unique gifts to the commission. I doubt, however, that we could have accomplished the task without those I've singled out above.

Off to Europe and the Alps

At the end of the Seattle meeting and with merger now certain, some commissioners sought me out and suggested that they would like to support me for leadership of the new church. I made no commitment to any of them. Edgar Trexler, editor of *The Lutheran* magazine, and Richard Koenig, editor of *Lutheran Partners*, were among several who told me they thought I was in the lead among all the candidates being talked about to serve in that role. I felt more unsettled than reassured by all of this speculation.

The day after we returned from Seattle to Minnesota, Corinne and I flew off to Europe to meet Chris when he finished his year of study at Bonn. We traveled to the Swiss Alps and then north to Denmark, Norway, and Sweden. It was good to get away from the pressures of all that was going on in the church in the United States. Yet I could not help but wonder what life would be like when I returned.

In my journal I described our first night in Switzerland:

> We stayed near the village of Grindelwald. The village itself
> is nestled in a valley between gigantic peaks on every side.
> That first night I hardly slept a wink. I felt like Jacob wres-
> tling with an angel of God. All through the night I thought
> about the future and what it might hold in store for us.
> Until now there had been some ego involvement. After all,
> it's more than a little flattering to think that one might be
> the head of a church of five million people.
>
> In the dark hours of that night I felt like I was going down
> and down into a black pit. It was as though life itself was

being drained out of me. Mom was sleeping so soundly beside me and I wanted so much to be rested for the next day in the mountains. But hour after hour the struggle went on. Finally, I found myself able to say, "There is nothing in it that I want for my ego. I don't need to be head of the new church."

When the struggle was over I fell into a deep sense of peace and contentment. I felt I was ready for whatever was ahead. I knew that God would give grace if the mantle fell on me. And I had the confidence to believe that God would also give me grace to allow someone else to lead and that another door would open for me.

In the short time that I slept I dreamed that I was leading a very large meeting and that I felt perfectly at ease doing it. When I awakened I was very tired and groggy. But reflection on the dream left me with a very profound sense of confidence in the future.

The LCA Council approves the Seattle actions

Meeting in New York City just a few days after the CNLC Seattle meeting, the Executive Council of the LCA gave strong endorsement to the recommendations of the commission. It was apparent that two things had happened: First, the demands of some for change had been answered to a sufficient degree; second, it was apparent by now from synod convention votes that the momentum at the grassroots was so strong that nothing could stand in the way of merger.

Some members of the LCA Executive Council credited their hard stand in April for forcing the necessary changes. Kinnison, chair of the CNLC, took a different view. The *Minneapolis Star Tribune* reported that he thought that

> . . . the belligerent stance of the LCA "didn't account" for the progress. He credited the "quiet negotiating and work" of several LCA leaders, including the Rev. Herbert Chilstrom, Minnesota Synod bishop, and the Rev. Kenneth

Sauer, Ohio Synod bishop, in bringing about understandings and compromises.

"A lot of work went on behind the scenes that won't get into the historic record" (7/2/86).

Approval from all three churches

The three churches had agreed to meet simultaneously in late August 1986 to vote on the CNLC recommendations: the ALC in Minneapolis, the AELC in Chicago, and the LCA in Milwaukee. Knowing how keenly disappointed people in the Milwaukee area were about my role in supporting the change from Milwaukee to Chicago for the headquarters of the new church, I was not entirely comfortable going to the convention in that city.

In Minneapolis the ALC went ahead with its vote and approved the merger proposal by a margin of 900 to 37. Delegates ". . . clapped, cheered, whistled, and threw confetti when the vote totals were announced" (*Minneapolis Star Tribune*, 8/30/86).

In Milwaukee the LCA vote was equally positive: 644 to 31. The same reaction ensued. As expected, the AELC vote was unanimous: 137 to 0.

The ALC also held out for the pension proposal that called for a nine percent figure as over against the LCA's twelve percent. I urged the convention to accept this compromise.

> It is a bitter pill to swallow. Are we willing to swallow . . .
> for the sake of the larger question? (*The Lutheran*, 9/17/86).

The lower figure was accepted.

On the issue of the site for headquarters Chicago was affirmed.

In spite of the CNLC action in June, the ALC held out for Milwaukee as the headquarters for the new church. But the conventions had agreed that when the ALC and LCA disagreed on an issue, the decision of the CNLC would prevail. Chicago was safe.

William Lazareth summarized what many had concluded all

along, namely, that the issues that had divided us in the entire merger process were not theological.

> There were no doctrinal differences among our churches that would be essential. What we did debate was not essential to the central issue of the church—its creed (*Minneapolis Star Tribune*, 8/30/86).

In August of 1986 I wrote a note to Art Arnold, my seminary professor and friend:

> I just returned from (Milwaukee). It was a good meeting. The Spirit of God was with us. It has been clear to me all along— and now more so—that God is calling us together.

What the three churches accomplished over that long and arduous process was summed up nicely by W. Kent Gilbert. This church, he wrote

> ... would bring together the various streams of Lutheranism that had been separated so long by ethnic origins, traditions, and theological views. It was a vastly different body from the largely German synod that Henry Melchoir Muhlenberg had envisioned in 1748. Within its ranks of more than 5,300,000 members, 11,000 congregations, and 16,600 pastors, there would be persons whose origins were traced to Africans, Asians, Pacific Islanders, Native Americans, Finns, Swedes, Norwegians, Danes, Dutch, Latvians, Estonians, Icelanders, and virtually every other group that had settled in North America (*Commitment to Unity*, page 531).

Who will be our leader?

With merger now a certainty, speculation about who would be the head of the new church got more intense with each passing month. My name was on most lists. The words of Fredrick Buechner became increasingly relevant:

If there was something about being in the limelight that
attracted me, there was also something in it that I recoiled
from. . . (Buechner, *A Sacred Journey,* page 99).

Reluctant though I may have felt, my name was emerging across
the church.

Already in March 1986 Clark Morphew of the *St. Paul Pioneer
Press* (3/17/86) speculated about the head of the new church. Like
others, he mentioned David Preus, Lloyd Svendsbye, H. George
Anderson, Martin Marty, and me among the leading candidates.
Svendsbye made it clear that he was not interested. Anderson stated
that such speculation was premature. "I have no other ambition or
desire to be anything but president of Luther College," Anderson
said. Morphew wrote that Marty, ". . . with his national reputation
and name-recognition, would be a 'shoe-in' if he does want to be
nominated." I said I was "honored and humbled," but, given the
enormity of the task, "One would have to question why anyone
would seek that job."

Marybeth Peterson, one of my assistants in Minnesota, came
back from a meeting in Philadelphia in April 1986 and sent a
memo saying that in conversation with national LCA staff persons
". . . you are the frontrunner." When I brought it home and left it
on Corinne's desk she drew a round face with a very worried look
at the bottom of the memo, adding the comment: "I love you very
much!"

While the three churches were still in simultaneous conventions
in late August, Martha Sawyer Allen, claiming she had contacted
twenty-four Lutheran leaders ". . . from all parts of the country and
of varying political views," wrote that "The Rev. Herbert Chilstrom
. . . is the top candidate to become the new church's bishop" and
that "The Rev. David Preus . . . is the other leading candidate."
These persons, said Allen, told her that "Chilstrom commands
an impressive edge and . . . Preus is considered a second, viable
choice." The persons she contacted

. . . describe Chilstrom as the right person in the right place at the right time. He is respected theologically and as a pastoral leader. He also has the charisma to present the new church to the world . . . and he is seen as a peacemaker and conciliator—someone who can blend the traditions of the three churches into a vibrant new organization. Chilstrom . . . also was described as someone who has taken courageous stands on controversial issues and has proven himself to be a leader on social issues. LCA leaders in the eastern part of the United States said that Chilstrom's midwestern roots probably will not deter Easterners from voting for him because he is respected within the entire LCA. Concern for his health is the only drawback cited by Lutheran leaders. Chilstrom had three operations in 1985, including one for cancer. . . . his liberal stands on social and political issues might not go over as well with some convention delegates. Some said Lutherans might want a leader who hasn't taken controversial stands (*Minneapolis Star Tribune*, 8/24/86).

From my hotel room in Milwaukee I wrote in my journal:

I just talked to Corinne. She'll be catching a plane to Milwaukee and will be with me here until Wednesday. I'm lonesome for her. We really enjoy being with each other— lovers and good friends.

She told me about the article in the Minneapolis paper today naming me as a leading candidate to head the new church. What do I do with all of this? It will make me feel awkward. I'll sense eyes on me—wondering what people are thinking—wondering if they think I'm trying to promote these things.

And what will I say when people bring it up this week? I can probably brush it off humorously by saying that people once thought Milwaukee would be the headquarters! Or I can remind them of what happened to some other Minnesotans—like Hubert Humphrey, Eugene McCarthy, Walter Mondale, the Vikings, and the Twins!

So what can I do—except the same as we have been doing—praying that God will give grace.

After I talked to Corinne tonight I turned out the lights and looked out the window from my room on the twelve floor. I looked south toward the airport. I prayed the "Abraham prayer" that we pray so often these days. As I prayed I noted a lighted highway that stretched out toward the horizon and disappeared from sight. And the prayer seemed appropriate again:

> Lord God, you have called your servants to ventures of which we cannot see the ending, by paths as yet untrodden, through perils unknown. Give us faith to go out with good courage, not knowing where we go, but only that your hand is leading us and your love supporting us; through Jesus Christ, our Lord. Amen (*Lutheran Book of Worship,* page 153).

And right now I'm remembering what Corinne said just before we hung up—"I'll stick with you no matter where this takes us. I love you."

Apparently my uneasiness about all this speculation was apparent to some at the Milwaukee convention. One pastor approached me and noted my troubled look. "Why don't you smile anymore?" he asked. "You have such a beautiful smile." I reflected later on what he had said.

> I wasn't surprised that I looked that way. It really was so very awkward that whole week. When I spoke on issues on the floor of the convention it was difficult to separate my concern for the issue itself and my concern for what people were inevitably thinking each time—"Will he be the head of the new church?" And when a close friend

said to me after the convention that none of the speeches
I gave did me any harm so far as new church leadership is
concerned—then I had confirmed what I felt, namely, that
people were indeed thinking those things.

With his name very much in the public media, I was surprised
to get a note from Martin Marty in September, 1986 stating that
"I hope to hear Good Things about you in the next year." I never
asked him what he meant by that, but one can assume that he must
have been referring to leadership of the new church. And it may
have been an early clue to what he affirmed several months later—
that he had no interest in the office himself.

In late November, 1987 I reflected in my journal how speculation since the Milwaukee LCA convention had mushroomed.

> Now it has become common wherever I go to be intro-
> duced as "one of the leading candidates to be the head of
> the new church." At one church the pastor . . . not only
> introduced me in that way, but added, "Maybe our bishop
> would like to make some comments about that." I wish I
> could have found a trapdoor and disappeared! Needless to
> say, you can be sure I said nothing of the kind.

> In some ways it's becoming almost comical. People are
> beginning to speak to me about being one of my assistants
> in the new church. Can you imagine that! The convention
> is still five months away!

> Am I afraid? Yes and no. I continue to believe that God
> gives grace for whatever comes. If I'm not chosen it will
> take more grace because then I'd probably spend the rest
> of my life known as the one who almost made it. And that
> would not be easy. In fact, that might be the most difficult
> of the two alternatives. And if I am elected—well, there's
> always the chance that I might fall flat on my face. But I've
> had these feelings of apprehension before in my life—and
> each time it seems there has been grace to handle it.

I went on to describe how helpful my reading of Ephesians had been.

> There is a section that speaks about wisdom as a gift from God. This is more than intelligence. It is wisdom that leads to good judgment and discernment. If God were to lead the church to elect me, would he not give me that gift? I believe so.

We went to Madison, Wisconsin, for Chris's graduation in early December 1986. While there I had another very significant dream.

> I was standing beside my mother in an open field. We were watching a huge plane take off. We both marveled at the sight. . . . Then we looked and saw another plane. It too was very large and powerful. It was flying low—in fact, just off the ground. There were many people in it. It headed directly into swamps, brush, and large trees. We wondered how it would get through all those obstructions. But it did. It just churned along, keeping on going in spite of the obstacles. We watched as it kept moving off into the distance.

> That dream said a lot to me about myself. At the time, Corinne and I were talking about what may lay ahead— the new church—the possibility that I might be elected bishop, etc.

> . . . although my mother and I never hit it off well, I have come to recognize a long time ago that I'm very much like her. I've never known anyone who worked harder or with more determination. Nothing was impossible. If something needed doing, you just did it. That was the significance of the airplane. Nothing would stop it. Push your way through!

Luther Northwestern Seminary presidency?

Early in 1987, after more than a decade of outstanding leadership, Lloyd Svendsbye resigned as president of Luther Northwestern

Seminary to take the call to be president at Augustana College, Sioux Falls, South Dakota. Almost immediately I was asked if I had any interest in being his successor. My nomination became official in February, 1987.

I wrote to Duane Hoven, chair of the presidential search committee and described my Holy Week respite from my usual schedule as bishop. It was a time for reflection and prayer. I told him that it would be a high honor to succeed my friend Svendsbye. Yet:

> I find no desire in me to become president of the seminary.
> I see no reason this conviction would change.

Was I so convinced that I would be elected head of the new church that I didn't want to close that door? Hardly. The reason was more deep-seated. I had been on the seminary board for more than a decade. I had seen the toll that job had taken on Svendsbye. While I had good friends, including respected theologians among the faculty, there were others who were, in my judgment, egotists of the highest order. With its deep roots in the former ALC, I also felt that the seminary needed someone out of that tradition.

I'm sure my thinking about the seminary was influenced significantly by a letter I received early in 1987 from Pastor George Johnson, an ALC national staff person in charge of the Hunger Program. Though we were not close friends, I knew of his work and respected his strong commitment to proclamation of the gospel and working for social justice.

> Excuse me for this next word. . . . I want to risk it. If you
> have to choose between Luther Northwestern and leading
> the new ELCA as its presiding bishop I want to encourage
> you to consider being available to the church as bishop.
> Luther/NW can find someone for president—plenty of candidates. But few fill the requirement of bishop. *You are one.*
> All of your previous training and experience has led to this.

And as Mordecai said to Esther, "Who knows whether you have come to the kingdom for such a time as this!"

It is a moment of opportunity for this beloved Lutheran church. May God give us leadership and courage to fulfill our calling.

I have no idea, of course, if I would even have been chosen had I decided to be open to that opportunity. But I must say in retrospect that I know I could not have even begun to do the kind of work David Tiede did as successor to Svendsbye. It turned out to be the best outcome for the seminary.

Do I have the energy? Would this be another setback for Corinne?

As we moved into early 1987 and the possibility of being elected head of the new church could no longer be ignored I faced two crucial questions: Do I have the energy for that task? And what about Corinne's call to parish ministry?

When health questions were raised by others, I always said I felt fine, my health was good. That was true, but only to a degree. Yes, I was able to do my work as the bishop of the synod and engage in many activities related to preparation for the new church. But did I have the vitality to undertake a task as daunting as head of the new church?

Since my prostate surgery in 1985 and two follow-up surgeries for hernias, I had been struggling to regain full physical vitality. One day I laid it out before God in one of the most honest intercessions I've ever prayed. It went something like this:

Lord, I have no idea what you have waiting for me in the years to come. I only know that if I am to lead the new church I will need more energy and vitality than I have now. I lay it before you. . . .

Call it what you will: coincidence, answer to prayer, psychological manipulation. I can only say that within two weeks I felt better

than I had felt in years. Regardless of what lay ahead, for me it was
an answer to prayer. I wanted to be hale and hearty for any possibility. If I had any reason to suggest that my health would not permit
me to accept the position as head of the new church, that excuse
was gone.

As to Corinne's call, she was having a wonderful parish ministry
at Bethlehem Church in south Minneapolis. She not only enjoyed
her relationship with the staff, but was fully accepted as a woman
pastor by the congregation. She was building programs in the congregation but also was gaining respect and acceptance from other
clergy in the area. Why should she have to pull up stakes again, as
she had done so many times in the past, because I was moving to a
ministry in another place?

We had long and serious discussions about these matters. I
assured her that my life did not depend on being elected head of
the new church. I felt certain that something would open up for me
in the Twin Cities area. I was ready for a new adventure.

We talked and prayed about this for some days. Before long
Corinne said:

> No, I simply can't stand in the way of this possibility. If this
> should be God's will for your life, then it's God's will for my
> life as well. We must let happen what will happen.

Though I still wasn't entirely at ease with this conclusion, I
agreed with her. Now my last excuse was gone. We would simply
have to wait and see.

More speculation

My principal confidant through all these months was Reuben
Swanson. He kept urging me to keep the doors open for leadership
of the new church. In early March of 1987, I wrote to him:

> The pressure keeps building as we approach Columbus.
> There are days when I feel like Jonah, ready to run from all

that seems to be down the road. But I've tried that before
and I know it is the wrong thing to do. So I remain open to
whatever the church calls me to do.

In an interview with *The Concord* at Luther Northwestern Seminary I was asked about my openness to the leadership of the new
church.

> To me it is a deeply spiritual question. It has to do with my
> calling as a pastor of the church. I have come to be able to
> say, let happen what will happen (4/7/87).

Corinne and I continued to wrestle with these questions. But we
had also come to some resolution. On the last day of March 1987 I
wrote in my journal:

> . . . both of us have a bedrock conviction at this point.
> And that is that we've lived long enough and been through
> enough so that we know we would not want to be in a place
> that is not the will of God—for us or for the church. To be
> elected head of the church if it were not the will of God
> would be an absolute disaster. It will be hard enough if it *is*
> the will of God! So we think we're as prepared as we can be
> for either outcome.

In the next day's mail the *Forum Letter* arrived. Richard John
Neuhaus opined (*Forum Letter,* 3/27/87) that if Anderson withdrew
from consideration, as had been rumored, William Lazareth was
the best candidate to head the new church—seminary professor,
church staff positions, head of the Faith and Order Commission of
the WCC, parish pastor. But he recognized that Lazareth's stances
on a variety of issues have ". . . bumped against the sensibilities of
some." Neuhaus went on to suggest that

> . . . an alternative reading of the situation is that front-run-
> ners are David Preus and LCA bishop Herbert Chilstrom.
> According to this view, the anti-Preus vote in the ALC will

go to Marty and the anti-Chilstrom vote in the LCA will go
to Bishop Kenneth Sauer of the Ohio Synod.

In his assessment of me, Neuhaus, his acid-ink pen never far out
of reach, suggested:

> Chilstrom, in the judgment of many, poses all the problems
> posed by David Preus. In addition, he is sharply criticized
> for being "trendy" on most of the issues that come down
> the religio-cultural turnpike, and having an ALC pastor as
> his wife is thought to be a neat formula too clever by half.

Neuhaus then put forward the best possible outcome.

> In our opinion, then, the best choices would be William
> Lazareth and George Anderson. If that turns out not to
> be possible, Bishop Kenneth Sauer is emphatically to be
> preferred among those now prominently mentioned. He
> has a strong sense of Lutheran identity, an appreciation
> of the momentous ecumenical decisions facing us, and
> a proven track record of pastoral sensitivity to the entire
> Lutheran family.

That same day I put down some of my thoughts. After reviewing
what Neuhaus said I wrote that

> In my judgment (*Lutheran Forum*) is kind of like a National
> Lutheran Inquirer—a cheap rag that parades under the
> guise of being theologically astute.

Neuhaus could not have known what would happen in the next
several days. As would soon become apparent, Neuhaus, always
certain he had the right slant on things, would be proven wrong on
almost every point.

Corinne and I, of course, were deeply offended by his snide
remarks about her call to ministry. Corinne wrote to him and I
wrote to Glenn Stone, Neuhaus's colleague at the *Lutheran Forum*
magazine. We explained to both how Corinne's call to ministry had

been completely independent of any connection with my alleged thirst for leadership of the new church. Stone agreed that Neuhaus had stepped over the line in his comments.

On April 29, 1987, the day prior to the opening of the Constituting Convention, Neuhaus wrote a tepid letter of apology that we did not see until we returned to Minnesota after the convention. We had suggested to him that he really didn't know us and had made judgments on the basis of faulty information. He began his letter by stating that it was a handicap for a journalist

> ... to get to know people personally. The views expressed ... pretend to be no more than the editor's judgment, which I hope is an informed and fair judgment.

In regard to Corinne being an ALC pastor, Neuhaus said that

> I do regret using the expression "too clever by half." I should have said "too neat by half" or simply "too pat." As you are undoubtedly aware, people have remarked on the fact that an LCA bishop married to an ALC pastor seems to anticipate neatly the merger. But I apologize for my unfortunate choice of words and will do so also in a forthcoming issue of the *Forum Letter*. I hope I will have the benefit of getting to know you better in the future.

We took him up on that last comment in his letter. After we moved to Chicago we arranged to meet him for lunch. The conversation amounted to little or nothing. Nevertheless, I think we managed to make our point.

Marty and Anderson step aside

Even though they had indicated informally that they were reluctant to be candidates for leadership of the new church, Martin Marty and H. George Anderson made it official in early April. The Associated Press reported that both men

. . . church historians and broadly respected among Lutherans, said they didn't want the top church post.

Marty said he

... had no call to the office of bishop and thus cannot assent to proposals to nominate me. . . . the post requires experience and qualities I lack.

Anderson said he wanted to preserve time for his family and ". . . continue my commitment to (Luther) college." He said that when considering a position like this one should have ". . . a feeling of anticipation or expectation," but in this case he hit a "blank wall." There was simply "a lack of inner call," said Anderson (4/2/87).

The day after I heard the news about Marty and Anderson I wrote in my journal:

I have no idea how this will affect the conversations and maneuvers going on out there. It's a strange time! When you are one of the candidates you are the last to know anything. In some ways, I regret that they have withdrawn. For one thing, either could have made a good bishop for the ELCA. Both are church historians and have good perspective on where we've been and where we should go. For another, if I'm elected I would not want to have people saying, "Well, if Martin—if George—had been elected things would have been better." In other words, I'd rather have one of them elected or else be elected myself with them on the ballot. Well, there are still some weeks to go and maybe one or both can be persuaded to change his mind—although I doubt it very much. Or maybe this will change the whole mix and someone, like Ken Sauer, will emerge as the dark horse and get elected. If so, so be it. Deos volente. . . .

Early in March 1987 I wrote to son Chris before I heard that Marty had asked not to be considered for leadership of the new church and said:

The pressure mounts as we move close to the convention.
We can't wait for it to come and put it behind us. . . . the
grapevine tells me that support for Martin Marty may be
growing in the East—and that if he doesn't pick up enough
votes they will switch to Bishop Sauer of Ohio. And there
are those who speculate that if the Eastern LCA does that,
then Bishop Preus will possibly be elected because upper
midwest Lutherans are determined to elect someone from
this area. So goes the speculation. . . . Makes life more interesting than I want it right now.

Speculation continued right up to the beginning of the Constituting Convention in Columbus, Ohio, in late April and early May
1987. Martha Allen wrote (*Minneapolis Star Tribune,* 4/26/87) that
"Two Minnesotans, the Revs. Herbert Chilstrom and David Preus,
are considered the leading candidates, although a host of other
names have been mentioned."

Last journal note before Columbus, Ohio

Finally on Monday, April 27, early in the week and before we flew
off to the Constituting Convention at Columbus, Ohio, I wrote a
lengthy entry in my journal, pouring out many sentiments.

As I drove back from Sandstone (MN) yesterday it all
seemed to come crashing down on me again—the awe-
someness of what lies ahead. Can I handle it if I am elected?
I have a feeling of wanting to run away like Jonah. But
nothing in me will really allow that either. It was this same
feeling that was plaguing me the other day. Then on the
way to work I was listening to Moby Dick tapes and these
lines came to me:

"As with the storm-tossed ship that miserably drives along
the . . . land, the port would fain give succor. In the port
is safety, comfort, hearthstone, supper, warm blankets,
friends—all that's kind to our mortalities. But in that gale,

the port, the land, is that ship's jeopardy. She must fly all
hospitality. One touch of the land, though it but graze the
keel, would make her shudder through and through. With
all her might she crowds all sail off shore. . . . better is it to
perish in that howling infinite than be ingloriously dashed
upon the lee—even if that were safety."

So it seems I really have no choice. I cannot turn back now. I
feel inevitably drawn out to sea—wherever it may take me.

I went on to write about what this would mean for Corinne:

Last evening we were at a picnic for the church council and
spouses from Bethlehem Church. It's clear that she is loved
and respected by these people—that she really belongs. If I'm
elected it will mean another time for her to be uprooted. Yes,
I too will be uprooted. But for me it would be different—as it
always has been. I would have a task and a clear mandate to do
something. But for her it would mean one more time to try to
find a niche, to discover a place where she can find fulfillment.

I continued with some thoughts about an important role I knew
she would fill if we were to move to Chicago:

I know she will find new community. Just the people who
will be moving to Chicago to be a part of the new church—
they in themselves will be people who will need exactly
someone like her to make them feel welcome and at home
in a new place.

I recalled Alvin Rogness's note to us after Andrew died. He wrote
about his sense that his deceased son Paul sat in "the bleachers of
heaven" cheering him on, I appealed directly to Andrew:

May I count on you to intercede from the bleachers of
heaven? Maybe even to cheer if the occasion allows for it?

I concluded by recalling a visit to my predecessor's grave a week
or two earlier. I was on my way to Rush City, midway between

the Twin Cities and Duluth. Because I was running a bit early, I stopped at North Branch on Interstate Highway I-35. Mal Hammarberg's grave was just a half-mile off the freeway. He had played a huge role in my life from the time I was a teenager. North Branch was his childhood home. I had been to the cemetery before.

> What came home to me again is the importance of living each day to the hilt—of being courageous because we have so little time to do things that are so soon forgotten. As I stood there the words of the morning hymn came to me:

> > Make clear our path that we may see
> > Where we must walk to be with thee;
> > And ever listen to thy voice,
> > That we may make thy way our choice.

> "To be with thee"—nothing else matters. If I can just keep that in perspective during these next days. We leave for Columbus tomorrow afternoon. Anxiety is mounting. I want to trust God completely. But I'm a human being and I feel overcome with uncertainty. It will be good to have it behind us—regardless of what happens. "Lord, I believe; help my unbelief."

Getting ready for Columbus

My first priority in preparing for the Constituting Convention for the new church at Columbus, Ohio, on April 30–May 3, 1987, was to make certain our Minnesota Synod delegation was fully informed of the actions that would need to be taken and the issues on which they would be expected to vote. Bubbling in the background, of course, was the question of who would be elected the first officers of the church and, especially, who would be the first bishop of the ELCA. There was absolutely no way of knowing what the outcome would be. I tried to be cool, calm, and collected. But that was difficult.

Final gatherings for the three churches

On April 29, 1987, the three merging churches met in separate sessions to hold their final conventions. At the LCA conclave a last vote was taken for merger. The outcome was 538 for and 19 against. The ALC did not require a final vote. David Preus urged ALC delegates to resist ". . . the temptation to gripe and complain about what is or ought to be" as they moved through the next days (*Detroit Free Press*, 4/30/87).

Winding up and winding down

What I have written about my life in the last years leading up to the merger may give the impression that I did little other than give my time to that enterprise. That was hardly the case.

My work as bishop continued as usual: preaching at a synod congregation nearly every Sunday and often during the week; finding pastors for congregations; working on urban and rural strategies; organizing new mission churches; preaching at funerals for pastors; ecumenical involvement; taping video Bible studies for use in congregations; preaching at anniversaries; ordinations, and installations; promoting the churchwide fund appeal; and much more.

I was also being asked to speak at events not directly related to my work as bishop in Minnesota: Luther Northwestern Seminary Convocation; Illinois Synod Convention; Worship Practicum; Association of Church Musicians; Deferred Giving Conference; an Upper Midwest Lutheran Youth Convention; and other events and places.

Yet in spite of all this activity, there was a growing awareness that we were doing many things for the last time. Whatever my future held in store, I was eager to get to Columbus and have it settled.

What I had said months earlier at the last convention of the Minnesota Synod seemed an apt closing for this chapter in our lives:

It is only fitting to end this final report to the final convention of the Minnesota Synod with thanks to God for what will be twenty-five years of unmerited grace. We move ahead in the confidence that the God of our Lord Jesus Christ, whose Spirit is the Creator of the church, will continue to be with us. To God alone be the glory!

Childhood home, Litchfield, Minnesota

With parents Ruth and Wally, 1932

Family, 1945
Front: Wally, Martha, Janet, Ruth
Back: Herbert, Lorraine, Adeline, Winnifred, Virginia, David

High school graduation
Litchfield, Minnesota, 1949

Augsburg College graduation
Minneapolis, Minnesota, 1954

Corinne Hansen and Herbert Chilstrom wedding
June 12, 1954
St. Peter Lutheran Church, Vermillion, South Dakota

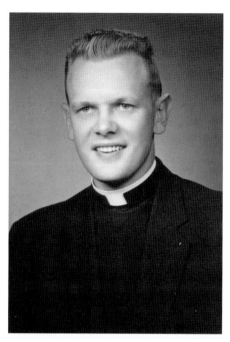

Ordination
June 22, 1958, Jamestown, New York

Family, 1970: Andrew, Corinne, Mary, Herb, Christopher
St. Peter, Minnesota

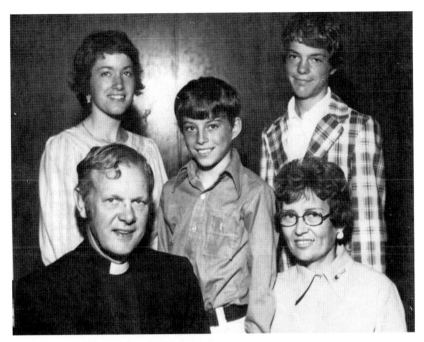

Elected Bishop of Minnesota Synod, LCA, 1976

Corinne's Ordination, June 16, 1985
Bethlehem Lutheran Church, Minneapolis, Minnesota

Elected (Presiding) Bishop of ELCA, May 1987

Meeting Pope John Paul II
November 1987, Columbia, South Carolina

Ecumenical Orthodox Patriarch Dimitrios
January 1988, Istanbul, Turkey
From left: Edgar Trexler, *The Lutheran* magazine, editor;
William Rusch, ELCA Office for Ecumenical Affairs

Queen Sylvia of Sweden
April 1988

My brother Dave, my lifelong friend and
pillar of faith

ELCA Church Council, 1995
Officers, from left: Richard McAuliffe, Treasurer; Lowel Almen, Secretary; Kathy Magnus,
Vice President; Herbert Chilstrom, Bishop

Chapter 11

Moving the ship out of the harbor: first term as presiding bishop (1987–1991)

Turbulent times

The Evangelical Lutheran Church in America was born in turbulent times. There had been enormous changes since the so-called glory days of the 1950s when mainline Protestant denominations flourished. Kent Gilbert summarized it well:

> The prospects for mainline Christianity in North America were . . . muddled. Cults were once again on the rise. Conservative evangelicals were fighting what they regarded as "secular humanism" being taught in the public schools. Television evangelists had large and lucrative followings. The scandals involving some of their number not only had an impact on the ministry of other television preachers but also spilled over to cause questioning among those tangentially related to the major church bodies (*Commitment to Unity*, page 482).

Globally, Islam was on the rise in many places where Lutherans had done work for more than a century. The entire scope of global mission work would undergo a great challenge. Though the merging churches had already begun to reshape the way they did mission work by accenting interdependence with the younger churches, we would also discover that supporting the worldwide mission, already evident prior to the merger, would become much more costly.

It was into this changing world that the new church was born.

Opening with Baptism and Eucharist: symbols of unity

The Constituting Convention began with a Eucharistic celebration. The defining moment came when the heads of the three merging churches—Will Herzfeld, James Crumley, and David Preus—poured water from separate flasks into a huge common baptismal bowl. In a post-convention editorial, Edgar Trexler captured the spirit:

> Everyone felt the new church come into being. Legal votes and banging gavels had been cold, but the worship was warm and soaring. As the water swirled into the font, each stream intermingled and became one (*The Lutheran*, 5/20/87).

Caring for the basics: seating, constitution, budget

The decision of the planners to seat delegates by alphabetical order without regard to predecessor church affiliation was a very wise move. There was no sense of separation between the uniting churches, no feeling that one was surrounded by persons of like mind when votes were taken, and no conversations on the floor about "those other folks." This made for a smoother legislative process, but also gave the convention the sense that we were already operating as one church.

The adoption of a constitution took place while elections were going on. The rules set by the CNLC called for little debate on the details of the constitution. It meant up or down votes on all related items. That was not greeted happily by some delegates. I think most, however, saw that it was the only way this could be done. Had we gone into extended debate over every jot and tittle of the proposed constitution, the convention could never have done its work in the allotted time.

The CNLC had brought to the convention a recommendation that the initial fourteen-month budget be set at $108 million. Conventions, however, do strange things. Enthusiasm sometimes outruns common sense. The delegates, hearing of all the great things this new church could do, decided to up that figure to $112 million.

In hindsight, it's clear that the convention was acting in a vacuum. Had we known that just a little more than five months later—October 19, 1987—the United States would experience a record market meltdown, we might have been more realistic. Even more important, had we paid heed to some of the studies undertaken by our predecessor churches, we might have been more cautious. Every study showed that income to causes beyond the local congregation had been in steady decline for at least three decades.

We might also have listened more attentively to church-planning gurus such as Lyle Schaller. He forewarned us that when there is major merger of church bodies, almost inevitably there is a drop in the total income from those churches.

As we would see, this budget, given what was happening in the churches, was indeed an impossible dream.

Excitement and disruption at Columbus

In the 1980s an advocacy group known as DMX had fomented much public disturbance in the Pittsburgh area. Using (and some would say exaggerating) the methods of the ardent social reformer Saul Alinsky, the DMX pushed vigorously for the church to confront business and industry, hoping its methods would bring change in society. DMX felt that the church had been too accommodating of these entities. Several ELCA pastors were active in DMX. They promised to make their point at Columbus.

Most delegates to the convention were unaware of DMX until

the group appeared in Columbus. On occasion they tried to crash
the business meetings. Sergeants at arms had to be posted at all
entrances to keep them off the floor. The local police were in evidence. They wanted no trouble to erupt during a church convention in their city.

The election of a bishop

Because the agenda provided for as many as nine ballots to elect
the bishop of the new church, and because other elections would
hinge on this one, voting commenced shortly after the convention
convened. The outcome of the first ballot, a nominating ballot, was
predictable. Sixty-eight names emerged. It included many favorite
sons and favorite daughters. The former included synod bishops
whose delegates supported them, even though they probably knew
the chances for election were slim.

Among the leaders on the first ballot were:

David Preus	284
Herbert Chilstrom	112
William Lazareth	101
Reuben Swanson	61
Kenneth Sauer	56
James Crumley	55
Barbara Lundblad	52
Kenneth Senft	44
Nelson Trout	24
Franklin Fry	23

It was no surprise that David Preus's name headed the list on
the first ballot. By the time of the convention, most delegates from
the ALC had probably concluded that he was their best hope. Of
the top ten nominees, Nelson Trout was the only other person out
of ALC background. Many saw that the outcome was apparent in
the early balloting: The two leading ALC nominees had fewer votes

than the total of their delegation. It then became a contest between LCA nominees.

I had enough votes to tell me that I would probably continue in the running for several ballots. But there was no clue as to what the final outcome would be.

As the balloting continued over the next days, I grew increasingly anxious.

By the third ballot the top nominees remained in the same pattern. It was impossible to ascertain any definite trends. I didn't sleep well. Whatever excitement I felt was undermined by the distressing thought that I might actually be elected.

It was about that time that a group of women requested a meeting with me. They represented those who supported Barbara Lundblad. It was clear by then that Lundblad would not be elected. Their question to me was whether I would be supportive of women were I to be elected. It seemed they were asking me for some kind of public statement in exchange for their promise to deliver Lundblad's votes to me. Not having asked anyone to support me, I saw no reason to change my pattern. I told them that my track record regarding support for women was clear and they would have to base their decision on what they had seen in my ministry as a synod bishop. That may not have been exactly what they wanted to hear, but it was the most I could promise.

In the meantime, my vote count went up with each succeeding ballot. It seemed almost certain that I would be one of the finalists who would be expected to address the convention. Now I felt growing pressure. With the rise in anxiety came more sleep loss. What should I say to the convention? What words were most important for them to hear from me? I wakened feeling exhausted from my fitful nights.

That is indeed what happened. On the fifth ballot I edged ahead of Preus by a handful of votes. It seemed clear that if votes fell somewhat along the lines of the two larger predecessor churches, Lazareth or I would be elected.

There was a panel during which the top five finalists sat on the
stage to field questions. Because I could hold the microphone close
to my face I felt confident in my responses.

It was at this point that something unexpected happened. When
he was eliminated, Kenneth Sauer, bishop of the Ohio Synod of
the LCA, did a very strange thing. As reported in the *Forum Letter,*
"Bishop Kenneth Sauer's 'releasing' his delegates to David Preus
over the noon hour recess made not a dent in the final outcome"
(6/12/87). This puzzled me. As an LCA synod bishop I knew Sauer
was extremely critical of the polity of the ALC. He was one who
spoke out forcefully against the ALC for its failure to understand
the "ecclesiology" that we needed for the new church. He surely
had little reason to support Preus. I was at a complete loss to know
what impelled him to act in that way.

On the sixth ballot my votes continued to climb. Now the final
four would be Chilstrom, Preus, Lazareth, and Lundblad.

Each of us would give a five-minute speech to the convention. I
felt uneasy as I mounted the platform with the other finalists. All,
and especially Lazareth and Lundblad, were proven stem-winders.
All three seemed to exude enormous confidence. If it appeared to
anyone that I felt as confident as they, then Lincoln was right, "you
can fool some of the people some of the time." Because of sleep
loss, my voice—never strong since I ruined it during my ministry at First Lutheran Church in St. Peter—crackled and sputtered.
Given my height, microphones have always been a problem. I tried
to adjust the microphone to my mouth but it kept slipping down. I
had to readjust it several times. All in all, it was a miserable performance. I was certain any chances for election were gone. And I was
not entirely sad about it.

In my speech I began by accenting the primary calling for the
new bishop of the church—to witness to the power of the gospel of
Jesus Christ. "Evangelism," I said,

is the first priority for the new church. If that is to be the
case, the bishop of the church must set the pace. Wherever
I went and whatever I did, I would witness to the good
news that God justifies sinners through Jesus Christ.

I went on to underscore the importance of giving much energy
to the administrative responsibilities that will inevitably fall on the
new bishop, including choosing highly-qualified staff and working
closely with elected boards.

I spoke of the importance of affirming our pastors and other
called leaders in their respective ministries. Nurture of the life of
believers in local congregations is at the core of our mission, I suggested. Here, I said,

is where the vast majority of our people experience the
faith firsthand. Here is where we baptize and teach. Here is
where we serve.

But we can become preoccupied in our local congregations, I said.
We need a vision for the whole world. Telling the story of world mission is the surest way to get our people involved in that vision.

I spoke of my burden to help the new church understand
how Scripture and our theology speak to increasingly complex
questions.

As for ecumenism, our dialogue with other churches does not
mean that we surrender our Lutheran identity. "I'm a Lutheran by
conviction and would conduct dialogue with other Christians out
of that posture," I said. "The vitality of ecumenism is in variety, not
conformity.

Because of our unique position among the Christian
churches, I believe the ELCA can play a pivotal role in deter-
mining where ecumenism will go in the next fifty years.

I put in a strong word for our partnership with sister churches
in the Lutheran World Federation. I suggested that it was time to

engage leaders in other religions of the world in searching for peace and justice.

I concluded with these words:

> We are bringing together three families of the Lutheran church. If I were elected bishop, I would want to make certain our separate traditions would not be forgotten. But at the same time, I would do everything in my power to be the bishop of the whole church, and to work and pray for the day—hopefully soon—when there would be a sense across the entire ELCA that we are a single family of faith.

My final sentences proved to be far more prophetic than I could have imagined at that moment:

> I know from experience that one cannot predict the unpredictable—the issues that will arise unexpectedly, the demands that will be made on the new church and its leadership. What we *can know*, however, is that God will give grace and strength for what we are called to do. We have the promise of the Spirit as our Guide and Counselor. It is only on that basis that I could dare to say "Yes" if I were called by the church to be its bishop.

Immediately after the speeches I met two of my staff members from the Minnesota Synod—Ron Peterson and Marybeth Peterson. I had the kind of relationship with both of them that precluded anything but complete candor. And that is what I got. Both said that it was the most poorly delivered speech they had ever heard from me. Here was confirmation of my own self-assessment. The vote that followed on the seventh ballot affirmed this. I lost forty votes, now leading Preus by only a handful.

Now I was certain all was over for me. Preus had hit a plateau. Given the number of votes that Lazareth had picked up after his dynamic address to the convention, I expected that he might well surge to the top. I felt a mixture of disappointment and relief, disappointment that I had not showed my best to the convention and relief that I would not have to endure this ordeal much longer.

I went to the men's room shortly after the vote. Richard Koenig happened to be there at the same time. Richard was editor of *Lutheran Partners* magazine and one whose judgment I respected. He stopped me for a moment and said, "Don't worry, Herb. The people heard what you said. They will think about it. You will be elected bishop of the new church."

I have no idea what happened behind the scenes before the next ballots were taken. I'm quite certain, however, that synod bishops met with their delegations and that a number of them persuaded their representatives that I should get their votes. Others may indeed have done what Koenig suggested: thought about what I had said, even though my delivery of those thoughts was, at best, second-rate.

In any event, on the eighth ballot the numbers for me surged again. Lazareth was eliminated. Now it would be between Preus and me.

It was clear that if the vote fell along predecessor church lines and if the folks from the smaller AELC supported me, as I expected, I would be elected. I had been through enough elections, however, to know that "it's not over till it's over." So the anxiety mounted as the ninth and final ballot was taken and we waited for the outcome.

Concluding that it was almost certain that I would be elected, I jotted a few notes on a small slip of paper.

Then it came. The vote was announced. I was elected by a substantial margin: 626 to 411. The final total showed that I had significantly more votes than the LCA and AELC delegations combined.

There was no doubt that the church had spoken and had spoken clearly and decisively.

As the delegation stood to applaud the election, I rose slowly to go to the front of the convention hall. A sense overwhelmed me that I can only describe as God-given. After days of high tension, I felt a deep calm that penetrated to the core of my being. As I had felt the call of God to all the places I had served until then, now that same feeling settled over me once more. It was a gift, a certainty that never left me in the more than eight tumultuous years that followed. On the highest peaks and in the deepest valleys in those years to come, I never doubted that my election was a call from God through God's people.

Corinne was waiting for me at the foot of the platform. Someone had sought her out and brought her to that place. With hands clasped as tightly as the day we were married, Corinne and I mounted the steps and walked to the podium. The convention continued to explode with applause and cheers. It was a moment to embrace, to give thanks, and, yes, a moment to savor.

I had learned my lesson about the microphone. This time I took it into my hand and held it directly to my mouth. With a few sketchy notes on that small slip of paper, I spoke extemporaneously, as I had done so often since high school.

I began by thanking David Preus for his exemplary churchmanship. "David Preus," I said, "represents all those people who have made a tremendous investment in being a part of the process." That comment evoked a standing ovation for Preus. He came forward to acknowledge the delegation's response. He moved to a microphone and said,

> We have elected a big man. He is big of heart, big of mind,
> big of spirit and destined to provide the leadership we need.
> I applaud him with all my heart. I look forward to serving
> with him, for him, next to him (*Forum Letter*, 6/12/87).

As I continued my address to the convention I acknowledged the weight of the "mantles of responsibility" from leaders in our Lutheran history, including Fredrik Schiotz, Franklin Clark Fry, William Kohn, Kent Knutson, Robert Marshall, and the leaders of our three merging churches. I gave thanks for my Augustana roots and its leaders.

I thanked Corinne, calling her "my wife and best friend"—and my children Mary, Christopher and, yes, Andrew as well. It was especially important to include Andrew, our deceased son.

I singled out my parents, sisters, and brother David for their love through the years.

I made reference to two of my treasured possessions: my great grandfather's Bible that came across the Atlantic Ocean with the emigrant family in 1853, and the bowl that held the water when I was baptized at my parents' farm home in 1931. "I have been blessed by generation after generation of families of faith."

I spoke of my vision for unity in the new church, the importance of ministry in our congregations; my commitment to the ecumenical movement; our connection with other Lutheran churches in the world. I referred to the new church as a ship ready to set out into the deep: "Some might want to remain in the shallow waters. But the only safe place is the open sea, no matter how stormy."

I concluded by thanking the delegates and asked them to "pray and pray and pray for me. Will you pray for us?" I asked. When the response seemed a bit tepid I asked again and heard a resounding "yes!"

I felt confident and apparently sounded as I felt.

Several hours later I met Chuck Austin at the convention. Chuck was a veteran news editor and writer for church publications. "Herb," he said "I've heard a lot of acceptance speeches. That was the finest." It seems I had gone from one of the worst speeches of my life to one of the best, and all in just a day.

Through all this election process I was grateful that son Chris could be with us, not only to experience the historic importance of those days for the church and for us as a family, but also to be a pillar of support for Corinne during that stressful time. As soon as daughter Mary heard about the election she sent a wire:

"DAD, HEARD THE NEWS. CONGRATULATIONS. THINKING ABOUT YOU. LOTS OF LOVE. MARY."

A hectic aftermath to the election

What happened after I descended from the dais was totally unexpected. I assumed that I would be able to plunge into the crowd, greeting old friends, fellow synod and district bishops, and other delegates to the convention.

Instead, I was met by a plainclothes officer from the Columbus Police Department. Because of the disruption by the DMX group from Pittsburgh, the authorities were taking no chances. The officer spirited Corinne and me away from the floor and toward a side door.

First press conference

The officer escorted Corinne and me through a maze of hallways to a press conference room. This proved to be a most daunting experience. Just when I was beginning to feel some relief, I found myself face to face with more than one hundred reporters from across the country and around the world. After I gave a brief opening statement, they bombarded me with questions I had surely thought about as a synod bishop. Now I was standing in an entire new venue. Now my answers carried enormously heavier consequences. From a variety of newspaper clippings I was able to reconstruct this summary of the news conference:

> At the time of our convention the fundamentalist world was being rocked by the Jimmy and Tammy Bakker scandal. They grabbed the headlines. One reporter suggested that ". . . stories of sex scandals sell better than stories about the naming of a bishop for a new 5.3 million member church" (*La Crosse Tribune*, 5/9/87) .

> When asked about suggesting that "evangelical" be included in the name of our new church, I said that "I did

so because I think we have to recapture a beautiful word that has to do with preaching the gospel of Jesus Christ."

When queried about ecumenical affairs, I admitted that this was an area where I lacked experience, especially on the global scene. But I also stressed my intention to "get up to speed" as quickly as possible.

I spoke about my love for preaching, noting that colleagues had sometimes cautioned me to slack up a bit. "I have to do it. It regenerates me."

How had I dealt with the tragedy of losing a son by suicide? I said that the experience had taught Corinne and me that the theology we had been taught was valid. "I know God is with people in times like that," I said.

I said that my greatest apprehension was whether I had the skills to bring the three churches together in unity. I was determined to spend the energy necessary to bring it about.

When asked about congregations that were threatening to leave the new church, I stated that "My concern is that they leave for the right reasons, and not on the basis of rumors. . . . we should send them off with our blessing."

One reporter wanted to know my views regarding the charismatic movement. I stated forthrightly that "I think of myself as a charismatic, even though I don't speak in tongues. To me, to be charismatic is to be open to the gifts of the Spirit."

I underscored my record of support for gay and lesbian persons during my tenure as Minnesota Synod bishop and welcomed these persons into the life of the ELCA.

Another reporter wanted to know my stance on abortion. I said I could only see it as "a tragic option" that would be chosen only if the health of the mother was in question or when a woman had been raped.

I did my best to reply to all of their questions. When it was over, I still felt that deep calm. But I knew that this was just a taste of what was to come. I had stepped into a demanding new and much larger world.

From the news conference we were escorted though another maze of hallways, and even a kitchen, to a service elevator that would take us to our room. From that point on I was a virtual captive of the DMX. Roaming freely among the delegates was not an option. This was completely contrary to my nature, to my way of relating to the people I wanted to know and serve. To this day I harbor a deep resentment against that group for robbing us of those moments when Corinne and I should have been free to be with those who had affirmed us so graciously.

Who will be secretary, vice president, and treasurer?

Following my election it was a foregone conclusion that the secretary must be someone from the American Lutheran Church.

I felt a bit uneasy when Lowell Almen approached me prior to any of the votes for secretary and handed me a sheaf of flyers promoting his candidacy. He asked if I would distribute them to the Minnesota Synod delegation. I assume he did the same with all of the synod/district bishops. In fact, *Lutheran World Information* reported that "Almen had contacted key people in the church bodies in recent weeks seeking support for his candidacy for the . . . post" (6/1987). I made no promise. This ran counter to my own conviction that one should not seek a call or an office in the church.

As I reflected on the issue, I realized that my views on this matter had no basis other than my personal convictions. So when our Minnesota Synod delegation met, I distributed the flyers and emphasized that this was in no way my endorsement of Almen's candidacy and that each should make up her or his mind on the basis of the one they felt best qualified for the office.

In the meantime, there were many in the ALC, and especially

district bishops, who were promoting Harold Jansen, bishop of the ALC Eastern District. I got a call asking if I would feel good about that choice. That put me into a terrible bind. I had nothing but the highest regard for Jansen as a good churchman and a fine bishop. Our personal relationship was longtime and solid. I would surely enjoy having him as a colleague. But I honestly could not see him in the role of secretary.

Then Jansen himself called. He wanted to know if I thought he would be a good candidate and if I would support him. Again, I was in a terrible quandary. This would be a crucial decision for him, for me, and for the new church. I simply could not give him my unqualified encouragement.

In the course of time, Jansen himself came to realize that this office was not for him. He went to a microphone and tried to pull his name from consideration, but it was too late in the parliamentary process.

Eventually, Almen was elected. As the editor of *The Lutheran Standard,* the magazine of the ALC, he was well known in that church. His competence as editor, his good judgment, and wry sense of humor had won many friends for him in and beyond the ALC.

After the convention Almen wrote of his understanding of the role of secretary, including the importance of working "under the leadership and direction of Bishop Chilstrom. . . . He is the bishop of the ELCA; I serve as churchwide secretary" (*The Lutheran Standard,* 5/22/87).

It became a foregone conclusion that the office of vice president should go to someone from the AELC, the smallest of the merging churches. The convention seemed to look to that delegation to give us a candidate. When the name of Christine Grumm surfaced I had no idea who she was. I had never met her or even heard of her. When I actually *did* meet her I was swept off my feet and left wondering if two such opposite personality types could work together. Short and given to wearing bright colors to accompany her platinum blond hair, Grumm was a woman to be noticed, a force with which to be reckoned. Her broad smile and strong voice captured your attention from the first moment. Could I, I wondered, somewhat of an introvert and preferring to make change by quiet persuasion, work with someone so obviously forthright and aggressive in promoting her ideas? I was "the man in black." She would be "the woman in red," so to speak. Given that the vice president of the new church would be the chair of the Church Council, I knew that this was one person I would be working with very closely. She easily won the election by a vote of 646 to 232 over Arnold Mickelson, the sixty-five-year-old former secretary of the ALC. One newspaper called it ". . . a sign that this new church does plan to make women equal partners in its leadership" (*La Crosse Tribune*, 5/9/87).

What I soon learned was that Grumm was not only a woman of enormous competence, but also one with a deep faith and a great love for the church. I would never have guessed at the moment of her election that we would become close colleagues in the coming years. I learned that our different personalities and styles of leadership actually worked for the good of the new church.

The treasurer would be chosen later by the new Church Council. There were two candidates: Robert Blanck from the LCA and George Aker out of ALC background. I knew Blanck, a Philadelphia lawyer, from our work together on the LCA Executive Council and the CNLC. I had nothing but the highest regard for him.

Aker, however, brought with him the experience of having been a banker. Though I had no knowledge of his work, he seemed like a good, successful person. I decided, reluctantly to throw my support to Aker. A big man with an ever-ready smile, Aker was the ultimate optimist. I would learn that what the church needed more than anything else in that office was a realist.

Ending and beginning with the Eucharist

It would be impossible to describe the sense of awe and humility I felt as I presided over the Eucharist on Saturday evening of the convention. With the theme "In the Unity of the Spirit—One Church Made New," Crumley, Herzfeld, and Preus poured wine from separate flasks into the common cup I held in my hands. As the wine mingled and then was consecrated, I felt the presence of the empowering Spirit as a force who would carry us forward as one people of God.

As fifty bishops and fifty lay persons moved out into the three thousand-member congregation in the auditorium one could feel the rich symbol of representation that those in this auditorium carried for the more than five million members of this new church. Everything from the past—years of hope for the unification of a major part of America's Lutherans, hard work that had been done by so many to bring greater unity, the arduous and at times fragile work of the CNLC, the frustration of not having at this table the "other Lutherans" in our land—all this and more came together at the celebration of Eucharist. Our vision for the whole world of Lutherans was accented as prayers were offered in Norwegian, Spanish, Indonesian, German, Zulu, Afrikaans, and Tswana. It was indeed the end of one era in American Lutheranism and the beginning of another—and all centered appropriately in the Eucharist.

It was also appropriate that Gunnar Staalsett, general secretary of the Lutheran World Federation, be the preacher for this service. This represented the commitment of the new church to the global Lutheran community. He said:

> The eyes of many are upon you as you take this important step toward becoming one in Jesus Christ. The task of Lutheran unity is still incomplete, but what you are doing here is a strong and hopeful sign (*The Lutheran Standard,* 5/22/87).

Gary Harbaugh, faculty member at Trinity Seminary, captured the moment:

> With uplifting and triumphal music resounding on every side, participant followed participant into the hall. Just when my senses had had about as many impressions, in came the erstwhile presiding bishops of the ALC, AELC, and LCA, distinguished by their service to the church. Finally, a tall, silver-haired, red-robed man entered—the newly elected Bishop of the ELCA—Herbert Chilstrom. With Bishop Chilstrom's entrance the eyes of the congregation focused once more on the worship center. Most surprising of all was the absence of the large red, blue, and black cross that had graced the wall during the day. The cross had been disassembled and reassembled as the table of the Lord. The gifts were placed upon it. Before the night was over, between four and five thousand people had shared the Word and Sacrament together for the first time as the ELCA ("Scandalon," 5/12/87).

I felt exhausted when the evening was over—exhausted, yes, but deeply at peace with all that had happened in those last several days.

Press reports

News of my election spread rapidly. Here's just a sampling:

The New York Times ran an article with a photograph of Corinne and me, one of the worst we've ever had taken. Reporter Ari Goldman gave his own slant on the election indicating that "One criticism heard of Bishop Chilstrom during two days of subtle campaigning for the office, was that he was not forceful enough to project the image the new church seeks" (5/2/87). Had he been following me around he would have seen no campaigning at all, subtle or otherwise.

In *The Christian Century*, Jean Caffey Lyles described me as ". . . a tall and trim white-haired figure exuding a pastoral warmth." She reported me as saying that I envisioned a church that is ". . . much more inclusive than it is—a church like that envisioned in the Book of Acts." The article also affirmed our role as a couple. "Both Chilstroms are known for showing their humanity openly and talking about their own struggles to help others in similar circumstances" (5/13/87).

The *St. Paul Pioneer Press* called the election ". . . a battle of the Minnesota giants of Lutheranism, both literally and figuratively. The vote reflected the young church's eagerness to move away from the deep tradition represented by Mr. Preus and toward the evangelicalism advocated by Mr. Chilstrom" (5/5/87).

One of the more interesting articles appeared in the *Fergus Falls Journal*, the newspaper that serviced the area around Pelican Rapids and Elizabeth, Minnesota, where I had served my first congregations after ordination. The headlines read: "Area Lutherans describe Chilstrom as 'go-getter.'" Victor Petterson, a pillar of the Elizabeth church and a dairy farmer, was quoted as saying that "Some pastors stressed damnation. He did, too, but he did it in a way that he didn't step on anybody's toes. He's very sincere and very set in his ways." "Outside the church," the article read, "he's described as a humorous man who's a good gardener and a self-taught carpenter."

Outpouring of support

In the days and weeks that followed the election an avalanche of letters, phone calls, and personal contacts brought assurance of support.

Before he left Columbus, *Robert Marshall* jotted a note. Knowing he had hoped either Martin Marty or William Lazareth might be elected the first bishop, I was especially gratified to sense that he had come full-circle. "Congratulations seems almost too mundane to be adequate to express my feelings about your election," he wrote. "'Thank God' sounds more fitting because the church and I can only be thankful that a person such as you is available and willing to serve as bishop. The task of shaping the structure, staff, and spirit of the new church will be overwhelming except that you have the Spirit, support, and skills that are needed. Little did I know at that moment how important his counsel would be in the years to come.

Reuben Swanson wrote to me a week after the convention remembering that "From the first time we chatted about the possibility of your being bishop of our church I have believed you could serve effectively and been convinced that someday this office would be given to you."

Surely one of the most meaningful letters was from *Edgar Carlson*, former president of Gustavus Adolphus College. In my years as synod bishop he had become a friend.

> You are so eminently qualified for that high post by native ability, experience, training, and personal qualities that members of the church will have great confidence in your leadership.
>
> I pray that God will enable you to see the fruitfulness that is in the seed as well as the harvest, so that you will not get discouraged. You have your values and priorities right, and your faith seems to have grown stronger and become clearer as it has been tested, both in trials and in triumphs. God bless you both.

Martin Marty wrote to remind me that he had suggested a few months earlier that "Great Things will happen to you this year. I can't think of a Greater Thing than what did happen. The combination of your experience, your spouse, and partnership across LCA-ALC lines, the fact you qualify to be a Lutheran theologian because of the suffering you've been through, and so many other factors give me good hope. I belong very much to the camp of those who think what the ELCA needs is not talkers-down, malaise-spreaders, gloom-sayers, and bet-hedgers, but morale-builders, under the power of the Spirit."

Patrick Henry, executive director of the Institute for Ecumenical and Cultural Research at Collegeville, Minnesota, had become
a friend during my days as bishop in. "It's rather astonishing," he
wrote, "that someone who puts together so many human desider-
ata—intelligence, warmth, openness, decisiveness, reconciliation—
should be asked to lead anything in our society. One just doesn't
expect a Herb Chilstrom to make it through the bureaucratic mesh.
But you did, and that's wonderful."

Peter Rogness, bishop of the ALC Southern Wisconsin District,
stressed that "Most of the delegates from this district, not surprisingly, were pulling for David [Preus]—he's been a fine leader, and
they respect his gifts. But there was almost universally among our
delegates a very positive feeling about the possibility of your being
our leader."

From *Jaroslav Pelikan* at Yale University came a handwritten
note. "It is my hope and prayer that under your leadership our new
Church will become an instrument of God for the deepening of the
'Evangelical Catholicity' you and I learned from Conrad Bergendoff
and, through him, from Nathan Söderblom. Please be assured of
my prayerful support."

Henry Horn was the highly respected pastor at University
Lutheran Church, Cambridge, Massachusetts. He was recognized
as a foremost leader in promoting good worship in the church. He
wrote that he was ". . . delighted not only because of your excel-
lence as a candidate . . . but that the Augustana Synod will now be
in front of us in our president. That brings the concept of church-
liness to the fore—something which one cannot talk about—one
just does!"

I did not know the eminent Lutheran church historian *E. Clifford
Nelson*, longtime professor at Luther Seminary and St. Olaf College. It was encouraging to read his handwritten word: "It is a joy
to think of you in this important position, which in my judgment
requires a bishop who is an authentic Lutheran, a churchman with

ecumenical wisdom, a solid theologian, a man of profound personal spirituality, and whose gifts are placed under the benevolent guidance of the Holy Spirit." I had read Nelson's book on Lutheranism in North America when I taught that subject to college students. In the weeks following my election I reread it, as well as his volume on the rise of world Lutheranism. The latter gave me the best foundation I could have had in readying myself for my new role on the international scene.

First Lutheran Church, my home congregation at Litchfield, Minnesota, sent a greeting that began with the promise that "We . . . salute you as our new bishop. We will support the new Lutheran Church in prayer, in time, in talent, and in treasure." It was signed by scores of members of the congregation. On the very last page, in shaky handwriting, were the words: *"Your Mother. Ruth Chilstrom."* By that time I wasn't certain that she had any awareness of what she was signing. Nevertheless, it was good to see her name on the list. I was pleasantly surprised and humbled to learn that First Lutheran decided to name its new assembly room "Chilstrom Hall."

The convention and my election—What does this mean?

Assessments of the convention and my election were numerous. One of the most frequently cited was by Richard Koenig in *The Christian Century (6/17–24/87)*.

Koenig wrote under the title "New Lutheran Church: The Gift of Augustana." He began by acknowledging that the convention was, in some respects "a surprise-free event" because so many actions were pro forma. In other ways, however, he called it ". . . an absorbing affair, offering an arresting tableau of Lutheran history on this continent and a redemptive conclusion to a difficult, sometimes conflictual passage." Koenig stated that the three final candidates ". . . clearly represented in their persons the major strands of American Lutheranism that were being woven together." Preus, wrote Koenig, represented the strong midwestern roots of the ALC in predominantly Norwegian and German culture.

Lazareth, a son of German immigrants, was the product of Philadelphia Seminary, the school that reflected ". . . a particular type of Lutheran confessionalism."

Chilstrom, wrote Koenig, ". . . represented another stream of Lutheranism:" the Augustana Synod, a church with historic ties to the Church of Sweden. In spite of those ties, "Augustana soon became known for its independent ways. In piety it was kin to its midwestern Scandinavian neighbors. In doctrine it felt drawn to the East and the Mt. Airy tradition, save for its German intellectualism." Over its more than one hundred years of history, Koenig wrote, there emerged what might be called "the Augustana ethos." Part of that ethos was a vision of a larger Lutheran unity in America.

Koenig noted that I was seen as a reconciler and bridge-builder.

> His election was a personal tribute; and it was also a recognition of the integrity of the ethos that shaped him and that provided the partners in the merger—at their weakest: the skittish ALC, the officious LCA and the truculent AELC—a zone in which to meet.

From this ethos, writes Koenig, emerged "The combination of a firm Lutheran confessionalism and a warm pietism."

Carl Braaten gave a rather positive assessment of my election:

> Why did they choose Chilstrom? For one thing, Chilstrom did not have a big bloc of delegates opposing him as did each of the others. He had the advantage of being an LCA bishop in ALC territory, and thus had the best chance of unifying the merging bodies. With the fewest liabilities, he was in the centrist position which usually decides the winner.

> In spite of rumors before and during the convention, that the bishop is "trendy" on the issues . . . those who know Bishop Chilstrom very well assure us that his is a living

piety anchored in the living Word and should not be
confused with the secularized pietism diverting the church
from its proper mission (*dialog, A Journal of Theology*—
Summer 1987).

Last days in Minnesota

As soon as got home, I crafted a reflective piece for the monthly
"Update," the newsletter that went to pastors and lay leaders of the
synod at the beginning of each month:

> It's Sunday evening. Four hours ago Corinne and I arrived
> home from Columbus. I sit here alone in my study wonder-
> ing. . . . Is it all a dream? Will I wake up tomorrow morning
> and find it was all an illusion?
>
> Feelings. . . . More than anything else—privilege. Can it
> really be that I should be so privileged? All this flow of his-
> tory that has come to fulfillment this past week. Why has
> God given this opportunity to me? I will never understand
> it. I can only say that when the decision was announced
> there came over me a profound sense of peace. I have
> learned in a smaller arena, the Minnesota Synod, that a
> bishop is a symbol as much as anything else. It is the office
> that is important. God calls persons because the office
> is essential. The fact that our Lord calls one rather than
> another through the church is a mystery. Like Jeremiah I
> wonder how it is that God can use me. But by God's grace
> and through the prayers of the people of God I will be
> given strength and wisdom that is not in me to fulfill the
> call to this office. The promise of the gift of the Spirit is
> what I claim now more fervently than ever.
>
> Now it is late. It is quiet. Eyelids are getting heavy. The
> pressures of the last days are subsiding and in their place is
> a deep sense of peace. I will sleep soundly tonight. And if
> I can manage to stay awake there will come again as a last
> prayer for the day:

Thy holy wings, O Savior, spread gently over me;
And let me rest securely, through good and ill in thee.
O be my strength and portion, my Rock and Hiding Place,
And let my every moment be lived within thy grace.

A new home for us and for the church

Corinne and I flew back to Chicago shortly after the Constituting
Convention. While a building had been purchased at 8765 West
Higgins Road, two miles east of the O'Hare International Airport,
it stood empty. Temporary quarters had been arranged in an adja-
cent building.

A real estate agent met us at O'Hare. We went off in separate
directions, I to the temporary office and she to hunt for a home for
us. After two days of intense searching, she found the Mission Hills
complex in Northbrook, which was ten miles north of the office. A
gated community, it offered the security I wanted for Corinne during my frequent trips out of town.

On my next trip to Chicago I walked from the Hyatt Hotel to
the empty building that would one day be The Lutheran Center. I
went to the eleventh floor and the corner where my office would
be located. I noted some green forest preserve space immediately
below my office, a place of sanctuary. But just to the left I could see
the endless stream of traffic that filled Interstate 90 day and night.
Snaking alongside the highway was the train that carried tens of
thousands of commuters to and from the airport ever day. Yes and
there on the western horizon two miles away was O'Hare International Airport, the world's busiest. As planes landed from the east,
one could almost catch a glimpse of pilots and passengers peering
out the plane windows.

Was this really that same boy standing there, the boy who had
rushed out of his grandparents' farm home more than a half-cen-
tury earlier to marvel at the flight of a small plane over the prairie
near Litchfield?

From that spot I could turn and look out in every direction, my view obstructed only by the elevator shafts that anchored the center of the unfinished building.

And that was the case on each of the eleven floors. It stood like a body without a heart and the other organs needed to give life. I found it difficult to comprehend how everything was going to come together over the next several months. There had been more than seventy-five hundred applications for the few hundred positions that would be filled for the new staff.

Corinne and I got settled into our Mission Hills condominium as quickly as possible. It would be our home for the next more than eight years. We had parking for our cars in the basement. Most days we bypassed the elevators and climbed the seventy stairs to our fifth-floor condominium. It was good exercise.

We looked out on a lovely scene that included a manicured golf course and the tops of giant elm trees where cardinals, the Illinois state bird, serenaded us. In almost nine years at Mission Hills I never played a single round of golf. Life was too busy for such a casual, time-consuming sport. When I was home we usually took a walk on the golf course before sunset. My commute to the office was an easy fifteen-minute drive, down I-294 to I-90 and then off the interstate highway to the office just before traffic into the city of Chicago began to get snarled.

I set up my home office in the second bedroom. On one of my first days in that place I wrote a note on a small piece of blue paper: "Help me fear no one but you." It was done both spontaneously and deliberately. I knew that with each unfolding day I would be the object of demands I could not possibly meet, of criticism that I could not possibly answer, of expectations that no human being could live up to. I knew I needed to listen carefully to the advice of others. But I also knew that in the end I had to be my own person. No matter how effective the churchwide staff and the high caliber of my assistants, I knew I would often walk a lonely road. I knew that my chief concern before all else had to be my relationship with God and the need to live in the will and purpose of God. That note never left my desk during our years in Chicago.

Farewell to our Minnesota home

There was little time to be nostalgic about leaving our lovely home in Minnesota. In a letter to Alvin Rogness, who had sent words of encouragement after my election, I wrote about the sadness that lingered:

> Thank you for your thoughtfulness in praying for us every day. You have no idea how much that means to us. Leaving our home in Edina was a very difficult time for us. I had left home for a trip to the West before the moving truck arrived. When I returned the house was empty. I was instinctively drawn to the basement where Andrew took his last breath. There I was able to do some grief work and take departure from a place that once held only fear and remorse, but in time became a place of consolation and renewal.

A modest beginning for a five-million-member church

June 1, 1987, was to be my first official day on the job in Chicago

Operating from our temporary offices put more than a little strain on our staff. The build out at 8765, however, moved along more efficiently than we had anticipated, thanks in large part to my seminary classmate Gerald Molgren who oversaw many of the details in that process. In early December I reported in the newsletter "On Occasion":

> If all goes according to schedule, we will be operational at 8765 on Monday morning, December 14. It cannot come too soon for most of our executive directors who wonder for whom the bell tolls as they sit in open space among a sea of desks, telephones, computers, and typewriters in our temporary space.

A month later in the same publication I was able to report that

> ... the arrival of warm bodies with smiling faces and arms
> filled with files and family photographs is giving what was
> a rather cold and impersonal building the character of a
> congenial workplace. I always have been of the opinion that
> those who spend most of their waking hours in an office
> should try to make it as pleasant as their home or apart-
> ment—where they usually spend less time.

Again, several months later I described my joy in seeing the
building occupied:

> For months I have looked down at our ELCA churchwide
> office as I have taken off or landed at O'Hare airport. There
> it was—a rather cold and impersonal configuration of
> glass and stone. Then, recently, I looked again as I landed
> late one afternoon. The building was full of light. My heart
> skipped a beat. Somehow what seemed so remote for so
> long was now here (*The Lutheran,* 3/2/88).

Tributes and an uncertain future for Corinne
Reporter Kim Ode wrote about the pain Corinne felt over leaving
her parish ministry.

> "I never did pray for his election, only that God's will be
> done. The end result was an overwhelming sense of peace
> for us. I woke up the next morning with my letter of resig-
> nation in my head. It's right, but it's sad for me."

Ode went on to say that Corinne,

> ... trim at 55, looks as proper as the Ladies Aid, but is as
> frank as a church treasurer. "I've always been gregarious and
> I guess I found life on a farm a little lonely. Anywhere the car
> went, I wanted to go. Even today, I want to be with people.
> If they're not streaming into my house, I want to be where
> they're streaming" (*Minneapolis Star Tribune,* 5/30/87).

In speaking to Ode about this new venture, Corinne told her:

> ". . . when two people struggle in a marriage, it's never at
> the same time, which is fortunate. We've learned to listen to
> each others' souls in depth, loving each other in this way. I
> do believe there is some special reason I was put together
> with Herb in this challenge and that I will come to it gradu-
> ally and that's exciting to know."

Corinne made our condominium into a restful and commodious place for us to live. It was my haven when I returned from travel and long days at the office.

She also used her time to pray. She rode her Exercycle and prayed for the entire sixty-five synod Women of the ELCA presidents, for the synod bishops and their spouses, for the churchwide staff, for our extended family, and many others.

Before long, invitations came for her to speak in various parts of the country. This, it seemed, was to be her calling in our early years in Chicago. She spoke at many congregations, synod assemblies, Women of the ELCA conventions, baccalaureate exercises at Muhlenberg College, the National Cathedral in Washington, D.C., and elsewhere. We always coordinated our calendars very carefully so that she was at home almost always when I was in Chicago.

Assembling a core staff

I had exclusive authority to choose only four persons on the entire Chicago staff: an administrative assistant, two additional assistants, and a personal secretary.

As for the three assistants, I knew that it was important to choose one from each of the predecessor churches. Yes, I wanted the best persons I could get. But I also knew that it would send a negative message to any of those churches if they thought I could not find at least one person in their church to fill one of those positions. It was also important to have a voice of familiarity from each of those churches, someone who knew people and history in each of them.

Robert Bacher

Because of my involvement with the LCA churchwide organization, I knew that Bacher was regarded as a top-flight administrator. His reputation was that of a sterling leader and a committed
churchman. He would be the first among equals of my assistants,
the executive assistant. Following my interview with Bob I had no
doubt that we could work well as a team. He would be the person
who would be chiefly responsible for my office when I was gone,
the person who would work most directly with other churchwide
staff, the person who would articulate my position on issues, the
one who would become my alter ego. Bacher filled that role and
filled it well for the more than eight years we were together.

I suppose my only regret in asking Bacher to be my chief assistant
was that this precluded naming him for another leadership position.
Robert Marshall, who knew Bacher well, told me later that he had
envisioned him as head of the Division for Congregational Life. That
was good judgment. Yet, because he served so well for me and my
successor, I can only wish that I might have been able to clone him.

Lita Brusick Johnson

Having a woman on my immediate staff and finding someone out
of AELC background was also important. Lita had been with the
Lutheran Office of Government Affairs (LOGA) in Washington,
D.C., for several years. She joined the CNLC when one of the
original members from the AELC had to resign for health reasons.
Though seemingly quiet and somewhat retiring, she quickly proved
to be an important member of the CNLC. She impressed her colleagues with the thoroughness and high caliber of her work. Her
knowledge of government affairs and of the mind-set of those who
worked in the power structures of the national government were an
asset needed in my office.

Lita worked hand-in-glove with Bacher in relating to the
churchwide staff and making certain that each unit functioned

interdependently with the others. For each Church Council meeting and Churchwide Assembly over the next eight years Lita would play a key role in making certain that agendas and reports were prepared well in advance. She was a first-rate administrator who maintained a masterful grasp on every detail.

Morris "Bo" Sorenson

Within days after my election David Preus invited me to lunch at the Minneapolis Club. The only topic of conversation was his recommendation that I choose Sorenson as one of my assistants. Sorenson had been head of global missions for the ALC and then one of Preus's assistants. I checked other references and learned that he was a team player and one who had superb administrative gifts. After a meeting with him I was convinced that we could work well together. Being able to concur with Preus's wish was also important for future relationships with the former ALC.

It proved to be an excellent decision. Bo and I bonded quickly. My only regret was that he was nearing retirement and served only four years.

Betty Fenner

I knew from previous experience that an effective and congenial executive secretary was essential. This is the person who meets people on their way into the bishop's office. Coming to that office is daunting enough for many people. Being welcomed by a pleasant, hospitable person makes all the difference in the world.

I knew the person I wanted: Betty Fenner. She had been the executive assistant for both Robert Marshall and James Crumley at the LCA headquarters in New York. But would she, a resident of New Jersey since childhood, be willing to move to Chicago? How relieved I was when she accepted. Having someone in that position who had a grasp of how a national church office works and who already knew many of the people who would take positions in

Chicago was an enormous advantage. I also knew that she could be absolutely trusted to keep sensitive matters in strict confidence.

Choosing churchwide staff—a small and difficult role

The boards for each major churchwide unit had been elected at the Constituting Convention. They met for the first time in late June 1987. At the opening worship I preached on the text from Ezekiel 34:11–16: the valley of the dry bones. I suggested to the combined boards that ". . . what we do these next three days here in Chicago is at least as important as anything that has happened until this time." Setting the parameters for each unit and selecting executives for them was critical to getting off to a strong beginning in the ELCA. I focused on the shepherding theme in Ezekiel.

There were nearly two thousand applications for about three hundred executive positions. Some job seekers applied for more than one position, bringing the total number to about seven thousand. Coupled with that, the personnel office did not handle matters well, prompting me to make a public apology (*The Lutheran*, 1/27/88).

As for me, one might think that being elected head of a church of more than five million would mean having major input in the choice of the heads of the major churchwide units. I had learned as part of the CNLC process that such would not—and could not—be the case. Transition teams had to do much of the vetting in order for the church to get off to an expedient start. In nearly every area of operation the field of candidates for each major position had been pared to two or three choices. I accepted this reality. Yet I also came to learn that even that intentional process left something to be desired.

When the boards of each major unit considered the nominees from the transition teams they faced an impossible task. For one thing, they were strangers to each other on those boards. Yet at that initial meeting they were expected to function as a seasoned board in doing one of their most important tasks: choosing a director for that unit.

The same was true for me. I was bombarded with all kinds of decisions about endless items, yet was expected to help ascertain the best candidate for each major unit.

There were, of course, complaints right from the start about the lack of balance in the persons chosen as final candidates for various staff positions. One head of a major division of the LCA, who was about to retire, wrote to me in confidence before final choices were made, complaining that the transition team had nominated no persons of color and few women for leadership of any of the major divisions and offices, other than that of Multicultural Ministries, where such a choice might be assumed. He urged me to take personal responsibility for reopening the process to rectify this fault. I found it impossible to comply with his wishes, not only because I, as a member of the CNLC, respected the process we had set up, but mainly because I did not know persons of color or women who would be better qualified than those already nominated. I could only promise to make necessary changes as the church moved through its early years.

A few comments are in order regarding some of the selections:

Ecumenical Affairs

The field of candidates had been narrowed to three persons: Eugene Brand, Daniel Martensen, and William Rusch. I knew that this choice was of eminent importance. This would be a major area of responsibility for me as the chief ecumenical officer of the ELCA. My experience was limited.

I had no definitive preference prior to meeting with each of them. After the interviews I was divided between Brand and Rusch. Both were experienced in the field. I felt either could serve me well. James Crumley leaned hard on me to opt for Rusch. I had no good reason not to choose him and finally gave him the nod.

ELCA Foundation

Before the Constituting Convention Harvey Stegemoeller was
chosen by the transition team to head the Foundation. He was a
proven fundraiser, having had a successful term as president of
Capitol University in Columbus, Ohio. At the time of my election,
however, he had not made a final decision about taking the post.
He called me on one of the first days following the convention to
inquire whether I would give him my support and would agree to
contact major gift donors during my time in office. I assured him
that I would be a good partner.

In my time in office Stegemoeller and I had a very fine relationship. I admired his excellent work. I was disappointed, however,
in his reluctance to engage me in what he had asked for. Not once
in the next eight years did he request my help in talking to major
donor prospects, even when I reminded him of our agreement.

Board of Pensions

I had little to do with the selection of John Kapanke as head of the
pension program of the new church. John had been with the LCA
pension program prior to the merger and was seen as the best
candidate for the new position. Kapanke's dilemma was that he was
a lifelong member of the Wisconsin Synod. Though there was no
requirement that he join an ELCA congregation, both he and I felt
it was important that he did so. He made the transition, joining Mt.
Olivet Church in Minneapolis. At a meeting of new executives in
Chicago, he received communion from me. It was the first time he
had communed in an ELCA setting. It was an emotional moment
for both John and me. He proved to be an excellent chief executive
for what soon became a multi-billion dollar program of pension
and health benefits.

Conference of Bishops

In the structure of the new church the Conference of Bishops
played a rather odd role. It met twice a year and just prior to the

biennial Churchwide Assembly. Later it also met for a separate annual study retreat. It had its own set of officers. Yet it had no legislative authority in the ELCA. It functioned strictly in an advisory capacity. Nine of the synod bishops—one from each of the nine regions—sat on the Church Council as advisors. Any action of the COB had to be forwarded to the Council as advice. Yet the COB may well have been the most influential body in the church. Nothing of major importance happened unless this group gave not only its advice but also its consent.

Edwin Bersagel was chosen as the executive director for the Conference. Technically, he was one of my assistants. In practice, however, he operated with such independence and in such close alliance with the secretary of the church that I never thought of him as an assistant. That would be rectified when Bersagel retired.

Division for Schools and Higher Education
Robert Sorensen was a fine choice for this office. He kept an important balance between the division's responsibility for our church colleges, on the one hand, and the campus ministries at dozens of secular sites across the country. Elementary and high schools of the ELCA also came under this unit's aegis.

Division for Congregational Life
Eldon DeWeerth had been on the national staff of the ALC but not as a chief executive. His was not an easy task. He struggled to bring this rather disparate unit into a cohesive unit. It became apparent after a time that it was not a good fit for him. He accepted the need for change but with feelings of keen disappointment. He went on to an effective parish ministry.

Division for Ministry
Joseph Wagner had also had experience on churchwide staff, in his case with the LCA Division for Professional Leadership (DPL). I had had considerable contact with him when he represented the

division at Minnesota Synod events, including leadership retreats. As a member of the LCA Executive Council I had come to see him as being as important to the division as its executive director.

The selection of Wagner was also made easier when the other candidate, John Tietjen, was elected bishop of the Metropolitan Chicago Synod. Wagner sometimes referred to the "Russian election" that got him into office. Yet even if Tietjen had remained a candidate, I would have favored Wagner.

This division was charged with one of the thorniest issues that faced the new church. The CNLC, as noted earlier, was unable to come up with a comprehensive definition of ministry. Early in the life of the ELCA the division realized that it needed far more time to work through this process.

Wagner grew into the position and proved to be a superb administrator. Over the course of time, he became a trusted advisor and one to whom I would turn at a crucial time for advice.

Division for Outreach

James Bergquist was probably the most ebullient of the chief executives. He had held a senior staff position in the ALC prior to merger and was thought to be the ideal person for the church's outreach program. Under his aggressive leadership the former ALC had organized scores of new congregations across the country.

After a relatively brief time in office, Berquist left his post and went on to serve effectively as parish pastor, college president, and seminary lecturer abroad.

Division for Global Mission

Mark Thomsen had a solid track record both as a missionary and as one who applied theological acumen to his task. He administered the division effectively and was highly respected by his staff. It was a large unit, coupled with hundreds of missionary personnel around the world. I gave him free reign to lead the division. Because of the size of the unit Thomsen and I had to work hard to make certain I was fully informed on what was happening in global mission work.

Division for Social Ministry Organizations

This division was the flashpoint for some of the most incendiary issues that came up in the early years of the ELCA. Social statements and position papers are almost always controversial. Charles Miller proved to have the steady demeanor and essential administrative skills that we needed during those times. He weathered some extremely stormy days.

When we tried to formulate a statement on human sexuality a year or two later, he proved his mettle. I can't imagine anyone who could have handled those difficult times better than Charles.

ELCA Publishing House

There was never any doubt that Albert Anderson should continue to head that important arm of the church. Every year under his direction Augsburg Publishing House had turned a handsome profit, part of which was given to the ALC churchwide organization.

It was only on his retirement we learned that we would have to pay a price for his tight-fisted management style. First, he failed to modernize the printing enterprise. Some referred to his "green visor" style of leadership. Second, he failed to nurture a good successor. When he left, the board of the publishing house tried its best to find a capable successor. In the years that followed, the publishing house fell into an unbalanced budget from which it is still straining to recover even as I write.

Having said that, one must also recognize the world of denominational publishing houses was changing dramatically. Between the aggressive actions of new ventures and the dwindling loyalty of Lutheran congregations to order books and supplies from our own publishers, one has to wonder if anyone could have been more effective in this role.

Women of the ELCA
Betty Nyhus, the executive director of the Women of the ELCA, may have had the position most like my own. With units in every synod, she had to divide her time between the Chicago office and the sixty-five synods. She brought very good leadership to the unit.

Space does not allow for extended descriptions of other executives who joined the staff at the outset: Ruth Ann Killion in Research, Planning, and Evaluation; Carol Becker in Communications; Paul Johns in Financial Support; Jerry Folk in Church in Society; Craig Lewis in Multicultural Ministries; Christine Christ in the Commission for Women.

The Church Council

The thirty-three member Church Council was, in my judgment, as fine a group as one could have elected to get a new church off to a good start. As I review the list of these persons now more than twenty-five years later, I cannot identify even one that I would consider a weak link in that chain of important leaders. In that tumultuous first year in the church's life these women and men were anchors of stability in rough seas.

Christine Grumm, who served as chair of the Church Council, was an experienced executive. She gave some the impression that she may have overpowered me. Michael McDaniel, bishop of the North Carolina Synod, was one of the advisory bishops on the council. He was quite authoritarian by nature and probably reluctant to see a woman take the lead. After the first meeting of the council he urged me to "be in charge" of the council. It was never a problem for me. Grumm and I had a comfortable working relationship during all of her years of leadership.

One of the major issues that surfaced at the first council meeting was the perception that we were not naming enough persons of color or those whose primary language was other than English to management positions in the new church. I pointed out, "While the distinction is not always easy to maintain, we must continue to remind ourselves that the quotas and goals for inclusivity were not laid on us as a legal requirement." I reported that this task was more difficult than many had anticipated. I stated, however, that up to that time twenty-three of the one hundred and sixteen executive staff were from those categories and that we would not forget the goals that had been set.

There was one person on the Church Council whose election troubled me—Robert Marshall. The dynamics reminded me a bit too much of the problems I had dealt with in the Minnesota Synod when a former pastor remained a member or came back to a congregation he or she had once served. How would I handle this? As a young synod bishop in the late 1970s I had felt a bit intimidated by the austere and somewhat authoritarian Marshall. Though I had moved away from that discomfort during our time together on the CNLC, I wondered how it would be in the new church.

I learned shortly after the Columbus convention that Marshall was coming to Minneapolis for an event at Mt. Olivet Church. I got in touch with him and asked if we might chat prior to his return home. In our conversation I spoke gently but firmly about my fear that he might be tempted to look over my shoulder. I made it very certain that I would not tolerate that kind of relationship. He assured me that he would not do so. It turned out to be an important step in my early tenure as bishop of the ELCA. Over the next years Marshall became a trusted friend and confidant.

The Church Council's initial meeting was held the first few days of June 1987. In the plethora of activities that preceded the meeting, it was scarcely possible for me to prepare adequately for the sessions. I was grateful for Grumm's competency.

At the worship service I preached on the lesson for the day, the Visitation, from Luke 1:39–47. I began by recounting how often I had been asked in the past month about how it felt to be elected the first leader of the ELCA. A few excerpts:

My answer has been consistent. Amidst the maelstrom of other reactions, one has been paramount. It is a sense of *privilege*. I know you share my feeling. To be elected to the highest governing body of this church; to be given such trust; to set the course that will determine its journey—yes, you too are people of great privilege.

Looking to the text for the day, I accented the theme of joy and hope that pervades the story of Elizabeth, Zechariah, Joseph, and Mary.

We also, like the two couples in our text, live in a time of conception and birth. For us it is a church. At its heart the good news of the gospel is that God keeps breaking into our world to give joy and hope at the most unexpected times.

The Conference of Bishops

In early August 1987 the Conference of Bishops held its initial meeting at Oak Brook, a suburb of Chicago. All sixty-five synod bishops had been elected in the previous weeks at constituting assemblies of synods. None had been installed.

At the opening worship service I preached on the text from Matthew 13:1–9, the parable of the sower. I raised questions about our usual focus on the sower of the seed rather than the seed itself. Neither, I said, should one get preoccupied with the variety of soils. Rather, one should look at the flow that runs through the text.

The sowing at the beginning, which continues under difficult circumstances, is all moving toward one single goal: a superabundant harvest. It is a parable of hope—a promise from God that the faithful sowing of the good news eventually will bring a good result.

Is there a better text for the first meeting of our Conference of Bishops? I read some excitement and anticipation out there at the grassroots. People are wondering what new things we will deliver to them. The best thing we can deliver is that which is always new—the promises of the Word of God.

If we as bishops are looked to as models for leadership in the church, then our primary calling in these initial years is to be purveyors of the good news. I urge you to waste no time in moving from one end of your synod to the other as its chief evangelist.

I wasn't fully prepared for my new relationship with this group. For eleven years my fellow synod bishops in the LCA had been a source of great encouragement. I looked forward to every meeting. I enjoyed the camaraderie of my colleague bishops and especially the good counsel I garnered from those who had been in office for many years. Even more important, many were my friends.

Now all that changed. Now I was in a new world, one that was different from that of the synod bishops. There was some slight distance between us now. I was looking to them to support the mission of the churchwide organization. Each of them, in turn, was becoming ensconced in his own synodical aegis. This separation, this slight separation, was difficult for me. One on one, nearly all of them were easy to be with. But when they came together as a group the dynamics changed. The fact that I was not chair of the conference made me feel at times that I was more of a guest at their meetings than an integral part of a group of leaders who had but one purpose and goal.

The one redeeming element in all of this in the first four years was that Paul Werger was elected to be the chair of the conference. Werger and I, as I've pointed out earlier, had a strong bond. He worked very hard to carry out a common mission between the synods and the churchwide organization. Yet that small distance remained between the conference and me. It would be there as long as I was in office.

Matters got more complicated when Kenneth Sauer succeeded Werger in 1991. In the last four years in office I felt that I had to work unusually hard to bring the conference along on programs of the church.

Because of my experience, I made the specific suggestion to the conference when I left office in 1995 that my successor be part of the executive leadership of the Conference of Bishops.

H. George Anderson handled his relationship with the conference better than I had done, possibly because of the suggestion I had made. At its meetings he seated himself at the head of the group, alongside the chair. I, in contrast, had often sat at the back of the room. That was a mistake.

Times for reflection

It wasn't until early August in the summer of 1987 that I found time to write in my journal.

> I've been so inundated by my new job that much of my deepest personal need has had to be set aside—including prayer and Bible reading. I'm not very proud of that and can't say I really have a good excuse—because being busy is never a good excuse for neglecting those things. Yet, that is what has happened.

Two months later I sat down with a reporter from *The Lutheran Standard* to share my vision for the new church.

> I would like to give a reading assignment to every ELCA member: the Book of Acts and Luther's *Small Catechism*. The Book of Acts tells us how the early Christians organized their church. Luther's *Small Catechism* helps us understand why we are Lutheran. Out of that center we can begin to face the issues of our world today.

I spoke of my need to educate myself as an ecumenist:

> I need to learn so much so quickly. I'm not frightened by
> that. I just wish I could snap my fingers and learn all I need
> (to know).

I reflected on my frustration in my mid-thirties when I felt
trapped and even wondered if I should continue in ordained
ministry.

> That brief period of testing resulted in greater confidence
> than ever that I was meant for the ministry. I am deeply
> grateful that I didn't go off in another direction.

I stated that I was opposed to abortion on demand, suggesting
that rape, incest, or the health of the mother would be legitimate
reasons for that procedure. I also made it clear that pastors who are
homosexual and remain celibate should be permitted to remain on
the clergy roster.

I spoke about the impact of Andrew's death, emphasizing that

> Healing will take the rest of my life. There is no point when
> you can say, "I'm now healed." Everywhere you turn there
> are memories. But to run away from the process is not the
> answer. It's through pain and grief that we are able to go on.

I told the reporter:

> There's a lot of ego involved when people say you will head
> a new church, but the new challenges take a lot more than
> ego. By the grace of God, each experience you go through
> gives you added confidence (10/2/87).

It was not until late fall of 1987 that the *Chicago Tribune* finally
seemed to realize that a major Protestant denomination had come
to town. In a wide-ranging interview Bruce Buursma, a religion
writer, described me as ". . . a tall and sturdy Minnesotan of pure
Scandinavian stock." I stressed to him that my vow was to make the
new church a clearly visible and important participant in the growing debates over moral and religious matters in American society.

"You can't avoid it," I said, "if you take the Scriptures seriously and if you take the life of Christ and study it carefully. . . . you recognize you must be involved in the world." I suggested that thorny questions such as AIDS, peace, and the economy must be studied by the church. "People forget that Jesus got killed. He said some very unpopular things. And we are in the risk business . . . we have to decide if we are willing to take the risk."

In addressing my primary role as head of the ELCA, I stated that ". . . while circumstances have changed, my call has not. My call is to preach the gospel and lead people toward responsible living" (11/23/87).

Unfortunately, there would be little attention from the *Chicago Tribune* over the next years. One might cite our location far from downtown Chicago as one reason for this indifference. But it is also a fact of life that Chicago is primarily a Catholic town where that church dominates many things, including the press.

In an article entitled "Chilstrom—the first 100 days," Tom Roberts, an outside reporter, did a story for *The Lutheran* magazine in the March 20, 1988, issue. Describing me as one who "does not need to shout or use gimmicks or convince anyone of his faith or commitment," he conjectured that I had been chosen because of:

> . . . impeccable personal integrity whose long suit was the art of compromise and reconciliation. Perhaps the worry that Chilstrom would not impress with dash and image was the highest compliment. He does not, by his own words, stand above the church. He has chosen to immerse himself in it.

I told Roberts that I felt comfortable with the fact that the leadership of the Church Council was a lay person.

> I work in very close cooperation with that person. I don't feel any inhibitions whatever in suggesting to the council directions in which we ought to go.

In the interview I spoke of my yearning for the ELCA to become more multicultural.

I shared with Roberts some of the discomfort I felt on occasion.

> He has found the job at the top to be lonely at times. He is
> uneasy . . . being in the public eye and being placed "on a
> pedestal." He does not like being "showered with compli-
> ments," and he feels most uncomfortable when he senses
> that his presence . . . makes others uneasy. "I think to
> myself, 'Hey, wait a minute. I grew up in a small town, in a
> big family, and I still have a lot of that in me.' Most people
> who have known me for a number of years feel that what
> they see is who I am."

In June 1990 on a trip to Switzerland for an LWF meeting, I wrote a long letter to Corinne. It was a moment to reflect on many things that had happened since my election in 1987. After lamenting how full to overflowing my life had become, I pondered on how good it would be to live three lifetimes.

> . . . one to get a real and comprehensive liberal arts edu-
> cation, one to do the work I love and that seems to be
> demanded of me, and one to do as I please—including
> sharing love with you. Instead, we have to jam all three into
> the same space. Maybe that's what heaven is for. . . .

> The (synod) assemblies went well. There's a lot of solid sup-
> port around the church. I only hope that someday someone
> will be able to look back at this period and see that some
> wise decisions were made for the sake of the church.

Preparing for installation: Once more—who lays on hands?
Long before the Constituting Convention, October 10, 1987, had been set for the installation of the new bishop, vice president, secretary, and treasurer. In its enthusiasm the planning group had reserved the cavernous University of Chicago pavilion.

I knew, of course, that the heads of the three predecessor churches would lay hands on me at the installation. But it occurred to me that the event could be of greater symbolic importance if some of the guests from abroad might also have a part in that element of the installation. Knowing that the participation of Archbishop Bertil Werkström from Sweden might be especially problematical, I consulted with David Preus at the LWF meeting in Sweden and Denmark in July. His immediate response was negative.

When I returned to the United States I wrote a lengthy letter to Preus outlining my thoughts. I stated that I was now leaning toward the inclusion of not only Werkström, but also Johannes Hanselmann, bishop of the Evangelical Lutheran Church in Bavaria and president of the Lutheran World Federation, and Kleopas Dumeni, bishop of the Evangelical Lutheran Church in Namibia. I suggested that their participation would be "a clear indication of our ELCA's commitment to our brothers and sisters everywhere." Furthermore, I suggested that this action would fit with what Preus and I had accented in recent years, namely, ". . . that Lutheranism in this country has 'come of age' and is ready to take its place as a mature partner in the larger church."

Among other sources, I noted the article by Warren Quanbeck, Luther Seminary theologian, in *The Sixteenth Century Journal*. In it Quanbeck distinguishes between a Lutheran understanding of succession and the Roman Catholic, Orthodox, and Anglican understanding. I quoted from Quanbeck:

> To say that the perpetuity of the church is the work of the Spirit is not to say that all human signs of continuity are valueless. They have their proper relative value. . . . Continuity in orders can be a valuable sign of the church's continuity with the apostles. A high estimation of traditional forms of worship and service can support and enrich the church.

I concluded my letter by suggesting that unless I could be persuaded otherwise, I would go ahead with these plans for the installation on October 10. I copied the letter to both Crumley and Herzfeld and solicited their advice and counsel as well.

The storm that erupted over the next several weeks reminded me not only that I needed to reflect more deeply on my intentions but also that tribal warfare was not dead in Lutheranism in America.

At the heart of the issue, of course, was the strong resistance in some quarters to the introduction of the historic episcopate.

I remembered, of course, the incident at my installation as bishop of the Minnesota Synod in 1976 when Robert Marshall refused to allow Werkström, then the bishop of the Harnosund Diocese in northern Sweden, to lay hands on me. But now Werkström was the archbishop and I was the head of the new church in the United States. Now if I wanted to push the envelope, I could insist that he be included.

Preus's response to my letter was strong. Focusing exclusively on the Church of Sweden, the point he made was that though "... the Swedish Lutherans do not claim to be holding the historic episcopate as a sacramental necessity," nevertheless, "... the Swedish claim to succession has taken on some kind of quasi-succession character. . . . This is not the time to raise the issue through an action at your installation."

When I checked with Herzfeld, he had no objection. He applauded the idea.

Crumley was more guarded. Though he said he would support me if I went through with it, his personal preference was to let the church make this kind of decision in a more orderly way and after careful study. Michael Root, a respected ecumenical theologian who was on the faculty at Lutheran Theological Southern Seminary, posed the same argument. He was strongly in favor of seeing the new church move in the direction of the incorporation of the historic episcopate. Yet, like Crumley, he believed it should come by means of church convention mandate.

One of the seminary presidents wrote a personal and confidential letter reporting that several persons had contacted him and were alarmed by the report that the bishop from Sweden might be involved. Like Preus, he made no mention of Hanselmann and Dumeni. He argued that having Werkström involved would have a negative impact on the integrity of the discussions on the subject of the ministry in the new church.

It was interesting that no one raised an objection to the involvement in the laying on of hands by Dumeni and Hanselmann, even though both had probably been installed into office by bishops in the historic episcopate. It was clear that the resistance was to the Swedish archbishop. Indeed, old differences die slowly.

I felt caught between a rock and a hard place. I recognized the intensity of the opposition to my plan. I had no need to stir up unnecessary conflict as the church was coming to birth. Yet I felt it offensive to exclude international representatives. And, quite frankly, I felt offended that the objections were so clearly centered on the participation of Werkström.

I decided that it would be good to consult with Conrad Bergendoff, one of the elder statesmen of the church and a man who knew the history of this question better than anyone I could think of. In his handwritten letter to me Bergendoff stated:

> The question of Apostolic Succession is a thicket with many thorns. Who recognized whom and to what end?

> Rome of course claims it, despite the Greek Orthodox Church. The Anglicans have sought to get in on the line, but Rome declines. The Church of Sweden has a case but doesn't consider it important. The rest of Christendom looks on in amusement.

After some comments on the complexity of the question, Bergendoff advised:

> We will have many problems. I would be in favor of letting this sleeping dogma rest in peace. I am hoping that the archbishop of Sweden will participate. That itself is significant. I hope the ELCA will help awaken the Swedish Church. But this requires no mythic succession—only succession in the Apostolic Faith.

Bergendoff's counsel made sense. I scuttled any plans to involve bishops from abroad. In retrospect, it was a good decision. As I have noted, it took several years for the ELCA to attain any sense of clarity on this issue. It was not until after I left office that the church was able to enter into full communion with the Episcopal Church, an agreement that included acceptance of the historic episcopate. And even then it could only be achieved by means of compromise.

At the time, I was rankled by the uproar over my plan. Now I feel more amused by it, and especially that the objections were centered on the archbishop from Sweden and not the others. In one sense, I was ahead of the times. Even the Church of Norway has now incorporated the historic episcopate into its church life.

After reading my account of this aspect of my installation, Dr. Maria Erling, church historian on the faculty at the Lutheran Theological Seminary at Gettysburg, observed:

> Your intended gesture would have communicated a "coming of age" moment for the ELCA. Your reflections on this time . . . in the church's new beginning help me see very clearly how difficult it must have been to achieve a working ELCA. It is really amazing that we have this church. God has really blessed us (8/15/08).

The installation of officers: glorious and disappointing

The gentle rain that fell on Chicago October 10, 1987, did not dampen the enthusiasm of the three thousand who attended the installations. Those numbers may seem impressive. But in the pavilion, huge and sterile, the congregation seemed to be swallowed up by all the empty seats. That took some of the edge off the excitement for the service.

Yet I could not help but feel upbeat and inspired. The service was planned with exacting precision. *The Christian Century* (10/28/87) called it "Lutheran liturgy at its best." Church leaders from around the world and across the country came for the installation of the new officers of the church. More than thirty of them marched in colorful procession with the sixty-five synod bishops, led into the auditorium by lithe dancers. The organist was my friend David Fienan from Gustavus Adolphus College in Minnesota.

Hymns from many traditions were sung prior to the service, including "Children of the Heavenly Father." The procession entered with "Holy God, we praise your name. . . ." Corinne, Mary, and Chris presented the sacramental gifts. Our godchild Jodi (Anderson) Belseth carried the pectoral cross, fashioned in England and a gift from St. Luke Church in Silver Spring, Maryland. The auditorium was festooned with colorful red banners. A huge baptismal font symbolized the coming together of the three churches.

The preacher was Donald Sjoberg, a friend since 1960 and presiding bishop of the Evangelical Lutheran Church in Canada. The synod bishops, a representative from each of the synods, a group of seminary students, and members from area congregations assisted with communion.

Though it was not all that I had hoped for, the service of laying on of hands was deeply moving. To feel the palms of my three predecessors resting on my head linked me with the event in Columbus a few months earlier when these leaders poured wine into the chalice I held that day.

In my "Greeting to the Congregation" I said:

> On behalf of all four of us who are installed today, thank
> you—all of you—for coming to this day of celebration. We
> believe you have come today for more than one reason. Yes,
> to see the officers of the church installed. But, more than that,
> you have come because you love Jesus Christ and his church.
>
> From the far corners of the world and from the United
> States have come representatives of other Lutheran
> churches. Scores of millions are represented by Bishop
> Hanselmann, president of the Lutheran World Federation.

The Christian Century opined that

> If there was a triumphal note in the service, it was to be
> found in the joy at the sign-of-peace exchange among all
> the worshipers: After generations of doctrinal discussions
> and disagreements, the majority of Lutherans in America
> could now be brought together in a union based on their
> confessional writings.

I presided over the Eucharist. Though I had done it hundreds
of times prior to that day, this was surely the most moving of all.
I could scarcely contain my emotions. I went to the section where
my family and relatives were sitting. Tears flowed as I communed
each one and recalled how much they had meant to me—sisters,
brothers-in-law, nephews and nieces, cousins, and, most of all my
godmother, Cornette. She had come in precarious health, determined not to miss this day in the life of the one she had promised
so long ago to remember in her prayers. In a note written by her
daughter Sharon later that same day Cornette said:

> Dear Herb:
>
> An exciting day for me was November 30, 1931, when I
> held you in my arms on your baptism day. It's especially
> exciting that 56 years later I was able to witness your instal-
> lation as bishop of the new church.

God bless.

In faltering handwriting she signed:

Love Auntie Cornette

This was also a moment of keen disappointment. Two who should have been at the service, weren't: my brother, Dave, and my son, Andrew. Dave had come down with the flu and had to remain at his hotel room. More than anyone else other than my immediate family, I wanted him to be there. Later, I wrote in my journal:

> It seems that he has had enough disappointments in life and enough suffering from his disability so that this could have been a day that he simply could have enjoyed to the hilt. That was hard for me to handle.

As for Andrew, I wrote

> Much harder . . . was missing you. We had planned to have Mom, Mary, and Chris bring the elements to the altar. I wasn't sure I could handle that—seeing them without you. Fortunately, they came only part way and were met by an assistant who received the elements from them and then brought them to me. Had they come all the way up to the altar I'm not sure I could have continued. I just made up my mind that I had to put my emotions aside as much as possible so the service could go on for the sake of the congregation. And that is what I did.

> That night when Mom & I collapsed into bed I could feel her trembling in my arms. I knew what she was thinking. In the midst of her tears she cried, "And Andrew never comes."

After I blessed the congregation we recessed with the hymn "Praise, my soul, the King of heaven; To his feet your tribute bring. . . ."

Later in the evening we had a festive dinner and reception for family and special guests at a nearby hotel. It was a time to relax, to greet, to laugh, to introduce family, and to hear greetings.

It was also at the dinner that I was presented with the certificate and medal from King Carl Gustav XVI of Sweden naming me a "Commander in the Royal Order of the Polar Star," an honor given to those of Swedish heritage "who have made notable accomplishments abroad."

The next morning on their way back to Minneapolis, godmother Cornette and cousin Sharon stopped at our place in Northbrook. She was too weak to get out of the car. As they drove off, I said to Corinne that I was reminded of the passage in Luke: "Lord, now let your servant depart in peace. . . ."

Later that day I flew to Switzerland for Lutheran World Federation and World Council of Churches meetings. On Wednesday a messenger at the hotel caught me on the elevator and handed me a telegram. It was from Corinne, telling me that Cornette had died on Tuesday. I wrote in my journal:

> I felt no sadness. Just a surge of gratitude. It's quite something to have someone follow you all the way from the waters of your Baptism to your installation as bishop and then die three days later.

From Geneva I wrote to my family.

Dear Sisters and Hubbies and All—

It's early in the morning. . . . Thanks again for coming to my big day—or days. What a memory! And thanks for that beautiful stained glass piece.

Serving the sacrament to family—to most of you . . . well, you have to know how very, very special that was!

And then there was the deep, deep disappointment that two people I wanted so desperately to be there couldn't be there.

It's at moments like that that the "Why?" questions come to the surface. . . for Andrew and David to be missing—well, one can only ask, "Why? Why?" It seems so unfair.

Yet—isn't that a picture of how it is with life? There is always that reminder that we live in a world that is so broken and complicated. And one is faced with the alternative at times like that to be bitter and angry and completely overcome with disappointment, or to believe that somehow there can be some good and some grace even in our disappointments. If nothing else, if it can make us just a bit more sensitive and a bit more tender, then that in itself can be a good purpose.

Travel, travel, travel

Though it started immediately after the installation with trips to Europe for LWF and WCC sessions, the major travel, by far, was domestic. I determined that the best way I could make myself visible to the church in the early months was to install as many synod bishops as possible. In that setting I could set forth my vision for the church to a large contingent of our pastors and lay leaders. I was able to install no less than forty-three of the sixty-five new bishops. The others were installed primarily by the three predecessor church bishops.

At the end of this five-month circuit of installations I wrote to my daughter Mary:

Today we had the installation for the new bishop here in Chicago. This is the forty-third one I've had—and the last one. It's a relief to have them over, even thought I must say I've enjoyed every one of them and it has surely given me a chance to see the church in all of its variety in every corner of the country.

One pastor sent a scathing letter suggesting that I had joined the jet set of those who flew about the country living in the lap of luxury. To help the leaders of the church understand what it was really like, I wrote a piece (December 1988) for "On Occasion," a newsletter intended for them.

> I surely have seen some marvelous sights in the past five months. Unfortunately, [the pastor's] letter arrived just after I had returned from a trip during which my suitcase was lost for six days, my reservation for two legs of the flight was not in the computer, and I was delayed in an airport without air conditioning on a day when that city set a high-temperature record.
>
> And I wish he were sitting beside me at this very moment. After a late night installation, an almost endless reception line, and a short night of sleep, I find myself sitting at the end of a runway. We have been out here for nearly two and one-half hours waiting for the fog to lift. Will I make the connection in Pittsburgh in order to arrive on time for the next installation?
>
> Marvelous—this life of a jet-setter!

Wanting to assure these leaders that I was trying to take care of myself in the midst of the hectic pace I was keeping, I also included a word about my personal schedule:

> Corinne goes with me on some trips. She also is traveling a good deal on her own, preaching and leading retreats. We try to plan carefully. We have determined that we can often take time "on the road" to be together or to enjoy a break with a friend: a delightful day's drive along the coast of Denmark; two days with family in South Carolina; a day with family in Alaska; a couple of memorable hunting days with Bishop Norm Eitrheim in South Dakota, after his installation; and in the next week, a few days at our lake home in northern Minnesota between installations at Rochester, Duluth, Fargo, and Moorhead. We are determined to keep our sanity and our sense of humor—most of the time, at least. And I can say what I said in June: It is a privilege to serve the church as its bishop.

A story that tells it all

Through the fall of 1987 the pace was unbelievable.

Sometimes a story is worth a thousand words. Because of my intense travel schedule I quickly accumulated enough air miles to qualify for an upgrade from coach to first class. It felt good to settle into that large, comfortable leather seat and have the full attention of the flight attendant on a trip back to Chicago from the West Coast.

My seat companion noticed that I was wearing a collar. Since he probably was not accustomed to seeing clergy in that section of the plane, he inquired about who I was and where I was going. I gave him a brief description of the new church—its more than five million members, nine regions, sixty-five regional organizations called synods, eleven thousand congregations, and more than seventeen thousand ordained ministers—and my role as the first bishop. I learned, in turn, that he was the CEO of a major American corporation.

He was intensely curious about the new church from an organizational point of view. The conversation went something like this:

"What did you do before you were elected to this position?" he asked. I said I had been bishop for some of the Lutherans in Minnesota.

"So you were never the head of a national organization or part of its staff until now?" When I said I had not been, he simply said, "I see."

"And what about your national staff?" he wondered. I explained that the commission that laid the groundwork for the ELCA had decided that no one on the national staff of one of the predecessor churches would have an advantage over new applicants. I estimated that about two-thirds of the new staff of more than six hundred had never served in those positions until now. He mused, "I see."

Then he asked about regional structure, the synods. I explained that forty of the sixty-five new bishops had never served in that capacity until the merger. He wrinkled his brow. "I see."

Next he wanted to know about our budget. I told him that the most optimistic estimate of income from the financial planning group had been $90 million for the first fiscal period. Then, I added, the convention decided we could do better and raised it again to $112 million. He wondered how we collected all this money. I explained that we had no idea what would actually be contributed because of our method of operation, allowing each local congregation to decide what it wanted to contribute to the synod and each synod deciding what it wanted to contribute to the national organization. Now he looked worried. "I see," he said.

After a long pause he looked at me and said, "Do you realize you can't do this?"

I looked at him and said, "You're probably right. But we have no choice. We have to do it."

Honors along the way

Whether one deserves them or not, honors come with an office such as that of presiding bishop.

I was named by the *Chicago Tribune* as one of the "88 People to Watch in 1988." Others included Jesse Jackson, Bonnie Blair, and eighty-five others of whom I have never heard anything significant since. So much for prophecy.

I also began receiving honorary doctoral degrees from a variety of institutions. Two of the occasions bemuse me a bit as I reflect on them.

When I came to Newberry College, Newberry, South Carolina, I discovered that the academic robe was mistakenly ordered for someone *five* foot, three inches, rather than *six* foot, three inches. When I suggested to the president that they might find a choir gown that would fit better, he insisted that I wear the one they had ordered. With a hem nearly up to my knees and sleeves scarcely reaching my elbows I looked like the ultimate nerd in procession. Corinne and my sister Chile were in the audience and had a difficult time suppressing their giggles.

One awarded by the Academy of Ecumenical Indian Theology and Church Administration in Madras, India, came at the instigation of the powerful lay leader of the Lutheran Church in India—Kunchala Rajaratnam. It was conferred with great pomp and circumstance. Some weeks later I received a letter from one of Rajaratnam's assistants suggesting that I might return the favor by recommending to one of our ELCA colleges that they confer a similar degree on Rajaratnam. He added that Rajaratnam's preference would be St. Olaf College. I explained in my reply that I had no such influence over our colleges.

January 1, 1988: the birth of the ELCA

I was out of Chicago on the birth day of the ELCA, installing Rafael Malpica Padilla as the bishop in Puerto Rico. The significance of the day, however, did not escape me. I wrote in *The Lutheran* (2/17/88) that

> I was wide awake at midnight, thanking God for the coming to life of our church. Outside the hotel there was reveling as Puerto Ricans welcomed the New Year with horns, sirens, firecrackers, and shouts of 'Prospero Ano!' This was one time when I did not mind losing sleep.

I went on to describe how at each hour, unable to sleep because of the noise, I prayed for the people of the ELCA as the sun rose on each time zone. At the end of the night I prayed for "my sisters and brothers in places like Anchorage and Honolulu and Pearl City and Sitka."

Back in Chicago the staff entered the new building for its first day of work on January 4. Secretary Almen conducted the entrance rite. Recalling our first days in temporary quarters, he commented that "At first we didn't even have a supply of paper clips. Try to run an office without paper clips. You can't do it" (*The Lutheran*, 1/27/88). By this time, fortunately, we were beginning to feel like a smoothly running organization, thanks to high competence and even higher commitment on the part of the staff.

"New Shoots from Old Roots"

When our publishing house asked if I would like to write the Lenten devotional booklet for 1988, I was inclined to tell them I simply was too busy with other matters. But after careful thought I decided that here would be one of the best ways I could connect with the grassroots of the new church.

I could find no better biblical resource for the booklet than the Acts of the Apostles.

In an introductory note I wrote:

> 1988 is a year of newness. It is the beginning of life for our Evangelical Lutheran Church in America. But is anything ever really new? Does not the new always depend on the old—the treasured past, the memory of great events, the gifts of grace through the years? Indeed, our new church has roots that go back to the Day of Pentecost and beyond. New shoots grow out of old roots!

It was a good decision. I felt firmly connected in Scripture reading and prayer with believers across the entire church.

Fort Myers: a watershed meeting for the Conference of Bishops

Setting the tone

The first meeting of the Conference of Bishops after the January 1988 birth of the ELCA was one to be remembered for many reasons. We met in March in Fort Myers, Florida. To set the tone for our sessions I preached on the Old Testament lesson for that week:

Numbers 21:4–9. It is the story of how the Israelites complained about the hardships of the desert:

> Why have you brought us up out of Egypt to die in the desert? There is no bread! There is no water! And we detest this miserable food!

I suggested that after a few months into the life of the new church many of us might feel that same way. In the midst of this hectic pace of life, we might be tempted to long for the good old days. But that, I said, is not an option.

> Life is such that you can never go back. The road to Egypt is already drifted over with sand. . . . the promise is not for Egypt. We all understand the feeling. But now comes the good news—and because of this good news we wouldn't *want* to go back. The same Lord who spoke to Abraham and Sarah, and Moses and Miriam, and Mark and Mary, and Paul and Priscilla—the same Lord speaks to you—"I will be with you. I will never fail you or forsake you."

> This is not to say that the road ahead will be smoother or easier than the road behind. No, it is only to say that the Lord will be with you if you venture out into that unknown and uncharted future.

> The promise is for the Promised Land.

The role of the conference

I delivered a major paper on the place of the Conference of Bishops in the life of the ELCA. After reminding them that the conference was not a policy-making body in any legislative sense, I moved quickly to use illustrations from our predecessor churches to under-score how crucial recommendations from synod/district bishops had been in those churches. I stated my conviction that the role of this group in the new church would be even greater. I stressed that those of us who worked in the churchwide offices needed to listen to our synod bishops, knowing that they were in more direct contact with what was happening in local congregations. I asked:

> Do some of you have gifts of the Spirit that will make your role particularly crucial in the unfolding life of the ELCA? I suspect you do. We cannot tell at this point who will play those roles. It will depend, in part at least, on the agenda the church and the world puts before us. Some will be better equipped than others to address those agenda items. Part will depend on the gifts you were given by nature. . . . And part will depend on how you allow your gifts and talents to flower in the church.

I concluded with a reference to the writings of Richard Norris about the influence of bishops in later antiquity. A bishop's effectiveness, he wrote

> . . . depended in part on the capacity of the people to acknowledge their bishop as one in whom they could . . . see themselves as Christians.

> If people can see themselves in you—that may be the ultimate answer to the question, "What is your role as bishop?"

What I prophesied about the influence of various synod bishops turned out to be true. Twenty years after the birth of the Evangelical Lutheran Church in America, I sat down and looked at the original sixty-five bishops. I ranked at least a third of them as clearly outstanding. Others did their jobs well, giving adequate leadership. Several should have left after one term but stayed on. A few either realized they were overwhelmed or wanted to return to parish ministry, knowing that their talent was better used in that setting.

Shall we ordain homosexual persons in relationships?
By far the most critical and divisive issue facing the conference was the action of three students—Jeffrey Johnson, James Lancaster, and Joel Workin—at Pacific Lutheran Theological Seminary. All three had

been certified for ordination by their respective synods in December 1987. Early in 1988 they made a public declaration that they were homosexual. "I see this more as my desire to be ordained, to be a parish pastor," said Johnson, "but to do that as a total person in honesty and above board with that church" (*Los Angeles Times,* 2/27/88). The three asserted that they would make no promise to refrain from having a homosexual partner. It was an in-your-face challenge to the church at its very outset to make a decision on this thorny question.

At Fort Meyers the Conference of Bishops decided to go into executive session for its discussion of the issue. This action, as might be expected, infuriated Edgar Trexler, editor of *The Lutheran* magazine. He felt that the conference was betraying the open meeting policy of the ELCA.

During the lengthy discussion, chaired by Paul Werger, a wide variety of views was expressed by synod bishops. A common denominator for all, however, was a conviction that any favorable action toward the challenge would have enormous negative consequences for our young and fragile church. It then became a matter of how to frame our response to the challenge.

When the exchanges seemed to move in the direction of a detailed statement regarding homosexual practice by any pastor of the church, I entered the discussion and urged the conference to avoid getting itself tied up in legalistic terminology. I counseled them to make a simple, straightforward statement, declaring that ". . . persons of homosexual orientation who seek to be ordained or who are already ordained will be expected to refrain from homosexual practice."

The Lutheran magazine published an extensive report on the Fort Meyers meeting. It brought an avalanche of negative reaction. When both James Crumley and David Preus agreed to write letters for the magazine, some bishops caught wind of it and intervened, persuading both men to withdraw their offerings. That, of course, further raised Trexler's ire.

I decided that I would try to put matters into perspective with a letter to all pastors in a special mailing.

I began my pastoral letter by pointing out that though homosexual pastors had been on the rosters of the predecessor churches, those bodies had no official *policy* regarding the issue. Nevertheless, it had become the *practice* of the churches not to ordain or retain in ordained status persons who were in a same gender relationship. I then went on to describe my personal journey in coming to grips with these questions:

> 1. I have never met a homosexual person who chose that orientation. On the contrary, these persons came to discover . . . that they were drawn to persons of the same sex.

> 2. I am convinced that many homosexual persons cannot change their orientation. Counseling and prayer may be effective in some cases. I am dubious, however, about some claims for a "cure." Because I have been willing to listen and to learn, I often find myself in church groups where I am aware of persons who are gay or lesbian. . . . I know them as sisters and brothers in Christ.

> 3. Homosexual persons are not more inclined than heterosexual persons to abuse others. . . . I must state emphatically that if we are to embark on a program to rectify an unhealthy situation in the church then we ought to devote our first energies to helping heterosexual pastors who are abusive or who are involved in immoral behavior.

I concluded the letter by suggesting that until the church could come to a common mind about this matter we would do well to abide by the practice of our predecessor churches. "Let us pray that in this, as in all difficult issues, the Spirit of God will be our Guide and Helper."

Going to Berkeley two months later to speak at the commencement ceremony at Pacific Lutheran Theological Seminary was no

easy assignment. I knew that sentiments were running strong in
support of the three gay students. And I knew that acting president
Walter Stuhr was also supportive of them. It was especially painful
to see the parents of these three men. Preaching on 1 Corinthians
2:2—"I decided to know nothing among you except Christ and him
crucified"—I accented the importance of a strong sense of call to
ordination. Our call supersedes any desire on our part to have our
rights recognized. "There is a limit to what the church can do to
meet our demands for our rights," I said. "Whether one is married, single, gay, a parent of several children, interested in graduate
studies, or what have you, the church cannot be expected to always
come up with an ideal call." I pointed out that in a later chapter
in that same book Paul outlined some of the rights he could have
demanded. "But Paul makes no such demands. Why? Because
demands for rights and privileges might hinder kingdom work."

I ended with an appeal to Christ-centered living and preaching.

> We would do well to sweep aside all questions—especially
> ones about our rights—and ask ourselves that one most
> important question: Are we fixed on that most important cen-
> ter to our ministry—to preach Christ and Christ crucified?

I think it was the best I could do under the circumstances. But I
knew in my heart of hearts that I longed to see the day when these
three young men could have their rights to be ordained honored by
the ELCA.

What I wrote in my journal in mid-May of 1988 shows where
my own thinking was at the time:

> The hassle over the three gay seminarians has died down
> a bit, but surely won't go away. Most people who write or
> talk to me are thankful for the pastoral letter I sent out
> several weeks ago. But there are people at both ends of the
> spectrum who are intensely angry at me. I believe I could
> support a pastor who was homosexual and in a long-term

covenant relationship. . . . But if I went public about that
it would cause such uproar in the church that the consequences, I believe, would be terrible. I believe I've done as
much as I can for now.

In retrospect, it seems clear to me now, more than twenty years
later, that the Conference of Bishops and, by extension, the ELCA,
had little choice but to take this kind of action. Some bishops had
come as far as I had in understanding gay and lesbian persons. We
were compromised. There is no question about that. Our personal
convictions were moving toward a new stance. But we were a small
minority among bishops and, again, by extension, among pastors and
laity of the church. The ship of the church was hardly out of port. We
were fragile. We were struggling to get organized. We were worried
about income to support the programs that had been mandated for
us to carry out. There seemed to be no choice but to act as we did.

Year after year the church could not find clarity on the homosexual issue. Every attempt to make some progress was met with
resistance. Change was happening, but little of it by official action
of the church. In the meantime, a growing number of homosexual,
bisexual, and transgender persons left the ELCA, lived in frustration and secrecy, or waited impatiently for some sign of hope.

In spite of many negative letters and phone calls, general reaction to my pastoral letter was overwhelmingly positive. Most were
grateful for what I had written. At their April 1988 meeting the
seminary presidents and deans passed a resolution in support of it,
expressing appreciation for

> . . . the care with which he has addressed the issue of
> homosexuality and candidacy for ministry, and to pledge
> our commitment to working with him and the church in
> implementing the implications of the church's position.

Among pastors in the field of psychology and counseling,
the response proved to be most interesting. Some pointed out

inconsistencies in the stance of the bishops and in my pastoral letter. They felt that the church was hypocritical. In contrast, others in the same disciplines insisted that reparative therapy was effective for homosexual persons and that the church must only advocate for a policy based on that assumption.

David Preus, in a handwritten letter in early April, 1988, said it was "very well done," but went on to caution me not to declare that the point of view of the Conference of Bishops was ". . . either the policy or accepted practice of the predecessor churches. Either is an overstatement as far as the ALC is concerned."

I felt a need to challenge what Preus stated. I reminded him that there were pastors in the former ALC, known to certain bishops, who had been open about being homosexual and celibate and had not been removed from the roster of pastors.

> I didn't claim it was a policy—because I don't think it was;
> I am convinced it was the practice—but stand to be corrected if persons actually were denied ordination simply because they were homosexual.

I closed my letter to Preus by suggesting that the best outcome of this discussion would be for the church to develop a broad statement on sexual mores and family life and ". . . leave the ordination question in the realm of pastoral care of the bishops."

I learned in time that such hopes were illusory. Over the next years I would come to the conviction that the gay/lesbian community needed the church to be clear and public in its stance.

More than a year later I had a provocative exchange of letters with Krister Stendahl, dean of The Divinity School at Harvard University. Stendahl was in the forefront of those urging the ELCA to ordain pastors in same-gender relationships. In October, 1990, he wrote:

> When I meet gay and lesbian Christians who tell me that
> they have searched their consciences long and seriously and
> that they cannot recognize themselves in Paul's description

in Romans 1 . . . then I trust them and I see more clearly
that Paul here uses the popular Jewish apologetic stereotypes of the Greeks as idol worshippers and homosexuals. I
think we have good reasons to accept that there are authentic homosexual persons who for all practical purposes have
never and will never experience themselves otherwise.

In my reply to Stendahl I affirmed what he said. But I also tried
to help him understand that my position as head of the church put
me in a dilemma. I reminded him that there seemed to be not one
positive reference to a homosexual relationship in the Bible.

I have moved to the place in my thinking where I can accept
the legitimacy of such relationships. I know many such
persons. But can I leap from that to urge the church to accept
ordination of homosexual persons who are living in an active
sexual relationship, without at least some modicum of scriptural authority? While I might personally be able to accept
such a person as my pastor, is it right and proper . . . that I
should urge the entire church to do likewise? . . . I believe
the church can only come to that place in the same way we
eventually accepted divorced persons in ordained ministry.

I also had some brief exchanges on this matter with Robert Marshall. Ever the taciturn, cautious person that he was, I sensed that
Marshall shared many of my views regarding the homosexuality
question. In reference to the request of one of the Pacific Lutheran
Theological Seminary students who sought ordination, Marshall
expressed support for the way Bishop Lyle Miller had handled the
situation. Then he added:

Thank you for your support beyond your official responsibility. I still hope that the scheduled ordination might be
treated as a synodical act. . . .

He was, in my opinion, advocating for some flexibility, for allowing some synods to do what might not be possible in others. That,

however, is my assumption. Marshall played his cards close to his vest. You could only guess what he was really thinking.

The colleges of the ELCA

On February 1, 1988, I met with the presidents of our ELCA colleges. I spoke about two things: what they could expect from the church and what the church could expect from them.

I said they could expect financial support—but not much. With college and university budgets rising swiftly, often with the infusion of government funding, it would be impossible for the church to keep pace. But I reminded the presidents that they should look at other benefits from church relationships, such as student recruitment in congregations, contact with church members who could give larger gifts through wills and bequests, participation by college presidents in decision-making conventions of the church, and the prayers of the congregations for the mission of its colleges. "You can count on me," I stated, "to promote all of them."

As for my expectations of them, I suggested several items:

> Care for the spiritual needs of faculty, staff, and students, including support for chaplaincies and promotion of the Christian faith.

> Renew campus chapel services where they had been discontinued. ". . . let the chapel bell ring again if they have been silent on your campus. And let it be a moment when we say without apology to everyone on campus that this is a time for reflection, for worship, for setting life in order."

> Make certain that every student is exposed in some way during their time on campus to what our church teaches about the Christian faith.

> Promote academic excellence. "Let me say it as forthrightly as I can: As your bishop I expect you to be presidents of the finest academic institutions in the world. The complexities

of conception, abortion, economics, war and peace, poverty, the environment—the list is endless. We cannot afford to be isolated from one another. We need you—indeed we *expect* you—to be at your best—yes, your *academic* best."

I concluded by assuring the presidents that

I as your bishop will do everything in my power to sustain and nourish our relationship as partners in a common mission and ministry.

In my first two or three years in office, I tried to visit as many college campuses as possible. I already knew that many of them had drifted far from the church. On one occasion when I received a mailing from the office of one of our colleges I wrote to the president stating that I looked in vain for any evidence that the college was related to the ELCA. As expected, I received no reply.

In contrast, I could not have been more warmly welcomed at most of our ELCA colleges. I was gratified to see that many treasured their connection to the church. In several places I was invited to deliver the commencement address and in a few instances I was awarded an honorary doctoral degree. On those occasions I accented the vertical and horizontal dimensions of the cross to remind the audience that life is ". . . a gift to be received and a gift to be given."

Among the families of faith our Lutheran church has been marked by our emphasis on the grace of God. It comes to us unmerited and undeserved.

Having been given the gift, we must do something with it or we will lose it. . . . the gift we have received is to be given away in unselfish service to others.

It was especially difficult to visit college campuses in the spring of 1988. This would have been the year when Andrew should have graduated, too.

I tried not to let it get to me. But how could I look into the faces of all those young men in the classes of '88 and not think about another young man who should have been their colleague? How could I help but wonder what might have been?

Dedicating our home: The Lutheran Center

Finally on November 13, 1988, we were settled enough in our new building to have a service of dedication. The move into our home had been a long, stressful, and, at times, frustrating process for the churchwide staff.

Naming the building was not a difficult challenge for us. As I recall, I made the suggestion to the Cabinet of Executives. After considering several alternatives, it was agreed that "The Lutheran Center" best described the building.

With the use of computers coming of age, many of us were on a steep learning curve to acquaint ourselves with this new phe-nomenon. I recall vividly the day I sent the first document from my home computer modem to the Lutheran Center. After following carefully the steps that had been outlined and pressing the "Send" button, I picked up the phone immediately and called the office. "Did the message come through?" I asked anxiously. I felt a bit put down when the person on the other end of line said casually, "Yes, of course it did." I knew I had taken my first baby step into a world that would soon revolutionize the way I and others did our work.

At the service of dedication I preached on 1 Kings 8:22–30. Recalling the spirit in which Solomon dedicated the temple in Israel, I reminded those gathered that God uses common elements—brick and stone, steel and mortar—to fashion places where we can do the mission of the kingdom. The name of the building, I said, is

. . . superficial, only a mark of convenience. More deeply
and more profoundly, we are a people and a place that are
marked by the name of God.

In May of 1987, within weeks of my election, I stood alone
in the empty bowels of 8765. Each floor was a forlorn
echo chamber. It was not a pleasant place to be. My only
recourse was to imagine what *would* be—and what *is* now.

And what has made the difference? Hundreds of people
who now come here with the mark of Jesus Christ on them.
Our bodies are the temples of God's Spirit.

Buildings come and go. And so it will be with this place.
One day, inevitably, it will have served its purpose. For
as long as we need it—and may God grant it many, many
years of use—it will be a place where God's name will be.

I drew a parallel with the sacrament we were about to receive.

Lowly, humble, ordinary elements of the earth. Yet, we
dedicate them because we want God's presence to be here
and to bless what we do. We are becoming a family of God
in this place.

"My name shall be there." God grant that it may be so.

Foundations for the future

In the midst of my travels hither and yon I kept feeling that I
needed to set into writing some fundamental ideas that could serve
as an anchor and guide for the new church. It came to a head in
the publication of "Foundations for the Future: the ELCA at the
Threshold of the Twenty-first Century." I based my writing on the
Apostles' Creed:

The First Article reminds us that "The theology of our
church must be rooted first and foremost in the theology
of God as the One who has spoken and who has created all

things." I challenged readers to contemplate the photograph of the earth from space and ask: "Where are the boundaries between nations? How are its resources to be shared?"

I reminded the readers that the Word of God is primarily Jesus Christ. I asked whether there is something in Lutheran history that gives us a reason to exist. "Yes, I believe there is. And we call it 'justification by grace through faith.'" Again I asked questions: "Is this message outmoded? Have we outgrown our need for it?" No, I insisted. "Grace is the only word that can give hope to the hopeless."

I suggested that living in the tradition of Martin Luther gave us no alternative but to make the work of the Holy Spirit a fundamental emphasis for the new church. ". . . it is only by the grace of the Holy Spirit that we can have faith to accept God's prior decision."

I concluded with an appeal ". . . to decide what kind of church we will be. Let us pray together that, based on this foundation, we will have the wisdom, strength, and courage of the Holy Spirit to follow the vision that unfolds for us as we move toward *anno domini* 2000."

Reflections: What it's like to be the presiding bishop

On April 30, 1988, exactly a year after I was in the throes of the election at Columbus, I took a few moments to put my thoughts and feelings on paper.

The meeting of the Church Council went quite well, all things considered. But when I learned that some of the executive directors were upset because they didn't think I backed one of their colleagues as much as they thought I should have, that bothered me a lot. And the homosexuality issue has been very hard to handle. I feel all right about the things I have done, letters I've written—but it hasn't been easy. I think the church may have moved one small step forward in understanding gay and lesbian persons. But it seems that people at both ends of the spectrum have been keenly disappointed with me.

I find the job lonelier than I had expected. I miss the staff back in Minnesota. It's not that I don't have good people to work with here in Chicago. That isn't it at all. Lita, Bo, Bob, Betty—and others—all are wonderful people. I think it's because the organization is so much bigger and because I'm on the road so much more than before. It's hard to establish deep relationships when you aren't around to sustain them.

Then, too, Corinne's role has changed. . . . Neither of us had any idea that she would travel so much on her own or be in such demand. It's hard to manage our schedules. Most of the time we work it out so that she's here when I'm home. But lately that hasn't worked as well. There have been things that both of us felt it was important for her to do, even when I'm home. That's an adjustment we're having to make.

I'll be ok when I can catch up with myself. . . . my devotional life is much in need of a shot in the arm. It felt good to read the Bible in a more leisurely way today. And I hope to do the same tomorrow.

Two weeks later I continued to write about some of the thorny issues that bubbled around the church and ended up on my desk. Most testy was the conflict that continued between Trexler and the synod bishops over the Fort Myers meeting. I went on to write about

. . . the general pressure of being bishop of the church. It's so incredibly lonely at times. No one really understands what it's like. And I can't expect it. I find it hard to sleep well. I often awaken in the night and can't get back to sleep again. I've learned not to get all wrought up about it—to just relax and rest anyway. But it isn't the same as sound sleep.

I feel that anything that goes wrong in the church is directly connected to me and that I bear some responsibility for it. I know that doesn't make rational sense. Yet, I am the one who gets the mail and the criticism. I feel I am exposed to anyone who wants to take a shot at me.

It does help to talk to others—like our pastor Troy. But that is helpful only up to a point. And I have a wonderful staff. ... Yet, they also can only walk with me so far. When I was a synodical bishop I had my fellow bishops to lean on now and then. I certainly have a listener in Corinne. Yet, she knows only too well that there is a limit there, too.

A week later I was feeling a bit more optimistic and hopeful.

The flap between *The Lutheran* and the Conference of Bishops is a tempest in a teapot. I'm gradually learning that "this too will pass" as these crises come and go. The church is strong. It will endure these things and God will bless it in spite of us.

Just after New Year in 1989 the staff of the "ELCA News" (2/1/89) interviewed me. Admitting that it had been "tough and demanding to put together a church of this size and complexity" and that it had been "a year of crisis," I also spoke of the "relief and satisfaction that we made it through the first year." I underscored my personal sense of call to the office, stating that "I have never awakened one morning without a sense of gratitude that I was elected bishop of this church. I feel overwhelmed by it, but have a deep sense that it is God's will for me." I also expressed my longing to get on with the work of establishing a clear identity for the ELCA by centering our common life in the proclamation of the gospel, nurture of congregational life, and strengthening of our awareness of our place in God's world.

Although we were still uncertain what our income would be for the first fiscal year, I had enough anxiety by that time to forewarn the readers that the ELCA, given our churchwide, regional, and synodical structure, "is an expensive church" and that "dollars are stretched to the limit." Little did I know at that moment what we would learn two months later: that the dollars were stretched *far beyond* the limit.

At a retreat for pastors and church workers in Pennsylvania's Lehigh Valley in February 1989, I was asked by three reporters from Allentown and Reading newspapers for an assessment of the first year of the ELCA. The *Reading Eagle* reporter John Smith described me as one who ". . . probably fits the ideal picture of a bishop with his distinguished bearing yet approachable manner. . . ." We covered a wide variety of subjects. At that point I had no certainty about income for 1988. I was beginning to realize, however, that we would probably miss our goal and spoke of "excruciating" decisions as to what important things will have to be deleted from the 1990 budget. Pointing to the root of the problem, I stated that "There are notable exceptions, but as a whole, Lutherans are not well-known for being generous givers."

I spoke candidly about how long it takes for a newly merged church body to come together. Noting that for some it took up to twenty years, I expressed optimism that for the ELCA it would come more quickly. Now, writing more than twenty years later, I think I was right. It did come more quickly. But that is a subjective judgment. Though it surely did not show itself in income for churchwide ministries, I believe that in terms of its spirit and sense of being one church, it did come about in the first decade.

By June 1989 we were seeing some changes among executive leadership. When the board of one division was in the process of selecting a new director, the field was narrowed to three. The constitution stated that all boards must consult with the bishop of their church prior to a final decision. When I expressed my preference for one of the candidates, some board members were incensed. They thought I was infringing on their autonomy. I wrote in my journal:

That made me very angry. If I can't even state a preference, that's rather pathetic. Sometimes I feel I am bishop of a church with more than 11,000 independent, autonomous congregations; and sixty-five independent, autonomous synods; and twenty-three independent, autonomous boards! This experience has intensified the loneliness I feel in this position in the church.

At times I had to preach to myself even as I was giving words of hope and encouragement to others. That was the case when I wrote for the November/December 1990 issue of *Lutheran Partners* magazine. In a meditation based on Isaiah 62 I asked pastors to remember that we:

> . . . walk into the most hopeless, joyless, distressful situations and dare to speak the same foolish, scandalous, unbelievable word that God's messengers have always spoken—that God will come, that the day of the Lord is at hand, that our God loves with the fervor of a bridegroom. Your arena . . . may not be the most hopeful place on earth. My own calling, I can assure you, is not an enviable one these days.

> But we have a privilege. We have been invited . . . to "draw near with confidence to the throne of grace." We can remind God that promises are overdue. And, having done so, we can speak words of comfort and hope to the people.

Then, of course, our frequent separation was a major challenge for Corinne and me. In early 1991 I was gone for several weeks at meetings in Geneva for LWF and Australia for the World Council of Churches. She wrote to me and poured out her frustration.

> This is the day I told you, once I got to Feb. 9th, I'd manage your being gone so long! This is the piece of time when I realize what all I've given up for the work you're in!!!! In some ways it is not good. And yet, there is no other way for it to work for us, I know.

It's hard having you far away. But you're safe. I think of all
the families who have loved ones in the Gulf War. Sometimes I just have to cry hard for them. And I pray.

The pace never slackened. After a good visit to the Virginia
Synod Pastors' Conference in January 1992, I wrote words that
describe well all of my more than eight years in office:

> I used Hebrews for Bible study. It felt good to get back into
> that book. How I thank God for those difficult Teaneck years
> when I did so much of the "spade work" for the preaching
> and teaching I've been doing ever since. There is so little
> quality preparation time. It seems I run from event to event.
> Speak, speak, speak . . . answer questions, questions, and
> more questions.

A few days later I was not feeling quite as upbeat about the life I
was leading.

> The conference here in Houston is not going very well for
> me. I think I've been on the road too long this trip. I need
> to accept less—and stay for a shorter time at each event. I
> just don't have the energy for this much. At each place they
> add on and add on—"As long as you're here." And I like to
> take advantage of the time as long as I'm in a place. I think
> jet lag is finally turning around. I thought the brief trip to
> Geneva for LWF would mean less trouble with lag—but it
> hasn't been the case at all. It still has taken a full week to
> break the circadian cycle.

In June 1992, while on a trip to Germany, I stood at the grave
of Bishop Hans Lilje, that towering giant of the German church
during and after World War II. I thought of what his life as bishop
must have been like. Did a person of his stature have to deal with

> . . . all the mundane, the difficult, the impossible, the frus-
> trating problems and issues that seem to assault me every
> day? I'm guessing that if one could know all about our

daily routine it might be very much alike. And how will I be seen and remembered? I can't know. I can only try to be faithful to whatever I believe God has called me to do each day—and hope and pray that it will make some good mark on the world.

I worried at times that my journal entries had become a dumping ground for the feelings of frustration that I felt I could not express in other places.

> That's good and wholesome. But I need to also make it clear that I get deep satisfaction out of what I do most of the time. Being in Minneapolis for [Al Anderson's retirement dinner], for example, was very affirming. Even though the crowd was mostly former ALC and even though there was some discomfort, the overwhelming feeling was one of respect and affirmation from those I met. That felt very nice. I thank God for it.

"Splendid misery" is how Thomas Jefferson once described the presidency. Much the same might be said about being presiding bishop. Indeed, it was splendid. How could one ask for a more interesting calling? But it was also quite miserable at times.

An untimely blow: the death of Betty Fenner

I have often said that the most unsung heroes in the church are those, mainly women, who serve as administrative assistants and personal secretaries. Sometimes I suggested, only in half-jest, that when I wanted to *really* know what was going on in an office or organization, the person to talk to was the leader's personal assistant.

Betty Fenner was that kind of colleague in my office in Chicago. Betty brought with her a wealth of experience. She was the perfect choice to be my chief personal assistant. Welcoming guests, keeping confidences, working efficiently, arranging my travel schedule, setting up appointments, and much, much more.

A single adult, Betty treasured her friends. On a lovely October weekend in 1988 she traveled with Pam Woolley to Brown County, Indiana, to enjoy the fall foliage and a small-town festival. As she was crossing the street on a picture-perfect Saturday morning, a driver, blinded by the morning sun, struck Betty. Emergency personnel quickly moved her to the intensive care unit at Indianapolis. I flew to Indianapolis. Betty had been unconscious from the moment of the accident. It was clear that she could not survive. I could only mutter under my breath, "Lord, have mercy! Lord, take her to yourself." I had my *Occasional Service Book* with me. As I held her hand I read the prayer of Commendation for the Dying, hoping she might hear me. I made the sign of the cross on her forehead as I pronounced the benediction over her. By the end of the day Betty was dead.

How ironic it was that this woman who had dodged New York City traffic for so many years should have been killed in a small Indiana town on a quiet weekend.

When she died, I lost not only a new friend but also an invaluable colleague. At her work station we found a poem she kept near her computer:

> I live alone, dear Lord, stay by my side.
> In all my daily needs be Thou my guide.
> Grant me good health, for that indeed I pray,
> To carry on my work from day to day.
> Let me be kind, unselfish in my neighbor's need.
> Spare me from fire, from flood, malicious tongues.
> If sickness or an accident befall, then humbly, Lord, I pray.

Those who do not know the value of persons such as Betty Fenner cannot comprehend how disruptive it is to lose such a person. And to have this happen at such a critical time in the early life of the ELCA was a major setback for me personally.

At her funeral service I suggested that Betty was like the first light of the morning.

She came softly into your world. Quietly, unobtrusively. She
was as gentle as a ray of morning sunshine. Yet, she could
not be denied. She was irresistible. She simply came—into
your day, into your life. And when she came, you felt
warmth. The source of the light we saw and felt in Betty was
Jesus, the Light of the world. She was like a prism. The light
of Jesus that shined into her soul and out from the person
God made her in her birth and in her baptism became a
riot of color that blessed you when you were with her.

I poured out my disappointment in my journal.

The psalmist says God doesn't slumber or sleep. But
sometimes I wonder! Why didn't something delay her just
a minute or two? Why didn't she forget something in her
room and have to go back for it? Is God so remote that
he couldn't have caused a little slip like that? How much
control does God really have over the world? I can see that
something like this might happen to someone who's push-
ing at the edges of life, taking risks, being stupid, chancing
something. But why to someone like Betty who wouldn't
think of testing God?

And why should I be left without someone as valuable
as Betty? I didn't have to train her. She knew what to do.
She'd think of things before I asked for them. Her head was
full of ten thousand details that no one else could know—
unless they had had her experience.

Who could step in to take Betty's place? I called Fran Forsman,
one of the competent Minnesota Synod staff secretaries who had
just retired. Yes, she would be willing to come to Chicago to fill that
important role until I could find a permanent replacement. She was
God's gift for a trying time. It turned out to be a highlight of Fran's
long career in business. After her stint with me, Fran wrote a kind
note expressing how gratifying it had been and how good it was:

... to observe you working with your people—to see the respect and admiration afforded you by all in the church— and rightfully so. And I'm so proud I can go back home and say, "Bishop Chilstrom hasn't changed. He's still the pastor/ friend we knew here in Minnesota."

She could scarcely have known how much I needed that word of encouragement after a year and a half in Chicago.

I turned back to Minnesota for a permanent replacement for Betty. I thought Rena Rustad, a staff person at the St. Paul Area Synod, might fill Betty's shoes. She learned the ropes very quickly, was loyal to me to a fault, and absolutely trustworthy.

The year 1989: "Nobody Knows the Troubles I've Seen"

The year of our son Andrew's death, 1984, was the worst year of our lives. However, 1989 was a close second. The ELCA was over- whelmed with a plethora of issues. For the church, three challenges were foremost. It is often said that money, sex, and in-laws are the bane of most young marriages. The same might be said of the newly formed Evangelical Lutheran Church in America. That is, if we think of other churches as our in-laws.

Money

Anyone who had served on the Commission for the New Lutheran Church (CNLC) or been involved in estimating income for the new church realized that we were skating on thin ice financially. I tried to sound hopeful. What other choice did I have? Yet as each month in 1988 passed, I became increasingly concerned about our finances.

Treasurer George Aker did a phenomenal piece of work in getting the church off to a strong start with the myriad finan- cial systems that needed to be put in place. But as I've indicated earlier, he was also the ultimate optimist. Some see the glass as half empty. Others see it half full. For George it was running over. Whenever I asked about the flow of income he would reply, "I feel certain the synods will come through." I wanted to believe him. But as we moved into 1989 and the end of our fourteen-month initial fiscal year I began to doubt his optimism.

My fears were affirmed when the final figures were in. Though we had under spent the budget by several million dollars, we still fell short of expenditures by nearly sixteen million.

Why this shortfall? It was difficult to measure at first. But as time went on and as we were able to analyze the flow of income more carefully, several factors emerged.

> 1. Congregations of the former ALC were accustomed to sending support for ministries beyond the local scene to both district and churchwide offices. The CNLC had agreed to follow the LCA pattern where all support went first to the synod offices and synods decided what part of it should be shared with the churchwide organization. In the new church many ALC congregations simply did not send to the new synod what they had sent to the district and churchwide offices prior to the merger. One bishop of a synod that was constituted almost entirely of former ALC congregations told me that very few continued to give that level of support. Multiplied across the ELCA, this amounted to many millions of dollars. Though I suspected this was a major cause for the shortfall, it would have been impossible for me to make any comments about it. In a fragile new church it would have been counterproductive.

> 2. The CNLC had agreed that if we were to meet our budget expectations, synod staffs would have to be limited to no more than two assistants, no matter how large the synod. Many synods, including some whose new bishop had been on the CNLC, set up operations with as many as five assistants.

> 3. Another factor was the uncertainty that always accom-panies the creation of a new organization, and especially

one as large as the ELCA. In 1988 income to local congregations rose by more than five percent. That was the good
news. The bad news was that little of that increase was
being shared with the synods and churchwide ministries.

4. Though it would be impossible to measure accurately,
I'm convinced that many congregations, thinking that
merger would bring savings, focused on local needs at the
expense of the larger mission.

5. A sharp rise in medical insurance premiums for clergy
coincided with the advent of the new church. What seems
most distant from the local scene is usually the first to be cut.

6. A long trend toward support of local and area ministries continued to flourish: food pantries, clothing depots,
homeless shelters, ecumenical projects. These and other
good causes soaked up contributions to congregations.
Occasional churchwide funding appeals had only masked
the trend. More and more was going for local congregational expenditures, for mission efforts in local areas, and
for pet projects of congregations.

It became necessary to begin immediately to restructure the
churchwide organization. The Cabinet of Executives took a first
crack at the unpleasant task. First, we agreed to freeze our salaries.
Cutting each churchwide ministry by an equal percentage would
be irresponsible. I admired them at the time, and still do, for their
high commitment to certain priorities. The prospect that most of
them would have to take significant cuts for programs that were
just getting off the ground was extremely difficult. But we knew we
had no choice. We agreed that support for three areas—seminaries,
new ministries, and global mission—should take precedence over
other programs. The Church Council affirmed the recommendations of the Cabinet of Executives. This meant cutting the church's
support for many ministries.

This decision set off a series of strong reactions across the church from a variety of interest groups. Several called for meetings with me. I entertained one delegation after another, all of them upset over the reductions in financial support. The most recalcitrant were the colleges. Robert Vogel, president of Wartburg College, organized a group of about a dozen college presidents who flew to Chicago. With Vogel taking the lead, they accused the ELCA—and me in particular—of abandoning our mission in higher education.

As I had said to them earlier, I reminded the presidents again that financial support was only one part of the relationship of the colleges to the church. It also included: access to congregations for recruitment of students, appealing directly to members of ELCA congregations for support by way of wills and bequests, and embracing the theological stance of the church to further their mission in higher education. I also pointed out to them that most churchwide entities had no alumni constituency to which to appeal for support. I urged them to redouble their efforts to garner financial support from their graduates and friends.

All in all, it was a most difficult session. In fact, I would have to rate it as one of my worst days in my eight years in office.

One of the college presidents who had not attended that meeting stopped by my office several weeks later. He apologized for the behavior of his colleagues and lamented their lack of understanding of what was happening in the new church.

All of these financial issues were on the front burner at the August 1989 Churchwide Assembly in Chicago. In retrospect, the comments of Peter Steinfels in *The New York Times* were exactly on target. He described the leaders of the ELCA as

> . . . anxious parents . . . hovering over the one-and-a-half-year-old denomination, trying to fend off serious trouble while this ecclesiastical infant learns to walk on steady feet and, someday soon, they hope, to run.

Uniting religious denominations is often a precarious and exhausting task in which the mechanics of merging can drain off energy from the very things the merger was supposed to achieve.

Steinfels reminded us of what an unusual and risky process we had followed:

Where other denominations carried out their mergers by stages, the new Lutheran church plunged in, as it united regional and national operations for about 11,000 congregations in three Lutheran bodies. It also elected new leadership, formed a new national staff, and began operating in a new headquarters building in new city, Chicago (8/23/89).

At the assembly I tried to be hopeful:

You will not like what we must say to you . . . fortunately, the short-range financial story is not the whole story. I hope the decisions we make at this assembly will be such that we will be able to look back . . . and say, "This was the turning point. . . . That was the moment when the church moved out of uncertainty and into a strong sense of identity and mission" (*Minneapolis Star Tribune*, 8/24/89).

Following the assembly I wrote a forthright letter to all of the pastors of the ELCA describing in detail our financial dilemma. I urged them to bring our needs to their congregations at annual meetings where budgets would be established for 1990.

Nothing would please me more than to be able to write to you a year from now, telling you that because of decisions made in thousands of ELCA congregations in the fall of 1989, the situation has changed and that our church will be able to move forward yet more boldly and confidently as we seek to carry out God's mission.

Unfortunately, my expectations were too rose-tinted. My appeal fell, by and large, on deaf ears. For the next two years we had to cut churchwide expenditures by several more millions of dollars in order to bring the budget into consonance with revenue.

It was hard not to feel personally responsible for this shortfall in income. On March 16, 1990, I poured out my frustration:

> My job is very, very hard these days. Because I have to make difficult decisions about budget cuts again, it seems everyone else is unhappy with me. It's a thankless job in some ways.

At one point I tried to convince the Conference of Bishops to launch a churchwide funding appeal. It, too, fell on deaf ears. The bishops were up to their own necks in trying to keep synodical ships afloat.

In the wake of all of the financial turmoil in the first year of the life of the ELCA we had to release not only a number of top executives, but also many support staff. It was an excruciating time for the church and for me personally. Many who had joined the churchwide staff came with spouses who had given up good positions in other parts of the country to move to Chicago. I received vitriolic letters and phone calls from friends of those who were released. In those months of transition it was difficult to even walk through the building because of the depressed mood that hung over us. If I didn't know where the buck stopped, there were plenty of people to remind me. There were moments when I wondered if a more dynamic leader was needed. Yet through it all I continued to feel that God had called me to that place at that time. It was an incredibly heavy load to carry. Fortunately, many on the churchwide staff carried it with me. And, of course, Corinne was a constant source of hope and encouragement. Without them it would have been difficult to pass through that time.

Sex

Yes, as in marriage, sex was a huge issue. I have already written about the challenge of the three gay graduates at Pacific Lutheran Theological Seminary. Edgar Trexler described that issue as one that ". . . blew the lid off the church in the first few months" (*The New York Times*, 8/23/89). Had that been our only sexuality issue, it would have been enough.

Synods were getting increasingly involved in sexuality matters at the same time. At their first assemblies in the spring and early summer of 1989, no less than thirteen of the synods passed resolutions asking the churchwide organization to produce a statement on matters related to sexuality and family life.

In retrospect, it was far too early for our newly born and fragile church to enmesh itself in a project as incendiary and volatile as human sexuality. Should I have announced to the church that our staff simply was not ready to undertake a project of that magnitude? I don't know. Appeals from synods, especially in such numbers, cannot be ignored.

Following the 1989 Churchwide Assembly, a task force with broad representation was set up and the process got underway. The aim was to bring a statement to the 1991 Churchwide Assembly in Orlando. Though the intention was to speak to a broad range of sexuality issues, it became clear in a short time that the issue on the minds of most people was only one: the gay/lesbian question.

Through the whole process people looked to me for leadership. Gay, lesbian, bisexual, and transgender persons and their supporters pushed me to be more vocal in advocacy for them. A group of congregations in the San Francisco area announced their intention to carry out unauthorized ordinations in October of 1989.

At the other end were those who maintained that anything less than condemnation of homosexual persons was an abandonment of our biblical heritage. One envelope contained nothing more than a card that read, "SHAME ON YOU."

The statement on ecumenism
And then there were the "in-laws"—those other churches not
in our immediate family. The decision by the 1989 Churchwide
Assembly to send the Statement on Ecumenism back for more
work was a keen disappointment. There continued to be a sense
on the part of some that the document leaned too much in the
direction of Roman Catholics, the Orthodox, and the Episcopalians. I believe, in retrospect, that it was more perception than
reality. Peter Steinfels of *The New York Times* thought the rejection reflected a division between "low Lutherans" who favored
strong congregational emphasis and anti-hierarchical tendencies,
on the one hand, and "high Lutherans" who were eager to heal
the sixteenth-century breach between Lutherans and Roman
Catholics.

Other challenges
As if these three areas were not enough, we were confronted with
calls for studies and statements in many other areas. Though our predecessor churches had developed materials in most of these matters,
there was a strong push for *this* church to stake out its place.

> Foremost among them was *the study of ministry*, inherited
> from the CNLC when it was unable to come to an agree-
> ment on the question. Though we knew the process would
> extend over at least five years, our ecumenical relationships
> depended on moving with dispatch.

> *Divestment of pension funds from companies doing busi-
> ness in South Africa* would evoke sharp differences among
> members of the church.

> Others expected the church to formulate something about
> *the environment*.

> Though *abortion* was not on the agenda for the assembly, a
> women's caucus called for immediate action.

Demands for inclusivity pushed us to hire persons of color or whose primary language was other than English. In this area we did well, far surpassing the ten percent mandate.

Lyle Schaller, like Steinfels, was probably right in observing that the formation of the ELCA was unusual when compared to other mergers. In most cases, those churches moved more gradually, giving themselves time to catch their breath between changes. For the ELCA, said Schaller, "It was like having quintuplets rather than one baby at a time" (*The New York Times*, 8/23/89).

Family

In the midst of all of the turmoil in the church in 1989, we faced challenges and testing within our immediate family.

Corinne began to feel unwell in the spring and early summer. She went into the hospital in early June for tests. We could not have known that she would continue to feel ill through the time of the August 1989 Chicago Assembly and on into the fall. When she was hospitalized again in October, we learned that she had a rectal sarcoma. It was an extremely rare form of cancer, one known to have occurred in only seventy people worldwide. No chemotherapy or radiation had proved to be effective. The tumor was removed and the surgeon said it should not come back.

We were relieved, thinking the ordeal was behind us. Unfortunately, it was not. She continued to feel ill over the next months. On my trip to Central America in March 1990 I wrote in my journal:

> The surgeon was so reassuring—that the cancer was discovered early, was encapsulated, and all. But sarcoma is a very virulent form of cancer. So we wonder. She was awake for a long time last night, worrying about herself. We're able to talk very openly and freely about it all. I touch her body when we pray and ask God to heal every cell. I don't know how I'd survive without her. I need her so very much.

Her fears were legitimate. The cancer returned again in 1993 and once more in 1994. Two more surgeries were required. Thank God, she has had no trace of it in the intervening years.

Corinne decided each time, with my consent, that only a chosen few should know about her cancer. She knew that if word got out, this would be the main topic of conversation wherever either of us traveled around the church. It was a wise decision. It did mean, however, that we had to carry the burden almost entirely by ourselves. And it was extremely heavy. It was hard during all these times to concentrate fully on my work. Though we prayed and tried to trust God, how could we help but worry? How could I help but be distracted at times?

In the midst of all this a persistent back problem laid me low. With constant pain in my legs, I began to stagger to the pulpit or podium at times. I joked that I had better take care of it before audiences thought I had been into the communion wine a bit. But it was no joke. Surgery was the only option. Fortunately it was successful and I had a quick and complete recovery.

And then there was my mother. As she moved into her 70s it was apparent that her memory was failing. A decade later she was deep into senility and confined to a nursing home bed where she lay staring at the ceiling for more than another decade.

In my journal in early 1990 I wrote that she

> . . . edges ever so slightly toward death. She could die
> tomorrow or live on for years. She is past the time she
> should die. I don't understand why God keeps her alive.
> Why can't my mother just quietly and peacefully die? I
> wonder. . . .

A retired pastor visited my mother on Good Friday in 1991 and wrote a poignant letter about his encounter with her:

> I told her it was G. Friday and wanted to share a brief devo-
> tion. When I quoted the first stanza of "O Sacred Head"

she tried to sit up. I took her hand, and she tried so hard to communicate something even to looking me in the eye as if something old familiar and beloved had a meaning. After prayer we parted.

I wanted you to know of at least this little incident, which might have been more than that to your Mom.

—Herb Hartig

In a letter to my cousin Helena Orup in Sweden I described what my visits to my mother's bedside were like:

She is just skin and bones. She reacts at times, but we cannot know if she realizes we are there or not. I usually sing "Children of the Heavenly Father" in Swedish for her, say the Lord's Prayer and the 23rd Psalm, and tell her that I love her. One can only hope that some of it gets through to her. If she could only breathe her last and die peacefully in her sleep we would be so grateful.

She would live on for another five months, all but completely out of touch with the world.

Then, of course, I continued to brood at times over Andrew's death. Those who have never lost a child, and especially by suicide, can never understand that this grief is for life. The wound remains open. One can only learn to live with it. It was during 1989 that I found enormous comfort and insight in writings by and about Dietrich Bonhoeffer. I learned that he had wrestled with a sense of hopelessness and thoughts of suicide. In my journal I wrote:

He seems to be one of the first in modern times to have some sympathy and understanding for those who take their own lives. There are indications of struggles with depression. He masked it well. But as his writings were analyzed and as friends pieced together different things he said, it became apparent that the thought of suicide plagued him at times. When he was in one of those moments of despair he wrote, "In such hours of trial no human or divine law can prevent the deed." Homesickness, hatred of imperfections, and doubts about goals in life—if one was afflicted by these then Bonhoeffer felt it was not proper to judge someone who took their life. "Suicide is a man's attempt to give a final human meaning to a life which has been meaningless."

Indeed, 1989 was a heavy year. "The loneliness of the road" was mixed with all of the distresses I've mentioned above.

As I go from one synod assembly or event to the next I find myself surrounded by large crowds of people. More and more know who I am. They give me standing ovations everywhere. Many, many tell me they are praying for me. They are kind and friendly. Yet, I find myself incredibly isolated. Yes, it *is* lonely at the top. I know I'm doing what God wants me to be doing at this stage of life. But it's very, very hard.

A note from staff member Bob Sitze in the fall of 1990, as I was recovering from back surgery and feeling almost totally exhausted, helped to put the previous year and one-half into perspective.

I want you to know how grateful I am for your strong leadership over the course of these first two-and-a-half years. I thank God when I think of:

Your strong personal testimony to your faith. . . .

Your understanding that leadership begins when a leader moves in a direction, and your willingness to be such a leader.

Your openness to criticism, your willingness to listen. . . .

Your approachability as a person.

I don't know . . . if you've spent much time wallowing in self-doubt. I hope not; but just in case the Devil should wrestle you into that position, you should know that you are an example for me how I should conduct my life as a leader/servant in the church.

Mission90 and the first Churchwide Assembly

It was decided that it would be most efficient and convenient to hold the 1989 Churchwide Assembly, our first, near our ELCA headquarters in Chicago. This was a good move. It would give voting members of the assembly a chance to see the Lutheran Center. It would give staff access to support associates and office facilities at the Lutheran Center. Many glitches were apparent to the delegation. Yet, all in all, the staff functioned admirably.

In my opening address to the assembly I urged them to keep in mind that

> . . . over and above and around and beneath us these eight days must be a spirit and an attitude that witnesses to our calling as people of the good news ("Nine West" 9/28/89).

In the midst of all of the turmoil in the church and the personal stresses in which I was engulfed, I knew it was time to present a vision to the church for the coming years. What emerged from my ruminations became known as the Mission90 emphasis. When I presented it to the Cabinet of Executives and the Church Council, they reacted very positively. I had meetings with the staff of churchwide units to share my vision with them. Again the response was positive. I also carried my plan to several synod assemblies in the spring and early summer of 1989. "I think I'm at my best," I wrote in my journal, "when I can share the vision of the church and mingle with laity and pastors in settings like those."

For the full Mission90 project I envisioned a several-pronged emphasis that I wanted to reach every congregation of the ELCA:

> A daily guide for common Bible reading called "New Ventures," using the about-to-be-published New Revised Standard Version and a publication with tips on how to witness to one's faith.

An accent on tithing as a response to God's grace.

A video series on "What Does It Mean to Be a Christian."

An evangelism program entitled "Bible Study-Witness."

A companion synod program that would link each of the sixty-five synods to a church abroad.

An emphasis on "Peace, Justice, and Care of the Earth."

By the time of the August 1989 Churchwide Assembly I was ready to present it to the delegation. I described it as:

> . . . a launching pad, a foundation, a starting place for our work together as we move through this final decade of this century and into the new millennium ("Nine West" 9/28/89).

Looking back from the perspective of more than twenty years, I believe that Mission90 may have been my single most important contribution to the life of our young church.

It is difficult to measure the effectiveness of the first two emphases. Anecdotal evidence suggested that many engaged in the "New Ventures" Bible reading program and that people here and there took the leap of faith to begin tithing. One Bible reader wrote that his reading had been "one of the most enriching experiences I have had in the church in many years. Reading it daily in this organized fashion brings fresh insight into the faith we confess." I jotted a note to Corinne in February1991 from the WCC Assembly in Australia about the Bible reading:

> I better get at my New Ventures reading. I'm thankful to be the catalyst that has so many people into the Scriptures. Who knows what may come of that! It's good we don't need to know. Just let it happen—whatever the Spirit does through the Word.

The effort to help congregations grow in membership was a keen disappointment. I asked two key staff persons, one from

Multicultural Ministries and one from Outreach, to take the reins on this effort. My idea was that they should study fifty of the most rapidly growing congregations of the ELCA in a variety of settings—rural, suburban, multicultural, urban, first-ring urban—and find out why they had increased their membership. I had hoped that we might learn lessons from them that could be employed in other settings. Why didn't it work? Was it because the reason for membership growth is so obvious and cannot be transferred to other settings? And what was the key? In my experience it always came down to effective pastoral leadership.

There is no question that the video series was highly successful. It was entitled, "What Does It Mean to Be a Christian?" I knew it would be costly. On a trip to Minneapolis I had lunch with Clair Strommen, the CEO at Lutheran Brotherhood. He liked what he saw and arranged for solid financial backing. Aid Association for Lutherans also came on board with support. Between them we had promises of several hundred thousand dollars for the full Mission90 program.

There were six segments in the video series:

    Grace
    Faith and sin
    Word, sacrament, and worship
    Community
    Stewardship
    Creation

Each video was filmed in a different setting across the country. Our intent was to give viewers not only some basic theological understanding of what the church should be and do, but also the sense that we are a church rooted in a wide variety of geographical and cultural communities.

My objective was that this would be a way for me as bishop, in a church of eleven thousand congregations, to visit every parish. I

wanted the series to be a "visual catechism," a simple, straightforward teaching of the basic elements of the Christian faith. Susan
Greeley from the Department of Communications proved to be a
superb project director. Her colleagues were equally competent in
producing first-rate video tapes.

We hit some early barriers with the videos. Staff in my office
thought the idea was too unsophisticated. We decided to run a pilot
of the first video with the Conference of Bishops. That was a mistake. It was not ready for showing. They panned it severely. I was
devastated. I wrote in my journal:

> I have never known deep depression, but surely felt its grip
> that night. I took a very long walk and then called Corinne.
> She could tell how deeply discouraged I was by the reaction
> of the bishops. In fact, she called back later in the eve-
> ning—something she's never had to do before. She could
> feel my disappointment and shared it. I have put so much
> effort into Mission90.

I soon recovered. I was confident of my teaching ability. I was
comfortable in front of the camera. I was also convinced that this
was the way to reach the laity of the church. I realized that the
criticism from my staff and the bishops was based largely on their
assumption that these videos should be aimed at the ordained pastors and other professionals in the church. My idea was different. I
asked myself, "What do my six sisters, all active members of local
congregations but not pastors, need to hear from me?"

Response was immediate, positive, and enduring. More than
ten thousand of the nearly eleven thousand congregations of the
church ordered the series. As I moved about the church people
would often come up to me and say, "I feel like I know you already.
Thank you for those videos." In the video "Sin and Grace" I decided
to speak about our son's death by suicide and how we, by grace,
survived. Typical of letters I received was one from Baltimore.

Your talk of your son's suicide, painful as it must be, allowed me to share my own pain at my youngest brother's suicide. . . . It allowed my congregation to express support and love for me that I somehow had been afraid of. Through this experience others asked about suicides of close relatives and we have all learned to support each other more.

About that same time a congregation at Fox Lake, Illinois, reported that as they watched the videos

. . . we experienced some lively discussions; we laughed together and cried together and prayed together; we learned more about ourselves, our faith, and each other.

Long after retirement I still meet pastors who thank me for the series and say that they are using it, especially in new member classes.

The same could be said about the companion synod program. It has been highly effective. I give enormous credit to Bonnie Jensen and Mark Thomsen in the Division for Global Mission for picking up this idea and putting it into effect. It would be impossible to calculate the number of ELCA members who have visited companion synods around the world or members of those churches who have visited companion synods in the ELCA.

When a woman in northern Illinois discovered that the idea of the companion synod program came from me she wrote and told of her visit to Tanzania. She had shared her experience across her synod. "My life has never been the same since I came back from Arusha! I have not been quiet since!"

The Bible Study-Witness segment of Mission90 was assigned to the faculty at Trinity Seminary in Columbus, Ohio. This was a carefully designed program. The intent was to acquaint people with the fundamental themes of the Bible and then aid them in practical ways of sharing their faith.

I was well impressed with the outcome. Unfortunately, most congregations that used Bible Study-Witness found it too demanding for the average member of their congregations. It flourished in a few places. But after several years it was not used. I had put a great deal of hope on this part of Mission90 and was keenly disappointed when it did not take root more broadly.

Getting back to the assembly itself, many came away with high optimism and enthusiasm for our young church. After hearing my opening address the Youth Convo adopted a motto: "Chill Out with Chilstrom."

One pastor said that he was

> . . . surprised by the spiritual aspects. I believe you set the tone in your opening address. The closing worship that you led was perhaps the most meaningful of all. I truly felt a sense of renewal as I assented again to the mission of the church. I left the assembly hall with wings on my feet.

Richard Jensen, Lutheran Vespers radio preacher, said:

> It struck me in many ways that the ELCA had its real birth during the course of the assembly. The spirit was excellent, the vision was clear, the courage was bold. This is a wonderful church.

A lay couple thanked me for having both "dignity and levity" when each was needed at the assembly.

Addressing social issues

As had been my pattern as a synod bishop, I tried to use my position as head of the ELCA to speak to a variety of crucial issues.

Corporate social ethics

On June 13, 1990, I delivered a major paper: "Purpose, Identity, and Action: Corporate Ethics and the Evangelical Lutheran Church in America." It was an attempt to outline some of the ways this young church would deal with complex issues.

I reminded listeners that until we developed new position statements for the ELCA, we would rely on the statements of our predecessor churches as a guide. I went on to say that we would be a church committed to dialogue, a church where a wide variety of opinions would be welcomed and respected. I stated, however, that discussion must eventually lead to action. As a church body we would need to speak a definitive word. We would need to formulate position statements.

> To choose not to speak as an institution is in fact to affirm the status quo. Silence is not synonymous with neutrality. To be silent is to make a decision.

I was quick to say, however, that such statements must never bind the conscience of individual members of the church.

Abortion

Prior to the adoption of a statement on abortion I was asked for my personal stance. When queried by a reporter in North Dakota, I said:

> I believe abortion never should be used as a means for birth control. I don't think we should ever in this society get to a place where a woman walks into [a doctor's office] and says, "I'm pregnant. I want to get rid of this." To me, that is morally indefensible. On the other hand, I recognize [that] there are some circumstances—the health of the mother, rape, and incest—where it ought to be allowed. There may be circumstances where the fetus is deformed or a case where there's a fatal disease, where [the fetus] may not be able to live to full-term or [much] beyond it, where a woman or a couple, in counsel with a pastor and their medical doctor may make a responsible decision for abortion (*Grand Forks Herald*, 4/21/92).

Economics

In a private exchange of letters in early 1990 with Dr. Walter Sundberg, professor at Luther Seminary in St. Paul, Minnesota, I outlined my view on economics:

> My own philosophy is that a combination of free enterprise
> and a network of support for those who cannot care for
> themselves adequately is the ideal economic system. We
> live in a very broken world and are always faced with hard
> questions about how to order our common life.

Rural life and the environment

In March 1990 I spoke at the annual Rural Ministry Conference at Wartburg Seminary in Dubuque, Iowa. My subject was the care of the earth. As I look back now more than twenty years later, it's clear that I was ahead of my times. I referred to my annual return to Otter Tail County in Minnesota where I had begun my ministry. Among other things, I said:

> I see soil at the bottom of the corn rows in fields that are
> not planted on the contour, and wonder what the next gen-
> eration will eat. I wonder how acid rain may be killing life
> in the lakes where my son and I love to fish. I read in the
> local weekly that the sanitation station is not able to handle
> all of the waste from that small community, and I wonder
> what is happening to fish and birds and people down-
> stream. I walk the ditches for a mile or two, picking up beer
> cans and thinking that maybe at least one small corner of
> the world will be better.
>
> We look at land as something to be conquered. If there
> is something valuable *beneath* it, strip it away. If there is
> something valuable *in* it, sift it out. If there is something
> valuable *from* it, extract it. And if you can get even more
> *out of* it by adding to it, change it. Above all, *use* it.

We must all finally come to recognize that the only way to ensure the future is to live in a sustainable way.

At its root we are looking at a theological problem. . . . salvation from a biblical perspective involves saving all creation. If we are wise, we will learn out of the depth of our faith what it means to live together in community, how to sustain life for the next generation, and how to enjoy the blessings of the earth that were given to us at the dawn of creation.

The role of seminaries in the life of the church

As I wrote earlier, I led the Church Council in setting priorities when funding had to be reduced for all programs. I was convinced that we must give special attention to the support of our seminaries.

I also had strong convictions about the role of the seminaries in the life of the ELCA. I had an opportunity to set forth those convictions at the installation of Dennis Anderson as president of Trinity Seminary, Columbus, Ohio, in March 1990. A few excerpts:

God calls and sets apart certain persons to be leaders in the church. Talents vary greatly. Vocational objectives differ. But in one way or another all have heard the stirring in their souls, a call from God to say something, to do something, to be something. . . . they are to proclaim a changeless Word in a changing world.

I went on to single out some basic areas that could not be neglected: biblical study, the theology of the church, the history of the church, preaching, Christian education, and leadership in worship. I called our eight seminaries

The single most important institutions in shaping the future of the church. . . . What will be preached and taught and advocated in the church ten and twenty and thirty years from now is what is happening in . . . the formative theological years.

At the Lutheran School of Theology at Chicago I preached on Isaiah 25, using the text as a basis for addressing the role of pastors in church and society. I committed myself to support for theological education and said:

> I will pray that Almighty God will raise up men and women to take their places in the pulpits and at the podiums across our land—in each and every place to point us beyond the mists and shadows of the moment, and to speak a clear word about the kingdom that is here and that is now and that remains forever.

As good as I felt about my relationship with the seminary presidents and most of the faculties, there were a handful among the latter who were persistent burrs under my saddle. In my journal in early 1990 I described:

> . . . some—especially among the seminary faculties at a couple of places and some self-styled "theologians"—who take pot shots at me. I can handle straightforward criticism. And I'm ready to discuss and debate issues. But some of them indulge in caricature and innuendo. That's so hard to deal with.

The majority surely were not of that ilk. Dr. Carl Volz at Luther Northwestern Seminary vented his frustration in a letter to me:

> The strident and sometimes irresponsible criticism leveled at the church in general and at you in particular in which several colleagues participate is embarrassing.
>
> I detect unmistakable signs of anti-clericalism. . . . In order to signal my own position with some visibility, I began wearing my clerical collar one or two days a week. . . . At first this departure from the normal dress code was greeted

with puzzlement, bemusement, and even hostility. After fourteen months of following this policy, almost all of the community accept it and some . . . encourage it. But it seems unfortunate that merely wearing a clerical collar can cause some people so much difficulty.

Volz continued:

After his return from the (churchwide) assembly, Pres. David Tiede addressed our first fall faculty meeting by insisting that LNTS change its negative image in the church from being "crabby" to one of support and cooperation.

Anniversary of the ordination of women

The ELCA marked the twentieth anniversary of the ordination of women in 1990. On July 11 I issued a statement in commemoration of that event. I admitted that when I was ordained in 1958, I looked negatively on the idea. By 1970, when it was approved, I was beginning to warm to it. By 1980, after I had been a synod bishop for four years and had ordained some women, I was fully on board as an advocate for it. By 1986, when I had walked with Corinne through her arduous struggle with a call to be ordained, I would have said, "I know, as I know God called me, that God also calls women to ordained ministry." My journey had been like that of the church itself. It was one of growing affirmation.

I went on to say, however, that

. . . it is a journey that is incomplete. There are still many unanswered questions:

Will the church give equal compensation for equal experience and equal responsibility?

Will our church call women to positions as senior pastors of large congregations, as presidents of colleges and seminaries, as executives of major agencies, where they will supervise male associates and assistants?

Will our church elect a woman as a bishop—synodical or
churchwide?

I pointed out that even among the theologians of the church
there remained resistance to the ordination of women, arguing
on the basis that the disciples of Jesus were only male, including,
I said (with tongue in cheek), ". . . the one who doubted, the one
who denied, the one who betrayed, and the ones who argued about
position."

I cautioned women to avoid "fighting like men" to achieve acceptance in the church:

> You will further the cause if you muster all the power of
> your feminine grace and wisdom for that discussion. And
> all of us will be the better for your having done so. God,
> who dwells in temples not made with hands (1 Kings 8:27),
> and whose ways are unsearchable (Romans 11:33)—this
> God came to us in the flesh and blood of a man, Jesus
> Christ. And this God keeps coming to us in the feminine
> winds of the Spirit, blowing where they will.

Homosexuality: the issue that would not go away

I surely did not want homosexuality to be one of the defining issues
of my years in office. But I learned, as I had already suspected during my years as synod bishop, that this question simply would not
go away. And, alas, now more than twenty years after the formation
of our church, it remains on one of the front burners.

What I wrote in my journal in early 1990 on the flight to the
LWF assembly in Brazil by-and-large characterized how I felt:

> I continue to wonder how I got into all of this and how
> I can carry such a load. We have some churches in San
> Francisco that have ordained practicing homosexual per-
> sons. One is the daughter of a good friend, Gerhard Frost.
> (Gerhard had died several months earlier). I feel so divided.
> I wish so very much that the church was ready to accept

such persons. But it isn't, by any stretch of the imagination. So I must do my duty. I must support denial of ordination for them. I feel very torn apart by it. At times I even wonder if I should resign because of the conflict between my conscience and the stance I must take as the bishop. If I spoke my mind, it would cause enormous disruption in the church. It would be irresponsible for me to do that. So I am trying to find a middle way, as is my usual pattern. I'm trying to do what I must do—reinforce that we can't recognize their ordination—yet, urging that the church continue to study the issue very carefully.

A little more than a month later I expressed my frustration in a letter to an attorney friend who is gay:

In many ways I can identify these days with your profession. I feel like an attorney who, for the sake of the law and in faithfulness to his profession, is having to argue the side of a case he would rather not take. Yet, that's the nature of the law, even in the church. I hope you understand fully what I must do in my capacity as a bishop, and will never think that I am anything but one hundred percent supportive of you and ready to defend you personally.

In the midst of all of this, I was getting pressure from every conceivable direction. In February 1990 James Crumley, after sympathizing with the burden I was carrying, wrote that he felt we must not waver from the church's policy on the ordination of homosexuals just because it was being challenged.

At the other end of the spectrum were pastors like Ronald Johnson at Holy Trinity Church in south Minneapolis. I had the utmost respect for Johnson. He had led his congregation to openly accept gay and lesbian persons. He understood my dilemma. He was not nasty. He simply felt that the church must change. He argued his case with both passion and acumen. He wrote on behalf of the council of the congregation:

If baptized gay and lesbian persons can function as effective participants in congregational ministry, it seems logical to believe that some of these persons have the gifts, interest, and call for the ordained ministry. If one accepts what appears to be the preponderance of scientific evidence as to the givenness of sexual orientation, the insistence on celibacy would seem to have the effect of compelling persons to deny expression of an integral dimension of their essential being.

In my reply to Johnson I asked:

Can you appreciate . . . how difficult it is to be the bishop of a church where, by my own estimate, eighty-five percent of the people are not ready to accept practicing homosexuals as ordained ministers? One is caught then with the reality that for the church at this time to approve the ordination of homosexual persons would almost certainly lead to deep division and, without any doubt in my mind, the loss of hundreds and hundreds of congregations. I travel around the church enough to believe that my sense of this is very accurate.

Thank you for being a very understanding person at this difficult time.

In middle ground I found support from such persons as Martin Heinecken, a respected theologian of the church, by then retired in Vermont. In a summary of our exchange of letters in April 1990, I stated that we agreed that

Some have such a profound homosexual orientation that change is not possible.

Homosexual persons are not sinners in some unusual sense.

The biblical witness affirms only a heterosexual, male/female relationship as moral.

Civil rights should not be denied because a person is homosexual.

Homosexual persons should be accepted as full members of the body of Christ.

All of the baptized are priests in the body of Christ, but not all are to be ordained. The church has both the right and the obligation to set standards. If there is to be a change in the church's stance, we need to be convinced of it.

As for the biblical question, key for both Heinecken and me, I insisted that:

One would have to practice eisegesis of the worst kind to find a text that one could stretch so far that it affirmed such a relationship. We might say that we do not have a biblical basis on which to condemn persons living in long-term, caring homosexual relationships with one other person. But can we extend it so far as to say that this opens the door to ordination of those living in such relationships? I think not.

Heinecken responded positively. He suggested, however, that I may have put some limits on God's power to change a person's sexual orientation. He cited recovery from alcoholism as analogous to a change in sexual orientation.

I wrote to Heinecken again in early July 1990, this time sending a copy of his letter and mine to the synod bishops and ELCA seminary presidents. Between the two letters I had been to Geneva, Switzerland, and had heard an excellent paper by Edward Schneider, an ELCA representative on the LWF Executive Committee, on the Lutheran dialectic way of dealing with difficult social issues. At our best, Schneider said, we walk carefully between those who are ready to ease standards without careful biblical and theological reflection, and those who use Scripture in a literal and legalistic way. Citing Schneider, I wrote that

. . . integrity in the theological task lies between those two poles. It is not only possible, but essential, that we be free to explore issues without fear . . . let us be open enough to be convinced, while we cling unapologetically to tradition.

Then I went on to tell Heinecken of an encounter with a young gay man who had come to my office since I last wrote to him. His story was typical of so many I had heard until then, and hundreds since. He had felt different since early childhood; he had sublimated his feelings of attraction to other males; he had prayed for change with no result. At a Lutheran campus ministry gathering he had heard the gospel of full grace and acceptance. His life had been changed. I asked Heinecken:

Should I have suggested to this young man, after hearing his story of grace, that he had one more step to take—that if he really wanted to know fully the grace of God, he should ask God to work a change in his sexual orientation?

Of course, you wouldn't suggest such a thing. We agreed in our previous correspondence that this is not the issue. We may set standards for ordination; but membership in the body of Christ is by grace alone.

As for the parallel with alcoholism, I asked Heinecken if it really fit:

It is true that an alcoholic, like a homosexual person, may be in for a lifetime of struggle with an inclination or an addiction. But doesn't sexuality take us in an entirely different direction? If one is to express one's sexuality fully and appropriately, it normally involves another person. We can say to an alcoholic, "Decide every day that you will not drink. Act like a person who does not need a drink." But can one say to a person with a strong homosexual inclination, "Act every day like a person who is heterosexual."? . . . Can you imagine some of the homosexual persons you have known "acting" as though they were heterosexual persons? I can't, as I think of some I have known.

I also asked about the heterosexual spouse of a homosexual person.

> Can you imagine what it would be like to be the spouse of such a person? I can't—and my conversations with some spouses leads me to believe that for them the hell is even worse. . . .

In 1990 I wrote a piece entitled, "The Ordination of Homosexual Persons." It reflects my thinking at the time. The paper was divided into four questions:

> *Is homosexuality a choice?* No, I believed it was not.

> *Can one change?* I suggested that it depended on the intensity of one's sexual orientation. For those with a "profound" orientation I was certain change was not an option.

> *How should one live?* I could not condemn those who have the freedom of conscience to live in these relationships. I believed the church should be fully supportive of such persons.

> *What about ordination?* ". . . a personal call to ordination is only half of the issue, I wrote. "The other half is the church's acknowledgement that it is appropriate to ordain certain persons."

Finally, I asked how the church should resolve this impasse. What has happened in these intervening years is exactly what I prophesied:

> Such a decision should not be made by the bishop of the church, by the Conference of Bishops, or even the Church Council. It is the kind of judgment that a Churchwide Assembly should make—and that only after careful study and reflections throughout the congregations of the church.

> The time may come when an assembly of the church will decide that persons in homosexual relationships ought to be ordained, assuming they qualify on other grounds as well. I would respect that decision. At this moment, however, I cannot in good conscience advocate for the ordination of persons who live in homosexual relationships.
>
> My strong hope and prayer is that all of us would be willing to search honestly for answers to these very puzzling questions. I would ask that we read widely, that we allow ourselves to come to know homosexual persons, that we engage in dialogue, and, above all, that we agree to pray for the wisdom and guidance of the Spirit of God in these matters.

Much more could be added to what was going on for me and the church in 1990. What emerges is that I was living in two arenas. Privately, I was having an intense personal struggle with the issue. I was not comfortable with what I felt I needed to say in public. My heart ached for those gay and lesbian brothers and sisters in Christ whom I felt were disenfranchised from a call to ordained ministry that was as strong and legitimate as my own.

In the public arena my concern centered in two areas: the need for more biblical study of the issue and my fear that any signal of change would bring chaos to our young and fragile church.

Relationships with evangelical and pentecostal churches

In 1991 I agreed to chair a six-member committee of the National Council of Churches (NCC) that would explore closer ties between its member churches and Roman Catholic, evangelical conservative, and pentecostal churches. The aim was to search for ways "to make a mutual witness together to the unity of Christ's body."

We had congenial meetings with representatives of each of these groups. It became apparent early on that the Roman Catholic representatives had little interest in talking to a council of churches.

Their emphasis was on church-to-church dialogue. Nothing came of those efforts.

With the evangelical conservative and pentecostal groups, however, we were somewhat more successful. In each encounter, stereotypes about each other were addressed. We learned that at the heart we had a great deal of consensus. Even here, however, the conversations did not have enough foundation in common interest to carry them on for more than a year or two. It was an intriguing venture but not one that deserved a larger investment of time and resources.

In our own ELCA I delivered a major paper on the subject. I noted that "evangelical/fundamentalist" churches were hardly ready for talks that would lead to greater unity in the gospel. There could be no agenda other than to get better acquainted with each other. I reminded listeners that our constitutional mandate was to "develop relationships with communities of faith for dialogue and common action." On that basis, I asked, "Is it not fair to conclude that we must be as open to 'interaction' with pentecostals as we are to 'dialogue' with Episcopalians or 'conversations' with Jews?"

I also emphasized that I had learned that there is no "monolithic evangelical conservative or pentecostal group of like-minded Christians." They are, instead, "a plethora of distinct denominations with innumerable varieties of doctrines and practices."

I stated that we must engage in conversation with these churches, not with an attitude of defensiveness or superiority, but with the aim to learn from one another. I reminded the audience that by their own admission, a significant percentage of our ELCA members view the Bible in the same literal way that fundamentalists do. These conversations could give us some clues on how to deal with these members of our own congregations.

I asserted that it is not in our best interest to react defensively when attacked by fundamentalists. Rather we should patiently look for opportunities for interaction. In the process we may discover ways in which we can link hands to address social problems that threaten to destroy our common life in community. If we know who we are, I stated, then we need not fear this kind of interaction.

Bishops accused of sexual abuse

Among the heaviest burdens I had to endure were allegations of sexual abuse leveled by women at two current and one former synod bishops. The accusations ranged from inappropriate touching to gross sexual abuse.

I would gladly have delegated these investigations to someone else. But the documents of the church were clear. I had to do this myself, no matter how much time it consumed.

All of the women were, in my judgment, believable. I could not dismiss any of the charges. In two cases, after a thorough investigation, I instigated the formal investigation process. And in both cases the men resigned on the day before the process was to begin. In the less serious instance, the bishop agreed to resign and was later called to a parish setting. Of course, the parish was informed fully by the bishop of that synod of what had happened.

Huge amounts of my time—at a juncture in the life of the church when I needed every ounce of time and energy to lead the church—were devoured by these cases.

In cases like these one must try to maintain objectivity. There are instances where women make false accusations, even imagining things that never happened. On the other had, I learned again through these instances that it takes an enormous amount of courage for a woman to come forward and lift charges against a pastor, to say nothing of doing so against a bishop.

I also came to appreciate the process the ELCA has in place for dealing with sexual abuse. The accused have a fair and equitable way of making their case before a jury of the church. If one is falsely accused, why resign before the process begins? For the sake of one's personal integrity, why not face one's accusers and insist on one's innocence?

What also emerged from these situations, and especially those involving the bishops in office, was another downside of the merger. When synods elected leadership, they often did not know well those who were candidates. Someone with an impressive record and good public presence could be elected. In contrast, in an established church body candidates for office are usually well-known and tested by long service in the church.

Once the dust had settled in these cases, I received words of gratitude from the women who had been abused. One wrote:

> I want to thank you for the note you sent me acknowledging my courage and thanking me for my willingness to testify. I appreciated your words and pray for all who have been affected by this tragedy. I also appreciate the difficult role you have had to play in the midst of this and know the decisions you have had to make have been difficult and painful. I have probably lost my call due to my senior pastor's close friendship with [the bishop] and I don't know where we will go. . . .
>
> I thank God for the legions of angels who have stood watch over me and bear me up. The healing process has begun and I know there will be setbacks, but I will keep praying and working toward wholeness.

A prestigious group addresses environmental issues

In early 1991 I was invited to serve on a task force whose aim was to bring together leaders in science, government, and religion to address the growing threats to the environment. Called "The Joint Appeal in Religion and Science" and funded by a grant from St. John the Divine Church in Manhattan, the group included such luminaries as Vinton Anderson, president of the World Council of Churches; Marc Angel, president of the Rabbinical Council of America; Edmund Browning, presiding bishop of the Episcopal Church; Carl Sagan, eminent astronomer, and his wife and coauthor, Ann Druyan; Senator Albert and Tipper Gore; James Hansen, director of the Goddard Institute for Space Studies; Archbishop Iakovos, primate of the Greek Orthodox Church of North and South America; Senator Robert Kasten from Wisconsin; Patricia Rumer, general director of Church Women United; Robert Schuller, pastor of Crystal Cathedral in Garden Grove, California; Senator Timothy Wirth from Colorado; and others.

Our goal was to develop recommendations that could be brought to the U.S. Congress and the president for enactment.

I learned that Carl Sagan, by then the star of the Nova series on Public Television, was an engaging and approachable human being. On one occasion I mentioned to him that I had an avid interest in gardening. He was fascinated by this. "I know all about the universe," he said, "but cannot identify one weed from another in my back yard." Sagan expressed wonder and awe at the magnificence of the universe. He was appalled by the degradation of the environment. "Even the birds don't soil their nests," he would say on occasion.

One of our smaller subcommittee sessions was held in Washington, D.C. We had an appointment with Senators Robert Dole (Kansas) and George Mitchell (Maine). When they were delayed for a time, we engaged in intense conversation about a variety of subjects, including religion. Sagan insisted that he was an agnostic. He could not believe, he said, without solid empirical evidence. I thought about Kierkegaard and the "leap of faith." Just as I was about to bring this out, lo and behold, a Jew, Rabbi David Saperstein, mentioned this very thing. After we have amassed as much information and insight as we can, he said, we must take a leap of faith. Sagan died several months later of a rare blood disease. I have no idea whether he ever took that leap.

Powerful as it was, nothing of great substance came from our efforts. We learned, once more, that the political world moves slowly and resists change. Nevertheless, I would like to believe that some impressions were made, some insights were put forward, and, who knows, some action in the years to come may have been influenced by our work. We can hope.

A vision statement for the ELCA

As we approached the Orlando Assembly I ruminated and chatted with others, including churchwide staff, about the need for a vision statement for the church. It was on a flight from the East Coast in June 1991 that it came to me. I think we were over Indiana at the time. It was a revelatory experience. I jotted it down on a scrap of paper:

> A church so deeply and confidently rooted in the gospel of God's grace, that we are free to give our life in witness and service.

I shared it with the Cabinet of Executives at its next meeting. They discussed it thoroughly and came up with only one suggestion, from Robert Sorensen. That was to add the words "joyfully" to the last part—"to give our life away joyfully in witness and service." It was an excellent suggestion. This statement was widely dispersed and became part and parcel of the life of the ELCA for many years to come.

In mid-July Lutheran Brotherhood sponsored a Lutheran Leadership Conference at Snowbird, Utah. That setting gave me an opportunity to spell out our statement in some detail.

> I reviewed how our Mission90 emphasis had evolved into our forthcoming assembly theme: "See, Grow, Serve."

> We were restructuring the church with a focus on mission. Because financial resources simply made it impossible for us to achieve what the CNLC had envisioned, we looked forward to a leaner structure. It would include:

> Learning, with an accent on innovative curriculum design for lifelong education in the parish.

> Witnessing, including new missions, support for existing ministries, and cooperation with other Lutheran churches

around the world. An important element would be equip-
ping the laity.

Serving, with the goal that others would look at our ELCA
congregations and say, "These folks really love. These
Christians really care. That church really serves."

I concluded with these words of hope: "We have a theology
rooted in the good news our world needs to hear. We have
well-equipped, capable pastoral and lay leadership. We have
financial resources. The question is, do we have the will?

Corinne's life during the first term

I want to write a bit about Corinne's life during my first term in
office.

Her first priority was to make our home a place where we could
both find rest and renewal. Because our condominium was on a
golf course, we often walked the fairways in the evening after the
golfers had gone.

We pick up golf tees as we walk—some nights forty or
more. It's a good time to talk. I'm grateful we have each
other and that our love continues strong and steady in the
midst of all kinds of onslaughts.

As I noted earlier, she started getting invitations to speak in
various parts of the country. Being an ordained pastor was a strong
asset. This opened the way for her to preach in many interesting
settings, including the National Cathedral in Washington, D.C. On
one occasion she preached at the baccalaureate service at Muhlenberg College in Allentown, Pennsylvania, when Coretta King spoke
at commencement exercises. She was especially involved in events
related to the Women of the ELCA, including their churchwide and
synod assemblies and area gatherings. She preached and led Bible
studies at a number of synod assemblies. She also continued her
ministry in doing grief presentations and leading workshops on

that subject. Her impact was more than an extension of my office. She carved out a ministry and mission of her own.

On one occasion I wrote about a trip she had taken to Minnesota where she spoke to more than thirty-five hundred people in various settings about global mission and outreach.

> What an ambassador for the ELCA. One of the best. And unpaid at that! But she seems to really love it.

The tension that hung over us in those first years in Chicago, however, was the question of how she could retain her call status as an ordained minister of the church. For all of her activity across the church, there was no entity that could issue a call to her. Finally a door opened. The Search Institute in Minneapolis was undertaking a broad study of adopted persons, a program instigated in large part by our initiative when we lived in Minnesota. They wanted Corinne to serve on the research team. This opened the door for her to be approved by the Conference of Bishops for a call to special service.

When the Search project was completed, she went on leave from call again.

During all of these early years in Chicago there was another matter brewing in Corinne's soul. As I indicated earlier Roland Seboldt, senior editor for Augsburg Fortress, Publishers, had heard her give an address on grief and tell the story of our loss of Andrew. He invited her to write a book for the church. She agreed and made preliminary plans with an editor assigned to her.

She would need to think and reflect on this for eight years. Through our first four years in Chicago, it continued to bubble up at times. Not until 1992 would she actually begin to write. Once she set herself to the task the words flowed almost faster than she could write. Out of it came *Andrew, You Died Too Soon.*

Should I stand for reelection?

The first term in office had been grueling. Though I retained a strong sense that I had been called to the task, I could not help but wonder at times if someone else might be better suited to pick up the reins for the next phase in the life of the ELCA. I had heard much affirmation from many sources as I traveled about the church. I also felt support from the staff in Chicago.

Nevertheless, there were moments when I longed to be free from the burden of the office. I suggested to my three assistants that leaving office would bring much relief to me personally. "I'm putting out the fleeces," I wrote,

> . . . looking to God to give me a sign to either clearly affirm or clearly disaffirm what the letter has said. I don't know where it will come from, but I am convinced it will come.

I didn't have to wait long for affirmation of my call. Within days I received a number of unsolicited letters of encouragement and support. Someone from the East Central Synod of Wisconsin sent a copy of a resolution of support for my leadership, and especially for the impact of the Mission90 program. At that synod assembly it got a standing ovation. In late May Corinne and I attended the gathering for pastors of larger congregations at Hilton Head in South Carolina. I sometimes felt an edge of criticism from some of them. This event, however, was unusually cordial and brought strong affirmation both at the gathering as well as in notes that came to my desk in the days following.

About that same time Corinne was in Minnesota for a St. Olaf College board meeting. She called Al Anderson from Augsburg Fortress, Publishers to see how he was doing after his illness.

> At the end of the conversation he wanted her to bring a special word to me—that we should go to Orlando with great confidence. He is convinced that the election will be over quickly and that I will be reaffirmed as leader.

A couple of weeks before the 1991 Orlando assembly I visited the ELCA Archives a few blocks from the Lutheran Center.

> It was good to see boxes and more boxes of materials from my predecessors in office [in the former church bodies]. It helps put things into perspective. My time is brief. I'll do my best, strive to keep my integrity, and leave the rest in God's hands.

Final chapel service before the Orlando assembly

I always treasured the chapel services at the Lutheran Center. Though my schedule was such that I missed many of them, when I was there it was a time to deepen my love and respect for my colleagues in every unit of the churchwide organization.

On August 6, 1991, I preached on the text from Exodus 16: 2–15. The Israelites are out of Egypt, trudging through the wilderness, not yet in the Promised Land. They grumbled, looking back through a cracked mirror on what now looked like a good life. At other times, they longed for what would surely be a much better life in the Promised Land.

I reflected on how easy it is for us to think that the good old days were only good. But when we think more carefully about them, we realize that those days had their painful times, too.

Neither, I said, does it help to think that future days will be without stresses and strains.

> If we wish for peace and assurance, it is not to be found in wistful longing for some future bliss or in illusory retreat to an assumed past security. It is to be found only in trust in our God who has promised that there will be enough for each day.

> Enough for the day. That's all we need. But it's more than enough.

The night before we flew off to Orlando I wrote:

> Lord, these next days are yours. Go with us. Give humility, wisdom, grace, patience, joy.

Chapter 12

Other ships on the seas: ecumenical and sister church relationships

Affirming our partnerships in the U.S. and around the world

Before moving on to the 1991 Churchwide Assembly and my second term in office, I want to write about some of the ecumenical and inter-church experiences that were a part of my life and the life of the ELCA during my time in office.

Looking back over my entire life, I must say that my journey in the life of the church has been like a ship that sailed on a rather small body of water for the first forty years. Though there were occasional forays into other larger seas, it was not until I became a synod bishop and then presiding bishop that I moved into places where I learned that God had many more ships than I thought, and many as seaworthy as our Lutheran flotillas.

Becoming the head of the new Evangelical Lutheran Church in America brought me out into the broad ocean where this new church, by comparison, seemed rather small, but never inconsequential. During the first years in the life of the ELCA, I gave the large majority of my time to its birth and organization, but it was also necessary and important to engage with other denominations and visit several places where we were in partnership with churches around the world. Some were living in deep distress, coping with unbelievable pressures. We needed to bring hope and encouragement to beleaguered sisters and brothers in Christ. In each place I sought to understand how best the ELCA could relate to them and be a full partner in interdependent mission and ministry.

Ecumenical affairs: source of both joy and distress

If I had one major area of weakness in my leadership of the church in its early months, it was in ecumenical matters. As I've indicated, I came into office with little experience in the field. Serving on the Faith and Order Commission of the National Council of Churches for a time had helped. And, of course, I had a plethora of contacts with leaders of other denominations on a regional level.

In the more formal aspects of ecumenism—study of the history of the movement, academic courses on the subject, participation in forging agreements between different religious groups, contacts with national leaders of other churches—in all of these areas I was a neophyte. Yet from day one in office I was to be the chief ecumenical officer of the ELCA.

By early 1989, thanks to the aid of our ELCA Office of Ecumenical Affairs and my own personal study, I was ready to speak with some measure of confidence about ecumenical matters. The setting was an ecumenical convocation at Newberry College in South Carolina where I delivered a major paper. By this time the statement on ecumenism that we intended to introduce to the 1989 Churchwide Assembly was taking shape. My address outlined some of its major points.

I began by reminding the audience that all of our predecessor churches, to one degree or another, had been in dialogue with other churches. Though many of us had grown up in communities where ethnic Lutheran churches had little to do with one another, some of our predecessor church bodies had been actively involved in the Faith and Order movement and in the formation of the National Council of Churches in the USA, the

World Council of Churches, and the Lutheran World Federation. I reminded them that well-known leaders of our predecessor churches, such as Franklin Clark Fry, Fredrick Schoitz, Robert Marshall, Kent Knutson, David Preus, and James Crumley, had been officers in those entities.

I stressed that the fundamental motivation for ecumenism is the Bible itself. Citing Ephesians 4, Colossians 3, and John 17 I stated:

> We do not believe it to be the will of God that the church be fractured. In the midst of our broken history of schism and division in the Christian church, we cannot shake ourselves free from God's call on page after page of the Bible that urges us to search for greater unity.

I spoke of ecumenism as a confessional tradition. Though the Augsburg Confession is our source for Lutheran identity, it is, at the same time, our springboard for ecumenical dialogue and cooperation.

> The gospel—the good news about Jesus Christ—this is the essential core of the one, holy, catholic, and apostolic church. Scripture is to be normative. The ecumenical creeds are to be the "chief symbols" of the church. Even when differences seemed inevitable, the Lutheran reformers spoke of latitude that would call for them to stay in fellowship with those with whom they had differences in certain theological formulations and practices. Fundamental to everything, and central to the ecumenical tradition, is Article VII of the Augsburg Confession, which states that "for the true unity of the church it is enough (*satis est*) to agree concerning the teaching of the Gospel and the administration of the sacraments."

> We in the ELCA believe that this foundational statement in Article VII liberates us from demanding absolute uniformity in doctrinal and ecclesiastical matters. No, it does not free us from serious, arduous, and at times fruitless

dialogue with other churches. But we can enter those
dialogues with the hope and expectation that the end result
of our efforts may be an agreement that we can express our
unity in concrete ways. Indeed, we are even prepared to be
led toward complete unity.

I recalled for the listeners that the Constitution of the ELCA
affirmed all of this by stating forthrightly that one of our primary
goals as a church was to "develop relationships with communities
of other faiths for dialogue and common action."

I reminded the audience that at the forthcoming Churchwide
Assembly in the summer of 1989 we would be considering a
landmark ecumenical statement: "Ecumenism: The Vision of the
Evangelical Lutheran Church." After outlining the proposals for
discussions with councils of churches and other church bodies,
I stressed that we live in a world where other religions also play
a major role in public life. I explained the four steps or stages of
"reception" that we would consider in the statement:

> *Ecumenical Cooperation:* our broad engagement with
> churches that were Christian but did not share our views
> on Word and Sacrament.

> *Bilateral and Multilateral Dialogue:* a stage of openness to
> new possibilities of cooperation with other churches.

> *Preliminary Recognition:* a stage where we would be ready
> to have interim eucharistic sharing and cooperation.

> *Full Communion:* the stage where so much common unity
> in doctrine is acknowledged that we must consider some
> form of union between churches.

I concluded my address with reference to the Third Article of the
Apostles' Creed:

> Our ecumenical venture is more than bringing peo-
> ple together for the sake of dialogue, discussion, and

formulation of agreements. It lies much deeper than that. We must be prayerfully tuned to the voice of the Spirit. Undergirding everything must be a commitment on the part of our church to pray for the wisdom to know where the Spirit is leading us.

In our ecumenical ventures, it would be safest . . . to remain comfortable in known traditions, to risk little. In our ecumenical ventures . . . the ELCA has chosen the high seas.

In spite of opposition in some parts of the church, William Rusch, head of the Office of Ecumenical Affairs for the ELCA, worked diligently at forging alliances with other churches. Unusually good progress was being made with the Episcopal Church. Opposition, however, was so strong, especially in the former ALC circles, that I urged both the Church Council and the Conference of Bishops to delay any action on Lutheran-Episcopal dialogue recommendations until the study on ministry had been completed.

Early in 1991 I wrote to Corinne while on my way to the World Council of Churches assembly in Canberra, Australia:

> I'm going to get started on an article for *Lutheran Partners* re. Luth/Episc relations. Wherever I go I find it misunderstood. I feel we have a huge mess on our hands & I'm not sure we can salvage it. But I guess I have to try. If I have any skills at making complicated things more clear, I'll need all of them now.

Later in the year, in a letter to Arland Hultgren at Luther Northwestern Seminary, I underscored my conviction on this issue.

> However the historic episcopate comes into the ELCA, formally or informally, it will make some difference. It is a sign. But signs carry their own significance. Just as the adopting of the title "bishop" was said to be "only a sign" and no more . . . yet it made a difference in the way we looked at the office of leader of the church and it made a

difference in ecumenical relationships. The irony—as I have pointed out to some friends of ALC background—is that it came first to that church, and even with the added qualification of "presiding." It seems strange that some of these same persons are so resistant to the next logical step—opening the door to broader communion with other believers.

I have learned from trusted friends out of ALC background that it is thought by some that the chief goal of my life is not my salvation but to bring the historic episcopate into the ELCA! If they looked at the matter objectively they would see that my only purpose is to try to make certain that the issue is treated fairly and debated evenly (8/16/91).

In the meantime, work on the Statement on Ecumenism resumed with the aim to have it ready for reconsideration at the Orlando Churchwide Assembly in 1991.

Our efforts paid off. At the Orlando Assembly the statement was enthusiastically endorsed. I give Bill Rusch and his staff the lion's share of the credit for nursing it along through a difficult time.

The LWF: cementing relationships with our partners

I was just catching my breath at the Constituting Convention in May, 1987, when LWF General Secretary Gunnar Staalsett invited Corinne and me to attend the meeting of the Lutheran World Federation at Lund, Sweden, and Viborg, Denmark, in early July 1987. This would be the fortieth anniversary of the LWF and it was important that I, as the new head of the ELCA, be present.

It was, of course, a special thrill for me to go to Lund, the place where my maternal great grandparents, the Carl Lindgrens, had lived, and to worship again at the cathedral where they had often gone for Word and Sacrament. They could never have imagined in their wildest dreams that a great grandson would one day come to that place to represent a large segment of the Lutherans in America. In my greeting to the LWF leaders I included these words:

> ... my great grandfather is buried only a short distance from the Lund Cathedral, not far from the grave of Anders Nygren. Unlike Nygren, my great grandfather was not widely known. He was a shoemaker who had his shop in his small apartment. He was a devout Christian with a vision for the world.
>
> One of the legacies he left for his descendants was his *Dag Bok*—his day book.
>
> One entry is of special interest. It is the record of a gift for "the black man Onesimus in Stockholm." Onesimus was an early Christian convert from Ethiopia who was brought to Stockholm for theological training. Christians like my great grandfather supported him. Later Onisemus returned to Ethiopia where he translated parts of the Bible and the Catechism for his people and preached the gospel for many years.

NCC, WCC, LWF—Where shall I focus my attention?

After my election in 1987 I knew I would be expected to assume responsibility in some of the inter-church areas: the National Council of Churches of Christ in the USA; the World Council of Churches; the Lutheran World Federation. Both Crumley and Preus were serving as officers and/or committee chairs in those organizations. Those terms were not contiguous with their terms as heads of predecessor churches. Thus, both could continue, if they wished, on those boards. Crumley graciously offered to step aside should I want to move immediately into leadership in those organizations. There was no guarantee, however, that I would be elected to the same positions. David Preus was determined to serve out his full terms.

I decided not to make an issue of it. My plate was full in getting the new church off to a strong start. Crumley was serving as chair of an important planning committee at LWF and it would have been disruptive to ask him to withdraw.

In time, and after careful consideration, I decided to forego membership on the central committee of the World Council of Churches. It seemed best to concentrate my energies on the National Council of Churches, where I would meet leaders of other Protestant and Orthodox churches in this country, and the Lutheran World Federation, where I would be working with Lutheran churches around the world that looked to the ELCA for leadership and assistance. I would let staff persons represent me at the World Council of Churches.

A meeting with John Paul II

On his first visit to the United States in the fall of 1987, Pope John Paul II was hosted by the University of South Carolina at Columbia. It was to be a gathering with United States church leaders.

But who was the leader of the newly born ELCA? Technically, Preus, Crumley, and Herzfeld were in office until the end of the year. And though I began my work on June 1, the ELCA would not be officially launched until January 1, 1988. I have no idea who worked out the logistics. Preus, Crumley, and I were all invited. I don't know if Herzfeld was excluded or could not attend.

It was a festive occasion with worship services, processions, a sumptuous banquet, and a small gathering of about two dozen leaders with John Paul. After a formal welcome and a brief address by the pope, each of us was given a medal to commemorate the occasion. When I shook his hand I said to John Paul, "I wish you much grace from the people of the Lutheran church."

The event was a keen disappointment for those who had hoped there would be any serious dialogue on issues that both unite and divide us. It was more of a public relations event than one of substance. I commented to the press that "the ecumenical move-ment is a glacier. It moves slowly, but it does move" (*The Lutheran Standard,* 10/2/87).

In my journal I tried to look at the meeting from a broader perspective.

> I was a bit disgusted with some of the Protestant lead-ers who took up more time than they should have with redundant comments. The pope made a few informal comments at the end, saying that this was indeed a historic moment. And that it was. Given the history of animosity between Protestants and Roman Catholics in the U.S., it really was a significant event. I feel deeply privileged to have been a part of it.

John Paul impressed me as a friendly, intense man of God. In the years to follow I would learn that he was not about to foster the spirit that had prevailed after Vatican II and the tenure of John XXIII. This would be a more rigid papacy, often characterized as the era of the man who led the Roman Catholic with an iron fist in a silk glove. We would see John Paul replace progressive bishops with more conservative, traditional ones. Even as he opened new doors of dialogue with non-Christian religious leaders, he never let it be forgotten that he was more than the first among equals. He was the first *without* an equal.

Ecumenical Odysseys: Rome, Istanbul, Moscow, London

From January 20 to 30, 1988, in the first month in the life of the ELCA, I embarked on an ecumenical trip to Rome, Istanbul, Mos-cow, and London. For the boy from Litchfield this was indeed an epic journey.

Six months later, in June of 1988, I returned to Moscow for the millennium celebration of the Russian Orthodox Church. On our flight back to the United States, we stopped for a few days in East Germany.

As I would learn on each step of these trips, Rusch had impeccable credentials and invaluable contacts in every place we visited. He covered every detail. Having Edgar Trexler, editor of *The Lutheran* magazine, along was also to my advantage. His longtime experience in international church news reporting proved helpful in many ways.

The fact that the first trip occurred during the ecumenical Week of Prayer for Christian Unity also heightened its significance.

Rome and John Paul II

Bill Rusch met me and guided me through the day at the Vatican, functioning so comfortably that one would have thought him to be a Vatican guide. We were greeted by Cardinal Joseph Ratzinger, the man who would succeed John Paul as Pope Benedict XVI. I described him as:

> . . . a German who heads the section on doctrine for the Vatican. It was primarily a courtesy call . . . it was a cordial conversation. We talked mainly about the ELCA, the dialogues Lutherans and Roman Catholics have had, and our hope for further conversations. I invited him to come for an official visit in the U.S. and he indicated that it might be possible the year after next.

Ratzinger suggested that if the mutual condemnations still standing from the time of the Reformation could be lifted, it would be a huge step in paving the way for fuller communion between Lutherans and Roman Catholics. I was pleased when the condemnations were dropped several years later. I see little evidence, however, that it has made any difference.

Next I stopped at the Office of the Secretariat for Promoting Christian Unity where I was greeted by Cardinal Johannes Willebrands, a Dutchman who headed that office. I had met him when he traveled to the U.S. with the pope.

As he emerged from his office he moved directly to me and gave me a warm embrace, touching me on one cheek and then the other. It was a very significant gesture. He surely didn't need to do that. I took it as a sign that the chemistry between us is good and that he wants to keep wide open the doors for communication between Lutherans and Roman Catholics.

After two or three other visits to high officials we went to a lovely restaurant in another part of Rome.

The next morning I awakened at five-thirty after a long night of good sleep.

It was an ideal morning for a walk. I went out of the hotel and turned toward St. Peter's Square. The eastern sky was just beginning to show signs of the dawn. There were very few people on the streets. The gates to St. Peter's were shut and it was dark in all of the buildings surrounding the Square, including the pope's apartment.

I had my camera along and took a number of time exposures of the fountains, the statue of St. Peter with the keys in one hand and of St. Peter's Basilica itself. As I strolled back and forth I found myself praying for Corinne, for Chris and for Mary. I prayed for my mother, wondering how she is doing and asking God once more to free her from the prison of her body. I felt a deep surge of gratitude for her. I thanked God—and her—for the strong body I had inherited, in part from her.

As it began to grow lighter . . . I looked up and saw lights in the pope's residence. No doubt he was getting ready for the day, including our visit.

As I continued walking back and forth, I went through my morning hymns. Some of the lines were especially important as I thought about what would happen later:

Direct, control, suggest this day

All I design or do or say,

That all my powers, with all their might

In thy sole glory may unite.

I was the fifth person to enter St. Peter's that morning. Where should I go in this huge edifice? I looked to the right and saw the *Pieta*. Yes, that was the place I needed to go first. Later that night I wrote:

Oh Andrew, I wept so hard for you as I knelt there. The body of Christ that Michelangelo fashioned is so much like your own—lean and muscular. A body of beauty and strength. A body of grace.

But also a dead body. I looked at the face of Christ—fallen back on the arm of Mary. And I thought of your face when I saw it that awful morning. And I felt such deep sorrow.

And then there was the face of Mary. I thought of the mothers who held you. How Mom loved you, Andrew! A sword has gone through her heart, too. She has a wound that will never heal.

It was time for the main object of our visit: the private audience with John Paul.

I had reflected on this visit when I arrived in Rome two days earlier.

So how do I feel as this is about to happen? Well, it may seem strange, but I really feel very calm and not at all apprehensive. In fact, I look forward to a very good visit with the pope. I suspect we both share the same sense of absolute dependence on the grace of God to carry out our responsibility.

And what will we talk about? I really have no idea. I'm praying that the Spirit of God will guide and direct us

in our conversation. My main purpose—here, as well as
in Istanbul, Moscow, and London—is to establish a firm
and congenial relationship with these leaders. Progress in
ecumenical ventures depends on a sense of personal trust
between leaders.

Rusch and I ascended the wide steps that lead to the papal
offices. As we passed through the long hall on our way to our meeting place, lined with one small chapel after another, I viewed exqui-
site art on every wall—paintings, mosaics, tapestries, and murals.

This is how I described the audience:

> Suddenly the door opened and a man in formal attire ush-
> ered us through an anteroom and into a large room where
> the pope had a desk at one end. As Bill and I entered he was
> already on his feet and moving toward us. He came directly
> to me and greeted me warmly. He invited me to take the
> seat at the side of his desk. He himself took his seat, but at
> the corner rather than behind his desk. He learned forward
> and looked directly at me—and remained in that posture
> for the entire audience.
>
> I reminded him that we had met briefly at Columbia, South
> Carolina last October. That prompted a number of reflec-
> tions from him. He talked of the people that lined the
> streets, of the pleasure of being welcomed in a place that he
> had previously known only as "the Bible Belt." He recalled
> the stadium event and his sermon on the family. I com-
> mented on the response of the congregations that night—
> the "amens" of appreciation for his words.
>
> I told him of my great joy over our meeting. I described my
> experience as a child—walking past the Catholic church,
> avoiding the priests and the nuns. I told him that I could
> not have imagined in my fondest dreams that I would ever
> experience a moment like this. I told him that it was truly a
> pentecostal moment.

He commented on the remarkable progress of the Lutheran/ Roman Catholic dialogues in the U.S. He felt that they had been a model for the churches around the world. In turn, I assured him that our ELCA would do everything in our power to make certain those dialogues continued and that we would work for their success.

Then it was time to make my main point. I told him that we have come a long way in our theological discussions, but now it was time that we worked equally as hard to implement some of those suggestions. It was time to take practical steps. I described how I had just joined with a priest to conduct the wedding for my niece Joy and her husband, Brian, last fall. I underscored how significant it would be if our devout young couples could come freely to the altars of both of our churches to receive the Sacrament of our Lord's body and blood. Although he did not make any promises, he seemed to agree that this is important.

We both spoke of the fact that there will probably always be differences between us. Yet, we must not stop talking and searching for ways to deepen our relationship. I told him of the exceptional relationship the Lutheran and Roman Catholic bishops had in Minnesota and how I treasured those contacts when I was a bishop in that place.

This was the pope's last interview for that day. We had been engaged in intense, animated conversation for about twenty minutes. I could see that he was very tired. The moment I picked up the hint that he was ready to conclude our conversation, I rose to my feet. I presented him with a leather-bound copy of my book on Hebrews, together with a medallion for the ELCA. On the inside cover of the book I had inscribed:

Your Holiness: May Jesus Christ, our Sacrifice and Great High Priest, be our constant source of grace and strength.

He presented me with a beautiful silver cross with the papal insignia on the reverse side. I continue to use it often.

> Then he pressed a button on the far corner of his desk. Suddenly the door in the opposite corner of the room flew open and three photographers swept into the room. We made a gracious departure and were on our way.

In the evening I hosted a dinner for Cardinal Willebrands and several of the others we had met in Rome. It was very informal with enjoyable conversation. After dinner Willebrands asked if he could light up one of his favorite cigars. I assured him that it was no problem, recalling for him that my father enjoyed cigars, too.

The better I got to know him the more I felt that Willebrands was indeed a prince of the Roman Catholic Church. Several months later when I was with him at the Russian Orthodox Millennium at Moscow I wrote of him:

> This warm Dutchman knows exactly how to put things. He's the best thing the Roman Catholics have going for them, including, in my opinion, the pope. Had Willebrands been pope instead of John Paul the climate of the church would be entirely different. He would have appointed bishops and archbishops and cardinals who would have carried forward the spirit of John XXIII. Instead, we are left wondering if we have not gone as far as we can go in our dialogues with the Roman Catholics.

Everything that has happened in Roman Catholicism since then proves that my prophecy was accurate.

Earlier in our visit I had shared with Monsignor Rodano, an American, that my mother was in very poor health. He accompanied us to the airport. He pulled me aside as we were leaving and said that he had remembered his own mother at mass that morning and had also included my mother in his prayers. When we left it was natural to exchange a warm embrace. We had come a long way from the days when we looked across the chasm and spoke of "those Catholics" and "those Lutherans." A fitting end to our time in Rome.

Istanbul and the Greek Orthodox Church

For our flight from Rome to Istanbul we removed our clergy collars. The secular Turkish government outlawed any public show of religious symbols. Only after we reached the walled compound of the ecumenical patriarch of the Orthodox Church could we change back into religious habit. We were met by Deacon Chrysostomos, our guide for our time in Istanbul. On our drive into the city I mentioned how awesome it was to come to a part of the world where Christianity had been embedded from the very beginning. In contrast, I said, the churches in the United States where I had been born and raised could trace their history for no more than one hundred years. He turned to me said gently, "Jesus is for everyone." It was a special moment.

Our meeting with Dimitrios, head of the Greek Orthodox Church, contrasted sharply with that of John Paul. The pope was robust, energetic, and engaging. He spoke impeccable English. Dimitrios looked frail and withdrawn. He spoke through an interpreter. Though he was "first of equals" among Orthodox patriarchs around the world, he seemed quite isolated from the real world.

All of this, however, may have been deceiving. After I gave him a copy of my book on Hebrews he presented me with a cross that was so beautiful that it nearly took my breath away. The splendid chain that was attached to it also caught my eye. Only later did I learn that it was the most costly kind of gold chain that is made in the Middle East. It became the cross that I wore most often in the coming years when I was not using the ELCA bishop's cross.

What was the significance of this gesture? Rusch had never seen the patriarch give a cross like this to any previous visiting head of a Lutheran church. It may well have been an affirmation of the work

James Crumley had done on previous visits and of the desire of the patriarch to forge closer ties with the ELCA.

In my formal remarks I accented how much we in the West needed the aid of the Orthodox Church in understanding the deeper spirituality that characterizes their worship and meditation practices. I described for them the formation of our ELCA, the study of ministry we would be undertaking in the new church and its importance for ecumenical relationships, and our desire to be of help to them in Washington, D.C. in advocating for greater freedom for the Orthodox Church in Turkey. They received it all very gracefully.

One of the subjects we covered during our conversation was the sensitive issue of the ordination of women. Dimitrios agreed that though his church did not ordain women, the subject would need to be addressed in future dialogues. He suggested that I bring my wife along on my next visit to Istanbul.

A high point of this leg of the trip was the opportunity to see the Hagia Sophia, once the center of the Eastern Orthodox Church and now a Muslim mosque. As Trexler put it later:

> Chilstrom was moved to tears at ancient Hagia Sophia church. . . . Huge round signs, with gold Arabic letters on black background, now hang in the nave (*The Lutheran*, 3/2/88).

In my journal I wrote:

> One can only stand there and imagine what it must have been in its days of glory—and what it could be again if the Christian churches had an opportunity to restore it! I said to our guide, an Orthodox professor, that I would at least like to make the sign of the cross. He agreed. I did.

> In the evening we were hosted at a lovely dinner on the top floor of a downtown Istanbul hotel. Our hosts were two metropolitans, Chrysostemos and Gabriel.

The main subject over dinner was again the ordination of women. They initiated the conversation and seemed eager to pursue it in this more informal setting.

They seemed to want to convey to us that they respected the position our church has taken and that they hoped it would not impede our dialogues. When I informed them that I was married to a pastor they found this to be most interesting! I described for them her journey of faith in coming to the conviction that she should seek ordination. They listened with great respect. They said they hoped I would bring her along on the next visit. They also wanted to say, however, that the possibility of ordaining women to the Orthodox priesthood was very, very remote!

The metropolitans also spoke at some length about the increasingly difficult time Christians were having in the countries of the Middle East where militant Islam was dominant. While some wonder if there is any hope for the Christian church in those places, Gabriel spoke confidently about the future. Many believers, he said— possibly hundreds of thousands of them—keep up the minimum of external signs that they were Christians so as to avoid trouble. Gabriel pointed to China as a parallel example, a place where it was also assumed that the church had been squelched until the bamboo curtain fell and millions of them emerged from the shadows. Even as I write these words Christian churches are being bombed by Islamic militants across the Middle East.

The next day I wrote that

I feel like I've walked into a home I've only viewed from a distance—a home I did not even care to come to. And now after just a little more than twenty-four hours in the house of the Orthodox I have been at a home that is warm, loving, deeply spiritual and, above all, profoundly hospitable. I want to come again!

Moscow and the Russian Orthodox Church

Coming to the Union of Soviet Socialist Republics (USSR) gave
me the feeling of stepping back at least fifty years in time. I was
suddenly transported to pre-World War II days in my hometown.
Automobiles and trucks were all antique-looking. My hotel room
was in the style of the old Lenhardt Hotel on main street in Litchfield, with floral wallpaper, fixtures that seemed ancient, a bed that
was most uncomfortable, and fifteen-foot high ceilings.

The long black limo that picked me up in the morning was waiting for me wherever I went.

> Ed and Bill followed in a smaller car. I find it quite amus-
> ing—and not a little distressing. For a supposedly classless
> society, they surely pay a lot of attention to class and rank.
> The bishops seldom walk since there's always a car and
> driver near at hand to take them wherever they want to go.
> People look at us, no doubt wondering who those dignitar-
> ies are in the big car.

Our meetings were held at the Danilov Monastery, a facility that
the government was restoring and returning to the church. In fact,
churches and monasteries everywhere were bring restored in preparation for the celebration later that year of the 1,000th anniversary
of the coming of Christianity to Russia. Much of the restoration
was being done at the behest of Mikhail Gorbachev. It was too early
in his time in office to make a balanced judgment of the man. As
we would learn, his motives were indeed genuine. After decades of
tyranny, his time in office was a breath of fresh air not only for Russia but for the rest of the world as well.

Our major contact with the church was Metropolitan Filaret,
the exuberant head of the church's Department of External Affairs.
Every move he made was grandiose.

> If you can imagine a "Russian bear" of a man, he is it! Long
> black hair, a magnificent black beard with just a touch of

grey, black robe with a beautiful cross resting on a rotund bay window. One could easily be overwhelmed by him if you had little confidence in yourself. . . . there was the Russian greeting—a touch first on one cheek, then the other, and then on the first cheek again.

We covered most of the subjects we had discussed in Rome and Istanbul. Filaret spoke of his satisfaction that this visit was a sure sign of serious theological dialogue with our new church. Among other things, I stated that one of the positive outcomes of the ecumenical movement was that Christian churches were looking outward for ways to make a common witness. All of them expressed the hope that the outcome of contacts between Gorbachev and President Reagan would be productive.

I went on to say that:

> When we reach out we learn not only about your faith, but we enrich ours as well. Each visit reaffirms our commitment to the ongoing dialogues (*The Lutheran*, 3/2/88).

After our exhausting day of conversation, I would have welcomed a quiet evening to myself. But we had tickets for the Bolshoi ballet, a treat of a lifetime.

> The theater itself was worth seeing. The chandeliers are magnificent leaded glass. It has the air of something out of the distant past. We had seats in the last row on the first floor level. They were slightly elevated so we could see the stage unobstructed. The stage itself was slanted a bit toward the audience, making it possible for one to feel drawn toward the dancers.

The next day we visited Zagorsk, a monastic community a couple of hours north of Moscow. The countryside reminded me of northern Minnesota in winter, with the roadside lined with endless miles of white birch and evergreen trees.

In our discussions with the head of the seminary, the dean, and the faculty, we all spoke of our hope for better relationships, not only between our churches but also between our countries. My strong impression was that the Soviet people were as eager to avoid a nuclear conflict as we were in the United States.

The day would end with an unforgettable dinner at Filaret's *Dacha*. I tried to capture its essence in my journal:

> Well, it was quite a dinner last evening! In fact, the whole experience was like a scene from a Russian movie.
>
> Filaret lives in a very exclusive section of Moscow. We entered his home by the main door. To one side was a quaint little chapel filled with icons and other art objects that have to be priceless.
>
> After a toast or two (by now I was really good at touching my lips!) we were welcomed to the dining room. I have sat at many luxurious tables, but never one more lovely than that one.
>
> There were several courses. Again, more toasts throughout the meal. I responded with a toast every time Filaret made one.
>
> We exchanged words of thanks for our days together; we pledged ourselves to further these relationships; we shared our hopes for peace in the world.
>
> As we left Filaret gave me a Russian kiss—three times on the cheeks. This time it was very vigorous—a sign that the visit had been good. As he and I stepped out to the car I was aware of the fact that a very nice rug had been rolled out over the snow and to the door of the car.
>
> Quite a night. . . .

The Anglican Church

Because of our flight delay in Moscow, we knew we would miss
the reception Archbishop Robert Runcie was to hold for me in
London. Later in the evening there was to be a small dinner at the
Athenian, an exclusive club.

With no time to go to the hotel, Bill, Ed, and I found a men's room
at the club, doffed our travel grubbies, and came out looking like a
million dollars and ready for a very proper English dinner party.

Unlike the endless toasts at the Russian dinners, there were
only two that evening in London, one by the bishop of York and
one by me. I had met this man earlier in the United States and we
had spoken about the death of my son Andrew. He had expressed
genuine concern and care for me. Now I felt bonded to him in a
special way again.

> Even though we didn't talk about it at the dinner last night,
> I could feel his sensitivity and love. It's strange how some
> people simply seem to know and to exude that kind of sym-
> pathy. I'm convinced it is a gift.

The next day we met with Archbishop Runcie at his office at
Lambeth Palace in London.

> He has an office that is just as you would imagine it to be
> in a palace. Very large and comfortable, with the charm of
> coal burning in a fireplace.

We covered the expected subjects. He was pleased with the progress of Lutheran/Episcopal dialogue in the United States. He called
it a model for the rest of the world.

We took the train to Canterbury.

> You can only really appreciate it by being there and seeing
> it with your own eyes. It's an experience of worship just
> to walk through the cathedral. We concluded our visit by
> attending the vesper service at 5 o'clock. . . . it was breath-
> taking—especially the choir of men and boys.

At the end of the trip I summarized my impressions in six points:

I thanked those who had paved the way in previous years, men and women who opened the first doors to ecumenical dialogue and cooperation.

The ELCA has an important role to play on the world religious scene.

The trip, taken so early in our church's life, was a clear sign to these fellow Christians that we will continue our conversations with them.

We are but one part of a great family of churches, all of us linked by the Lutheran World Federation, which are serious about ecumenical relationships.

Our accent on Word and Sacrament as the primary signs of the church positions us uniquely for participation in ecumenical matters.

The task of clarifying our understanding of ministry is absolutely essential to the future of ecumenical work.

A retrospective on the first trip

It was, as I have written, a significant trip, giving important ecumenical partners the assurance that this new church would keep the pace in pursuing further dialogue. It was also important for me personally, given my prior lack of experience in international church relations.

Yet it has to be said that the timing was wrong and left an impression with the members of the ELCA that I was more interested in the excitement of traveling to exotic places around the world than in tending to the business of bringing the church together at a critical time. I, of course, could try to explain its importance; I could point out that my days abroad were only a drop in the bucket compared to the time I was spending organizing the church and visiting as many places in the ELCA as was humanly possible. For me, having taken office seven months earlier, it seemed that this church had already been up and running for some time. But in January 1988 at the grassroots they were only taking their first uncertain steps into this new arena. To see my trip highlighted on the cover and in the pages of *The Lutheran* magazine left a wrong impression. Perception is reality. The reality for the church was not a good one. The trip could have been delayed for at least six months or more. The leaders of the churches in Rome, Istanbul, Moscow, and London would surely have understood the timing.

It was, in short, a mistake on my part. A mistake that it would take a long time to overcome.

For this reason, when I was preparing to leave office in 1995, I wrote in a memorandum to my successor, unknown at the time, that he or she would be wise not to make a trip like this shortly after taking office. I also suggested that a conversation with the editor of *The Lutheran* and other communications personnel about how to handle publicity about these trips would be in order.

One thousand years of Christianity in Russia

In early June 1988 I was in Moscow again, this time for the celebration of the 1,000th anniversary of the coming of Christianity to Russia. With greater freedom and support from the government, the Russian Orthodox Church was determined to share its history with Christians from every corner of the world. Knowing that this was an unrepeatable event, I kept a detailed journal of each day's activity.

Metropolitan Filaret, the Russian bear who had entertained us so royally in January, met us at the airport. The Ukrainian Hotel, built during Stalin's era, again reminded me of my hometown hotel in the 1930s: florid walls, high ceilings, a hard bed with an equally firm pillow half the size of the bed, no air conditioning, street noises outside the window.

Given my earlier exposure to the spirituality of Orthodoxy I decided to make one of my major aims on this trip to acquaint myself with its deeper streams. My companion was Henri Nouwen's book *Behold the Beauty of the Lord: Praying with Icons.*

> I determined before coming that I would be as open-minded as possible—that I would try to plumb as deeply as I could into the spirituality of the Orthodox people. Why have we Protestants robbed ourselves of this marvelous avenue for revelation?

The opening worship was at the Church of the Epiphany. I knew it would be several hours long and that the worshippers would stand through all of it. I noticed, however, that there were chairs for visiting dignitaries. Was I one of them? I wasn't sure. I noted other Lutheran bishops from Europe in that section. But I was the new kid on the block. I played it safe and stood. After an hour and a half I began to sense the rhythm of the service. The interplay of antiphonal liturgical chant between cantor and choir drew me into the service, though I could not understand a word. I began to get a second wind.

> Just then Gunnar Staalsett, general secretary of the Lutheran World Federation, turned from his chair and motioned for me to come and take his place. I whispered to him that I was doing fine. "No," he says, "I want all of the Lutheran bishops to be seated together." Now after two hours I began to feel the flow of the service at an even deeper level. In fact, I found myself wondering how we American Christians can expect to really find communion with God in services that last less than an hour. These Russians seem to think that nothing can be left out at the risk of spoiling the rhythm of the liturgy. Maybe they have something here.

After almost three hours into the service, a hush fell over the congregation. I could hear whispers passing from one to another and the name "Pimen."

The doors opened and he emerged from one of the partitions that divided the congregation from the altar. Having met him in January, I was not surprised at his appearance. He moved very slowly, covered with colorful robes and wearing a miter. He could only shuffle forward with the help of an assistant. His mouth was drawn, his complexion pale. When he began to speak I was surprised by the vigor of his voice. His opening words were of interest to those of us who are Lutherans. He greeted "Eastern, Roman Catholic, Lutheran, and other Christians. . . ." The fact that he singled out Lutherans rather than lumping us with other Protestants was interesting. It may be indicative of the good relationship that has been built over many years between Lutherans and the Orthodox.

In the evening we were guests at a delightful string concert. I was seated between Gunnar Staalsett, the Norwegian who was general secretary of the LWF, and Andreas Aarflot, bishop of Oslo. Each number was introduced by a woman who blew away any stereotypical thoughts one might have that Russian women were not very handsome. She was ravishingly beautiful.

> Each time she appeared I could feel the Norwegian heat rise on each side of me. After one of her introductions one of the Norwegians said in a stage whisper, "She alone would have made the evening worth our visit!"

That night I wrote:

> Jet lag is such a terrible, ugly, disgusting thing. I'm wide awake at 12:30 a.m., and there's no sleep the rest of the night. There isn't even a wisp of fresh air in the room. It could just as well be a sauna. How on earth will I get through this day?

At daybreak buses took us to Zagorsk for the general meeting of the Orthodox Church. Bill Rusch and I took seats at the very back of the room. That would soon change.

With arms flailing in the air Bishop Theodocius shouted
across the rows, "Bishop Cheelstrom! Bishop Cheelstrom!
Follow me." We made our way past the Orthodox bishops
who sat facing each other at long tables and on up to the very
front where there were about twenty-five chairs for dignitaries immediately behind the table where the metropolitans
were seated who would chair the assembly. Never before have
I had such a profound feeling of being "called up higher."

I did my best to stay attentive through greeting after greeting,
most of them not translated. I jotted in my journal:

Now the long night is beginning to get to me. I am desperately trying to stay awake. Meanwhile the temperature is
rising higher and higher and the speeches are getting duller
and duller. Brevity is not the mark of Germans, Italians,
Greeks, and Armenians. How will I survive this? I notice
Aarflot get up and leave. I decide that if he can do it, so can
I. They will think that I am just making a pit stop.

The air outside isn't much cooler. This had to be the hottest
day I have ever known. (Later we learned that it had been
the hottest day on record for that day in 109 years.) I look
for a place to sit down. There are no chairs or benches anywhere. I see a shady spot over in the corner of the courtyard
and sit down on my briefcase. Behind me is an iron fence. I
lean against it and fall into a sound sleep. Half an hour later
I awaken and look over to a short flight of stairs in another
corner of the courtyard. I'll sit there for a few more minutes.
I lean back and soon I am asleep again. I'd better go back in.
Even though I'm only one of twenty-five dignitaries, someone may be wondering if I'm really that constipated!

What followed was the high point of the week in Moscow. Nine
saints of the Orthodox Church were canonized. As each name was
mentioned a picture of them was carried in and a brief word was
spoken about the life of each. Among them was a woman.

I find myself wondering if we Lutherans have gone too
far in denying the reality of the saints. The Orthodox do
not think of these as persons who do not need the grace
of God as much as others, but who have responded in
unusual ways to that grace. They become examples in
godliness. They are very much alive. They are with us in
the true church. They can help us. Have we Lutherans
come down so hard on justification by grace alone that we
have deprived ourselves of other aspects of grace? And as a
result, do we discourage a life of discipline and piety among
our people? I wonder. . . .

I continued to reflect on passages from Jeremiah and on the
writing of Nouwen.

I find I have to go back and read again the earlier chapters
in Nouwen. It has to be chewed word by word and then
gone back over again to see something you missed the first
time. And that is also why people can look at an icon over
and over again and see something new each time. And so
it is with Scripture—a new thought jumping out of an old,
familiar passage.

Over dinner the next evening I engaged in conversation with
Natasia, a teacher and one of the interpreters. "Nalalie," as she
preferred to be called, made it clear that she was not a believer. Her
primary interest was in psychological therapy. She spoke of her
father who had been wounded in World War II and left an invalid
for life. Our conversation turned to the Russian war in Afghanistan.
"It was a grave mistake," she said. She described a young student in
one of her classes, a veteran of that war. "He has no wounds, but a
wounded soul. He is an old man before his time."

Now the United States is repeating that same mistake in the
Middle East. We count the dead and the wounded. But who can
count the "wounded souls"?

Back at Zagorsk for another session of the assembly of the

Orthodox Church, I walked between lines of faithful lay folks. Most of them were elderly women with heads wrapped in scarves, the babushkas.

> I look into the faces of all those old women and think to myself again that they are as responsible for the survival of the church as the robed priests at the head of the procession. They kept praying, lighting the candles, attending worship—when others abandoned the church. . . . here may be the real beauty of the Soviet people.

On this day Billy Graham joined the dignitaries at the front.

> We shake hands and introduce ourselves. Billy is having trouble with his receiver, so I turn around and help him figure out how it works. . . .

After the session I ran into a reporter from *Newsweek* magazine. He told me that the joke among the reporters was that it was now clear who will succeed Pimen as patriarch of the Russian Orthodox Church.

> "His name is Gorbachev! Who else could give approval for a new cathedral in Moscow? Who else but Gorbachev?"

I ran into Billy Graham again at a dinner. This time he was chatting with a Methodist minister. The Methodist asked if I would use his camera to take a picture of him with Graham.

> The thought crossed my mind that I should ask him to do the same for me. But then I looked at Billy and decided that . . . it would be an imposition. Up close, Billy shows his age. . . . Does he wear some makeup to give him a tanned look? I think so. And is that dye in his hair? No doubt about it. I wonder how long he can go on. And what will happen to the movement when Billy is out of the picture? It must be a terrible burden to feel that so many are so dependent on you. . . . There are some advantages to the organized

church. Those of us in leadership could drop dead or depart the scene suddenly and the church would go on. Maybe a bit of disruption, but nothing like a movement that is so centered on a single personality.

The next day was the great public celebration of the millennium at the Bolshoi in Moscow. Seated on the stage next to Patriarch Pimen was Raisa Gorbachev.

> She is well-dressed, but looks pale and drawn. Entertaining Nancy Reagan must have taken its toll. Periodically, she leans over and speaks to Filaret. It is apparent even from a distance that there is a warm and comfortable relationship between them.

There are greetings and greetings and more greetings. Finally there is a break and everyone rushes for the bathrooms.

> Quite a sight! Outside the door stand the assistants to the bishops, holding the hats of the bishops. After taking my turn at the urinal, I look back at quite a sight. There lined up at about fifteen urinals is an array of the high and mighty and the low and ordinary. I decide that it makes no difference whether you pull up your robe or pull down your zipper; nature has a way of equalizing us when we get down to basic needs!

In the evening we were treated to a magnificent concert with full orchestra, a dozen professional choirs, and a seminary chorus of seventy voices. I was enthralled.

> Will I hear anything like this before I get to heaven? I doubt it. Many of the performers may not be believers, but how can they sing these great religious songs and not be moved by the message? Will some of them become believers tonight? I hope they all get converted before they die. We certainly will need them in the heavenly orchestras and choirs.

The next day we were invited to the Supreme Soviet, the official government chamber, at the Kremlin to meet Andrei Gromyko, the veteran Soviet foreign minister. I can only catch the essence of this experience by citing a long section from my journal.

> As I enter the chamber Metropolitan Filaret . . . is just coming up the aisle from the front. He notices me and grabs the arm of the man who is supposedly an interpreter. Through this third party Filaret is saying something about "Bishop Cheelstrom . . . a question to Gromyko . . . a speech. . . ?" I really don't understand what he is trying to tell me. Is he suggesting that I give a speech?
>
> Finally, Gromyko enters with Karchev, the minister of religious affairs. Then comes Patriarch Pimen, slowly descending the stairs. . . . He has assistants holding both arms. The contrast between the two old contemporaries is stark. Gromyko looks very vigorous and alert; Pimen appears frail and worn. Gromyko, the survivor—serving every leader from Stalin to Gorbachev in just about every important post in the government. Pimen, the sufferer—spending at least ten years in camps at hard labor and severely beaten at times. One could only wonder what thoughts ran through their respective minds.
>
> Now Gromyko says he will take questions . . . Karchev sees me and suggests to Gromyko that he call on me next. I observe that some groups outside the Soviet Union use clandestine means to smuggle religious literature into the country. Will *perestroika* mean that there will be a free flow of literature into the country and permission for the Orthodox Church to publish whatever it wishes? This has never been a problem, says Gromyko. Literature can come in—but under the principles of the government, of course.
>
> As I reflect on Gromyko's answers to the questions it becomes apparent why this man has survived so many

changes. . . . He is the consummate politician. Each time
he answers you think you are getting a straightforward
reply. But as you reflect on it you realize he has only artfully
dodged you.

When the session is over I notice that Billy Graham is in
a small group near the front. I decide to go over and get
better acquainted. Again, I am struck by how old he looks
when you get close. I thank him for his greeting at the
Bolshoi yesterday—and especially his observation that
we hear the Word of God through many avenues, including the liturgy. I tell him of my growing appreciation for
the Orthodox Church and its rich heritage of worship. He
agrees—it has been an experience of deepening respect
for him, too. I tell him of growing up where there were no
Orthodox churches and thus I had not come to know them
until very recently. He told of the same background. In fact,
he said there was a Lutheran church not far from his home.
He often wondered if those Lutherans could be Christians! Now, he told me, one of his daughters is married to a
Lutheran and they belong to one of our ELCA churches in
Florida. As he described his schedule for the next several
months, I had a feeling of sorrow from him—like a man
trapped who cannot get away from the movement he created. Maybe he doesn't feel that way himself. But I couldn't
help but wonder.

I notice Gromyko is still standing at the front, greeting
people who want to shake his hand. I decide it's an opportunity one should not pass up, so I join the line. When I get to
him I say, "I greet you from the Lutheran Christians in the
United States of America and the Caribbean." The man next
to him starts to translate, but Gromyko interrupts him. There
is laughter. I wonder what it's about. Kishkovsky (an Orthodox priest friend from the U.S.) says that Gromyko told the
interpreter he didn't need to interpret such plain English!

The last day of the millennium celebration was to be its high point—an outdoor service at the Danilov Monastery. Now the weather had changed and it was bitterly cold, no more than the high forties fahrenheit. The service went on and on and on. I was especially moved to watch the faithful receive the sacrament.

> Each makes confession to the priest. Sometimes it is a rather lengthy conversation. The supplicant bows as the priest drapes his stole over their head and pronounces absolution. Then the priest dips a spoon into the cup and lifts a piece of the wine-soaked bread to the mouth.

There is much for which one might criticize the Russian Orthodox Church. Its survival for one thousand years, however, testifies to the deep spirituality that I discovered on this sojourn.

A memorable visit to East Germany

I had agreed to stop in East Germany on the trip back to the United States. Feeling completely drained after the events in Moscow, I wondered about the wisdom of tacking that visit on to our trip. But once I arrived at the home of Bishop Johannes Hempel and his wife in Dresden I realized the importance of it. I felt almost overcome by the sense of gratitude they exude over our coming. I begin to realize how much it must mean in a country like this, where the faith is suppressed on every hand, to have believers visit from the West.

> They told us we must sign the guest book. I began to understand . . . how repressive this country is. I must enter not only my name, but my place and date of birth, information about my position, my passport number, etc. The Hempels told me that periodically they must bring their guest book to the police station to have them check it.

> After visits to the city and the church offices, the Hempels took us to their place in the country. It was a barn converted into a

summer residence. He removed several casual chairs from the home and placed them on the patio. Then he heaved a huge sigh of relief. Here, said Hempel, they were free to talk. He assumed that their driver and gardener were paid by the state to report any suspicious activity. On a walk out into the countryside Hempel stopped at a high vista. Here at this spot, he said, away from any threat that their words would be heard, he and his son had a very deep conversation about the meaning of life.

After our return to the bishop's home in the city we shared wine and exchanged gifts.

> I can't believe how my feeling has changed since last night. To think that I might have missed this! What better way to end the trip than to be with these remarkable strangers-become-friends.

Those who have not experienced the suppression of the former East Germany will never know what it was like to walk from East to West Germany.

> Freedom! There may be much wrong with life in America; we may have more than our share of problems; we may have much to correct. But I wouldn't trade.

After my return to Chicago I wrote to Billy Graham suggesting that he and I might be catalysts in bringing mainline Christians and evangelical conservatives closer together.

> For many years I have had the growing conviction that there are many believers in our churches who share similar convictions but have no good means to express them. I would describe them as I often describe myself—evangelical conservatives with a radical social conscience.

I proposed a very private meeting that would include such persons as: Carl Henry, Mark Hatfield, Martin Marty, Tom Skinner, Coretta Scott King, Lowell Erdahl, Cardinal Joseph Bernadin,

Ron Sider, and Paul Simon. I added that we might also include a respected scientist in the group.

Graham replied a few days later, stating that he was honored to be asked but certain that his board would not allow him to be involved in the proposed meeting because of his heavy preaching responsibility and his advancing age. "I thank God for the burden he has given you and pray for wisdom and strength for you as you set it in motion."

It would be several more years and as a part of my work with the National Council of Churches before I could pick up work toward this vision.

Partnerships around the world

Now I want to bring my readers along as I revisit some of those other ships, some of those other waters. I want to give you some perspective on how important it is for all of us to break out of those smaller ponds. I want to accent our membership in this larger family of faith.

Madagascar

Just days after I was elected in May 1987 I received an invitation to visit Madagascar in September 1989. It was the centennial year of work in that country by Lutheran missionaries from the United States. I decided that it would also be good to visit Namibia on the same trip. Corinne was able to travel with me.

I found that the church in Madagascar had its own unique character. Mysticism runs deep in the psyche of these people. It was clear that missionaries had also been influenced by it. Speaking in tongues, healing services, accent on the work of the Holy Spirit—all were apparent during my visit.

Two memories stand out from this trip. One was the unusual influence of a native Christian woman, Nenilava. By this time she was an elderly person. Though the church did not ordain women,

she was such a commanding personality that even the most prominent men in the church, including a medical doctor, went to her for
advice and counsel.

We visited her at her home. She was unable to walk. The aura in
her presence, however, was overwhelming. Like a Deborah from
Old Testament times, she simply commanded respect and awe. We
had a most satisfying conversation with her.

A celebration of the centennial at the old Fort Dauphin included
a parade down the main street. All of the ordained clergy were to
march in procession. Corinne had her clerical collar along. The
missionaries suggested she join us. The male clergy hardly knew
what to think of this—an ordained woman among them! But they
accepted her warmly and were even a bit bemused to see her in
their parade. Not many years later, that church began to ordain
women. I would like to believe that Corinne's participation in that
parade may have played a small part in bringing them to accept
women into the ordained ministry.

Namibia

Known at the time as Southwest Africa it would become today's
Namibia. When we visited it was under the oppressive thumb of
the South African government, its neighbor to the south. Early
German settlers had transformed parts of the country into reflections of their native land. If you were dropped into Windhoek, the
capitol city, and had not been told where you were, you might think
this was a lovely city in Bavaria.

It did not take long, however, to discover that the black majority
in Southwest Africa was on the verge of revolt. The presence of the
South African military was everywhere. Roads were clogged with
armored vehicles. In the middle were the churches, trying to bring
peaceful change. Surely one of the towering figures I met during
my eight years in office was Kleopas Dumeni, bishop of the church
in northern Namibia. His silvery hair stood in stark contrast to

his unusually black skin. He exuded both love and authority at the same time. He lived with constant threats to his life.

As we drove around the northern part of the country where Dumeni was bishop, we noted that whenever we got off the main paved roads there was a pickup truck always in front of us. We learned later that this vehicle was there to protect us in case a bomb had been planted in the roadway. It was sobering to think that others were so willing to sacrifice themselves for our safety.

Anna, one of Dumeni's daughters, had been killed just prior to our visit when a bomb blew up in a bank lobby. After one meeting we noted that the bishop and his wife were standing by a fresh grave behind the church. We learned that it was Anna's grave. Corinne and I could hear them singing. Having lost our son Andrew only a few years earlier, we felt drawn to them. We joined hands and surrounded Anna's grave. We listened as they continued to pray and sing. Though we did not understand their language, it made no difference. Four heavy, grieving hearts from different continents of the world were melded in oneness in our sorrow and hope.

One of our traveling companions in Namibia was Ralston Deffenbaugh, an attorney from the ELCA who had played a key role in helping indigenous leaders to forge a constitution for the country. Later he became head of Lutheran Immigration and Refugee Service (LIRS).

The Baltic States

In May 1990 I was invited to visit the Baltic States. Corinne accompanied me on this trip as well. The timing was critical. The Soviet Union was breaking up and the churches were in turmoil. They needed words of encouragement and promises of support from the ELCA.

Shortly after we checked into the hotel in Tallinn, Estonia, the phone rang. A woman's voice, heavy with a Russian accent, asked, "You vant a voman?" I replied, "No thanks" and hung up. Corinne asked who it was. When I explained it to her we had a hearty laugh.

It is the only time in all of my millions of miles of travel that I have been propositioned. Is that a compliment?

The foreign minister in Estonia told us that his country had announced its independence. He predicted that the entire Union of Soviet Socialist Republics would break up into separate nations. In Moscow and St. Petersburg everything seemed to be in disrepair. In Latvia and Estonia it seemed better, due, the foreign minister claimed, to the Lutheran work ethic that pervaded in those countries.

In the midst of the upheaval the churches were experiencing renewal. There were so many requests for baptism and confirmation that pastors could scarcely keep up with them.

Nicaragua

Among my companions on a trip to Central America was Rafael Malpica Padilla, then bishop of the ELCA's Caribbean Synod and later executive director of the Division for Global Mission. Malpica's fluency in Spanish was an asset on this trip.

Because of the turmoil caused by President Ronald Reagan's support of the right-wing governments of Central America, travel to that part of the world was dangerous. Reagan had named Nicaragua an "evil empire." At a Jesuit university I spoke candidly to the priest who was head of the school. I asked about some of the negative characteristics of President Daniel Ortega and the Sandinistas. He agreed that there were problems, but then quickly reminded me that our United States was also born in a revolution, that the press had been muzzled during both world wars, and that the Japanese had been ill-treated during World War II. I had to agree that the situations were not entirely dissimilar.

In my journal I describe a meeting with one of the Christian base communities in Managua:

> We're in a very simple room in one of the poorest neighborhoods in the city. There are about fifteen to twenty people with us, sitting in a circle. Most are women. They

sing. They tell their stories. An older, heavy-set woman
says three of her sons have been killed in the war. I've only
lost one son. How can I even imagine her sorrow! There
are angry remarks about U.S. imperialism. We listen. They
sing some more. No matter how angry they are at the U.S.
government they do not seem to transfer that hate to those
who come to visit them. At the end of the evening they pass
out deep fat-fried soy and lettuce pastries. Do I eat one?
I can't be rude. I take one and nibble at the edges. I can't
afford to get sick at the very beginning of the trip.

At the U.S. embassy we met with officials who played the party
line, fully supportive of the U.S. government's opposition to the
Sandinistas. But I was reminded by local pastors that some embassy
staff confessed privately that they had feelings that the United
States was on the wrong side in Central America. Such is the cap-
tivity of embassy staff around the world.

After much uncertainty and confusion we learned that we would
be able to meet with President Daniel Ortega at a country club
where he was to address writers from around the world. Here is
how I describe it in my journal:

We are ushered through the crowd, down to the lower level
of the central building, and into a small waiting room that
looks out on to a sunken garden. We wait . . . and wait.
After a while we see a soldier come by the window with
a mine detector. He carefully goes through the garden
outside our window, poking the detector under the leaves
of plants.

We wait some more. [We are told that] this is the room
where Henry Kissinger met with Ortega when the Central
American Commission visited here several years ago. The
story around here is that Kissinger asked Ortega to leave
the room at one point in order that the delegation from the
U.S. could discuss its strategy. For a guest to ask his host to

leave was regarded as a very rude gesture and actions like this only intensify a sense of anger toward Americans.

Suddenly Ortega enters. He shakes hands with all of us and takes a seat next to me. He's a very handsome man. Slight build. Dressed in green khakis, open shirt, light jacket. He welcomes us. I tell him about our delegation, give him a description of the ELCA, inform him of our support for the Central American Peace Plan, of our opposition to arms aid either to the Contras by the U.S. or to other groups from the Soviet Union. I tell him of our work through the LWF in Central America and of our visit to Monsignor Mandragon. He listens with great intensity.

He responds very softly and deliberately. He says he has nothing against the Catholic religion or the followers of Catholicism. He says his conflict is with the hierarchy. He wonders why our Lutheran church does not do more in Nicaragua. He seems in no hurry to leave.

Ironically, I am writing this account just a bit more than twenty years after the visit to Nicaragua. Ortega has morphed into a very different man from the fellow we met in 1988, the left-wing revolutionary and darling of intellectuals around the world. Now he is president again and acting just as rigidly and oppressively as his right-wing opponents had acted. Such are the affairs of the world.

El Salvador

Our flight to El Salvador was supposed to arrive at seven-thirty in the evening. Instead, we got there just after midnight. Bishop Medardo Gomez was there to meet us and usher us quickly through customs. Little did I realize at the time that this would be the beginning of a lifelong relationship with one of the most remarkable, courageous men I have ever known. Whenever I'm asked to point to one of the most memorable aspects of my years as presiding bishop, I invariable mention my times with Medardo Gomez.

The drive from the airport into San Salvador is about twenty miles. It was along this road that Bishop Gomez was captured a couple of years earlier and held under threat of death for three days. It was also along this road that the four American nuns were murdered. That night I wrote:

> I guess I should feel some fear. But somehow I don't.

We went to Resurrection Lutheran Church where Gomez served as pastor. The witness of believers was powerful. Later we visited the Roman Catholic Cathedral and the tomb of Archbishop Romero. The blood was still on the floor at the place where he was shot. We also learned that for many people Gomez was now the one who fills the role of Romero in the minds of the common people.

Over dinner we were joined by Phil Anderson, an ELCA pastor, and Kirsten, a Danish lay worker. They are the LWF representatives, along with Phil's wife, in El Salvador. They spoke of the danger they live with—and the potential dangers our delegation faced. If there were any trouble, it would likely be from a bomb planted someplace where we might visit. They tell us of a Swiss citizen who was shot by the military just two days ago in the area near the refugee camp we will visit in a couple of days

The next day we drove far out into the countryside to visit a refugee camp. "We are now in the war zone," Gomez says as we cross a bridge. I'm beginning to understand that there are no safe places in this country. I wrote of one incident:

> Some military pull us over. They ask for our papers. Gomez and his people seem quite unfazed. Cecelia, head of the social work of the church and quite a woman in her own right, is very casual about it all. We examine flowers along the road as we wait.

As we moved on, the conversation with Gomez picked up again. What happens to this small, fragile church with all of its programs if you should die or be killed? I ask. In other circumstances that might

seem a rude question. But not here. Gomez answered very deliberately. "I am praying that God will spare me for at least two more
years. Then the programs we have started should be on firm ground.
Then the work can go on, even if something were to happen to me."
I'm beginning to understand why he's held in such high regard.

Our destination was a village called Los Ranchos. The people
had been driven out by the military because they were suspected
of collaborating with the guerrillas. They fled to Honduras. Just a
week earlier a procession of them had been allowed to return.

As we entered it looked for all the world like a war zone. Everything was in shambles. Here and there in the woods one can see a
family huddled under a plastic cover. There were a few utensils here
and there. Scraggly chickens and ducks wandered about. Mud and
more mud. On the side of the church are scrawled the words: "Viva
las Lutherana Iglesia"—Long live the Lutheran church. Though
mostly Catholic, they were grateful for what our church had done.

As the people gathered it began to rain harder. I was asked to
greet them.

> I tell them that I was baptized as a small baby, but now God
> was baptizing me again. They understand and break out in
> spontaneous applause. I pronounce the benediction over
> them. Hats come off the men. Everyone makes the sign of
> the cross. This is a family of God in the most indescribable
> situation. I feel hope here, unlike any place I have been in a
> long time.

At another village we visited more refugees. It was beginning to
get chilly. The female head of the community offered us a hot, sweet
coconut drink and a cob of field corn. I wonder about the sanitation, but it has clearly been boiled. No matter about sanitation. It
tastes wonderful. I felt marvelous hospitality in a place where they
can hardly afford to give me this food.

Gomez seemed in no hurry to return to the city. It was getting
dark. After being stuck in the mud twice, we finally got to a better

road. By that time it was pitch dark. Later I wrote about the next frightening moments:

> Suddenly Carol Smith [ELCA communications officer who was traveling with us] lets out a gasp—"Oh no!" I look up and see a group of young soldiers barricading the road. Suddenly all of the images rise before my eyes—stories I've heard earlier in the day about shootings and targeting foreigners. I feel a pull in the pit of my stomach.
>
> Since my socks were wet and I had taken them off I decide to put them on slowly and give myself a chance to think—and pray. I pray for a deep sense of complete surrender to the will of God. The fear recedes. As I move out of the van I chide myself for not keeping on my clerical shirt. Even though it was soaking wet and I would surely have got a bad cold, it might have been my salvation right now. Maybe there's a devout young Catholic among the soldiers who would have mercy on me, thinking I'm a priest.
>
> Bishop Malpica asks one of the young soldiers if he can step down the road a bit and take a leak. No problem, says the young man. Malpica tells me that they tell him to watch out for the "land mines." I feel alarm. Later we understand that they may have been referring to "cow pies."
>
> I look into the faces of the soldiers. Most appear to be not more than fifteen or sixteen. I see their fingers on the triggers of their M-16s. I think again of how old men require young men to fight their wars and die in their places.

Over breakfast the next morning our group discussed the encounter with the soldiers:

> I tell of my absence of fear most of that time. I wonder if it may have something to do with the loss of Andrew. After that trauma, is there really anything else to fear?

In the afternoon we visited an orphanage where several hundred children left parentless by the civil war are cared for. The buildings are ramshackle, but the love for the children is palpable.

> Bishop Gomez asks Bishop Malpica and me to come forward. We sit on a bench in the front of the chapel and the children sing to us. I cannot hold back the tears. Malpica translates one of the songs:
>
>> "Why, mother, are so many walking without shoes? Why do I always have to eat salty food? Why does my brother look green and why is his belly full of parasites? Where is my father?"
>
> And another:
>
>> "Dear Daddy Jesus, why don't you answer? My mother prays to you and my daddy doesn't come. Why?"
>
> As they sing two small boys snuggle up to me. One puts his head on my lap and wraps his arms around my leg. Now the tears really flow!

Over dinner that evening I conversed with two lawyers. Working for human rights, both knew they lived under a sentence of death. Seven of their colleagues had been shot by death squads in the past two years. One of them described an incident with the police:

> A death squad entered his home, pinned him to the floor with a gun to his head, and told him that if he didn't stop handling human rights cases his fifteen-year-old daughter would be raped and he would be shot.

I wrote a letter that night to Mary and Chris and mailed it after I returned to Chicago:

> They thanked me for coming. They said that when prominent persons like me come to El Salvador it makes it safer for them because the police and the military are less likely to harass them. This has been a very hard trip—but words like that make it seem worthwhile.

The next day we visited the American embassy. As in Managua, it is like a fortress.

> What a sad, pathetic feeling comes over me when I think of how hated we are in places like this. The personnel are very congenial. I go out of my way to thank them for the difficult work they do on our behalf.

> The head of the American embassy staff gives us a briefing on the situation. It is what we should have expected. It follows exactly the State Department line. It is optimistic. I keep thinking of all I have seen and heard these past several days. I look around the room at other staff persons and wonder what they *really* are thinking about the situation. What would they say if they could be totally honest?

When Gomez and I emphasized that it is the church's mission to do relief work, we are told that it only plays into the hands of the guerrillas.

A visit with the well-known priest Jon Sobrino was another highlight of this trip. Known for his strong accent on liberation theology, Sobrino differed from many others in that school of thought in that his emphasis was rooted in sin and grace, making him a good ally for our Lutherans in El Salvador and elsewhere.

> We can learn from the poor, he says. God speaks to us through them. When we believe we have heard a word from God telling us what to do, we can "sin boldly"—take a risk for the cause of justice, knowing that we live in grace and forgiveness.

In the evening we were entertained by the Gomez family in their home. The meal was simple but delicious.

> I ask if I can have a prayer of blessing on their home before we leave for the hotel. It is a holy moment. In this situation one can only wonder if we will see some of these people again.

Tonight Matthew 25 seems right, but so hard to read—"I was
hungry . . . thirsty . . . naked . . . in prison." "When did you
see me?" Today, today I saw you. . . .

Before our group left El Salvador, Gomez and I were to meet with
the head of the government, Jose Duarte. But he was too ill to see
us. So it was agreed that we would see the second in command, Vice
President Castillo Claramont, at the national palace—their White
House. The driver tried different streets but all are blocked. We
decided there is only one thing to do—approach one of the barri-
cades and explain to the military police that we had an appointment
with the vice president. I described the next scene in these words:

> We park about a block from the soldiers. The street is abso-
> lutely abandoned. Four of us agree to approach the soldiers.
> It's an eerie feeling to walk down this street with eyes on
> us from buildings along the way. The soldiers glare back at
> us. We approach the commander of the group and explain
> our purpose. He seems quite gentle and understanding. He
> instructs us to go to the far side of the area and explains
> how we can get in.

After I outlined the purpose of our visit, Claramont, like the
embassy staff, insisted that the guerrillas are communists and that
we are only aiding their cause. When I ask about Romero, he says
he was no doubt a kind and compassionate man, but also naïve, a
used man.

At a meeting with ecumenical leaders I learned about the complexities of working with the government. Religious groups that
cooperated with the government, such as the fundamentalists
and the Jehovah's Witnesses, got preferential treatment for speedy
building permits in choice places. Roman Catholics, Lutherans, and
Baptists, who called for human rights, faced endless delays.

On our last night it was time for a party, for an exchange of gifts,
for greetings.

> It's clear that we have meant much to them. And how can
> I measure what they've meant to me! In my comments I
> tell them that what I have seen here—hope shining in the
> darkness.

As we landed in Miami on U.S. soil the next day. . .

> One thought grips me—that I feel so bad about feeling so
> good to be back on U.S. soil.

> What a world. Lord, have mercy. I can never be quite the
> same again. . . .

After my return to Chicago I issued a statement in which I criticized the support of the United States for the Contras in Central
America.

> "We are deeply concerned about Central America. We
> have asked our government to oppose military aid to the
> contras. . . . we do not believe the conflict will be solved by
> military means" ("ELCA News," 8/31/88).

Several months later I went to Washington, D.C., with a representative group of religious leaders to meet with Secretary of
State James Baker and his chief assistant Margaret Tutweiler. I sat
directly across from Baker. Each of us in our group shared with
them what we were hearing from our church leaders in Central
America; namely, that military forces supported by our government
were abusing innocent men, women, and children. I can still recall
vividly how Baker stiffened, looked around at us and said, "Our
contacts tell us that this is not true." The attitude of both Baker and
Tutweiler was cold and dismissive.

Some years later, reports coming out of El Salvador confirmed
that what we had heard was true. Graves were unearthed where
bodies of innocent children killed by the military forces were
found. The sorry mess called "The Iran Contra Affair" came to light
and the complicity of the Reagan administration was apparent.

These times with Medardo Gomez bonded us forever as bothers in Christ. In June 1990 I wrote to Corinne from Geneva and told of Gomez's arrival for the meeting of the LWF Executive Committee: ". . . we have been through quite a bit together in ways that transcend language—and I know we both feel it."

Back to El Salvador

I had no plans to return to El Salvador as soon as I did. At the LWF assembly in Curitiba, Brazil, Medardo Gomez approached me with a request. Having been living in exile in neighboring Guatemala, he said he felt it was time to return to his native land. He went on to say that it would be good if I would accompany him.

My initial reaction was one of caution. Though I knew that the civil war was less intense, I also realized that the situation was still dangerous. I said to Medardo that I was not afraid to die, but asked if there were any reason to be concerned. Medardo's disarming response was one I should have expected: "We will have to trust God." I agreed to accompany him.

One of the highlights of the trip was to meet Emily Green, a young woman who was in Sunday school in St. Peter, Minnesota, when I was pastor of that congregation. She came from one of our strong families in the congregation. Now she was in El Salvador as a volunteer in one of the orphanages. "I feel that the seeds that were planted long ago are bearing fruit," I wrote in my journal.

Though I felt secure during my visit, I left with a heart made heavy over my concern for Medardo.

> I see a sign above the terminal—"San Salvador." How odd that this troubled place should be called "The Savior."

> I see bunkers and soldiers along the runway opposite the terminal. I haven't had a moment of fear down here. But I fear for Medardo. On the way to the airport I looked at two of his children who went with us in the van and prayed that they will not lose their daddy.

To England, Germany, Scandinavia, and the Middle East
In late 1990 I traveled with Edmund Browning, presiding bishop
of the Episcopal Church to England, Germany, and Scandinavia
during the Advent season. Though I had been to England, Browning had never been to the Lutheran centers in Germany, Norway,
Sweden, and Finland. Our wives accompanied us. The hospitality
in the Anglican and Lutheran centers was warm and genuine.

Surely the highlight of the trip for me was to preach at the Lund
Cathedral in Sweden on December 9, 1990. Here, as I have noted
earlier, is where my maternal great grandparents had worshiped. I
preached on the text from Malachi 4.

Pointing to the words of Malachi, the prophet who spoke to a
people who had forgotten their responsibilities for worship and
generosity, I reminded the listeners that we lived in a similar world,
one in which we have lost hope. But the message of the prophet is
clear. When we forsake God, God does not forsake us.

> The prophet would remind us that the way to restoration
> begins with repentance. But it does not end there. We need
> to hear that other important word from Malachi—the word
> of hope. It is often at the point of our deepest despair that
> we are finally ready to hear God's promise of hope for the
> future. It has been my experience that one most often finds
> hope where it is least expected.

Corinne and Patti Browning returned to the United States while
Ed and I flew to the Middle East where we were part of a delegation
of U.S. church leaders who would meet with religious and political
leaders to try head off what became the first war with Iraq under
George H.W. Bush. Our delegation fanned out in different directions: Gaza, Israel, Syria, Jordan, and Iraq.

The words I had spoken in Lund came to life in the harried streets
of Gaza and Jerusalem, the places I had been asked to visit. We
made little impact. The depth of animosity was nearly impossible to
describe. In a letter to my family following the trip I wrote:

The hate one feels from Jew to Arab and Arab to Jew is so intense that one wonders if reconciliation is possible without even greater bloodshed. Fortunately, there are some small groups here and there that are trying to bring some understanding to the chaos.

The Arabs are completely befuddled by American foreign policy. For years and years the Palestinian Arabs have wondered why we have allowed the Israeli government to take over more and more of their land—land they have lived on for many, many generations. Why have we not sent our armed forces to defend them, as we have Kuwait? They do not admire [Saddam] Hussein. But when compared to the Americans, they wonder if he is really that much worse. What can one say to them?

Eastern Europe

In early December 1991 Corinne and I traveled to Eastern Europe—Austria, Czechoslovakia, and Hungary. In Czechoslovakia we met with President Vaclav Havel.

When Havel came in there was a stir of excitement in the room. I was stunned by how common he looked. He is short—maybe five feet, seven inches at most. He was dressed very casually—slacks, open shirt, pullover sweater, and jacket. A president of a country? We sat directly across from one another. He greeted me, but then seemed at a loss for words. I told him a bit about our church, our relationship with the Lutheran Church in Slovakia, commended him for his fine speech at the U.S. Congress, and suggested that it was a model that made a strong impact on our country, and assured him of our prayers.

Havel obviously understood English perfectly, but answered in Czech. He thanked me for my assurance of prayer, and indicated that he received it not just for himself but for all of his people.

There were big demonstrations going on at that time so he apologized that he could not visit with us longer. We said we understood and were on our way.

In Bratislava we met with the head of the new parliament. He was a devout Roman Catholic and had been part of the underground church during the Communist era. Though he was very gracious, I found myself wondering if he had the needed skill to handle his role.

> Can one step into such a responsible position without
> significant political background? It was the same question I
> wondered about when I was with Havel.

In Budapest, Hungary, we met with leaders of the Lutheran churches in Yugoslavia. Their land was so war-torn, so unsafe, that we could not even think of going there. So they came to us. We could see the war unfold in front of us as the three leaders of the Lutheran churches in Yugoslavia argued with each other. The head of the Slovakian-background church stressed the need for unity in the country. His church had suffered little.

But the head of the German church in Serbia gave a completely different account. His people had suffered greatly. Many had been killed, including women and children. He pleaded for help. He could not understand how the United States could be involved in defending Kuwait against Sadam Hussien and then look the other way when his people were so oppressed. He surmised that it must be because they had no oil. And he was probably right, though the United States did eventually get involved.

In Romania we saw a country that was completely ruined after years of Communism. Everything, I wrote in my journal, seemed wired together and ready to fall apart. The Lutherans were fleeing the country—the Hungarians to Hungary and the Germans to Germany. And that in spite of the fact that the Germans had been there for more than eight hundred years. When I suggested to Bishop Klein, who had just lost his wife to cancer, that it must be very depressing at times, he looked at me with deep sorrow and said, "Yes, it really is."

The most emotional part of the visit to Romania was at an orphanage where some seventy abandoned children lived. When we walked in the door many of them rushed up to us and clung to our legs, eager for the slightest show of affection. Under the Communists abortions were illegal and doctors were imprisoned for doing them. Women would have their babies and flee from the hospital, leaving the child for others to care for. Now abortions were permitted again and there were four for every live birth.

I wondered,

> Sad . . . but what is the answer? Is it better to allow abortions—in the early stages of pregnancy? Or should they be brought to full term and birth, to be neglected in orphanages and starved for affection? Where is Solomon?

Corinne was along at our own expense. We did not feel justified in having the church pay for her, even though in other church bodies it was unheard of that the spouse of the head of the church would pay her own way. We simply looked on it as a good time to be together and to see an interesting part of the world.

India: a sensual, troubling experience

In March 1992 Corinne and I visited India with several other ELCA staff persons. After our return I wrote:

> No matter what I had heard from others, one had to go there to experience what it is like. . . . it assails all the senses. The exquisite beauty of the Taj Mahal. The filth of Calcutta. The beautiful flowers. The sight of people picking through garbage heaps. I have found it hard to put all this together. To fly from Delhi and be here in our comfortable condo in Illinois and then fly off to Albuquerque a couple of days later for the bishop's conference—it's almost more

that I can bear. These stark contrasts between the haves and
the have-nots. And where does one start to rectify all this?
Does one just give?

I noted that everywhere we went in India they begged and
begged. First we would be honored, then asked. They would present us with framed documents. I soon learned to look beyond the
first paragraph—down to the last one. They all began with praise—
usually excessive and flowery. But eventually they got around to the
main point—give us this, give us that.

> As one looked around there was surely a need for what they
> asked for. But again and again I found myself asking if this
> is the way—just to give. . . . one wonders. One could invest
> a million dollars on one street corner in Calcutta or Guntur
> and wonder what lasting impact it would have.

I had to ask myself how one puts all this into our appeal to
people to support global mission. Is this how to use the limited
resources of the church?

> I only know that India has left me with more questions
> than answers.

A visit to Ethiopia

Though I scarcely had time or energy for it, leaders of the church in
Ethiopia pleaded with me to visit them. A large issue for them was
the confiscation of church-owned property by the socialist government. The presence of the Lutheran World Federation in Ethiopia
had been substantial.

I visited with both government leaders and the U.S. ambassador
while I was there. I laid out a strong case for return of the properties to the church.

I saw no evidence of any moves on the part of the government
while I was there. I learned later, however, that my visit had been
significant and that it may have been a key factor in the government's
eventual agreement to return those properties to the church.

At the final banquet, attended by government and church leaders, I had an opportunity to give a brief greeting. I mentioned the
emotional ties I felt with Ethiopia because of my great grandparents
in Sweden who had contributed to the support of Onesimus, an
Ethiopian who had been educated in Sweden and who returned to
his native land to become the chief founder of the Mekane Jesus
Church. The Ambassador from Sweden spoke to me later and said
she was very touched by the story.

The place of the ELCA in the larger Christian world

In this chapter I have tried to give the reader a small taste of my
experiences beyond our own church. It is easy to forget that our
church cuts a wider swath in the larger Christian world than most
members realize. But, more importantly, we need to keep these
doors open for our own benefit. Much as we treasure the gift of our
own history and the way we understand the essence of the Christian faith, we have much to learn from other Christian churches.
Every contact with these brothers and sisters in Christ helps us to
realize that the Spirit of God is at work in ways we could not even
begin to imagine.

Chapter 13

Keeping the ship on course: second term as presiding bishop (1991–1995)

The 1991 Orlando Assembly

A surprise at pre-assembly meetings

As is customary at a Churchwide Assembly, the Church Council and the Conference of Bishops met prior to the formal opening of the assembly. The usual agenda for these sessions is to make certain these important groups are up to speed on the assembly schedule and to review the issues that might call for their special attention.

This time, however, these meetings evolved into something quite unexpected. Yes, the usual business was covered. But at both sessions there was an eruption of anger against editor Edgar Trexler and *The Lutheran* magazine for what some called the "negative slant" of many articles in recent issues. Christine Grumm, chair of the Church Council stated that the tenor of some articles maligned all leaders of the church for being irresponsible in handling the finances of the church. Others voiced their concern that these articles undermined the unity of the church.

The same scenario unfolded when the Conference of Bishops convened. At the conclusion of my report there was a time for questions and dialogue. At the very end Bishop William Lazareth rose and lambasted *The Lutheran* for "regurgitating stories like one might expect from cheap, third class, secular publications."

At its meeting the next morning the Church Council passed a strong resolution calling for review of editorial policy.

Now some twenty years has passed. As we look back on these incidents it's fair to ask: Were the Church Council members and the bishops unduly critical of Trexler? Did he in fact do damage to the image of the church? Or was his a prophetic voice, the view of one who saw coming what others did not want to acknowledge?

The opening of the assembly

"Here it is," I wrote in my journal,

> the day we've been looking forward to for so long. I must have been asked a hundred times, "Are you ready?" I tell each one that it's like preaching. You use the time you have to prepare as well as you can and then comes the moment when you must go to the pulpit and let it fly. So in a little more than an hour the opening service will begin. I've gone over and over the sermon. I think I'm as ready as I can be. Now I pray that the Spirit will take what I have and wing it into their hearts.

This assembly would center itself in the Lord's Prayer. In my sermon at the opening worship I used the text from Matthew 6:7–13, focusing on how remarkable it is that Jesus taught us to use such a familiar term as "Father" to address God in prayer.

> Whenever we pray this prayer, we are agreeing with Jesus that the God we believe in is a God of intense grace and mercy, a God who cares as dearly for us as any parent cares for a child, a God who will sacrifice life for the sake of the child.

After referring to the role of mothers in *Oliver Twist, East of Eden,* and the life of Augustine (it was his commemoration day), I suggested that what Jesus is telling us in the Lord's Prayer is that God can only be known in this intimate way through Christ himself.

> We are invited into the family. We are Native American and Asian and Caucasian and Hispanic and African American. We are American-born and foreign-born. We are male and female. We are old and middle-aged and young. We are all of that and more

> But most important of all, we are the children of God. We are born into one human family. We have been through the same waters of Baptism. And now, as we embark on these days together, we are invited to the family table. . . . God, like a loving and forgiving parent, is here to welcome us again. . . .

Reelection to a second term

Any doubt I had about a second term was erased when David Hardy announced the results of the first ballot. I needed 75 percent and 750 votes. I had 74.1 percent and 741 out of 1,000 ballots cast. William Lazareth was second with 37 votes. I was easily re-elected on the second ballot with more than 86 percent of ballots cast.

That night I wrote in my journal:

> So how do I feel? Relieved. Even though I felt confident it would turn out that way, there's a certain level of anxiety that persists until it's over. It's clear that people really do long to get beyond some of the negative spirit that has pervaded in some places. I think this assembly will be a solid turning point in that regard.

> One thing that troubles me is that no "heir apparent" came to the surface. Those who got a few votes—Lazareth, Sauer, Lundblad—are not leaders for the future; the first two, too old, and Lundblad has only a very limited following. Will God make it clear who should step in four years from now?

A successful assembly

By all accounts, Orlando was a very positive event for the ELCA. *The Lutheran* described the difference between this assembly and the previous one in Chicago in 1989. If editor Trexler shared some of the negative views he had been reporting prior to the assembly, it seems that he, along with others, was expecting a better future.

> Two years ago . . . the joints and seams of the merger hammered out by three Lutheran church bodies were plainly visible. But this year with new-found unity, the delegates seemed ready to smooth the rough edges and make the union work. With courtesy and decorum they sought compromises to diffuse explosive issues. With few exceptions, votes did not split along regional or predecessor-church lines. Working their way through the full-platter agenda, high-spirited participants resolutely aimed at leaving Orlando united (10/2/91).

I give major credit for the success of Orlando to the leaders of the churchwide units. They had learned many good lessons from our first assembly. Presentations were superbly well-done. I was intensely proud of all of them, including my own staff and the staff of the Office of the Secretary.

For the first time, this assembly used electronic voting machines, with a device at each voting member's fingertips. We had our concerns about how it would work. In a short time, however, everyone seemed completely at ease with the system. It speeded up the process, not only for elections, but also for voting on the adoption of many other matters. The ELCA Office for Communications reported that the chief technician for the company that provided the system had worked with a large number of conventions of various kinds. He said, "Bishop Chilstrom is the easiest person he has ever worked with on electronic balloting." I should have signed on the spot to moonlight at other conventions!

We brought recommendations for restructuring to the assembly and they were approved. These changes would make it possible to do our work within budget expectations and also to eliminate some of the duplications the Committee for the New Lutheran Church (CNLC) and the Constituting Convention had created for the church.

In my report to the assembly I projected optimism. And for good reason. Our churchwide staff was functioning effectively. In the weak spots we were making good replacements. I reported that membership in the church had been up slightly in 1990. After so many years of decline, including in our predecessor churches, I suggested that this might be "a temporary blip on the screen," but hoped that it was a first sign of the beginning of a new era.

The one ominous harbinger of things to come was that though income had increased again in local congregations, the receipts to the synods and the churchwide organization had actually declined. Income to the churchwide organization would remain flat for the next twenty years. And membership would decline by more than half a million. I could not have believed this in 1991 at Orlando.

There had been growing complaints about social statements. There seemed to be an impression that they originated with the churchwide staff. I reminded delegates in my report that social statements almost always originate in response to resolutions from synods. I also emphasized that social statements do not bind the conscience of any ELCA member.

We had many major challenges to address at the Orlando assembly:

"Ecumenism: The Vision of the ELCA," refined and much-improved since the last assembly, passed with enthusiastic support. I give major credit to William Rusch. Whatever other difficulties he posed for some in the ELCA, in this task he and his staff did a superb job. The statement became a model for other denominations and churches around the world.

"The Church in Society: a Lutheran Perspective" was another notable action at Orlando. It stated unabashedly that this church would not shrink from its responsibility to address critical social and ethical questions.

The assembly took a stance opposing the death penalty, recognizing that certain crimes might deserve imprisonment without parole.

Adopting the "Statement on Abortion" stretched to the limit my patience as presider. The same was true for the assembly. There were a few voting members who persisted in bringing up minor points in the document, sometimes over and over again. We finally succeeded in adopting it, a document that also still stands as a model for other churches. Declaring that "human life in all phases of its development is God-given and therefore has intrinsic value," and stating that abortion is "an option only of last resort," it also recognized certain exceptions: when the mother's life is endangered, when the fetus is so abnormal it would probably not survive, and in cases of rape or incest.

Just prior to the assembly, Cardinal John O'Conner of New York had sent a letter to delegates urging them to take a stance protecting the unborn. I called his action "most unfortunate." It was a blatant incursion into the affairs of another church body. But it also represented one more instance that, no matter how much progress we had made in dialogue between our churches, Rome still regarded itself as the one true church in the world.

The Bible studies on the Lord's Prayer by Dr. James Nestigen from Luther Northwestern Seminary were a high point of the assembly for many. What happened in subsequent years is a mystery to many. He became more and more reactionary, attracted a fairly large circle of supporters, and was even a leading candidate for the office of presiding bishop when Mark Hanson was elected.

Another superb vice president

When Christine Grumm resigned as vice president to take a position with the Lutheran World Federation, I held my breath. We

worked so well together that I feared I would be in for a disappointment. My fears were short-lived. By a margin of just one vote Kathy
Magnus was elected Grumm's successor. I—and the church—could
not have been more fortunate. Magnus and I worked as well
together in my second term as Grumm and I had in my first. She
proved to be a churchwoman of the highest order. Like Grumm,
Magnus chaired the Church Council with confidence and aplomb.

Almen's reelection

I was genuinely pleased over the reelection of Lowell Almen as secretary for the church. I told him often that this was the right place for
him. This was his calling, a setting where he blossomed from year to
year. He was appreciated by voting members at churchwide assemblies and across the church for his excellent work.

A launching pad for the next four years?

Newspapers across the country carried headlines like that in the
Reading Eagle in Pennsylvania: "Lutherans UNITED" (9/14/91).
"Voting members came with a commitment to become the ELCA
and they did. The key now is to carry that back to the rest of the
church." Foster McCurley, a parish pastor in Pennsylvania who had
had experience as a churchwide staff person with the LCA, said,
"The mature debate on sensitive issues was really impressive. It
surpassed my expectations."

I was feeling very upbeat about Orlando. While on vacation
after the assembly at our lake cabin, I wrote to my sisters and their
spouses:

> It went so very well—way beyond what we could have
> expected. Many prayers, including yours, were answered.
> I feel like I am finally at the place where I can take charge.
> And now for the first time I can have a major role in choos-
> ing some staff. It makes a big difference in how loyal people
> are when they know they are there because I want them.

I was especially heartened by a post-assembly letter from Robert Marshall, my mentor and role model:

> Although your leadership of the convention two years ago was so commendable that I thought there was little room for improvement, this year you were superb.
>
> Your helpful but firm dealing with troublesome overtures and your unlimited good humor was a joy to watch.

George Cornell, religion editor for the Associated Press, caught a bit of my humor. After "bungling momentarily in trying to clear up a parliamentary tangle, he remarked, 'Swedes wake up early, but not fast'" (*Lakeland* [Florida] *Ledger*, 9/21/91).

I also appreciated the unique perspective of Gunnar Staalsett, general secretary of the Lutheran World Federation:

> I fully expect that Orlando will come to be seen as the point when the ELCA began to function as a mature, responsible, and aware church body. It was reassuring to observe an increasing consciousness that the Church acts as part of the larger communion of Lutheran churches.

Coming down after Orlando

Corinne and I went to our lake home for a time of rest after the assembly. Unfortunately, I decided to interrupt it several times for what I thought were important trips to events around the country. I was excited about what had happened at Orlando and wanted to spread the enthusiasm. It was a serious mistake not to take time for complete rest and relaxation. I ended up completely exhausted by the end of the so-called vacation.

Yet my enthusiasm remained high. On my sixtieth birthday Corinne and I had read Psalm 103 for our morning devotions:

> As for mortals, their days are like grass; they flourish like a flower of the field; for the wind passes over it, and it is gone and his place knows it no more.

I wrote in my journal:

> I want these next years to be harvest time, years of bold-
> ness, a period of my life when things I have done over the
> earlier decades will come to some natural and strong con-
> clusions, a time when I can make maximum impact with
> whatever gifts I have. But if that is to happen it has to be in
> the context of the Word for today—that I am dispensable,
> vulnerable, passing, like the flower that fades. Who remem-
> bers those we once thought so great? And that is how it will
> be with me. Soon forgotten. But that's all right, so long as I
> can be fully used during these days that God has given me
> to be the leader in the church.
>
> Of course, any day could be the last. With all the travel I
> do I am vulnerable. I pray I will be spared a scary, pain-
> ful, or lingering death. If I could have the choice, it would
> be to have a good mind and reasonably good health and
> Corinne's companionship until our late 80s and then death
> in my sleep.

"Focusing for Mission"

The Orlando Assembly gave us the green light to proceed with
restructuring the churchwide organization. We called it "Focusing
for Mission."

I had received a warm letter of congratulation on my reelection
from Harold Midtbo, former vice president of Standard Oil of New
Jersey and a board member and mentor when I was dean at Luther
College in New Jersey in the 1960s. In my response to Midtbo, by
then retired from his business position, I said:

> I remember so well from my days at Teaneck how you
> would give clear counsel out of your experience in both
> business and the church about the need to make a difficult
> decision when staff changes were imperative. One must
> always keep clearly in mind the good of the church and

then try to deal as kindly as one can with those who must
be separated. I learned that good lesson from you!

It is one thing, of course, to restructure. It is another to implement the changes. I wrote to my family that:

> It's so hard to tell nice, committed people that they are
> going to be replaced. Yet, you have to do it for the sake of
> the church. Now if the funds come in as promised. . . .

In my own office, with the departure of Bo Sorenson, we had
agreed that we would replace him and add a fourth assistant. I
looked in two directions. I needed relief both in handling administrative detail as well as in relating the office to those in the building
and the wider church.

I asked Craig Lewis to fill one position. He was head of the
Commission for Multicultural Ministries. He and I had had a close
personal relationship. Being African American, he also brought
better balance to my staff.

I envisioned Lewis picking up two roles. First, that of chaplain
to the churchwide staff in Chicago. Second, I could not begin to
go to all the places in the ELCA where we needed to communicate our vision for the next four years. I had seen Lewis walk into
settings where there were hundreds of typical ELCA members,
almost entirely Caucasian, and have them in the palm of his hand
in moments. He was a superb preacher and communicator.

I asked Lee Thoni to fill the other spot. Bo Sorenson had been a
first-rate administrator. I had seen enough of Thoni's work in one
of the divisions to believe that he could pick up that slack, especially in aiding me in answering the mountains of correspondence
that came to my desk every day.

Unfortunately, Lewis never took the initiative in the two areas I
had assigned to him. When he had an opportunity to move on to a
non-church position with a Chicago-area bank I encouraged him
to take it.

Thoni worked very hard for me. We had a good personal relationship. He was dogged in handling detail. Coming on to a staff
where others had served for four years, however, made it somewhat
difficult for him to fully enjoy his work. Our friendship remained
strong after he left the staff just before my final term ended.

One of the more controversial decisions I made was to recommend a clergy couple, Mary Ann Moller-Gunderson and Mark
Moller-Gunderson to head the Division for Congregational Ministry. They were on the staff of the Milwaukee Area Synod as a team
and were highly regarded in and beyond that synod. Peter Rogness
agreed to let me contact them but was not happy at the prospect of
losing them from his staff.

After interviewing several candidates, the search committee
was convinced that the Moller-Gundersons were easily the best
candidates.

A few weeks later, on a visit to Southern Seminary, James Crumley voiced his strong reservation about the decision. He could not
understand how a couple could head a major division. I stood my
ground, pointing out that many successful business enterprises
were headed by a married couple.

In retrospect, I do not rue that choice. My only regret is that
Mary Ann did not stay for a longer time. She felt a strong call to
go back to parish ministry, where she has flourished for many
years. Mark stayed on and was joined by another co-director of
the unit, Wyvetta Bullock. They served as an effective team for a
number of years.

After eliminating a position in stewardship emphasis and meld-
ing the rest of the unit into another division, several pastors of
larger congregations pounced on me. I tried to respond patiently to
each one who contacted me.

The personal trauma of making these changes came out in a
journal entry in December 1991:

> Today was a hard day. We . . . said good-bye at a luncheon
> to three of the executive directors. . . . On days like this I
> hate my job. How can one be pastoral and still run such a
> large and complex organization? Can one do those things
> without eventually losing one's pastoral heart?

In spite of the difficulty of the transition in staffing, I was feeling
very good about the general tone of life at the Lutheran Center. In
my last journal entry in 1991 I wrote:

> It feels more and more like a family. It has taken a long time
> for this to come about, but how good it feels! Relationships
> are becoming more and more solid. I feel more and more a
> part of the staff family. With my travel schedule, no won-
> der it has taken so long. I enjoy circulating the building.
> Invariably, I get involved in several conversations and learn
> a good deal about what is happening.

We also continued to strive for a multicultural staff at the
Lutheran Center. That was not always easy. With only two percent
of the church non-Caucasian, it was difficult to find people of color
for key positions. Nevertheless, more than twenty percent of the
churchwide staff was from these communities in the church.

At the November 1991 Church Council meeting two surprising
things happened.

Robert Marshall, who had been nominated to serve on the
executive committee of the council, was not elected, and Franklin
D. Fry, nominated to the standing committee for the Office of Ecumenical Affairs, also was not elected.

> Who could have expected the day to come when (Marshall)
> or someone with the name "Fry" would not be an auto-
> matic election? It's a good lesson learned for those of us
> who think we can go on and on.

Within the Lutheran Center and at the Board of Pensions in
Minneapolis I set aside times to meet with each unit for a brown

bag lunch. In these informal settings I had an opportunity to get better acquainted with the support staff and to share with them my vision for the ELCA and their place in that mission. I also announced plans to meet with synods in regional configurations to lead in Bible study, reflect together on the interdependent nature of the ELCA, and discuss other pertinent issues, including how to find resources for our common mission. In this connection I called on synod bishops to take the lead in presenting churchwide needs to each of their synods.

Sexual abuse in the church

I spoke forthrightly to the Church Council at that same meeting about the need for the church to face up to the growing number of sexual abuse cases we were seeing.

> It might be tempting for some in the church to say that this is not an issue over which we have to worry. Unfortunately, that is not the case. While the vast majority of our lay and ordained leaders in the ELCA are persons of high integrity and strong personal morality, we also have to deal with the very real fact that there is more abuse in the church than we may have realized.
>
> We must strive to make our church in all of its expressions a safe place to work, to receive counsel, to worship, and to take part in activities (Church Council, 11/8–11/91).

With the issue gaining ever more attention in the church and in the media, I decided to write a major article on "Clergy Sexual Abuse: Some Perceptions" for the May/June 1991 *Lutheran Partners* magazine.

I began by reminding the readers that ordained ministry is a vulnerable calling. We are invited into the private, intimate lives of many parishioners.

It is doubtful that sexual abuse is more common than it was

in previous generations, I said. But because of changes in the law regarding sexual abuse, victims are more willing to come forward.

I reminded them that pastors have power over those who come to them for help. They are usually trusted. But that trust can be an opening for misuse. The pastor represents more than a profession; the pastor also represents God for some people.

A pastor, being a sexual person, may be attracted to others in addition to a spouse. I cited Peter Rutter: "It is entirely natural to have sexual feelings and fantasies in any relationship of importance. The ability to avoid *acting* on these feelings is the central challenge of maintaining respect for sexual boundaries."

I pointed out the consequences. For the victim: rage, shame, guilt, broken marriages, and emotional trauma. For the abuser: guilt, emptiness, loss of faith. For the church: loss of confidence in the church and its leadership, loss of members.

Though homosexual abuse is often accented as the chief issue, I stated, by far the most common instances of abuse are by heterosexual male clergy against female members of congregations.

In an increasingly litigious society, the church must take strong action in sexual abuse cases in order to protect the resources of the larger body of believers. "Our calling to ordained ministry is not a right; it is a privilege. We are always subject to the expectations of the church to live lives consistent with the gospel."

I concluded with four suggestions on how to avoid crossing sexual boundaries:

> Do not share your own personal problems with someone who comes to you for counseling.

> Avoid compromising situations insofar as it depends on you.

> Give time and attention to your own needs for intimacy, affection, and nurturing.

> Care for your personal devotional life. There is no absolute guarantee against temptation and sin. But one thing that can

help us find the grace we need for that moment of temptation is the reservoir of our devotional life.

A vision for the seminaries

At about that same time I met with the presidents of the eight seminaries of the ELCA. In regard to financial support for them and all the other ministries of the church I suggested that it was time to be realistic about our expectations.

> We know now where we are financially. We have a very good picture of what this church is going to do . . . I want to suggest to you very strongly that . . . we . . . "get real" ("ELCA News," 11/20/91).

In line with financial expectations, I urged the seminary presidents to guard against compromising on the fundamental elements of a good theological education: Scripture study, the theology of the church, church history, preaching, Christian education, and leadership in worship.

Having said that, I also pressed them that we try to be flexible as we moved through the study of ministry.

> My hope is that out of the study of ministry we will understand ways to enlist other people in the ministry of the church in places where it is difficult for us . . . to provide ordained pastors. If my prognosis has any merit, we would do well to rethink our whole program of training for persons who are not seeking ordination but who want to serve the church in some clearly defined capacity. It is a fact of congregational life that non-ordained staff often have a greater impact on the members of the church than the pastor—who is often overwhelmed with administrative detail. And yet these other staff persons, more often than not, have little or no solid theological training

A year later we were looking at the same scenario. I asked myself,

Where will we find the resources to keep our eight seminaries vital? And should we keep all eight of them? And
how would we close any of them? Loyalty to them is as
fierce as to anything we see in the church. The only thing
that might change that pattern is the absolute necessity to
do so for financial reasons. I dread that day.

As I reflect on these words in early 2011, I observe all eight seminaries, though still struggling and, in some cases financially on the
edge, alive and mostly well.

The Lutheran Church—Missouri Synod: a peculiar relationship

One of the more surprising and interesting early contacts after I
took office was with Ralph Bohlmann, president of the Lutheran
Church–Missouri Synod. Bohlmann paid me a visit not long after I
moved to Chicago. We had lunch together. Something unexpected
happened. We bonded almost immediately. It was the first of several private conversations we had during my time in office.

I learned over the next years that there was a private person
quite different from the public person. Bohlmann seemed comfortable, even eager, to share with me some of the frustrations he lived
with as head of the Missouri Synod. When I suggested cautiously
to some of the former LCMS persons who were in the ELCA that
Bohlmann had a softer side, they seemed surprised, even unbe-
lieving. When the leadership of the two churches met annually he
retreated into the more rigid pattern that was expected of him.

Concordia Seminary

I was pleasantly surprised to get an invitation in the fall of 1991
from President John Johnson to deliver two lectures at Concordia
Seminary, St. Louis. One was to be given to the faculty, the other
to the student body, faculty, and guests. It had been suggested by
one of the faculty members that I speak on the subject, "God Language" to the faculty and on ordination to the larger group. Only

at the last moment was I asked to speak about the ordination of women in the ELCA. Not being one known to dodge bullets, I welcomed the challenge.

In the faculty lecture I began by asserting that we have more in common between our two churches than many may think and that in areas where we have substantial disagreement, many are learning the art of disagreeing without being disagreeable. I also spoke positively about the good relationship I enjoyed with LCMS president, Ralph Bohlmann.

I focused on two points in my faculty lecture on inclusive language.

First, that God is beyond all human reference, including sexual identity. Like Job, we must confess that we know only the vague "outskirts" of the person of God. Like Job

> . . . we stand dumb. We know so little. . . . we bow to the
> God who is beyond all human comprehension.

I moved on to other places in Scripture where the invisible, immutable nature of God is accented: Solomon, Isaiah, Romans— ". . . who has known the mind of God?"—Revelation. I cited Luther: ". . . let us shun that inquisitiveness of the human intellect, which wants to investigate His majesty."

What then about Jesus? Could the human expression of God have been female rather than male? Using Hebrews as a reference point, I alluded to the idea that Christ as human male was in that form only "for a little while."

> I see no need to insist that Christ is eternally male. Ulti-
> mately, it seems to me that we must insist that God is
> beyond all human reference, including sexual identity.

In the second part of the lecture I accented the importance of respecting the language of the Bible. We agree that in direct references to the person of God, Scripture is consistent in using male terminology. But in secondary references there is more variability. In symbol God is the Mother who nourishes Israel. The Spirit in Old Testament sources is usually feminine.

I said that I have sympathy for women who say they feel like second-class citizens because of our exclusive use of male language. Yet,

> . . . it is confusing to believers when we begin to use language that is not consistent with what we find in Scripture.

Having said this,

> . . . we should be sensitive to the problem we create when we use male terminology and images to the point where it becomes obnoxious.

Then I threw somewhat of a bombshell into the lecture. I pointed out that in my presentation to that point I had not once used "he" or "him" in reference to God. I asked if anyone had noticed. No one had. This illustrated my point, namely, that we can exercise more care and in the process be more inclusive in our references to God.

My lecture was received very cordially by the faculty. At the end President Johnson remarked (*Saint Louis Lutheran*, 1/15/92) that:

> It seems to me that in the last hour we have had two stereotypes broken down—that bishops never talk about controversial topics and that bishops are not very involved in theology.

In my address to the larger group on ordination, I fell back on my Augustana roots, underscoring that the call to ministry is an irresistible gift of grace from God, given through the church.

I reviewed how our predecessor churches had decided to ordain women and the positive influence this had had on those churches and on the ELCA.

Reaction, as one might expect in that setting, was quite mixed. Some thanked me for my "precise language." Others questioned my premises.

A painful change in leadership

It was customary for the heads of our respective churches to greet the national assembly of the other. I traveled to Pittsburgh to do this in the summer of 1992. Just before I flew to Pittsburgh I learned that Bohlmann lost his bid for reelection. Their convention was deeply divided and in a state of shock. And, of course, it put me in a very awkward position.

As I was introduced, a huge number of delegates rose from their chairs and exited the convention hall. I suppose if I were to have given them the benefit of the doubt, I might have assumed it was time for a beer. No doubt the better conclusion was that it was a statement of rejection.

I had some time to visit with Bohlmann and some of his supporters before I left Pittsburgh. Later I sent a letter that included these excerpts:

Dear Ralph:

You have surely been on my mind a great deal since I was in Pittsburgh a week ago. And you have been in our prayers. I am guessing that the full impact of what happened did not hit you until your return to St. Louis. And I think I can say the same. . . . it didn't seem real until I actually left your convention and returned to Chicago.

. . . please know of the sincerity of my comments to the delegates in assuring you of my gratitude for your partnership these past five years and of my promise to continue to hold you in my prayers as you move into an uncertain future.

Bohlmann's reply characterized our relationship:

Your warm and thoughtful note meant more to me than I can possibly express.

I hope our paths will indeed cross from time to time so that we can discuss the future relationships of our church bodies more privately, but also exchange whatever thoughts we might have on a variety of subjects. I have come to value our friendship very much, and pray that the Lord will provide us with continuing opportunities for contact and sharing. Pat and I . . . are deeply grateful for your continuing love and friendship and pray His blessings upon you, your family, and His whole church.

A bit later his handwritten note in response to another letter I sent to him typified again our mutual respect:

Your personal note meant a great deal to me at a particularly difficult time—and to Pat, too. I'm so embarrassed about the way some people behave and bring pain and shame to Christ's church. But in the process God's grace— and the love of His people—seem more real, too. Thanks so much for your thoughtfulness, Herb, and continuing blessings to you and Corinne.

—Ralph

In a 1995 memorandum to my successor I put into perspective the difficulty of relating to the Missouri Synod.

It is like living next door to a dysfunctional family. No matter how much you may like some members of the family, it is impossible to relate to them as family so long as their internal conflict remains unresolved.

A call for joint Lutheran/Roman Catholic eucharistic celebration

In late April 1992, Viterbo College, a Roman Catholic school at La Crosse, Wisconsin, honored me with the "Pope John XXIII Award" for my work in bringing reconciliation to diverse religious communities. I took the occasion to call again for joint eucharistic celebration between Lutherans and Roman Catholics. It was another bold gesture, one that would surely not come to fruition for many years, if ever. But how could one not make the appeal?

I began by noting that on the previous day the president of
the Lutheran World Federation, Dr. Gottfried Brakemeier, had a
private visit with Pope John Paul II at the Vatican. Among other
things, Brakemeier urged the Holy Father to join with Lutherans in
the quest for coming together in the Lord's Supper. I went on:

> We will probably always be separate members of the family.
> In fact, there may be value in our separate organizational
> identify. But though we be different branches, there is only
> one Christian family. Is it not possible that we have suf-
> ficient agreement between us in our understanding of the
> gospel and the Sacraments, so that we could at last share
> the Eucharist?

I asked whether in an increasingly secular society, in a world
where all Christian churches face difficult obstacles, is it not time to
make a strong witness to the world by, at the very least, coming to
the altar together?

I invited them to join me in the hope and prayer that the conversation yesterday in Rome would bear fruit.

> I am convinced that John XXIII would smile approvingly
> on such a venture.

A call for Corinne

At long last, the door opened for Corinne to be called to her first
love, parish ministry. We had been members of St. Luke's Lutheran
Church in Park Ridge since moving to Chicago. When the parish
decided to add an associate pastor to their roster in the summer of
1992, the call committee could think of no one they wanted more
than Corinne. And she was more than ready for it.

Getting the call, however, was not a piece of cake. As was often
the case in the early years after women were approved for ordination, it was *women* who often most opposed calling a female pastor.
I was on a trip the day of the call meeting at St. Luke's. I was certain

she would get the call, but she was not. When I reached her she said
that she did indeed get the votes needed, but far from unanimous.
I, of course, asked if she was disappointed. She exploded with, "No,
not at all! I'm grateful just to get the call!"

Her colleague, Pastor Ken McKnight, explained to her that a
group of women had been working hard to defeat the call. That
didn't bother Corinne. She told him that she was certain she would
win them over after some time.

That is exactly what happened. When we retired in 1995 McK-
night gave her the names of the women who had tried to frustrate
her call. As she predicted, they had become her friends and ardent
supporters. As with the call to Bethlehem Church in Minneapolis
in 1985, Corinne once again paved the way for another woman to
be her successor.

I was in Madras, India, on the Sunday Corinne was installed at
St. Luke's Church. In a written greeting delivered to the congregation that day I said:

> Though I may be a bit prejudiced, I can say without quali-
> fication that we are getting one of the finest pastors in the
> ELCA at St. Luke's today. I have known it for many years;
> the rest of you will soon find out for yourselves.
>
> As you gather for worship at St. Luke's, it will be late eve-
> ning in Madras. I am with you in my prayers.

To my cousin Helena Orup in Sweden I wrote that this means that

> . . . she will be my pastor! I think that is rather nice. How
> many people can have their pastor right in their own home
> to go to whenever they need to! I know the people in the
> congregation will love her very much.

Facing reality and proposing radical change

The high spirit and hopefulness we felt at the 1991 Orlando Assembly did not last very long. I have often read that presidents of the

country who serve a second term face diminishing results of their efforts the second time around. By early fall 1991 I began to wonder if that would be true in my case as well.

As noted earlier, a factor that would plague me for the next four years was the election of Kenneth Sauer as chair of the Conference of Bishops. The spirit of cooperation between Paul Werger and me during the first years in the life of the church could not have been better. I have told him many times since then that I cannot imagine how we could have survived those years had he not been chair of the conference.

With the succession of Sauer, that changed. Now initiatives from me would be countered by Sauer in some way, often subtly. I tried to make the best of it, but always felt frustrated.

The other reality that became clear by the fall 1991 meeting of the Conference of Bishops and the Church Council was that income projections for 1992 from across the sixty-five synods were increasingly negative. We were learning again that no matter how hard we pushed stewardship efforts, the church was very vulnerable to the rise and fall of the general economy. Overall income did not fall. Congregations, for the most part, paid their bills and supported their pastors and local staff. Synods took some minor reductions in support. With their hands on the financial till, many would make certain that most synodical staff and programs continued. Once more, it would be the churchwide mission that would take the largest hits. Other denominations, among them the most conservative, were seeing the same patterns.

I was incredibly dismayed by all of this. What should one do? If we were to fulfill our Churchwide Assembly mandates, I had no choice but to put difficult alternatives before the bishops and the Church Council. The churchwide staff under the leadership of Robert Bacher went through a lengthy process of self-study, looking at proposals for change in multiple areas.

In March 1992 what I called a good news/bad news scenario

unfolded. We had met the budget for 1991. What a relief it was to finally operate in the black. Good news.

Unfortunately, what we had feared for 1992 was unfolding: projections of reductions in revenue from synods. I wrote in my journal:

> It was hard to tell unit leaders that we'll have to cut back to 95 percent expenditure authorization. Yet . . . it didn't seem quite as hard this time. In the previous cuts much of the problem had to do with faulty budgets—expectations that were unrealistic and a certain impatience that we couldn't rectify it more quickly. But now . . . everyone is hurting—local congregations, synods, institutions, and even European churches. I'm afraid we're in for more major adjustments in the structure of the ELCA.

By April 1992 I was ready with a set of proposals for the Church Council. I observed that many deep changes were occurring within the whole of our society and our church—changes that call us to revisit our understanding of the role of national or churchwide structures.

I went on to speak about the "devastating ripple effect" the reductions in churchwide income had had on every ministry that looked to us for support: Lutheran Immigration and Refugee Service, Lutheran World Federation, seminaries, colleges, social service agencies, and many more. I asserted that the latest reductions meant that we had no choice but to cut out some constitutionally mandated ministries of the church.

I proposed that we:

> 1. Reduce the number of synods by a fourth or a third. I suggested that our CNLC ideal of sixty-five synods left us with a structure that was more expensive than we could afford.

> 2. Phase out the regional centers for mission, with synods to pick up their work.

3. Phase out and eliminate funding support to the colleges and assign it to synods.

4. Establish an annual fund appeal—"Vision for Mission"— for churchwide mission.

5. Reduce the number of churchwide units.

6. Establish a single formula of support for churchwide ministries that would apply uniformly to all synods. This would mean that synods could not unilaterally reduce their percentage support for the churchwide mission. An alternative would be for congregations to remit funds directly to the churchwide organization.

I pointed out what was obvious, namely, that the direction of the ELCA was more and more toward a federation of sixty-five synods, a pattern that was out of sync with the vision we had at the birth of the church.

I concluded my report to the Church Council by stating:

It would be tempting to do nothing, to allow things to drift, to make the best of it; but I would be derelict of my responsibility if I did not share with you some initial suggestions as to what I believe may contribute to the long-term good of this church.

Yes, I agreed, our financial dilemma was fomented in part by factors beyond our control—fine-tuning our new organization, increasing healthcare costs, and a weak national economy.

Yet, I am firmly convinced that we have a deeper problem—one that will not be resolved by the reorganization we have done thus far or by an improved economy. A realistic look into the future tells me that we are looking forward to diminishing churchwide resources, staff cut after staff cut, and lower morale—unless we look radically at what are the core functions of the churchwide

organization and take action that will free up resources so
that [those] functions can be carried out effectively. This
will mean the elimination of helpful activities that are
currently contributing much to the vitality of our church
("ELCA News," 4/7/92).

I knew, of course, that my proposal to reduce the number of
synods would be impossible to enact. Why then would I even suggest it? First, the CNLC had theorized that having smaller synods
would mean that bishops could pay closer attention to the needs of
congregations. And, in so doing, it was assumed that we would see
a better response to the needs of the church beyond the local scene.
What I had seen in my first four years as bishop did not convince
me that the synods, even the smallest of them, were doing any better in this regard than we had done in the much larger Minnesota
or Central Pennsylvania Synods of the former LCA. Second, it was
a simple economic necessity. If we were going to fulfill the demands
laid on the churchwide organization it would mean major reorganization of the whole church.

Let me inject here a bit of whimsy about what the ELCA might
have looked like had my recommendation on synods been accepted:

> Regional structure would have been retained but the offices
> would have been closed and the work of those entities
> would have been lodged in one of the synod offices. That
> bishop would have been responsible for coordinating the
> work that needed to be done on a regional basis.
>
> The synods would have numbered thirty-eight.
>
> Region I: (Office in Seattle)
> Washington/Alaska
> Oregon
> Montana/Idaho/Wyoming
>
> Region II: (Office in Phoenix)
> Northern California/Nevada

Southern California/Hawaii
Arizona/Utah/New Mexico/Colorado

Region III: (Office in Fargo)
North Dakota
South Dakota
Northern Minnesota
Southern Minnesota
Minneapolis/St. Paul

Region IV: (Office in Tulsa)
Nebraska/Kansas
Missouri/Oklahoma/Arkansas
Northern Texas/Northern Louisiana
Southern Texas/Southern Louisiana

Region V: (Office in Chicago)
Northern Wisconsin/Upper Michigan
Southern Wisconsin
Western Iowa
Eastern Iowa
Greater Chicago
Outstate Illinois

Region VI: (Office in Toledo)
Lower Michigan
Indiana/Kentucky
Northern Ohio
Southern Ohio

Region VII: (Office in New York City)
Upstate New York
New England
Metropolitan New York/Northern New Jersey
Eastern Pennsylvania/Southern New Jersey

Region VIII: (Office in Harrisburg)
Central Pennsylvania
Western Pennsylvania

Maryland/Metropolitan Washington DC
Virginia/West Virginia

Region IX: (Office in Atlanta)
North Carolina
South Carolina
Tennessee/Mississippi/Georgia
Florida/Bahamas
Caribbean

When current synod bishops read these lines they will probably bend back from their desks and have a rollicking good laugh. Yes, I knew that any hope of such a radical restructuring of the synods was unthinkable in 1992. In the end, I backed away from recommending these changes. The upheaval would not have been worth the cost savings.

Having said that, as I look at the church now more than twenty years later, I cannot help but wonder if this is not exactly what was needed in order to rescue the vision we had for the mission of the churchwide organization.

Let me get back to the world as it was in 1992.

Because of reports from synods of reduced income for 1992, we made immediate five percent cuts in churchwide unit budgets, reduced staff, and delayed filling new positions. Further complicating this grim picture was the decision of the Church Council at that spring 1992 meeting to increase pension contribution rates for pastors. Though the action was deemed necessary to help pastors in smaller congregations, it meant a further cut in funds received from local churches for the synodical and churchwide mission.

In that same action the council approved a recommendation from the Board of Pensions to initiate a mail order prescription program. That brought an outcry and angry letters and phone calls to my office from ELCA members, including one of my brothers-in-law, who were local pharmacists. It was not something I needed at that moment.

Over the next several months my recommendations were discussed by a number of entities across the church with the goal that the Church Council would take action at its fall 1992 meeting.

One of the good things that came out of this process was the launching of the Vision for Mission annual appeal, a source of funding that has proven to be a good avenue for over-and-above giving for thousands of ELCA members since its inception.

Another was what happened among the seminaries. Thanks in large part to the work of Joseph Wagner and his Division for Ministry staff, the presidents heard my message about facing reality. I was with them at their meeting in Pittsburgh in mid-June 1992. After some posturing and petty self-interest it was apparent that all eight were committed to developing a churchwide system for theological education—within the context of resources available. That was a healthy breakthrough and one that served as a good model for the college presidents when they met later in the summer.

Nothing came of my suggestion that we explore a different way of funding the churchwide mission, such as having congregations forward monies directly to Chicago as well as to synod offices. This had been the pattern in the former ALC. It was clear that there was no support for this method. Synods wanted to retain control of the flow of funds.

The same was the case with my suggestion that we lock in a percentage that each synod would retain and a percentage that would go to churchwide needs. Synods wanted to continue to negotiate and be free to change those numbers.

Funding for seminaries remained as it had been—from both synods and the churchwide organization. Grants to colleges from both synods and the churchwide offices were reduced.

I spoke candidly to the college presidents in July 1992:

> Our discussion . . . needs to be set in the framework of
> reality. The ELCA has no reserve/endowment fund. We
> cannot afford any longer to build a budget on the basis of
> an expected turnabout in the near future. We must put
> together our best estimates and then plan and execute our
> mission accordingly.

While this candid assessment was not greeted with good will
by either seminaries or colleges, I look back now and see that it
may have been one of the best things that happened to them. They
enhanced their fundraising staffs and worked more deliberately at
raising larger sums from alumni and friends. And in neither case,
as some had feared, did the relationship of these schools to the
ELCA suffer any diminishment. In fact, it could be argued that it
even strengthened those ties when seminaries and colleges went
directly to individual donors for gifts.

It is hard to measure the success of efforts to strengthen stewardship and fundraising through such units as the ELCA Foundation,
the Division for Congregational Ministries, Lutheran Laity Movement, and other entities. The ELCA Foundation was surely successful in its efforts. But much of its work was devoted to handling wills
and bequests for congregations, social service agencies, and other
causes. Not a great deal came to the churchwide organization. And,
of course, the delay in realizing the benefits of some gifts made it
difficult to see any dramatic impact.

As I traveled from one end of the church to another and tried
to awaken the church to the gravity of the situation, it became
more and more clear to me that my influence was limited. I
wrote in my journal about the core issue that I was confronting—
authority and power.

> Constitutionally I have authority, but no power. In contrast,
> the Conference of Bishops . . . has little authority but all
> kinds of power. The fact that funds flow from congregation

to synod and then to churchwide means that the power is
with synods. I am at the mercy of the synod bishops. If I
want to move anything, I need their approval. There seems
to be so much hesitation on their part to move ahead. Even
Mission90 did not get much support from them. I had to
move ahead on my own, and only after it was well underway
did the bishops acknowledge that it was a good program.

Yes, of course, there were the issues external to all of this. But at
the heart of it was the authority and power question. Unless I could
influence the synod bishops by persuasion, the churchwide mission
would continue to suffer.

After the fall 1992 meeting of the Church Council, I tried to put
matters into some historical perspective. "It's clear," I wrote in my
journal, "that denominations are becoming something that we did
not envision when we put this church together."

I went on to ponder how I might be seen in twenty-five years.

I am inclined to believe that it will be kindly and very positive. But who knows. I do my best, my limited best.

Sauer resisted the idea of an annual offering—the Vision for
Mission Fund—for the churchwide mission. Even though we had
received $1.5 million in a special offering in 1991, he insisted that
each synod would need to approve such an offering if it were to be
continued. He also announced that his synod, the Southern Ohio
Synod, would launch its own appeal to raise funds for scholarships
for its companion synod and for starting a new mission congregation. From one who had spoken so vociferously about the danger of
a federation of synods, that came as a rather strange move.

Sauer also accused me of moving too rapidly. Though he said,
on the one hand, that "I believe, with you, that we must act or
we'll go slowly sliding further and further downhill," (9/3/92), he
also feared that we weren't spending enough time reflecting on
"ecclesiology." We had heard this same charge from James Crumley

through the entire CNLC process, but without a clear statement from him as to exactly what he meant by the term. Now we were hearing it from Sauer, but again without a clear definition of what he had in mind. For me and those working with me, that was not the issue. We saw ourselves in a growing crisis regarding funding for churchwide ministries and felt the need for immediate action.

Then Sauer charged me and my staff with not consulting carefully with him and the leadership of the Conference of Bishops about the process for restructuring and financial support for the churchwide mission. I reminded him that it was my responsibility to set up the agenda with the help of my assistant for synodical affairs, Thomas Blevins, and Lowell Almen, who served as secretary for the conference. When Blevins read Sauer's letter he went into orbit. In a lengthy letter, Blevins reviewed in detail for Sauer the conference call he and Almen had had with Sauer and the other leaders of the conference in which all of the details of our proposals had been carefully spelled out and the agenda for the forthcoming meeting of the conference was agreed to. In his suggestions for the agenda of the conference, Sauer recommended that, along with other items, we discuss a lengthy article by Robert Benne, one in which the author criticized the churchwide organization for being too authoritarian and for pursuing a social agenda that was too liberal.

A pattern was becoming clear, and it would play itself out in the coming years: No matter what I proposed, Sauer would oppose. It was also becoming evident that in Sauer's mind the Conference of Bishops was pitted against the Church Council. "There needs to be a strong word from the conference that it is not merely responsive to the . . . Church Council" (9/3/92). Gone were the days when every effort had been made to coordinate the work of the conference and the council, a time when the two groups worked in tandem. We were becoming engaged in a power struggle between these two bodies—the one, the Conference of Bishops, which had great power but little legislative authority; the other, the Church

Council, which had legislative authority but little power to initiate or change without the consent of the Conference of Bishops.

In the midst of all of this turmoil over funding and my increasingly contentious relationship with Sauer, I poured out my soul to Reuben Swanson in a confidential letter in August 1992. In addition to the impasse over proposals regarding funding, I mentioned to Swanson that Sauer was also continuing to complain about the quota system the church had approved at its inception. I wrote to Swanson that I had challenged Sauer to come up with a new proposal for representation, but got no response. After telling Swanson about the plethora of issues that were crossing my desk I observed that

> . . . at meetings of church leaders I hear the same chorus from every church, no matter how large or small, no matter how liberal or conservative. It is a time when we must choose our priorities, setting aside important but less essential facets of our mission.

The actions in the Southern Ohio Synod were an omen of what was to come in other parts of the ELCA. More and more synods launched fundraising efforts. As they did, less and less funds flowed to churchwide mission efforts.

It is fair to ask whether the Achilles' heel of all this was the decision of the CNLC to recommend the LCA process for funding the mission of the church beyond local congregations. That process called for local congregations to send all their dollars to the synod and for the synod to share some of them with the churchwide mission.

In contrast, congregations in the former ALC had sent support dollars to both district (synod) missions and to churchwide missions. It was a fatal mistake not to follow the ALC process. This method would have given each congregation a sense of partnership with both synod and ELCA mission work.

After the merger too many congregations lost a sense of that larger partnership with the church beyond the synod. With each passing year the ELCA evolved more and more into a federation of sixty-five synods and more than 10,000 independent congregations.

Now more than twenty years have passed since these seemingly insoluble issues confronted the church. I have no regret for what I stood for at the time. The mandate from the CNLC and the constituting convention of the church was clear. My charge was to work for one church with three equal expressions. Were the actions of Sauer and others only "the first shots across the bow," forecasting a very different church from the one we had envisioned, one in which local congregations and synods and independent entities would be the center of the action? Possibly so. That does not make me feel even a smidgeon of regret for having fought so hard for the broader vision.

New detractors: "Call to Faithfulness" and Braaten and Jenson
After having survived the attacks of the Fellowship of Evangelical Lutheran Laity and Pastors (FELLP) in Minnesota, and the incessant barbs from the *Commentator* and *Forum Letter*, I thought I might have some respite for a time. The decision of Richard John Neuhaus to convert to Catholicism left very few teary eyes across the ELCA. I night have known that others would be waiting in the wings and ready to fill the vacuum.

In 1990 three independent Lutheran journals—*dialog, Lutheran Forum,* and *Lutheran Quarterly*—sponsored a conference at St. Olaf College, Northfield, Minnesota. Titled "Call to Faithfulness," the event drew almost one thousand participants. Given the success of the first gathering, the planners announced "Call to Faithfulness II"—in June 1992. The *Christian Century* described it as a confab for "those who were generally united in the belief that the ELCA administration in Chicago—'Higgins Road'—has been unfaithful to the Lutheran tradition." They went on: "This charge of infidelity is nothing new. Such rumblings have haunted the ELCA since its formation in 1988" (7/15–22/92).

Though there were a number of speakers, the *Century* reported:

> By far the most galvanizing speeches addressed the per-
> ceived infidelity at Higgins Road. Theologian Carl E.
> Braaten, director of Northfield's new Center for Catholic
> and Evangelical Theology, received a standing ovation for
> a fiery oration titled "The Gospel—or What?" Braaten
> blasted the "various mutations of the gospel that have ema-
> nated from synodical offices and the churchwide units" and
> accused the ELCA administration of buying into the plural-
> istic theology of religions that reduces Jesus to one of many
> great religious leaders in history. Declaring that "heresy and
> apostasy are as much a possibility in the modern church
> as in the ancient," Braaten said the new pluralistic theolo-
> gies smack of Arianism, the ancient heresy that denied the
> divinity of Christ.

The hot button issue of the conference, according to the *Christian Century*, was the quota system of the ELCA. Robert Benne
from Roanoke College said adopting it was like planting "a decon-
structive virus right into the center of our nervous system. . . ."
Gracia Grindal climbed on board with a much-applauded speech
in which she asserted that the quota system "represents the failure
to trust the democratic process in the church."

I was invited, apparently as an afterthought, to address the event.
Again, not having the reputation—or the good sense—to avoid
fiery trial, I accepted the invitation. I knew I would be facing a
mostly hostile audience. Speaking under the theme, "We Can Love
the Church—the Whole Church," I began with what some in the
audience may not have expected. I affirmed the importance and
legitimacy of independent movements in the church. I reminded
the audience that there is even a section in the church's constitution that applies to free movements. The key to their effectiveness, I
suggested, is their adherence to the Pauline word, "Let all things be
done in love."

I described the church as imperfect, yet able, in spite of that imperfection, to be a channel for God's grace. I reminded the audience that nearly every letter in the New Testament was written to a congregation or group of Christians in some state of conflict.

But what about the church in its expressions beyond the local congregation? Here, too, the church

> . . . is broken, it is incomplete; it is a disappointment at times. Yet, because the whole church is under the gospel, these other expressions are also the church. Judging from mail I receive and conversations I am engaged in around the church, it is my impression that we have a long way to go in fully appreciating the church in its fullness, including all of its many visible expressions.

I went on to observe that when I read some bashing of institutions and synods and the churchwide expression, I was left with questions:

> Why is it so often done by those who are beleaguered in their own settings? How much of it is related to life in a culture where so few trust anyone or anything beyond the local community—and possibly not even there? How much is rooted in a dim memory of "the good old days" when pastors had a different social and educational status vis-à-vis lay parishioners and women?

Who then, I asked, calls the church to accountability? In Scripture there is more than one answer to that question. At times Paul asserts apostolic authority. Pastors are also called to speak both *for* and *to* the church. But we also find in the Bible, such as in Acts 15, that there are councils—assemblies, if you will—that speak for the whole. In the ELCA we vest that authority with the Churchwide Assembly and the Church Council.

As for quotas, I observed that the church decided that decision-making needed to be rooted in representative bodies that affirm the gifts of both clergy and laity, both men and women, both Caucasian and African American and other people of color. ". . . the gifts and perspectives of all need to be employed in the shaping of policy and practice that affect all."

Must we always use our current formula? No, I said.

> There is no reason we cannot decide at some point to exercise that same evangelical freedom to change the nature of representation if there is clear reason to do so. But I would forewarn you not to think that we would thereby have no quotas. If we decided, for example, that assembly representatives should be equally divided between clergy and laity, that is still a quota. Or if we decided, by some formula, to include more theological professors, that is still a quota. Or if we decided that representation should be on the basis of baptized and confirmed believers, we would have a delegation with only a handful of ordained clergy. Or, we could move toward the Episcopal system, with a house of bishops and a house of delegates. My point is that there is no way to move away from representational principles of some kind.

I concluded by asserting again that no matter how we organize the church, we will always live with imperfection. I urged the listeners to join me in searching prayerfully, and lovingly, for ways the ELCA could more fully embody what God expected us to be.

> I can honestly say from the depth of my being that I love this church. Though congregations, synods, the churchwide organization and, yes, independent organizations and publications, are imperfect and faulty expressions of what we might hope; though we must continually call all of them to faithfulness; though they will need constant renewal; yet, for all of that, we are together the church of Christ.
>
> I love this church—the whole church.

Unfortunately, Braaten and Jenson could not resist the temptation to carp incessantly about what they thought was heresy in the ELCA. I could live with that, knowing that "this too will pass." I was also hearing in many parts of the church that there was growing discontent with their emphasis. "What I hear," wrote one pastor,

> . . . is that the conference may have run out of gas. How many times can you go over the same ground and how long will people listen to unfair criticism? I see no need to be with them again, assuming they would want me.

I look back on these encounters and ask whether I should have bothered to speak at the Northfield event. Would it not have been better to just turn the other way, to ignore them? Did I enhance their cause by engaging them as I did?

There is no easy answer. I feel confident in saying that I would do it again. Our churchwide staff was being unfairly attacked. I knew how hard staff members worked and how faithful they were to our church and its teaching. Who else should have defended them if not I? And was I not correct in challenging their misguided rhetoric about the quota system?

I always appreciated the churchmanship and theological acumen of Herluf Jensen, both before and after he served as the bishop of the New Jersey Synod. In his 1992 Christmas greeting, written after he had retired from office, he added a handwritten note that helped put all of these encounters with detractors into perspective. After noting that he still subscribed to a number of theological journals, he commented:

> I get very frustrated and upset by the fulminations against the ELCA by various neoconservative theologians and their bigotries, of which they seem remarkably unaware. We pray for you and hope you are doing well.

At last—goodbye to my mother

On December 12, 1992, having heard that my mother had stopped taking nourishment, I wrote to her pastor and said,

> What a marvelous birthday gift it would be if she could go to be with the Lord before her ninety-second birthday. Christmas would be special to all of us, but particularly for her.

I told him that in the previous two weeks I had had the strange sense of the "collective unconscious," giving me the strong feeling that this was different from previous times when she seemed near death.

My brother Dave is very sensitive spiritually. He had had the same feelings. When she retreated so completely from any contact with the world, and because visiting her meant a walk across town in the cold winter weather, Dave had not gone to see her as often. But just before she died, he felt an urge to go there. Soon after her death I spoke to Dave on the phone. He said to me, "Something just told me, Herb, to come down here."

And that is what happened. She died just two days before her ninety-second birthday. The baby who had taken her first gasp of air in far away Mälmo, Sweden, now quietly drew her last. She died in peace. Thanks be to God!

At her funeral service I gave a brief greeting, thanking many, but especially my brother, Dave.

> Each of us in our own way has tried to do what we could for mother. But he has been with her through everything. It is no surprise that when she seemed to lose touch with the rest of us, she still responded to him. He was the last of us to visit her before she died—and that was the way it should be. When I talked to David on the phone shortly after she died, it was he who comforted me when he said, "She's home with Dad now. She's at the golden door. There's where Dad was waiting."

For me personally it was the end of a long and sometimes complicated journey with my mother. I had come to accept many of her idiosyncrasies. And she had done the same with me. I was at peace and in full reconciliation with her long before she died. To this day I still say that I am much more my mother's son than my father's son. I inherited more of her spirit than his. I give thanks for that. Had her mind not failed her, she would have been full of the same energy and zest for life that I feel in my seventy-ninth year. It is her gift to me. Again, thanks be to God!

And now—again—let's talk about sex

Everything else that we wrestled with in the early years of the church, and still today more than twenty years later, pales in comparison to our attempt to develop a statement on human sexuality.

As I have mentioned earlier, I was looked to for leadership and did my best, in the midst of all of my other responsibilities, to stay engaged. In October 1991 in a lengthy memorandum to Karen Bloomquist, director of the process, I gave a detailed response to an early draft of the proposed statement. My suggestions, numbering more than one hundred, included everything from simple word changes to major text revisions. Among other things:

> Rather than "Many Voices in One Body," as had been recommended for the title, I suggested it be called: "A Discussion among Believers: Human Sexuality and the Christian Faith."

> I argued for a definition of sex that would always cast it in the broadest possible context, avoiding the idea that it is primarily genital in nature.

> I suggested that the section on the biblical basis for the discussion on sexuality was too heavy. It needed to be rewritten in language that ordinary laity would understand.

> I urged a stronger accent on the role of the church in healing broken relationships.

At the end of the memorandum I added some comments that, from the perspective of almost twenty years later, seem prophetic of what the whole study process turned into:

> Karen . . . at the moment I must confess to a fairly high
> level of frustration. I am not sure we are ready to send out
> this material as a study document. I am not at all certain
> that we should proceed according to the schedule. I believe
> that even the earliest draft needs to be more carefully
> defined than what we have before us. As we know, many
> conclusions are drawn from material that is intended only
> to be preliminary and for discussion purposes.

I went on to reinforce what I had noted earlier; namely, that we could only discuss other areas of sexual relationships after we had strongly underscored the church's primary affirmation of hetero-sexual marriage.

> If we state it in that way, can we not go on to say to our peo-
> ple something like the following: "While the tradition of
> the church and our strong affirmation is for genital sexual
> activity to be within heterosexual marriage, we recognize
> that there are many . . . questions that the church needs to
> discuss at this point in time."

A year later, in a memorandum to the planning team at the Churchwide Center I summarized the disjointed journey of the study process:

> Reading my mail inclines me to be pessimistic over the
> prospect that this church can reach any kind of consensus
> on a statement on human sexuality.

To reinforce my point I gave the team just one day's mail on the subject that had come to my desk. "I think," I said, "that we need to prepare ourselves for the debate that lies ahead."

Early in 1992 at the Academy of Synod Bishops at Mundelein, Illinois, I did just that. The evening before delivery I wrote in my journal:

> Tomorrow I . . . lecture to the bishops about human sexual-
> ity and ordination of homosexual persons. I will speak the
> truth and with integrity. But can I say those same things in
> the broader circle of the church? I wonder. . . .

I tried to prepare the synod bishops for this discussion in
the church. I felt they needed to know my stance on the key
issues, and especially the one that always overshadowed our
discussions—homosexuality.

I began my lecture by stressing those things regarding sexuality
about which we could be certain:

> It is good to be human, male and female.

> Sex is good, a gift from God.

> Sexual intercourse is good within the context of a lifelong
> heterosexual marriage.

> Sex is intended both for pleasure and procreation.

> Like everything else, sex is distorted by sin.

> Any statement of the church, I said, must affirm these
> points on which we have broad and historic agreement.

In other areas, I suggested, we do not have uniform agreement in
the church, such as sex prior to marriage, sex after marriage, and,
most thorny of all, same-gender sex.

In the rest of my comments, I stressed that what I shared was my
opinion, not a certain word from God or from the church.

> It is not possible, I asserted, to change something as funda-
> mental as one's sexual orientation.

> If one cannot change, how should one live? Here, I said,
> one must be careful when applying Scripture. Jesus
> allowed for divorce, but not remarriage, or so I inter-
> preted the text. Yet we have moved from that rigid stance
> to a more flexible one.

What does the Bible say about same-gender relationships? I reviewed in detail the few relevant texts. We are left with as many questions as answers, I said.

I went on to ask what the church should do while we continue to debate these issues.

I asserted that we should ordain those who are homosexual but not living in a same gender relationship, and who qualify on all other grounds.

We should not ordain those living in such relationships. I gave two reasons:

The disruption and division it would cause in the church. "The unity of the church is important. Where there is absolutely no doubt about an injustice, the unity of the church may have to take second place. But where there is uncertainty and disagreement—even among those most able and competent to explore Scriptures and the Confessions of the church on a given issue—then I believe the unity of the church must take precedence.

The silence of Scripture. While I agree with those who believe that a long-term relationship of consent between adults of the same gender is not condemned by the Bible, I must hasten to point out that neither is there affirmation of such a relationship.

What about blessing same-gender partners? While I resisted calling such relationships a "marriage," I urged the bishops not to discipline pastors who felt free in conscience to bless them.

I concluded my lecture by reading one of the many pain-filled letters I had received, this one from a lesbian person whose father had been a Lutheran pastor. Like so many, she felt disenfranchised by her church. She wrote:

Please, be merciless no longer. If not for my sake, and for the one I love, and for our families, then for your colleagues, our fathers, and for the sake of the Lord of Love and Compassion, whom you have otherwise so ably served.

Reaction to my lecture was interesting. Two or three of the bishops commended me for what I said, indicating their full agreement. A few expressed surprise that I had come to this point in my thinking, neither affirming nor disapproving my lecture. A few, by their demeanor, were clearly upset and opposed to my views. Most were silent, showing strong evidence that this was a subject they would just as soon ignore in the hope it would somehow go away.

Three months later, as the discussion about sexuality and homosexuality bubbled up across the church, I sat down and wrote a draft letter that I thought I might send out as a public statement to the church. It was patterned after the lecture I delivered to the bishops at Mundelein. I shared a rough draft with my four assistants, asking each of them to respond with suggestions. Only Lita Johnson replied in writing. She found herself caught up in the same dilemma, having personal convictions about justice for gay and lesbian persons, but worried about the impact on the church if a letter of this kind were to go out. She feared that a pronouncement of this nature from me might polarize people and lead many to think that I was trying to force my opinion on the outcome of the study in progress. I typed up a final draft of my letter on April 11, 1992.

The next day, April 12, I wrote a note to myself and attached it to the proposed letter:

> As much as I might like to do something with [the letter], I am trapped by my office. Not only would it cause enormous turmoil within the church—consuming most of my energy for the next three years—it would also have ecumenical consequences. The Orthodox would probably pull out of the NCC for good—and much more. And there is also the double standard. Even though one explains it, it is still hard to say that gay/lesbian persons should have full rights— except to be ordained. This dilemma seems insoluble.

In the meantime the Division for Social Ministry and the task force charged with drawing up a draft proposal on human sexuality continued that process. And as they did, the mail piled up not only with the division but also on my desk. I had daily reminders that no matter how democratic our process, the buck stopped with me.

By mid-June 1992 my pessimism over the prospects for developing a statement had grown. I poured out my frustration on a page of my journal: "Sometimes I think the church will be the last to become comfortable with gay and lesbian people. That saddens me. But it's reality."

Through 1992 the discussion continued across the church. In November I wrote in my journal that

> My mail reflects deep division. I feel caught between wanting to speak out on it as a justice issue, yet know that it is also a church unity question. Where does one go? How does one keep one's integrity when one must publicly take one stance, yet privately wish the church would be more flexible?

Debating sexuality in the ecumenical arena

It was about this same time that the issue came to the surface at a meeting of the National Council of Churches (NCC) board meeting. The Universal Fellowship of Metropolitan Churches of Christ (MCC) had been requesting membership in the NCC for ten years. When that came to naught, they asked for "observer" status. At its Cleveland meeting the NCC engaged in intense debate. The black churches and the Orthodox Church threatened to drop membership if even "observer" status was granted to the MCC.

Once again, as in the ELCA, the issue of justice versus unity confronted some of us. And, once again, I found myself between a rock and a hard place. And, once again, I sought middle ground by urging the board to delay action on the request in order to buy some time for more discussion. But I also warned the board that there was a limit to our patience, that many of our churches were moving to the place where concern for justice may outweigh our concern for unity. By a narrow margin, the board decided to delay action. The result, unfortunately, was no action.

Following the vote a number of supporters of the MCC gave impassioned speeches, mostly pointing to the injustice of the NCC in not even allowing them to sit with us as observers. Many left the meeting, but I stayed and listened. The afternoon ended with many standing with our MCC sisters and brothers in a circle and singing—including me.

I was very torn. Later in my room I wrote:

> Isn't it dangerous to go against your conscience? And how can a leader of a Lutheran church do that? Wasn't that what gave us birth—Luther's insistence that he could not compromise conscience—"Here I stand."

The next morning, before flying back to Chicago, I arranged for breakfast with Leonid Kishkovsky, the ecumenical officer for the Orthodox Church and a former president of the NCC. My plan was to speak forthrightly about my stance on the homosexuality question.

I wrote extensive notes in my journal about our time together:

> He is a good and wise man. I know him well enough to know that I could share openly with him.

> I . . . reiterated what I had said on the floor the previous day—that I had voted for no action because I wanted time to see if we can resolve this without forcing the Orthodox and other churches to leave. But I said that in so doing I was going against my conscience. That, I said, is an intolerable conflict for me. While I have convinced myself that I must do so for now for the sake of Christian unity, I could not keep on doing so. I asked if he saw any chance that there was a way through this dilemma.

> Leonid seemed very sensitive to my personal dilemma. He talked about the Orthodox position, that they have a

deep concern for gay and lesbian persons. But he said the problem with the UFMCC is their insistence that being gay or lesbian is normal, even a gift from God, and that the Orthodox simply could not tolerate that viewpoint. In other words, they must change is what he was saying. I spoke of my grave doubts that this was possible.

Leonid did listen respectfully. We are good enough friends so that there was not even the slightest trace of defensiveness in our conversation.

I had to leave it at that. Whether Kishkovsky changed his views even slightly, I will never know. It was one of those instances where one must simply plant a seed and hope it will one day grow into something one will never know about.

I wrote later that day:

Some say that this may be the most divisive issue we have had to face since the slavery question. I think that is true. In this conflict, however, it is not one region of the country against another. It is division *within* every structure in our society. And that is what makes it so difficult to deal with. Not only the church, but also political parties, institutions, communities, the military, and, most of all, families— everything and everyone is involved.

What is God calling me to say and to do? I'm not sure. Lord, give me the wisdom of Solomon. And give me courage and good judgment.

Abandonment of the study on sexuality

By early 1993 there were calls to abandon the ELCA study on human sexuality. Some thought the church simply could not handle this incendiary subject. At the March 1993 meeting of the Church Council I urged that we remain steady and push ahead toward the goal of adopting a statement at the 1995 Churchwide Assembly.

I learned in time that the goal was indeed unattainable.

Time for a change in my ministry?

In late November 1992 Dick Jensen announced unexpectedly that he intended to leave his position as preacher for Lutheran Vespers. After ten years he felt it was time to move on. He visited with me and said he wanted me to play a major role in the choice of his successor.

Within days I started asking myself, "Is it possible that *I* might be the one to succeed Dick?" Dick talked about the possibility that the broadcast might be done from someplace other than at the Lutheran Center in Chicago. That set me to thinking that we might move to our lake home and I could do the broadcast from Concordia College in Moorhead. I kept counsel only with myself, not even hinting to Corinne that I had such ideas.

We took a break at Thanksgiving time and flew to Pelican Rapids for some rest at our lake home. During that time I mentioned it very cautiously to Corinne. We spent an entire morning mulling it over and looking at every facet of the possibility.

I assured her that any move must have as its first priority that she find a satisfying call to parish ministry in the area around Pelican Rapids.

I also had to ask whether it would be an appropriate time for me to make a change. I reminded myself that at the time of my election in 1987 I had speculated that the challenges and stresses of the office might well call for something less than two full terms. Now I was wondering if this opportunity might be good reason to leave after six years. I felt certain that one term was not sufficient to get the church settled. But I also wondered if eight years was too long, if one could keep that pace without paying an enormous price.

My radio ministry while a parish pastor in St. Peter had been a positive experience. I had also had enjoyed listening to Lutheran Vespers during my years as bishop in Minnesota. At that time it was broadcast on Sunday evenings. After a busy day on the road it brought refreshment and renewal to me as I began a new week. I realized the power of that media.

Now I wondered if I might concentrate on an opportunity like this and build it into something that might last several years into the next decade.

I sat down and outlined reasons for and against such a move.

The next step was to meet with Dick Jensen to see how he would react to the idea that I might be his successor. He was quite stunned at first. Such a thought had never occurred to him. After thinking about it for a day, he came back to my office and said he felt very positive about the idea. I found this very affirming.

Following the meeting with Jensen, I met with Eric Shafer and John Peterson from the Department of Communication. They, too, were shocked at first. Not surprisingly, such a thought had never occurred to them. They gave it some consideration and came back with strong words of affirmation. Again, this seemed like a green light.

Several days later Shafer and Peterson returned again to meet with me. Now they were less certain. As Peterson put it, on a personal level he saw me as a very pleasant, approachable person who would undoubtedly succeed in the role as Lutheran Vespers preacher. But on another level, said Peterson, "You are a nine-foot gorilla." What they were telling me was that it was just about inconceivable for them to envision me moving from the office of bishop of the church in the prime location in the building to a cubicle in their department.

For the first time I began to see what became more and more apparent in the coming weeks; namely, that once you've been in such an office it is virtually impossible for others to conceive of you as fitting into any other slot in the churchwide structure.

In spite of this challenge to my thinking, I kept persisting. I decided to consult with two persons I could trust for an absolutely honest evaluation and forthright opinion, Joe Wagner from the churchwide staff and Bob Marshall as one who saw things from the outside and who had himself stepped out of office in an abrupt and surprising way in 1978.

Both men listened carefully to my case for leaving and for becoming preacher/director for Lutheran Vespers. Both affirmed my capability to do that ministry. But both said emphatically that it would be a mistake. Wagner affirmed the widespread respect he sensed for me in the church. He knew of no one who questioned my integrity. Even those who may disagree with me, he said, know that my life does not depend on being bishop. But he also spoke of the rhythm that the church goes through in each four-year cycle, that programs and themes tend to flow in that pattern and that for the head of the church to leave in the middle of it would be disruptive for the church and for everyone on staff. I knew, of course, that this made sense.

Marshall said that no matter how I tried to explain it, people would not understand why I would leave in mid-term. Here, though he never said so directly, he may have been speaking from his personal experience.

A conversation with Corinne over dinner at Bailey's restaurant near her church in Park Ridge one evening was probably the clincher. She gently pointed out that I have been pursuing the Lutheran Vespers opportunity and that this is something I've never done. I had always waited for an opportunity to come and to accept it as God's providential intervention in my life. Now I was reversing field. *I* was pursuing this call. Little wonder I felt more and more uneasy about it.

Sometime during this process Corinne left a note on my desk at home. She had been reading the Book of Acts in her devotions:

> Powerful word for today—Acts 27: 27–44, tried to escape from ship! "Unless stay in ship cannot be saved. Take food—help you survive . . . not lose a hair! Took bread— gave thanks broke it—began to eat. Then all escaped. Love, Corinne

I was ready to accept what I knew deep down was inevitable. I must stay in office for the full term. After our visit at his home in

Hyde Park, Marshall sent a handwritten note saying he was "honored by your visit and grateful for the chance to have a relaxed conversation about the church and your work. The Lord keep you and guide you." Having heard of my mother's recent death he also reminded me that

> Your mother's life of hard work and profound Christian faith has also a reward in your life of faith and your hard work in the service of the Lord and his church. Many of us know we are the beneficiaries of your dedication and the upbringing that helped produce it.

Those words only added to my certainty that I must stay in office. God had not called me to do what was easy. I knew I must keep my hand to the plow.

In my response to Marshall I wrote of the help I had received from the lament psalms during my mother's long descent into death. "I pleaded with God to set her once strong and vibrant body free from the bondage of a cruel old age." Then I came to the crux of my struggle:

> I got so very excited about the broadcast possibility, as you could tell. But I found no peace until I let go of it and committed myself in a fresh and new way to the call God has given me to lead the ELCA. I still feel that six years is more than enough for a task of this magnitude. But I found that the struggle with another possibility has brought me back to the church's call with renewed vigor and enthusiasm.
>
> . . . thanks for being my pastor at a very critical time.

"All right, Lord, you win," I penned in my journal on December 17.

> I'll stay with the call to be bishop of this church. Just saying that makes me feel a peace within that is a relief. Now I'm sitting here shedding tears—tears of relief. Yes, I dread the heavy load of this office. But I also remember Christ's

promise that when we come to him—surrender our load to him—"his yoke is easy and his burden light."

A few days later, in a brief handwritten note, Marshall wrote:

Herb: HALLELUIAH!

—Bob Marshall

Why did I want to leave office?

I've given an inordinate amount of space to the matter of the Lutheran Vespers opportunity. It may seem that I wrote far more than was necessary. Yet it was a critical issue in my time in office and the consequences for either choice—leaving or staying—were enormous for me and, possibly for the ELCA as well.

So why this fascination with a change? There is no doubt that the major factor was that I was feeling deeply compromised over the sexuality study and my role in leading the church in this troublesome arena. On November 1, 1992, I wrote in my journal:

I was awake very early this morning. I thought about yesterday's mail—that which had accumulated over Thanksgiving weekend. Among the letters ten related to sexuality issues. Nine very negative toward gay and lesbian persons. One from a young woman who is a lesbian and who writes with gratitude for what she believes I have done to change attitudes, but who also says that she will probably have to pursue her call to ordained ministry in the UCC. She describes poetically how difficult it is to be so out of sync with the rest of the world, how painful it is to be judged as a "genetic defect," how she longs to be accepted for who she is, what she is.

I wrote about how these letters make obvious one more reason why I wanted to think about leaving office in the next several months.

I feel like I'm living a lie. I'm losing that one gift without which I cannot go on—my integrity. I have always said to my colleagues that one can endure anything if one keeps that one thing—one's integrity. Every response to every letter on the subject is an exercise in delicate diplomacy. But it has come to the point where it is so intense that I wonder how much longer I can keep doing it without losing my soul.

I simply do not agree with where I believe the majority of the church is at on the subject of homosexuality. I've met too many beautiful, caring, sensitive, deeply committed Christians who happen to be gay or lesbian through no choice of their own.

As I wrote I realized that I had moved another step down the road since I had spoken to the bishops.

I am convinced that the church should allow for the ordination of practicing gay and lesbian persons, assuming they are qualified on all other grounds. We should permit congregations who want to call them to be able to do so. If they abuse others, we should treat them just as we do heterosexual persons who do those things. If I said this publicly, it would really blow the roof off the church.

I wondered if I might be a better catalyst for change if I were not in the office of bishop.

Could I speak up more openly, being more certain that my voice in that status would not be as disruptive?

Added to this inner conflict regarding sexuality issues was the weariness of travel. In a letter to Corinne from Japan in early August 1993 I wrote: "It's been a very good day in every way. But I'm so weary of travel and travel and travel." Maybe I am too conscientious. I felt compelled to fulfill my duty on boards, and especially on the LWF Executive Committee. I wanted to be a living presence and witness of support to our sister churches around the globe. I continued to believe that it was important for me to be at as many synod events as possible, believing this was the best milieu for engaging the pastors and laity of the church.

Another crucial factor was Corinne's role as a pastor at St. Luke's parish in Park Ridge. From the moment she began in September 1992, it was apparent to me that she was back to her first love—parish ministry. She had done yeoman's duty as the wife of the bishop of the church in its first five years. She had traveled to every corner of the church to speak to groups of every size and constituency. Her influence had been deep and profound. Unfortunately, she was too often seen as an extension of my office rather than as a pastor in her own right.

Yes, it seemed I had good reason to consider stepping out of office in mid-term. But, no, there was no way I could do so. I simply had to pray for renewed energy, enthusiasm, and wisdom to keep some balance in our lives until 1995.

At the spring 1993 meeting of the Conference of Bishops in South Carolina, Wayne Weissenbuehler, bishop of the Rocky Mountain Synod, took me aside and said that several of the bishops had urged him to speak to me about being open to staying in office beyond 1995.He said that he and others knew of no one other than me who was not beholden to some interest group in the church. He said that I have the freedom to speak on issues and to take stances without worrying about pleasing some special interest people. I said nothing about my plans. I just said I would give it some thought. But in my heart of hearts, I knew that I could never remain beyond 1995.

Gratitude for a superb churchwide staff

In January 1993 we had a special occasion at the Lutheran Center to honor all those who had been with us for the first five years in the life of the ELCA. In my journal I called it "a deeply satisfying milestone." There was a sense on that occasion that we were settling in for the long haul. It could mean that these next two and one-half years would bring some reaping of the results of the hard work it had taken to set this ship on its course.

Given what would happen in that next chapter in the life of the church, we would need all of the talent and dedication that I saw in that group that day.

U. S. church leaders conference

One of the most interesting annual events on my calendar was the gathering of U.S. church leaders in Washington, D.C. It was the most representative group of which I was part, encompassing every denomination from Roman Catholic to Southern Baptist to Mennonite to Quaker to Lutheran Church—Missouri Synod, and many more. The meetings were always strictly confidential. The press knew nothing of these events. It was a place where anyone from any background could bare their soul and be certain nothing would leave the room.

At each gathering, among other items, two leaders were asked to speak on the subject, "Fulfillments and Frustrations." My turn came in February 1993.

As for fulfillments, I singled out the privilege of proclaiming the good news of the gospel and especially of the satisfaction I felt from the Mission90 emphasis in the ELCA.

As for frustrations, I spoke of my difficulty in being forthright regarding my stance on the gay/lesbian issue. I walked through my journey of coming to understand homosexual persons and my conviction about doing justice for them. "I have changed my mind," I said. "I now believe that they do not choose that orientation and that they are no more moral or immoral than heterosexual persons. It is a justice question for me."

But this, I stated, put me in conflict with that part of me that yearns for the unity of the church.

I wondered if saying these kinds of things about gay and lesbian persons at that meeting, where more conservative leaders were present might evoke strong reaction. To my surprise, no one attacked me. No one even challenged me. On the contrary, even those from the most conservative churches identified with my dilemma. I came out of this meeting feeling grateful that though the ELCA was riddled with homophobia, I actually had more freedom to deal with this question than most others in that room.

Gathering of pastors of larger ELCA churches

For the most part, Corinne and I enjoyed attending the gathering of pastors of larger ELCA churches. The majority were solidly in support of the ELCA. At the spring 1993 session, in addition to preaching, I used part of my time to give them a preview of what I expected the statement on human sexuality to be like and to share some of the same convictions with this group that I had presented to the bishops two months earlier. The reception was good. Richard Boye, pastor at Elim Church in Robbinsdale, Minnesota, wrote to me later, stating that "though it is a bit tough for me as a conservative, I saw the ministry to homosexuals in a new light after your thorough explanation to us . . . I know this is a thorny issue, and I hope that it is not divisive in the church."

This was exactly the kind of reaction I hoped for, namely, to help people to think about the issue without stirring up animosity and ill will.

An avalanche of thorny issues

As the year 1993 continued to unfold, I would learn that all of us on the churchwide staff would need every ounce of the renewed commitment and energy we were feeling. Ending 1992 in the black was, of course, a source of encouragement. Though it was done mainly by cutting some programs, it was, nevertheless, a good feeling to know where we were at in terms of income from synods.

My resolution to complete my second term surfaced in a message I delivered at the meeting of the Conference of Bishops in

March 1993. Preaching on Matthew 4:1–11, the temptations of Jesus, I reminded my colleagues of our own temptation to run from the difficult challenges we face as leaders in the church.

> Do you and I spend much time reflecting on that original commitment we felt when we first heard God's call to be a pastor, when we were ordained, when we were elected to the office of bishop? What has happened to it?
>
> Jesus discovered the freedom and authority to fulfill his ministry by accepting death. From his temptation and on, the cross looms larger and larger. Yet, it is also from this point and on that he takes on a freedom and an authority Satan could not give him. It is the freedom and authority that comes to one who is so deeply related to God and who is so deeply committed to the kingdom that nothing—not even the cross—can deter him.

I suggested that we needed to connect our responsibility to serve the church and the world with our baptism.

> Do you serve like one who has already died? Where is that ultimate source of your freedom and authority? Is it in your election? Is it in your gifts and talents? Or is it in your baptism into the death and resurrection of Christ?

I stated that when the Christian community singles one out and sets one apart for leadership, it is even more sobering and even more radical.

> To be called to live out your baptism in the public arena should strike fear in us. To wear the mark of the cross in an office where you are under constant public scrutiny is awesome.

I said to them that we would not dare to do it were it not for the promise of Christ to be with us in our baptism journey.

> I do not have much time left to do what is courageous, to stand for what I believe is right, to speak a clear word.

I cannot step into a pulpit without praying, "Lord, I'm a dying person, speaking to dying people. This may be my last chance. Lord, give me a clear, ultimate word."

None of the bishops knew, of course, about the caldron of temptation and fear and turmoil out of which this message had emerged. For me, however, it was clear that there was now no turning back. Whatever challenges lay ahead, I was prepared to face them.

And come they did. One pressing issue after another was landing on my desk, each indicative of stress across the whole ELCA:

Gays in the military

President Bill Clinton, in what many considered a bold move, declared that the military must institute a "don't ask, don't tell" policy regarding gay and lesbian persons in all of branches of the services. I came out publicly in support of Clinton's policy. In an Associated Press report (*Washington Post*, 4/3/93) George Cornell, Associated Press religion editor, commended me for a "clear, forthright comparison" of the ELCA stance with that of Clinton's proposal.

> While the church does not ban gay people from becoming pastors . . . it has a clear set of standards and expectations for all clergy, including that gay clergy abstain from homosexual relations. We judge them by their behavior rather than on the basis of sexual orientation. Also, church standards for heterosexual ministers forbids sex relations outside of marriage.

Reaction to my support for Clinton's proposal was strong. Letters kept coming in for several months, nearly all protesting my support for Clinton's policy. It was interesting to note, however, that when I visited a number of synod assemblies during those months most who talked to me about this matter were grateful for my action.

In time I would come to the conviction that even Clinton's stance—and by extension, my own—was prejudicial toward homosexual persons in the military. Thus, I could only be grateful when that policy was finally eliminated for our service personnel. Once again it was clear that the sexuality issues were at least as controversial as slavery, and that in this instance, as with slavery, the church would be a follower rather than a leader.

The study of ministry

In my report to the Church Council in March 1993 I noted that the study on ministry was moving forward with good prospects for approval by the Churchwide Assembly later that summer. The task force, after very thorough study and intense debate emerged with, among other things, a recommendation that the ELCA approve the creation of a diaconate and that these persons be ordained into that office.

We knew this would be a controversial issue for some. I had no worries about the former AELC. John Tietjen and others with roots in the Missouri Synod had good memories of the work of teachers and deacons in that church. Tietjen had made several forceful statements during the CNLC process insisting that as Lutherans we had the freedom to create such orders in consonance with needs in the church and the world. I did, however, have major concern about how this proposal would fly in circles where the former ALC was predominant.

I had urged Joseph Wagner and Paul Nelson, director of the study, to be in close touch with David Preus, James Crumley, and Robert Marshall, knowing that the strongest opposition might come from them. To the best of my recollection, Marshall made no public comments. Preus and Crumley, however, came out swinging, with strong statements of opposition to the diaconate. Their resistance, however, stemmed from quite different perspectives.

In mid-March 1993 Preus sent an open letter to a representative group he described as people "I have worked closely with through the years." He felt that the report focused too much on what he called "professionals" in the church. He thought the task force was moving too deliberately in the direction of establishing orders in the church "at a time when the church needs to treasure its flexibility." He felt no compelling need for an order of deacons. He worried that we were losing the necessary focus on the importance of word and sacrament ministry. Not least, he argued that establishing an order of deacons would "inevitably be viewed as a way to provide another large group with the IRS housing perk, thereby further feeding anti-clericalism."

Crumley's opposition was rooted in his experience in Lutheran-Roman Catholic dialogue. He insisted that we are not free to constitute any ordained orders other than that of pastors. "If Word and Sacrament," he wrote, "are the marks of the church, do they not define ministry, so that we may conclude that the ordained ministry is 'constitutive' of the church. . . ." This uniqueness, he insisted, must be maintained. "To ordain deacons to the same service is ecclesiological confusion."

Crumley went on to posit that having just one ordained ministry would open doors to ecumenical cooperation. Citing his experience with the Lutheran-Roman Catholic dialogue, he argued that ordaining deacons would interrupt our progress toward resolution of our differences with them regarding ministry,

When I shared Crumley's views with Paul Nelson, director of the study of ministry, he took sharp issue with Crumley's stance. Nelson pointed out that even in the Roman Catholic Church there were different orders of ministry. He agreed that we need to accent the uniqueness of word and sacrament ministry. But having a separate rite for ordaining deacons, said Nelson, served that purpose.

In my report to the Church Council I commended the task force for its good work. I charged the members of the council to base their reaction to the report of the task force on their own careful study of the document and not on "letters and other mailings that, in some cases, are riddled with inaccuracies." As for a set apart order of deacons, I told the council that I "fully and enthusiastically support the proposal." I also felt a need to point out the obvious, namely, that one in five of those on our current roster of ordained ministers was not in what we normally think of as "word and sacrament" ministry.

Cancer again—a trial we didn't need

During this tumultuous time in the church Corinne was enjoying immensely her ministry at St. Luke's. It was evident to everyone that this was the place where she belonged. Her impact on many lives in the parish and beyond was evident on every hand.

We were completely unprepared for what happened in early June 1993. After being assured three years earlier that the surgical procedure had removed all evidence of the deadly cancer, she began to feel distress again. The sarcoma was back. After surgery she was assured once more that it was all removed. Now she realized that the Chicago surgeon actually had had very little experience with this type of cancer. It was apparent that she needed another source of help.

In my journal I wrote:

> It's hard to think of the unthinkable. We take life for
> granted, in spite of the forewarnings we've both had
> through our bouts with cancer. But we want so much to
> have some free years together. It is unthinkable to contem-
> plate the possibility of the death of either of us. I know it's
> wrong to live that way. In fact, I just edited a sermon that
> will appear in the next *Lutheran Partners* that says exactly
> that—we must be reconciled to our death if we expect to be
> free to live. But that's easier said than done. I pray for her
> health and vitality.

A week later I was in Norway for an LWF meeting. Corinne's condition was constantly on my mind. I wrote that there may be one benefit to all of this:

It makes us more courageous. We know more than ever that we don't have forever to do what we are called to do, to stand for what is right.

Some days later, while still in Norway and feeling very eager for Corinne to join me, I reflected again on how impossible it would be to carry on without her.

The loneliness is very real. I'm surrounded by so many congenial people. "Friends" one might say. Yet, when you are at the top of the organization there is always an invisible shield that separates you from others. It's there, always. And it makes for loneliness. That's why I want Corinne to live. And that's why I want some years—many years—for us to fully enjoy each other.

Corinne flew to Norway to join me for an excursion to the north of Norway with Dave and Elisabeth Wold. We met at Alta and drove through Lapp country to North Cape and on to Kirkeness where we boarded the King Olav for a cruise down the west coast to Bergen. Then we took a tour through the Hardanger Fjord and back to Oslo for our flight to the United States.

We had been consulting with Robert Mandsager, her brother-in-law, a surgeon in Iowa. He recommended that we get an appointment with Dr. Stanley Goldberg, a world-famous expert in colorectal surgery. We made a trip to Minneapolis and soon learned that this man indeed deserved the acclaim he had earned in his specialty. Corinne began flying to Minneapolis every three months for an ultrasound, the only effective diagnostic tool.

Through all of this we once again walked a lonely road. Once more we agreed that making this information public would not be in our best interests. Being asked wherever we went about her condition would only be a distraction. As we had done earlier, we informed only a handful of our family and best friends.

Nevertheless, this was one more burden of concern to pile on to our already stressful lives. It was constantly in the back of my mind during the unfolding months of 1993.

Firm resolve

Though I was not conscious of any personal changes in the way I was carrying out my ministry, others seemed to note a new resolve as I faced increasing challenges. The *Milwaukee Post-Crescent* ran a story headlined "Bishop Not Afraid of Tough Issues." Citing abortion and gay rights as the most divisive, controversial questions we were facing, I stated that "we've made a lot of people on either extreme unhappy over the stands we've taken" (6/12/93). The *Harrisburg Patriot-News* headlined an article with the words, "Church Leader Blunt on Issues." Focusing on my support for Clinton's policy regarding gays in the military and intervention in Bosnia, the article quoted me on the first issue as saying that

> There are many moral, highly-principled gay and lesbian people who have always served in the military and who still want to serve their country.

A profile in *Sweden and America* magazine summarized where the church, and I, were at as we approached mid-1993 and prepared for the Kansas City Churchwide Assembly:

> By all measures, the merger has been a tempestuous one, but six years of relocations and adjustments have finally resulted in a firmly established church body running more efficiently and gaining new confidence. Much of that is to Chilstrom's credit.

Was this an accurate assessment? I'd like to believe it was. But I would be the last to judge.

Corinne's book

Just prior to the 1993 Kansas City Churchwide Assembly, Corinne's book *Andrew, You Died Too Soon* came off the press at Augsburg

Fortress. While I was traveling in Japan a few weeks before the assembly, Corinne sent a letter informing me that the book was out. She bared her soul about what it meant:

> I must say I feel bittersweet about having the book public now. Deep satisfaction from doing the "I must" & vulnerable to open deep feelings of grief to the world. But do believe it will help many to open their hearts & lives to God in their grief & that in so doing God will be glorified & the *kingdom will come.*

Now almost twenty years later, letters and phone calls continue to come from appreciative readers. Every year she receives a letter from a professor at Wartburg College who uses her book in one of his classes. He asks the students to write a brief description of what it meant to them to read the book. These readers tell of how the book opens their minds to new perspectives on suicide and adoption. And this is only a small example of why the book continues to be a strong sales item for Augsburg Fortress.

The 1993 Kansas City assembly

Leaving office

I decided it would be well at the beginning of my report to share with the assembly my plan to leave office at the end of my second term. After giving thanks for the strong vote of affirmation at Orlando in 1991, I said that from the beginning of this second term, I decided that 1995 would be a good time for the church to elect its next leader.

> After a time of prayerful reflection and conversation with my family, I took out my appointment book, turned to the back pages where I keep long-range notations, and inserted the words, "October 31, 1995. Amen!"
>
> Those of you who know me well know that I'm not a sprinter. I'm a distance runner. A good distance runner

does not slacken the pace when moving into that last stretch. In fact, a distance runner quickens the pace. And that is exactly what I intend to do in these next two years.

In my report to the assembly, among other items I emphasized that

> Bringing together a church of our size had been an arduous task. I suggested that it might take at least twenty years until we achieved a sense of broad unity. "We may have been naïve in thinking that in one or two years we would have a solid identity."

> I warned the assembly to resist the temptation to place a moratorium on the discussion of complex issues, naming especially the human sexuality discussion. I urged that we find a way "to discuss potentially volatile issues without risking division of this church." The key, I suggested, was to keep our focus on the faith of the church and to remember that no statement of the church is binding on individual members.

> I also urged the church to press on with our attempts to establish lasting ecumenical bonds with other churches.

The study on ministry

Highest on the agenda at Kansas City was the report of the task force on the study on ministry. The final action on diaconal ministry was probably a good compromise. Though some wanted these persons to be ordained, it was clear that support for it was lacking. Nevertheless, having diaconal ministers as "a public ministry that exemplifies the servant life, equips and motivates others to live it" got overwhelming support from the voting members of the assembly.

Looking back now I ask if the action has made a difference in the life of the ELCA. I doubt it. It seems that only a small number of persons have pursued this vocational option. One wonders if having ordained diaconal ministers might have resulted in a better response.

Other assembly actions

I felt proud of many of the other actions taken by the Kansas City Churchwide Assembly.

> "Caring for Creation: Vision, Hope, and Justice" was a social statement that was cutting edge for its time and a clear commitment of the church to preserving the earth.

> A delicately balanced statement of concern for our sister churches in the former Yugoslavia caught up in the war in Bosnia.

> A positive word of support for persons abused because of their sexual orientation was at least a small step in laying some groundwork for the forthcoming discussion on human sexuality.

> A statement on racism that overwhelmingly affirmed the so-called quota system, assuring minority representation at all levels of the church's life.

Response to the assembly

As is always the case, reaction to the assembly was mixed. One woman was so moved by the worship services that she sent a post-assembly donation to defray some of those expenses. James Crumley thought the worship experiences were "more of a variety show than a Lutheran liturgy." He was not alone. I pointed out that we had been criticized at Orlando for being too traditional and the worship committee was responding to a changing church, one in which members came from a variety of cultural backgrounds. It is a never-ending issue in the church.

In his usual gracious manner, Robert Marshall responded to my announcement of leaving office and also commended me for my leadership of the sessions.

> I want to thank you for your faithful diligence in office during these years when the new church organization has been

struggling to find its way. The responsibility of presiding at the Assembly provides a symbol for all the rest of your work. You must maintain intense concentration while attending to technical details at the same time that you strive to be fair to every speaker and still retain a clear sense of proportion and propriety that will benefit the progress of the whole enterprise.... I was constantly amazed at your composure and good humor in tedious and provocative situations.

Coming from a man who had not only presided at many conventions himself, but who had also been on the Church Council from the beginning of the ELCA, those words were particularly heartening.

My own assessment of the Kansas City Churchwide Assembly was that it turned out to be better than I expected. I feared that it might be boring. But it wasn't—at least not from my perspective and from what I heard from others. There was a sense of unity that prevailed at the assembly. I felt a prayerful spirit, a confidence that in spite of difficult times, we are beyond the point where we need to fear serious division.

My announcement that I intended to step out of office when my present term ended caught many by surprise. The most common reaction I heard was that folks were not prepared for it. They simply had not expected it at this time. But these same persons said that the more they thought about it the more sense it made.

Where are we headed?

It was during this time in mid-1993 that I found myself asking again where the ELCA was headed as a church. I reflected on a conversation I had with Eric Shafer, director of the Office for Communications, after I had attended many synod assembly meetings in the spring and early summer.

I told Shafer that as I moved from synod to synod I sensed that the ELCA, like most other denominations, was moving toward local and regional configuration. I said I didn't like it. I feared that our loss of a churchwide identity was regrettable. "I will fight it all the way," I wrote in my journal.

> Yet, there is a limit to how much one person can do. I hear everywhere of fund drives for local and synod causes. Yes, I know they have always been there, but what I see and feel now is almost a withdrawal from the larger scene. I heard the other day that only one in eleven younger adults watches a regular news cast. We know they are not join-ers—including the church. One can only wonder where this is going. The point is that I sense withdrawal—a kind of "tribalization" that seems to be happening.

In the fall of 1993 after the meeting of the Conference of Bish-ops, I put similar thoughts in writing:

> The gathering of the synod bishops last week was, as usual, mixed. . . . They see themselves as the center of the church, synods as the places where the church is working best. I don't like to disillusion them, but I think that a bit myopic. The interdependence we envision in the constitution is something that doesn't come easily. I get much personal affirmation from them. I worry sometimes, however, that it doesn't extend to the churchwide staff. I don't think they realize how much affection we have for each other on the churchwide staff and how we hurt when some are criticized—often unfairly.

"Making Christ Known"—evangelical outreach

In the fall of 1993 it was our clear intention to accent evangelism. We affirmed again our mission statement:

> A church so deeply and confidently rooted in the Gospel of God's grace, that we are free to give ourselves joyfully in witness and service.

This was stage two of Mission90. My aim was to visit as many synods as possible in my final two years in office to encourage congregational outreach. I focused on Luke/Acts as the basis for energizing the church. Again and again, others had acknowledged my teaching gifts. Now across the church and in as many places as was humanly possible I wanted to engage pastors and lay people in discussing how the insights of the church in the first century could help us to be an evangelizing church as we moved toward the twenty-first century.

Synods set up area workshops where members of congregations could learn how to do evangelism. A sampling of my travel in October and November of 1993 for this emphasis found me in places like Seguin, Texas; the Ozarks; Denver; Puerto Rico and the Virgin Islands; eastern Pennsylvania; Sacramento and San Francisco; Minneapolis; York, Pennsylvania; and Jamestown, New York. This is the pace I maintained until I left office. I reminded folks wherever I went of the seventy-five million in our communities who were not part of any church; that only a third of our members were at worship each week; that the place to begin is with prayer and family devotions in our homes; that as worship preferences change we must hold on to the fundamental elements of confession, preaching, Scripture reading, prayer, good hymn singing, offering and the sacraments.

Human sexuality: All hell breaks loose

A muddled release of the draft and the aftershock

Could we have anticipated what happened in October 1993? On October 19 through 21, I was at a pastors' retreat in the lovely Ozark mountains, leading them in the study of Luke/Acts. In the middle of my lecture, I noticed a stir in the room. I saw newspapers being passed from table to table. I could not help but see that bit by bit I was losing their attention.

At the end of the lecture I soon found out the reason for the disruption. Copies of the *St. Louis Dispatch* were being circulated with a front-page headline story about the ELCA draft statement on human sexuality. I was caught completely off guard, as was the entire church. The intention had been that all pastors of the church would receive a copy of the draft before it was released to the press. Only later did we learn that a staff person in Chicago had released an advance copy to a reporter on the promise that the reporter would hold it until it was officially released by the Division for Church in Society. Complicating matters even further was that actual release of the draft statement was delayed for technical reasons. The reporter, probably realizing he had an irresistible coup, wrote an article and released it to the media through the Associated Press.

The account spread like a prairie fire. Even *The New York Times* picked it up with the headline, "Sexual Policy Stalls Lutherans." Religion editor Peter Steinfels reported that our four-year effort to produce the document "has nearly foundered since reports of a first draft alarmed members of the 5.2 million-member denomination" (11/26/93). Edgar Trexler was reported in the story as saying, "The proposed statement . . . is mortally wounded." He was right.

Little wonder that people at the grassroots were disturbed. The AP report highlighted parts of the draft that would almost surely incite strong reaction. Like others, Steinfels relied on the AP report that led off the story with the assertion that the document "declared masturbation to be healthy, homosexual marriages to be biblically supported, and condom distribution among teenagers to be a moral imperative." Most every newspaper across the country did the same.

To his credit, Steinfels recognized the difficulty of dealing with human sexuality.

> The episode illustrates how volatile the prospect of revising traditional teaching on sexuality can be in American churches, especially when complicated theological discussions get distilled—or sensationalized—in news reports.

Reaction from pastors and bishops

Pastors across the church were incensed, and rightfully so, that they had not seen anything until it hit the public media. There were scattered reports of congregations taking action to cut their giving to synod and churchwide causes. Some bishops reported their phones were "ringing off their hooks" with irate callers. At least two synod bishops denounced the draft. In contrast, other bishops reported only minimal reaction to the draft statement and newspaper accounts. Robert Isakson, bishop of the New England Synod, was quoted in the *Christian Century* as saying:

> The church cannot be helpful by refusing to talk about difficult questions. The purpose of dialogue is not to have controversy but to glean insights about issues people are wrestling with in their lives (11/17–24/93).

An avalanche of angry protest

For us in Chicago, it was like mayhem. Hundreds of irate phone calls came in the first days. Over a period of a few weeks, the Division for Social Ministry was inundated with thousands of letters of protest. I alone received seven hundred letters, most of them so angry and incendiary that, as I was wont to put it, "they nearly burned the finish off the top of my desk." For several weeks I got one or two letters a day suggesting that I resign. I canceled a planned hunting trip to South Dakota at the end of the month and spent every free moment with my staff answering the overwhelmingly angry mail.

Three prominent professors at Luther Seminary—James Burtness, Gerhard Forde, and Craig Koester—released a public statement attacking the biblical basis for the way the draft had dealt with homosexuality. Twenty-three of their colleagues at Luther signed on to the letter. Another thirty-two full-time faculty did not sign. In spite of President David Tiede's insistence that it was not an official statement of the seminary, it became known as that in many places. None of the seven other seminaries responded in this way.

They seemed ready to study the draft carefully before making any such judgments.

I chose not to take on the Luther Seminary professors publicly but pointed out to at least one long-time acquaintance, Philip Worthington, what I thought were the faulty bases for their case:

> Their inconsistency in the application of biblical interpretation. If they used the same hermeneutical principles regarding divorce as they did with homosexuality, we would have to ask tens of thousands of divorced persons to leave the church.

> Their posture was entirely lacking in pastoral concern for our brothers and sisters in the church who are gay and lesbian through no choice of their own.

Damage control

Our initial effort to stem the tide was to report to the media that the draft was exactly that, a *first* draft of a *possible* statement on human sexuality. I wrote that the draft document:

> . . . has no official standing in this church. Our intention is that this first draft will be studied carefully by folks like you and that you will send your comments to our Division for Church in Society.

We tried to make it clear that the draft could be amended and even abandoned entirely over the next stages of the process.

The report in the *Christian Century* was headed with the words: "Chilstrom: Read the sexuality report." I was quoted as saying, "Do not base your reaction on the assumption that the newspaper reports are accurate and complete" (11/17–24/93).

We accented the core of the draft that a permanent and loving relationship with deep commitment is at the heart of a Christian understanding of sexual activity.

In an interview with the *Chicago Sun Times* (10/25/93), I stated that our church was not about to bury its head in the sand and ignore the pressing issues of our times, including human sexuality. I also suggested that the AP account had missed the nuances of the draft statement:

> Masturbation may be appropriate and healthy, unless it becomes compulsive or hinders development of life-fulfill-ing relationships.

> While heterosexual marriage is normative, it is inappro-priate to use Bible passages to condemn all same-gender relationships.

> Sexual intercourse should be reserved for marriage. Those who do otherwise should practice safe sex with the use of condoms.

> Education regarding responsible sexual conduct is a moral imperative.

> Even if a statement is finally adopted, it is not binding on any individual member of the church.

On October 27, I sent a special mailing to all ELCA pastors. I apologized for the mistake that had been made in giving a copy of the draft statement to the press before pastors had received their copy in the mail. This gave them "a serious disadvantage in know-ing how to respond to those who raised concerns with you." I pointed out that the media reports had skewed the content of the draft. "The major focus of the material got minor attention."

I went on to accent the major points they needed to keep in mind:

> The draft had no official standing in the church. This was only the first step in a long process.

> Until the Churchwide Assembly considered a final draft in 1995, there would be thorough discussion and revision of the document. I pointed out that an assembly has several options when considering any proposed statement:

> It can accept it exactly as received (this has never
> happened); it can reject the proposed statement in its
> entirety (this has never happened) it can delay action
> on a proposed statement (this has happened); or it can
> revise the text and adopt it as amended (this is what
> usually happens).

I asked if our church could be "a source of healthy and thorough reflection in a society that needs help with issues relating to human sexuality." I reminded the pastors that members of their congregations were engaged with sexuality issues in their daily lives: adultery and infidelity, promiscuity, sexual abuse, sexually transmitted diseases, discriminatory behavior toward others, prostitution, pornography, and much more.

I concluded with a plea for their partnership in this difficult but important task. . . . "we are all invited to participate in the process of discovering the mind of this church in this complex area."

In a follow-up letter to the synod bishops in November 1993 I took full responsibility for what had happened:

> I recognize as the chief executive of this organization that
> the buck stops with me. I apologize for what has happened.
> I am deeply sorry for the trouble that this situation has
> caused so many of you. I grieve over the sense of betrayal
> and mood of broken trust so many pastors and others feel
> as a result of what has happened.

I went on to urge the bishops to

> pick up the pieces and fulfill the various crucial tasks at
> hand. I solicit your help and cooperation. At the same time,
> I appreciate the leadership that you have provided.

I reminded the bishops that all of this had started, not at our offices in Chicago, often maligned as "Higgins Road," but with resolutions that came from a number of synod assemblies early in the life of the church calling for this very thing: a statement on human sexuality. I refreshed their memories about how the ELCA had agreed to develop social statements and how task forces, including this one, were constituted with broad representation.

I challenged the bishops to think about how the draft document would have been received had everything worked smoothly and as we had intended. Suppose, I asked, pastors had received it in advance of the public release. Would the challenge for us be much different?

> All of us would still have been faced with the enormous task of clarifying and teaching. . . . if you believe, as I do, that good can come from the most unfortunate situation, then the attention the draft has drawn gives us a "teaching moment" that we seldom have at our disposal.

I said to them that this was a moment for a synodical bishop, as one who carries a teaching responsibility, to put in writing exactly what it is that was of concern to them, point out where changes needed to be made, and what they would recommend as an alternative or as a revision.

I urged the bishops to be proactive in seeking out media opportunities to set the draft into proper perspective, mentioning that I had been on several outlets around the country and that "even the Chicago papers seem to know we're in town!"

When the Church Council had its regular meeting, the sexuality report, as expected, was high on the agenda. The council decided that it might be well to add more persons to the task force, including some synod bishops, in order to bring broader perspective into the ongoing process of refining the draft. The council also decided to add two more years to the development timeline, extending it to 1997. As we would see, this made no difference whatever.

In public statements I spoke of the obvious—that homosexuality was *the* issue.

> I think the jury is out on so many questions about homo-
> sexuality. The best we can do is frame the issues and urge
> courageous and calm discussion (*Minneapolis Star Tribune*,
> 12/10/93).

Support and affirmation

Initial reaction to the draft document, as I've noted, was mostly
vitriolic. As weeks passed and as more and more actually read the
draft, the tide began to turn. Even those who did not agree with
parts of the draft sent words of encouragement.

A tongue-in-cheek article by Jim Klobuchar, columnist for the
Minneapolis Star Tribune in the heartland of Lutheranism, brought
a bit of comic relief. The eye-catching headline read: "If Lutherans
don't like sex, why are there so many of them?"

> No one is as creative as the Lutherans in finding grounds
> for internal brawling and hair-tearing. The latest is sex.
> With most people, sex brings thrills and propagation.
> Lutherans are different. With Lutherans it brings revolt and
> indignation.
>
> The unlikely lightning rod for all the fuming is a tall, white-
> haired prairie bishop from Minnesota, Herb Chilstrom. . . .

After calling the Chicago offices a fortress rather than a headquarters, Klobuchar, as a good columnist should do, pointed out
the inanity of what was going on.

> None of the recommendations or statements are sensa-
> tional. The objections deal with the actual or perceived
> conflicts between those and what's read in the Bible.

Klobuchar noted that this process was scheduled to come to a
head at the church's gathering in Minneapolis in 1995. He urged
local officials to "Get the armory ready" (12/2/93).

It was good to have a bit of humor in the midst of those heavy
days.

At Luther Seminary, other heavyweight scholars such as Arland Hultgren, Paul Sponheim, Robert Albers, and Terence Fretheim began to work on materials that were in sharp contrast to what their colleagues had published.

Some positive words of understanding for me in my difficult role also emerged.

Elisabeth Wold, wife of one of our bishops, sent a note to Corinne expressing the support we felt from many of our colleague bishops and spouses.

> You and Herb are in our thoughts and prayers so much in these days of emotional and financial stress in our ELCA. How quick we all are to express our freedom in Christ without love! I am often aware of how lonely Herb's and your place is; and so I want you to know how deeply I respect and love you.

I discovered that when I was directly engaged with people in grassroots settings the discussion was usually sane and sensible. It was the mail that dragged me down.

Two weeks later I wrote in my journal again, this time about the need to keep matters in perspective.

> Because I have had so many hundreds of letters in opposition to the draft on human sexuality, I tend to think the whole church shares the views that come in letters. But I would guess that they are not truly representative of many in the church—possibly only a minority.

Will Herzfeld, the former head of the AELC and a strong supporter of what I was doing, spoke to me forthrightly in February 1994, suggesting that I may have done as much as I could at that time. To say more, he counseled, might be counter productive.

Putting things into perspective

As I moved into my final year and a half in office, I found it important to help others put our young church into perspective. At the
spring 1994 meetings of the Conference of Bishops and Church
Council I took time in my joint report to try to give these leaders
of the ELCA an understanding of how I saw the current and future
life of our church.

I had just attended the annual meeting of U.S. church leaders,
the group that embraced the broadest configuration of churches
in the country. Given our tendency as a young church, which
had begun with such high expectations, to beat up on ourselves, I
reported that nearly every leader painted a picture like that of the
ELCA: financial shortfalls, membership decline, and the need for
reorganization.

I cited the work of Douglas John Hall who traced our problems
back to the halcyon days following World War II. While record
numbers of churches were organized and memberships and financial resources grew, we were living in denial of what was actually
going on around us. What emerged was "cultural denomination-
alism" that had little to do with the radical nature of apostolic
Christianity, said Hall. What must emerge, he insisted, is a remnant
church whose primary mission is service and prophecy.

I also referred to the work of Langdon Gilkey. He suggested that
the decline of the church is linked to the decline of Western civi-
lization. How can we survive this decline? Gilkey isn't certain, but
thinks it may be through spiritual renewal—especially in worship.

I mentioned several others, including Loren Mead, Martin Marty,
and Robert Wuthnow. The latter notes that the major tensions of our
time are not *between* denominations, but *within* them. The call is for
major restructuring to meet this new challenge.

I reserved major attention for William McKinney. He thinks
denominations have a future if we stop listening to the fringe

groups in our churches and pay more attention to the broad middle. These folks are committed to the fundamental evangelical message of the church, but are also ready to heed the church's call to address complex social issues. He says we need to declare an armistice between the extremes in our churches and work for "a reinvigorated middle."

I said to the bishops and the council that if there is wisdom in these observations, it

> . . . means that business as usual is out of the question. It means that if this church has a future, we must move into it without losing our anchor with the past.

I reminded them that further reduction of the churchwide organization was not an option.

> We must be prepared for changes that will reach beyond the churchwide structure. We cannot put off indefinitely the question of the reduction of the number of synods. While that action may lie beyond my tenure in office, I would not be accountable if I did not raise the question now.

I talked about creeping congregationalism in the church:

> For decades there has been a gradual but continuing decline in the percentage of congregational income that is shared with synod and churchwide mission.

I said that there is only small comfort in knowing it is happening to others as well as to us.

> We need to ask ourselves, Is this the kind of church . . . we want to be?

It was, to be sure, a hard-hitting report. I showed the freedom I felt in wanting to make my last months in office as productive as possible. I did not want to be a lame duck bishop. After reminding these groups that every generation in the church had to deal with a divisive issue—slavery, predestination, language, inerrancy, Communism—we needed to keep our focus on that glue that holds us together: our Confession of Faith.

Did these two key groups take up the challenge I laid before them? I have no evidence to show for it. Like it or not, I was going out of office and they were no doubt beginning to think of a future under some other leadership. Surely no bishop at that meeting was ready to forfeit his or her fiefdom. And I know of no mention from my successors about reducing the number of synods. Yet I believe even now that the challenges I laid out in the spring of 1994 were what needed to be heard at that moment in the life of the young church.

Meanwhile, we continued to make cuts in grants to various groups. In a letter in May 1994 to my brother-in-law Fred Sickert, a chaplain supervisor in California, I described what it was like to sit in my chair:

> One time its sem presidents, then college presidents, then peace activists, then the gay/lesbian community, and on and on. After meeting with the chaplain reps yesterday I had a session with reps from the minority communities. I think some of these folks are beginning to realize that we don't print money here in Chicago and that we are directly dependent on funds that come from congregations through synods. When I asked the persons at the meeting yesterday if their local congregations had increased their giving to their synods there was a strange silence in the room! What often puzzles me is that folks who see volcanic upheaval in their own fields—such as medical care, hospitals, etc.—can't seem to understand that the church, too, is in the midst of that kind of change.

I got a bit of comic relief the next week when I was in New Orleans for a synod assembly. The announcement for the service at the St. Louis Cathedral said that "Bishop Herbert Chilstrom will bring the message and we will sing praises to his name."

Temptations to bail out

As we moved into the synod assemblies in the spring and summer of 1994, several bishops who could have stood for reelection were choosing not to do so. It seemed that some of them, as well as heads of churchwide units, were experiencing what I had gone through more than a year earlier. In a letter to all of them in early June 1994 I urged them to take the longer look.

> These are difficult times to be in leadership. I need not say that to those of you who serve as synod bishops and heads of churchwide units.

I went on to cite a passage from Henry Melchoir Muhlenberg's *Diary of a Colonial Clergyman*:

> Frequently Muhlenberg had to try to mend the relations between pastors and congregations following quarrels.

I said I knew the temptation to look at other opportunities and to think that there must be something more rewarding to do in ministry. I reminded them of that broad middle in the church, full of supportive folks who were their allies in difficult times.

> These are the folks you and I meet in our congregations and at area meetings. Remember them when you get discouraged. They are praying for us who share leadership responsibilities.

I'm sure I was indulging in a bit of introspection when I went on to say to those who were leaving office that

> To one degree or another we must live in a situation where others look through us and beyond us as they think about who will succeed us and as they weigh the needs of the church under new leadership. We need to be careful not to be defensive. Our shortcomings have left gaps that need to be filled and mistakes that need to be corrected. But let us also give thanks for those areas in which God may have

been able to use us for some good in this church. Let us serve with love and enthusiasm as long as we bear responsibility for the office or the position. And, above all, let us be constant in prayer that God will raise up those who are needed for synod and churchwide offices.

The heaviness of that time was also evident in my journal entries. In mid-April 1994, after hearing that the Lutheran Church in Canada had all but dismantled its national organization, I wrote that:

We may be there in some years. I don't know. Visiting synods for assemblies and Mission90 events is almost always an upper. I'll put full energy into the remaining months.

Dealing with the lame duck syndrome

With only a year left in office, and knowing it was unthinkable to try to initiate new programs, I had to decide what kind of bishop I was going to be for my last months in office. I had a choice, I could coast, letting programs in place carry themselves forward. Or I could be proactive, giving myself energetically to what I felt was of highest priority.

Choosing the latter course was a no-brainer for me. I wanted to, and needed to, stay as engaged as possible with the church. And how would I do that? I would keep on trying in my quest to visit every synod before the end of my term in office.

Of course, I had to attend to the other demands of my office during this time: leadership at meetings of the Church Council, work with the Conference of Bishops and the Cabinet of Executives in Chicago, fulfilling my role as a vice president of the LWF, and much more. But first and foremost, I would devote my time to being the chief pastor of the church.

I used the 1994 synod assemblies to interact with as many synods as possible. I loaded my calendar, often going from one assembly to the next. In my report to the assemblies I laid out three things that pleased me most about the ELCA and then two that concerned me most. Then I opened myself to give and take questioning with the voting members.

My three gratifications

1. We are a word and sacrament people. "Lutherans," I said, "have never been very big on structure and organization. But one thing we are big on—one thing we insist on—is that the Word of God is faithfully preached and taught and that the Sacraments are faithfully administered."

2. We know we are called to reach out to the world. "It's time to take our light out from under the bushel and let it shine." We need not surrender witnessing to the fundamentalists, I said. "I like to think of our 11,000 congregations as 11,000 mission stations. In those places, you are in the front lines of our witness to the world."

3. We have such an exceptional churchwide staff. "I wish you could know them as well as I do. They are deeply dedicated brothers and sisters in Christ. I count it a privilege to work with them."

My two concerns: neither was a surprise to the listeners

1. We need to increase support for the ministries we have agreed to do together through our synod and churchwide organizations. Congregational giving had increased since the birth of the ELCA. "The problem is in our vision and in our giving. We need an even broader vision of our calling to witness and serve, not only in our immediate community, but in the whole world."

2. We are called to unity. Merging our churches at that moment in history had been a gargantuan challenge in itself. Addressing complex social issues had stretched us, especially in the area of human sexuality. But this was not new for the

church. Every generation had faced a major threat to unity. "I would plead with you to remember that we can disagree on some of these issues so long as we are held together by what is central to our faith. And what is that? The answer lies in where we started—Word and Sacrament."

I concluded by admitting that I could not predict where we were headed in some areas. But I was certain beyond doubt that "the glue that holds us together is secure. As long as we keep in focus our first and primary commitment to the proclamation of the gospel and our faithful administration of the sacraments, we will be a strong church. That is what I pray for, over and over again. I know you are with me in that prayer."

In my report to the Church Council on October 3, 1994, I shared my enthusiasm for what I was doing:

> The Mission90 events in synods are giving me the opportunity to continue the pattern I have followed since I came into office—to be at the grass roots of the church as much as possible. I am grateful for the excellent response in most synods.

I spoke about what a special privilege it was to lead our pastors and lay persons in study of the Bible and in discussion regarding our response to God's call. "I am overwhelmed," I said "by the commitment and dedication of so many in this church."

It was about that time that I received an enormously encouraging letter from H. George Anderson. He had expressed no interest at the time in being my successor.

He blessed me with the perspective of a church historian.

> From my point of view, you have been exactly the right person to lead us into the venture of a new Lutheran church. It has been so important to have a spiritual leader with a good theological basis to help focus the eyes and the energies of the church on significant goals.

There have indeed been many difficult times and disappointments, but they certainly were not of your making.

He went on to observe that all of the major denominations were
facing the same difficulties to one extent or another.

I believe that you helped us avoid some of the worst pitfalls
that those stresses have created elsewhere. In a time when
there has been much criticism and unfair one-upmanship,
you have remained above the battle and have tried to let all
members of the church know that they are important and
that you care about their life and faith. Your ability to listen
to complaints and criticisms and then come back with
caring and thoughtful answers has impressed me at many
synod meetings and pastoral gatherings. Thank you for
your pastoral ministry.

It was a "word in season."

Worship in the ELCA

A constant source of satisfaction during my time in office was to
participate in worship events in many different venues. When the
presiding bishop was present it was usual for these events to be
planned carefully and carried out effectively. Now and then, however, I found myself in settings where worship was ill-prepared and
even more poorly conducted.

I had an opportunity in September 1994 to give a major address
on worship at the Worship Leaders Network event. It was an ideal
place to spell out my convictions on the subject.

I began with a citation from Brueggemann's book *Israel's Praise*:

Praise is the duty and delight, the ultimate vocation of the
human community, indeed of all creation. Praise articulates
and embodies our capacity to yield, submit, and abandon
ourselves in trust and gratitude to the One whose we are.

I went on to speak of how we had tried to make our worship experiences at the Lutheran Center a model for the whole church.

As for the church at large, I noted the dramatic changes I had experienced in my lifetime—visual arts, free-standing altars, baptismal preparation and practice, the participation of children in coming to the altar for a blessing, children's sermons, the lower age for communing children, and much more.

While I affirmed these changes, I also underscored my delight in seeing that our *Lutheran Book of Worship* was the anchor at most of our congregational services.

> When led with enthusiasm and with a sense that the leaders are a part of the worshipping community rather than performers, the *LBW* works well . . .

I also lauded the creativity I witnessed in many places as congregations sought to relate worship to the everyday lives of parishioners and visitors.

As for so-called contemporary worship, I recalled my own experience:

> We soon learned that it takes just as much talent and forethought and just as much attention to detail to have a good contemporary service as it did to have a good traditional service.

The danger in this kind of worship, I said, is that those who attend may be inclined to watch rather than participate. If the performance of the leader is not up to expectations, people tend to tire of it very quickly.

I concluded with a word of warning. Seeing a tendency to develop worship materials in local and synodical settings, I found it important to say that in some areas we need to do things together and through well-established processes. Through worship we build identity. In a mobile society, where members move frequently and where few people live in the community where they grew to adulthood, we need the kind of worship resources that help us say, wherever we go, "This is my church."

Theological education: seminary clusters

We had learned in our predecessor churches that merging seminaries simply would not work. Philadelphia and Gettysburg may have been only a couple of hours distant from each other but were also on different planets. The same was true when some thought it would make sense to merge Luther and Wartburg.

Was there a way, however, for the seminaries to be more effective if they were clustered into units of two? Under the leadership of Joseph Wagner, the Division for Ministry staff, and the excellent cooperation of the eight seminary presidents, this plan worked out far better than we could have expected. I said to the Church Council at its October 1994 meeting that:

> We are looking at a radical change in the way this church goes about preparing its leaders for ministry in a radically changed world. A spirit of cooperation has marked the successes of this work to date.

Who will succeed you?

As we moved toward the end of 1994 I was surprised, and a bit dismayed, that there seemed to be so little discussion across the church regarding a successor to my office. There were, of course, some "wannabes." But none of them seemed to garner any enthusiasm. I began to wonder if Bishop Wayne Weissenbuehler and some of his friends were right—that there was no one out there with enough support to step into such a difficult role at that time.

At a meeting for pastors and lay professionals in the Southeastern Minnesota Synod in the fall of 1994 I was asked during a question and answer time if I had any recommendations for a successor. I, of course, refused to take the bait.

But at the Church Council meeting in October I decided to inject a bit of levity. At the end of my regular report I tacked on this addendum:

> Let me add one more word. I was in the Southeastern Minnesota Synod . . . for an event for pastors, AIMS, and lay leaders. During the Q and A exchange I was asked about many things, including whether I would give some names of persons I think are best qualified to be my successor. In that setting, of course, I refused to respond to the question.
>
> In this setting, however, and strictly off the record, I *do* want to say a word. I am convinced that there is, in fact, one person who is preeminently well-qualified to lead this church during the next stage of its life. This is a person of deep and known personal piety. He has had years of experience in administrative work. He is a superb negotiator, having helped bring together many who were in dispute— surely a quality we need in this church. He is both gentle and tough at the same time. If he is willing to become a Lutheran and be ordained, I'm convinced Jimmy Carter is our man.

I held them in suspense and treated them to a good laugh.

In late November 1994 I said to Corinne over dinner that H. George Anderson would be an excellent candidate.

In mid-February 1995 I made these notes in my journal:

> I'm guessing . . . it will go down to the assembly . . . and that it will hang or fall with the speeches the seven finalists give to the voting members.

The sexuality draft: managing a discussion, moving an elephant

My role seemed clear as the discussion on human sexuality continued. Frustrated as I was by how few in the church were ready to deal with the nub of the issue—homosexuality—I kept reminding myself that I was the bishop of the whole church, including those with whom I disagreed. But I also needed to moderate the discussion in the church and, when possible, advocate for a change in attitude toward gay and lesbian persons. I often suggested that a church the size of the ELCA was like an elephant. One could poke and push and shove and cajole. But movement is always slower than we might expect.

I said to the Church Council that we are not a papal church. Final authority does not reside in the office of the bishop of the church. "Many have appealed to me," I said,

> to act decisively—so long as it is in accord with their own opinion! Others have urged me to speak out in a prophetic way, setting out my personal stance on all matters related to human sexuality. I have refused for what I hope are obvious reasons. The moment I were to take that step the debate in the church would galvanize around my opinion rather than on the drafts and the orderly process we have approved for the development of a social teaching statement.

Then I made what is in retrospect a rather radical suggestion: To remove from the "Visions and Expectations" document the sentence:

> Ordained and commissioned ministers who are homosexual in their self-understanding are expected to abstain from homosexual sexual relationships.

I asked if it could not be possible that we might allow congregations that felt free to do so to call a pastor who was in a faithful same-gender relationship.

> Given the fact that we respect and guard the prerogative of local congregations to make the final decision regarding the calling of ordained and commissioned ministers, no congregation need fear that it would be forced to call anyone it does not wish to call, no matter what its reasons may be.

This approach, I argued, would not only lodge the decision where it belonged, but would also highlight the pastoral responsibility of synod bishops in helping the call process.

I was, of course, far ahead of my time in making what I thought was a sensible suggestion. We would soon discover that the issue was so hot that resolution was impossible.

A few weeks later in an interview in the *Fargo Forum* I acknowledged the difficulty we were having with the sexuality discussion and stated that "we . . . have to agree that this issue is going to take us a lot longer to deal with" (7/9/94). In the *Petersburg* [Alaska] *Pilot* I noted that in my travels about the country I had encountered parents of gay and lesbian children who expressed gratitude that the church had the courage to address what was for them a very personal issue—the relationship of their children to the church. "They're reluctant to speak out openly, but in private they thank me" (8/11/94).

I also appreciated the perspective of Lowell Erdahl, bishop of the St. Paul Area Synod and a member of the task force that drew up the draft statement. In 1995 he looked back and framed his views in words that could well have been my own. Like me, he had been involved in many discussions regarding the draft. And, like me, he had discovered that in nearly every case the outcome had been very positive.

> Whatever some may think of it, that statement has made a great contribution to our church and helped to alleviate an immense amount of ignorance and prejudice. There was no doubt some cost in decreased contributions but if it saved even one gay or lesbian person from committing suicide or giving up hope in God and the church, I believe it was worth it. Thank you for your patience and steady presence during these turbulent times.

I have said over and over again that anyone who takes up that first draft now all these years later will find it solid and surely good ground from which to draw up a balanced statement on human sexuality. Regretfully, it came before its time and before the church was ready to deal with something so volatile.

The crisis in the Sierra Pacific Synod

The waters got even muddier in the fall of 1994 when St Paul's Lutheran Church in Oakland, California, decided to call a pastor who refused to comply with "Vision and Expectations." Though it was a synodical matter to deal with this crisis, there was no way that I and the Conference of Bishops could not be involved.

In a letter to Robert Mattheis, bishop of the Sierra Pacific Synod, I poured out my agony. Knowing that Mattheis shared my sentiments about gay and lesbian persons, I traced for him the story of my personal journey and change of mind. My struggle was intensified, I told Mattheis, by my own involvement in the shaping of our current policy that precluded persons in same-gender relationships from being on the clergy roster. "I believe it was the only option for us at a time when this church . . . was too new and fragile to deal with it in any other way."

I concluded that Mattheis might have no option other than to move ahead with a disciplinary process to remove St. Paul's Church from the roster of ELCA congregations. I reminded him that a committee of the Conference of Bishops, which included two members whom I knew had children who were homosexual, had come to the same conclusion.

Having said that, I made two points to Mattheis that I thought might be helpful:

> For those of us for whom this is a justice issue, we must ask how an unjust policy can be changed. By now it is clear that it will never be done by a legislative action of this church. It will only happen when a synod bishop decides that he or she will be the first to "look the other way" and take no action against a congregation. . . .

Knowing that there was strong support in his synod for not bringing disciplinary charges against the congregations, I suggested that Mattheis might well decide to be that first bishop. But that left questions.

> What would be the consequence beyond the Sierra Pacific Synod? It is hard to judge. Surely you would be criticized by many. My guess, however, is that you also would have solid support from many, including some synod bishops.

The second problem Mattheis would face would be that he would be accused of ignoring ELCA policy, I wrote, however, that ignoring church policy for pastoral reasons was not unprecedented.

> I have in mind the practice of a growing number of pastors [who commune] younger children and even infants. The policy adopted by our predecessor churches in 1976 and reinforced since then clearly precludes the communing of infants.

I reported to Mattheis that at a recent gathering of pastors in the Eastern Washington/Idaho Synod a spot survey showed that at least one-fourth to one-third of them were ignoring the rule and were communing younger, uninstructed children.

I concluded with a word of encouragement:

> . . . if you choose to take no action against St. Paul's Church you will have my personal support. That will not be easy for either of us. But who ever said this task would be easy!

Mattheis wrestled with the matter for almost two months. By then he decided that the pastoral way was the best and only way to deal with the congregation. "I have read and reread (your) letter as I have thought about how I might respond to the situation," Mattheis wrote. "My hope is that we might take a small step toward justice for people who daily struggle with being different and who are, in my experience, committed and faithful disciples of our Lord

Jesus Christ." He would simply keep them on the roster of congregations of the synod and declare St. Paul's to be vacant, that is, without the leadership of a pastor on the ELCA roster. The congregation continued to support the mission of the synod and the ELCA. In fact, their giving put some other congregations to shame.

As I was about to retire in late 1995, Mattheis put matters into perspective:

> Without your strong support and encouragement I do not
> believe that I would have acted as I did. . . . I sensed your
> pastoral heart and your desire to place a sense of right
> above the path of expediency.

Once again, I was far ahead of my time. Though it could not have worked at the time, what I suggested to Mattheis is exactly what happened later. Some synod bishops did in fact begin to look the other way and permitted good, faithful pastors in known and stable same-gender relationships to remain on the roster of their synods.

I could scarcely have expected that the ELCA would in fact take legislative action nearly fifteen years later when the 2009 Churchwide Assembly officially endorsed the freedom of a congregation to call a pastor in a faithful, lifelong, committed, same-gender relationship. At that assembly I wept for joy. Finally, this church was being honest. Finally, my own long journey was complete. And to have lived long enough to see that St. Paul's Church in Oakland was welcomed back into our ELCA family of congregations has only been an added satisfaction.

The consequences, of course, have been excruciatingly painful. Hundreds of congregations have left the ELCA and tens of thousands of members have withdrawn from congregations that remain in the church. It is clear as I saw earlier, that homosexuality is at least as divisive in church and society today as was slavery a century and more ago.

Preparing for retirement

Crossing over into 1995 seemed to be a time when Corinne and I were increasingly eager to put our lives into perspective. That included our marriage and all of the stresses we had encountered during our Chicago years. On January 28 I wrote in my journal:

> As I move toward the end of my time in office we're trying to ready ourselves for the next stage of life. We've discovered that it's not simply a matter of packing our bags and possessions and moving to another place. No, we've discovered that the past almost eight years have taken an enormous toll on both of us. Yes, we've survived. Yes, we love each other deeply—beyond words. But we also have been facing the reality that it takes careful planning and a lot of frank and open communication to make the transition.

At times I found myself so eager for retirement that I almost felt guilty about it.

> I look forward more to retirement than to heaven. Is that a sin? Do I have my priorities wrong? I'm not sure how to deal with that seeming conflict. Maybe it's a matter of how we deal with the various stages of life. Maybe as we move toward the later years of life there will gradually be a longing for the life beyond—as I've seen in others.

I also tried to sense what it would be like to be out of the limelight. One morning our prayer included the phrase, "Rank me with whom Thou wilt . . ." I wondered:

> Can I handle it when I am out of office and no longer ranked with the high and mighty? I surely hope so. I know there is freedom only in being in the will of God and finding joy and release in my relationship with Christ.

Final synod assemblies

Once again, as I had done in all of my years in Chicago, I loaded my spring and early summer calendar with synod assemblies. There was no better place to be in direct contact with more of the leadership of the church, lay and clergy, than at these places.

In my message to all of the synod assemblies I accented our unity in the gospel in the midst of the challenges that faced us. I reminded them that it takes time, much time, for an organization the size of the ELCA to build identity. It happens event by event, year in and year out. I gave special praise to the churchwide staff, commending them for the enormous adjustments they had gone through in our initial years. I deplored the giving patterns of our membership and how this has hobbled our work at every level, including our support for global mission and the Lutheran World Federation. But I also commended our members for the magnificent way they had responded to disasters and the Hunger Appeal. I urged them to engage fully in our discussion of complex social issues and our ecumenical ventures. I invited them to join me in the prayer that the Holy Spirit would guide us in the choice of my successor.

Two synod assemblies from 1995 are etched deeply in my memory:

The bombing of the Federal Building in Oklahoma City

Most memorable of any synod assembly I've ever attended was the Oklahoma/Arkansas gathering in April 1995.

The previous day I was in New York at LaGuardia Airport for a meeting of VISN, the religious cable network on whose board I was serving. The Greek Orthodox representative arrived late. When he entered the room he reported that he had just heard on the radio that there had been an enormous explosion in Oklahoma City. He had only sketchy details.

As the day unfolded we heard more: that it had been the Federal Building, that many had been killed, that the terrorist was unknown. I thought about my schedule for the next day. I would be flying into Oklahoma City for the synod assembly at Chickasha. I wondered what was in store for me on this trip.

On the flight from Chicago the next day the passengers were acting very casual about it all, until the pilot announced the beginning of our descent. Silence fell over the cabin. I happened to be sitting in a window seat on the side that gave me a clear view of the city below. The smoldering hulk of the building was in clear view. I could not comprehend the massiveness of what had happened: how many children, women, and men had been killed. I speculated that this must surely be the deed of a mideastern terrorist.

At the synod assembly the bombing dominated everything else. It seemed that voting member after voting member knew someone who had been killed or the family of someone who had died.

Only later, of course, did we learn that the perpetrator was a homegrown American terrorist. I learned once again how easily we make judgments and how wrong we usually are.

Southern California (West)

In California I encountered an explosion of another kind. The turmoil that had been brewing all across the church over sexuality issues concentrated itself in the Southern California (West) Synod where there was to be an election for bishop. The race came down to two candidates whose views on sexuality issues were diametrically opposed. William Bartlett had made it clear that he was strongly opposed to any move to bless or ordain homosexual persons. Paul Egertson was known to be very open to inclusion of gay and lesbian persons in the life of the church. Egertson won by a narrow margin. After the convention it became known publicly that Egertson had blessed a same-gender couple. California, with all of its cultural and religious differences, played itself out in the election.

The uproar spread beyond the synod. Part of it boiled over in a heated exchange of letters with James Crumley. Charging that

Egertson had "deliberately and intentionally violated the constitution and bylaws of the ELCA and of the synod by conducting same-sex blessings," Crumley implied that I had no choice but to bring charges against Egertson.

In my response to Crumley I informed him that I had not known that Egertson had blessed same-gender couples at the time I installed him as bishop. I also pointed out to Crumley that in the ELCA we made no distinction between a parish pastor and a bishop. Thus, if one were to bring to trial a bishop for this cause, one would need to do the same with all pastors who had conducted such blessings. That, I suggested, would lead to chaos, given the growing frequency of such occasions.

The more serious issue, I wrote, was to ascertain the basis on which one would take such action. There was no specific word in any ELCA document about this matter. And if one were to look to the social statements of predecessor church bodies, as we had been doing in other matters until the ELCA developed its own social statements, we would still have slim grounds on which to conduct a trial. I suggested that in some areas pastoral care rather than canon law may be the best avenue to follow.

In a second letter Crumley acknowledged that disciplinary action may not be constitutionally warranted. These kinds of action, however, are what he called "a departure from the way Scripture has been interpreted and from the tradition of the Church." In this instance, he thought that "pastoral advice and counsel" were in order.

Before my final letter to Crumley on this matter, Egertson, with strong urging from me, announced to the Conference of Bishops that he would not conduct same-gender blessings while he was in office. Even in his own synod he had probably encountered enough pressure to lead to that decision.

I shared this information with Crumley.

> I think [Paul] understands the point you made in your initial letter, namely, that the office [of bishop] itself calls for conduct that may be different at times from what one may have known as a pastor in another setting. A double standard? Yes, I suppose so. But those of us who have served in the office understand the difference in terms of the responsibility that goes with the call to be a bishop.

This, however, will not make the issue go away, I wrote:

> As [pastors] come to know gay and lesbian persons who do not fit the stereotypes we have carried with us for so long, as they sense their commitment to Christ and their love—often anguished—for the church, they will inevitably seek for ways to welcome them into the family of faith, including those in relationships.

After referring to Acts 10 and the need for the apostle Peter to be converted in his thinking about who belongs and who does not belong to the kingdom, I suggested that

> . . . time will make it clear that many in our churches . . . need to be "converted" in their attitude toward gay and lesbian persons. They may see that inordinate attention to order may impede the faith. It will take years. And in the interim, to the dismay of our gay and lesbian sisters and brothers, we will need to continue to study the issues, seek ways to minister to and with them, and try to maintain order in this church.

Final meeting with the Conference of Bishops

Just prior to the 1995 Churchwide Assembly I had my final meeting with the Conference of Bishops. I made two important recommendations, both aimed at resolving frustrations I had lived with for eight years.

First, I recommended that the Constitution be amended to make my successor a member of the executive committee of

the Conference of Bishops. I suggested that this change would
bring the conference into a pattern similar to the Church Council, where the vice president chaired the council, but where the
bishop of the church was a member of the executive committee of
the council. In retrospect, I believe this was an important move to
help my successor feel like more of an integral part of the leadership of the conference.

I made a second important recommendation: to change the title
from "bishop of the church" to "presiding bishop." I probably could
not have done this any sooner. It would have been seen by some as
self-serving. But now as I was leaving office I felt completely at ease
in doing so. I explained that this was not necessarily an issue within
the church.

> But the moment one steps outside the ELCA ... there is
> confusion. Again and again I have had to explain the nature
> of my office by stating that it is "like being a 'presiding
> bishop.'"

Both recommendations were welcomed by the synod bishops
and approved by the Church Council with no discussion.

In thanking the bishops for their partnership over eight years, I
pictured them as "my parish."

> You have been in my regular prayers. And because old hab-
> its die hard I suspect I will be working my way across the
> church for some time to come, remembering each of you by
> name, and, especially, the person who will succeed me.

And so it continues to be to this day . . .

The 1995 Churchwide Assembly
Minneapolis, a good setting
Though the site for the 1995 Assembly had been set long before
I decided to retire in that year, I was especially pleased that this

gathering would be in my home state. Since early childhood when I gazed in awe on the city from the windows of a Greyhound bus, through my years as a student at Augsburg College, and more than a decade as a synod bishop, this was home ground for me. It would be the ideal place to end my formal years in ministry. And, given the density of Lutherans in the area, it would also be an excellent place to hold the assembly.

Actions of the assembly

Gathering under the theme, "Making Christ Known: Hope for the World," the voting members looked at an agenda that was not as heavy as usual.

> Adoption of a statement "welcoming gay and lesbian persons as individuals created by God." At its meeting just prior to the assembly the Church Council decided to postpone indefinitely any recommendation on the Statement on Human Sexuality. It had been projected that the 1997 assembly might act on it. Though it was a bitter pill for me to swallow, I was enough of a realist to know that this simply could not be done during my watch.

> The clustering of the seminaries was approved, a tribute, as I've suggested earlier, to the excellent work of the Division for Ministry and the seminary presidents.

> Strong action on violence against women.

> The adoption of a comprehensive statement on global peace, with an accent on the responsibility of the United States for poor countries.

> To the disappointment of detractors who had argued against the use of quotas since before the church was organized, the assembly decided by a strong majority vote to keep them. It was a milestone decision.

An affirmation that "this church will not discriminate against persons who carry the AIDS virus in its calling or employment practices."

An evening of affirmation

Surely a highlight of the assembly was the August 20 evening of tribute to Corinne and me on the mall outside the convention center. Charles Anderson, who had been one of my assistants in the Minnesota Synod and then bishop of the Southwestern Minnesota Synod, chaired the evening with skill and good humor. Corinne's word of thanks, tied to her experience of faith as a child, was a highlight. And surely having in attendance Martin Marty, who had written the forward for Corinne's book and had been a colleague of hers on the St. Olaf College board of trustees, and Archbishop John Roach, who had become a friend during my years in Minnesota, was deeply appreciated. And, not least, sharing the evening with our children and so many from our families and circle of friends— it was simply overwhelming. An evening never to be forgotten.

The Servus Dei Medal

Receiving the Servus Dei Medal at the assembly was a singular honor. Fashioned from solid silver by a design created by the distinguished sculptor Ralph Joseph Menconi, it is about five inches in diameter and shaped in the form of an ancient coin. On one side are symbols of the Hebrew and Christian faith. On the other is the name of the recipient and the years served in leadership.

First created to honor leaders of the former Lutheran Church in America, this meant that I stood in the company of luminaries such as Franklin Clark Fry, Robert Marshall, James Crumley, and many others. It was indeed a most humbling experience for this boy from Litchfield, Minnesota.

My report to the assembly

In my report to the assembly, the accent was on gratitude. In the opening phrases I praised the churchwide staff, synod bishops and their staffs, regional coordinators, and "a network of others who are related to the churchwide organization in one way or another."

I singled out Corinne for special praise:

> Because it is important for the bishop of the church to be with the people of the church, I have spent more than four of the past eight years away from home. It is not a thing to choose. How grateful I am for a life partner who loves this church as much as I do, who prays faithfully for this church, and who has been my most important source of encouragement these years in office.

In a statement of my vision for the church I said that "we must pray that the winds of the Spirit will blow among us and convert us from a settled church to a mission-driven church."

In my longing to see the church come together in greater unity I described what I saw as a healthy church. It is one

> . . . that lives in creative tension between two extremes, framed by two questions: How much unity shall we demand? How much variety shall we tolerate?

Departing from my prepared text, I added these last moment handwritten comments:

> Now and then we hear from those who long for a unity to come in the future, or a unity they thought we had in the past. Or we hear some say, "The ELCA is such a large church and there are so many 'special interest' groups. How can we ever achieve a sense of unity?"

> As for the past, have we forgotten our history lessons? When we were in those smaller enclaves where most members were of the same ethnic background—German, Danish, Norwegian, or what have you—did we have a good sense of unity? No, not at all. Then, just as now, there were tensions in the church, often leading to division.

As for the future, I said it was naive to believe that a time will come when there will be no issues with the potential to divide us.

> Regardless of the issues . . .what holds us together is our agreement on gospel and sacraments.

In retrospect, and as is often the case, those off-the-cuff comments may have been the most important part of my report.

I concluded my report with an allusion to comments I had made in my acceptance speech on May 1, 1987:

> I likened this venture to a ship departing its safe harbor and heading out into the deeper waters. I predicted that there would be storms, as there surely have been. But I also reminded us that the deeper waters are the safer waters. Your faith, deeply and confidently rooted in the gospel of grace, and your witness and service, given joyfully and freely—these have been our strength and hope.

Press reports

There was, as expected in that Lutheran stronghold, good press coverage. Under the headline "Lutheran group's 'rock' is retiring," Clark Morhpew, religion editor of the (St. Paul) *Pioneer Press*, wrote that I had been

> . . . the rock, the force of stability that carried the ELCA through the toughest years of its young life.

After citing the stress of the financial shortfalls in the first three years, Morphew wrote that:

> . . . through it all, Chilstrom remained calm and confident that the church would pull through and remains strong.

To Martha Allen at the *Minneapolis Star Tribune* I said:

> When I see my own weaknesses and all the imperfections of the church I wonder how it can all go on. But it's God's church and God's going to see to it that through thick and thin God's word will be heard (8/18/95).

Steven McKinley, writing for the *Christian Century*, wondered if "Minnesota nice" may have had some influence on the assembly:

> Voting members of the assembly didn't want to hurt anyone's feelings. They enjoyed being together. Those who were present will go away describing it as an excellent experience.

McKinley also raised the kinds of tough questions that haunt me and anyone who leads a church:

> What difference does it make to a local congregation who the presiding bishop is?

> Will local congregations pay any attention to statements on peace, sexuality, or sacramental practices? Or is the denomination as Lutherans have known it in the past an anachronism, to be replaced in an evolutionary way by some whole new kind of structure?

The election of H. George Anderson

Speculation prior to the assembly

As I mentioned earlier, no viable candidate to succeed me in office seemed to be emerging after my announcement at the 1993 Kansas City assembly that I would leave office in 1995. In my journal in March 1995, I noted that there were some names floating about, including H. George Anderson. Of his potential election, I wrote:

> It would give the church the stability we need as tough issues—like the ecumenical proposals of '97—come to the front.

My concern grew with each passing week as we approached the 1995 assembly. Then one morning over breakfast I said to Corinne, "I wonder if H. George might be open now to a call to lead the church."

When I got to the office that same morning, I heard that one of George's friends had spoken to him and that George had agreed that he would not withdraw his name from consideration. I felt enormous relief. I had absolutely no doubt that he would succeed me, though I knew, of course, that assemblies had a mind of their own and that strange things could happen.

On May 25 a teleconference was held by a group whose purpose was to ferret out names of potential candidates for bishop of the church. A copy of that conversation came to my desk. On the list were about thirty-five names. I scanned them and jotted this note on the margin:

> I predict the final seven (in alphabetical order) will be: Almen, D. Anderson, G. Anderson, C. Maahs, P. Rogness, D. Tiede, K. Sauer.
>
> Final three will be: G. Anderson, D. Anderson, D. Tiede.
>
> And Geo. Anderson will be elected.

My prophecy was partly right. As the voting progressed at the assembly, H. George Anderson led on every ballot. What became apparent, however, was that voting blocs had been at work to elevate three of the candidates: April Ulring Larson, bishop of the La Crosse Area Synod; Richard Foss, bishop of the Eastern North Dakota Synod; and Donald McCoid, bishop of the Southwestern Pennsylvania Synod.

Larson, the first female synod bishop, was probably the candidate many women wanted to see finish strong in the balloting. But she also carried respect in wide circles across the ELCA. Why didn't I see in advance that she would be among the finalists? I suspect it was because I knew the church well enough to realize that no female could win over a male candidate. There was still too much anti-female sentiment across the church. That has changed since then. I would not be surprised at all to see the ELCA elect a woman as presiding bishop in the next decade or two. Larson and many others have paved the way.

As for Foss, I was mystified by how he amassed so many votes. Was this the "anti-sexuality statement" vote? Foss had played his cards very carefully on that issue. He made comments from time to time that led one to believe he was strongly opposed to any attempt to move it forward. He also emerged as a confident and able orator at the assembly when he gave his speech as one of the finalists.

It seemed to me that McCoid's support came primarily from the so-called "evangelical catholic" folks, and mainly from the eastern United States.

On the final ballot Anderson won easily by a vote of 698 to 334 over Larson.

When I announced the outcome I said with tongue in cheek that I had seen a vision unfolding on the lofty ceiling of the assembly hall. It read, "*LET GEORGE DO IT!*" It was a huge relief to pass the mantle to him.

Martin Marty commented that

> If anything made Anderson acceptable, it is that he's the
> embodiment of both sides of the church. People in the East
> and South identified with him. Anderson was president of
> Lutheran Southern Seminary in South Carolina for more
> than twenty years and people in the Midwest identify
> with him because he's at Luther College. H. George won't
> make headlines or bold statements, but that doesn't mean
> he won't act when he feels it necessary (*Minneapolis Star
> Tribune*, 8/21/95).

Mark Hanson, who had just been elected bishop of the St. Paul Area Synod and had no idea at that moment that he would succeed Anderson in another six years, said:

> [Anderson] brings a sense of history, openness to the
> future. He won't have to earn respect, integrity, or honesty,
> because he already has it. At a time when we get too quickly
> discouraged he's . . . not a cheerleader, but an encourager
> (*Minneapolis Star Tribune*, 8/21/95).

In the *Christian Century* article cited above, Steven McKinley reported that:

> The more the voting members saw of Anderson, the better they liked him. He gave off a quiet confidence and hopefulness they found reassuring. [He] spoke movingly of his own experience of adoption, of the death of his wife, and of his experiences as a single parent. Through the whole process he came through as a leader who could be trusted. After the assembly one synodical bishop remarked that Anderson might be the ELCA's version of Pope John XXIII.

McKinley also captured a moment of high spirit after the election. He described how one of the speakers carried a basketball onto the stage at the Target Center and passed it to Anderson with the suggestion: "The ball is yours now, but put us in the game—we want to play."

> Anderson spontaneously threw the ball out into the crowd, and it bounced around the auditorium like a beach ball at a football game. For Lutherans, this is an uninhibited good time.

Post-assembly decisions and reflections

Corinne and I could scarcely wait to get to our lake home for a few days of rest and recovery. I sent a note to George.

> Waking up here at our lake home yesterday was a delight. And the prayer for the day seemed just right: "Let your continual mercy, O Lord, cleanse and defend your church; and because it cannot continue in safety without your help, protect and govern it always by your goodness; for you live and reign with the Father and the Holy Spirit, one God, now and forever. Amen."

The next day I wrote a nine-page, single-spaced letter to George with a detailed description and evaluation of each of the heads of churchwide units. Two weeks later I wrote another memorandum to George, this time more than thirteen pages in length, describing each of the sixty-five synod bishops and evaluating their effectiveness and potential.

After he took office Anderson sent a note of thanks for this invaluable help in getting started in his tenure as presiding bishop.

> I want to repeat how helpful it has been to have the "orientation" materials. . . . As close as I was to the general life of the church, I had no background on many of the personalities and issues that are so central to this office.

From our lake home I also wrote to my family:

> It's such a relief to leave the office in the hands of someone I respect as much as George . . . there are problems George and I will have to deal with in relationship to staffing changes. One of those decisions kept me awake most of the night. I'm just glad I have someone like George who tends to see things from the same perspective as I do.

That same day I wrote to Bob and Alice Marshall:

> It was good to have both of you at the assembly. I hope you both know how special you are to us and how much we have appreciated your support these past eight years. Thanks, Bob, for your wise counsel that I continue in office when I was sorely tempted to bail out. In my heart of hearts I knew I had to stay on. But I needed to hear it from your perspective.

Mark Hanson: a future leader for the ELCA?

In my final weeks in office, I installed several of the newly elected synod bishops. Among them was Mark Hanson in the St. Paul Area Synod. It is interesting, given what happened six years later, to read again what I wrote to George Anderson in late 1995 after that event:

A very enthusiastic installation with a large crowd in attendance. I find myself increasingly impressed with Mark Hanson. I keep hearing about his good judgment, fiscal conservatism, sensitivity to people, blend of biblical insight with passion for justice.

An avalanche of accolades

I found myself saddened that Corinne could not be with me in my travels in the last weeks in office to hear how much love and gratitude I was hearing for her, and especially the impact her book *Andrew You Died Too Soon* was having far and wide.

Of all the letters of gratitude that came in those last weeks, four or five came to the top.

John Reumann, professor of New Testament at Philadelphia Seminary and a fellow member of the CNLC, said he wanted to thank me

> . . . for the many things you have done as pastor, teacher, and bishop for the church and our Lutheran churches in the USA. Who can count up the hours, the meetings, the trials and despair at times, as well as the joy and satisfactions among the people of God in faith? You know, as well as I do, what a capable and dedicated wife means in such a life. Only Corinne as a pastor has probably had to give up much more than my wife has, in her own career. Therefore Martha and I join in thanking you both for what you have given to the benefit of us all.

April Ulring Larson, our first female synod bishop might have been expected to bring a feminine touch and write as she did:

> You have been like the parent who holds a colicky crying baby, pacing through the night, caressing, nursing, and rocking the infant through the screaming and sobbing. Many of us have wondered long and hard from whence comes the reservoir of your endless compassion, love, and patience for this church. You have told us often. It is Jesus Christ.

A letter from James Crumley meant more than most. As the record shows, we had had a somewhat rocky history of differences of opinion. But we both knew that beneath it all we were bound together as brothers in Christ and in the gospel ministry. He wrote that

> ... there were many facets of the whole [assembly] process that made us feel very positive about the ELCA. Thanks, too, Herb, for your willingness to be our bishop for these eight years. I know how heavy the load has been on you and how frustrating the "settling-down" period must have been for you. But we're now well on the way.

My daughter Mary sent what was probably the most appreciated note of all. She has a way of finding the right words for the right moment. For my October 18th birthday she wrote:

> Now may be the opportunity to tell you how much I admire you as both a man and a father. I also think the church was very fortunate to have such a wonderful man to work as diligently and faithfully as you have for so many years. I am hoping and praying that the years ahead will be as rewarding for you both. Much love and admiration. . . .

It may seem like an exercise in self-aggrandizement to include these accolades in this autobiography. But when I put them into context it helps to understand how much they meant to me, especially in the retrospective as I write these words more than fifteen years after leaving office. Because of falling membership, decreases in income, and the constant pressure from detractors—and especially those with objections to the sexuality draft—I have tended to have a rather dim recollection of my final two years in office. These letters, mostly forgotten, have emerged from musty file boxes like a fragrant breeze of grace after all these years. I have been reminded again of so many satisfying contacts with good and faithful people across the entire church. And, more important, I have been able to recapture memories of so many good things that happened in those final two years, all made possible by God's grace.

In March of 1995, when many of these letters were streaming in, I read a book review in *The New York Times* about Franklin D. Roosevelt. Written by a friend in whom he confided and shared thoughts and feelings never revealed to the public, Roosevelt comes across as a man who shared many of the same feelings that I had while in office. He confessed to a good deal of self-doubt. A magnificent communicator, he had misgivings about the effectiveness of his speeches, wondered each election time if he should stand for another term, questioned decisions he had made, and even considered resignation from office in order to be the U.S. representative to the United Nations. As a lad growing up in that era, I had only known the public Roosevelt, the one who exuded complete confidence in everything he said and did.

As I pondered all this, I saw much of myself in what I was reading. I reflected on my own self-doubt about my ability to communicate, the quality of my preaching, about remaining in office, about decisions I had made. In late March 1995 I wrote in my journal:

> In the end, one finally has to be content to let history be the judge. And that won't happen . . . for many years to come. In the meantime, I'll live with my doubts, accept the good words of commendation that come my way in these last months in office, and leave it all in the hands of a gracious God who knows all things, including my sins and shortcomings, and who forgives.

Final chapel service

We would leave Chicago on my sixty-fourth birthday, October 18, 1995. The day before, the churchwide staff gathered for the last chapel service during my time in office. As I looked over their faces that morning I realized how closely we had bonded during those years. We had struggled with enormous issues; we had endured unjust criticism; we had supported each other in mistakes we had made; we had prayed for each other; we had brought stability to our young church. Now it was time for me to move on and to leave everything in their capable hands as they welcomed George Anderson.

Given that October 18 is the Festival Day of St. Luke, I chose appropriate lessons: Isaiah 35:5–8 and Luke 1:1–4; 24:44–53:

> Some of you know that some time ago I wrote two words in my date book on the last day of October, my final day in office. They are: "Amen!" and "Hallelujah!"
>
> I confess freely that when I first wrote them I had just one thought in mind. I was looking forward to the end of my time in office and the beginning of the next stage of my life when things should be less hectic. These eight and one-half years have indeed been taxing. On this last jaunt I was gone for more than two weeks. Corinne was able to travel with me—a rare treat. We enjoyed the time together very much. But as we were heading for the O'Hare baggage claim last Sunday evening . . . she looked at me and said, "I'm certainly glad this trip is over." I looked back and asked, "Is that 'trip' with a small 't' or with a capitol 'T'?" I must confess that I am relieved that this long "Trip" is over.

I want on to say that those words "Amen" and "Hallelujah" had taken on a somewhat different meaning the past several weeks.

> "Amen!" is also the word we use to express the sense that something has been completed. "Amen! Yes. It shall be so." I am profoundly grateful that I have in my heart a deep sense of completion. No, not that everything was done that could be done. But life has a way of coming to certain passage points where we are able to say, "It's enough. Amen."
>
> The "Hallelujah!" has also taken on a deeper meaning for me. I praise God and sing "Hallelujah!" for the privilege of sharing the good news of the gospel in so many places and with so many people. How could anyone be so privileged!

I pointed out that the gospel lesson *was* from the opening and closing sections of Luke.

> He begins by saying that the purpose of the gospel is that others might know about Jesus. And in the closing paragraphs he goes back to the basics, speaking about the suffering and resurrection of Christ.

> That is how I have tried to shape my ministry in these first years in the life of the ELCA. I will sing "Hallelujah!" for years and years to come.

The mantle slips away

Later that day Corinne and I packed the last of our possessions into a rental trailer. The next morning, my sixty-fourth birthday, I went to the office for a brief time. Then we hit the road, Corinne driving ahead in our sedan and me following in our Blazer with a trailer in tow.

Our plan had been to travel as far as the Twin Cities the next day, stay overnight, and complete the drive to Pelican Rapids and Lake Lida the following morning. After a good meal we looked at each other with the same thought in mind, "In another four hours we could be at 'home' and sleeping in our own bed. Let's go for it." And we did.

It was a beautiful starlit night as we drove west from Minneapolis on Interstate 94. Suddenly I felt warm tears streaming down my cheeks. I was startled. "What's going on?" I pondered. Soon I realized what had prompted this unexpected outpouring of emotion.

First, it was the sense that with each passing mile away from Chicago a small part of the heavy mantle was slipping from my shoulders. Relief! What a relief! Gratitude! Gratitude that God's grace had sustained me in these arduous years.

But there was a second and equally strong emotion. As I looked into the gleaming taillights of our sedan ahead of me, I was overwhelmed with a flood of gratefulness that Corinne had been my companion through these times. I could not have done it without her help and support and encouragement. We had been tested to the limit in every way, and we had endured.

It had been "A Journey of Grace" all the way.

Thanks be to God!

Epilogue: retirement

When asked by those about to retire what they might expect in the coming years I have but one reply: "Surprises."

We began this time of life as we had planned. Corinne took a part-time call as an assistant in a local congregation. Given her relatively brief time in parish ministry, that seemed good. That is, until she realized again that there is no such thing in church work as "part time." After a year she was ready for full retirement.

As for me, I plunged into life at the lake and in Pelican Rapids. First on the agenda was to build a storage barn for garden and lawn equipment. Then a greenhouse to satisfy my love for gardening year-round. What a thrill to go there in the dead of winter to enjoy those tender plants. Besides gardening, I now had ample time to indulge in my other favorite hobbies—fishing, hunting, golf, travel, and photography.

A Habitat for Humanity project was an enormous relief from office detail and travel. To recruit fellow retirees and help construct a home for a needy young family gave an immediate sense of fulfillment after a career that often lacked concrete satisfaction.

Leisurely travel without meeting tight schedules and important dignitaries was a pleasure for us. Our itinerary has included New Zealand, Switzerland, Ireland, Costa Rica, Iceland, Alaska, Scandinavia, and other beautiful corners of the globe.

Writing at a more deliberate pace has brought much enjoyment. In addition to this book and one on my family history, a few of the major published works have included:

What Does It Mean to Be "Evangelical"?
The Interpretation and Use of the Bible When Dealing with Difficult Social Issues

Money and the Judeo-Christian Tradition
Politics and the Pulpit
The Crisis in the Middle East
The Meaning of Churchmanship
The Loss of a Son
The Church and Human Sexuality

Corinne and I are also currently working on a year-long devotional book that will be published by the Augustana Heritage Association in June, 2012.

Now there was time to enjoy seeing daughter Mary and son Chris move ahead in their careers.

Soon invitations to preach and lecture here and there began to come to both of us. Now, however, there was no sense of obligation to accept as many as possible. We could pick and choose. And that is what we continue to do even as I write.

Along the way we discovered Arizona. After a winter or two in that moderate corner of the country we built a smaller second home. It has been our winter refuge for more than a decade.

Possibly most satisfying of all was to become a Minnesota Master Gardener. For a time I served as the garden editor for *Lake and Home* magazine. After transforming our lakeshore grounds to a park-like setting, we decided it was time to return to our most favorite place of all—St. Peter, Minnesota, with Gustavus Adolphus College only a short walk away. As I write I am serving as the interim director of the college's Linnaeus Arboretum, a 130 acre expanse of flower gardens, hundred of varieties of trees, a wide native prairie, and an interpretive center for educational offerings for college and community.

Through all these years Corinne has enjoyed entertaining guests at our table with good food and lively conversation.

And now I'm about to cross the threshold into my eightieth year. Other than significantly limited vision due to glaucoma, I feel incredibly blessed with vitality and enthusiasm for what lies ahead. I know, however, that even at best life is now more fragile and my days are numbered. I feel certain that the major purpose of my life has probably been completed.

I come to this moment with both fear and confidence. Fear, because of my low vision and because I may not be spared the kinds of debilitating diseases some of my friends have encountered.

But confidence, because I believe my Savior will be with us all the way. What lies beyond this life is a mystery I can leave in the hands of a gracious and loving God.

So I come back to the questions I pondered at the outset of this autobiography: How much do we determine the outcome of our lives? How much of it is controlled by powers beyond us, including the intervening grace of God? There is no clear answer. Indeed, it seems that the best possibility is that there is that golden mean I wrote about in the opening paragraphs. Yes, our personal decisions are of great consequence. But only within a larger circle of the will and purpose of God. That's the best I can do with this conundrum.

As I look back, I share the sentiments of Laurens van der Post. In *A Walk with a White Bushman* he writes:

> I came to live my life not by conscious plan or prearranged design but as someone following the flight of a bird. My life has not been planned, I have always taken what was on my doorstep . . . and yet looking back on it, more and more it has a definite shape, a pattern as if planned in advance.

What better way to conclude than with the good words of that grandest of America's twentieth-century theologians, Reinhold Niebuhr:

> Nothing worth doing is completed in our lifetime; therefore, we are saved by hope. Nothing true or beautiful or good makes sense in my immediate context of history; therefore, we are saved by faith. Nothing we do, however virtuous, can be accomplished alone, therefore, we are saved by love. No virtuous act is quite as virtuous from the standpoint of our friend or foe; therefore, we are saved by the final form of love, which is forgiveness.

It has been, and is, "A Journey of Grace."

INDEX OF NAMES